Software Project Management

Sanjay Mohapatra, *PhD*
Director, Batoi Systems Pvt. Ltd
Visiting faculty at IIT Mandi, IIM Ranchi, and IIM Raipur
Previously,
Professor, Xavier Institute of Management, Bhubaneswar (XIMB)

Cengage

Australia • Brazil • Canada • India • Mexico • Singapore • United Kingdom • United States

Cengage

Software Project Management

Sanjay Mohapatra

For product information and technology assistance, contact us at **asia.infoindia@cengage.com**

For permission to use material from this text or product, submit all requests online at **www.cengage.com/permissions**

ISBN-13: 978-81-315-1484-9
ISBN-10: 81-315-1484-6

Cengage Learning India Pvt. Ltd.
T-303, 3rd Floor
DAV Complex, Plot 3
Mayur Vihar Phase 1
Delhi-110091

Cengage is a leading provider of customized learning solutions with employees residing in nearly 40 different countries and sales in more than 125 countries around the world. Find your local representative at **www.cengage.com**

Cengage is committed to creating inclusive and diverse products, including perspectives that represent the diversity of people across all backgrounds, identities, opinions, and experiences. If you have any feedback related to this, please contact us at **support.cengage.com**

To learn more about Cengage products, platforms and services, visit at **www.cengage.co.in**

Printed by:
Rajiv Book Binding House
D-1518, DSIIDC Industrial Complex,
Narela, New Delhi 110040

Printed in India
Print Number: 02 Print Year: 2024

Dedicated to
My Father Dr. B C Mohapatra

AND

Late Dr. Sushila Mishra, and
Late Parmananda Mishra

PREFACE

The software industry is steadily expanding in India. Today, India is a leading destination for the IT and IT-enabled services worldwide. The IT and software industry is a major economy player in India. Mainly based on IT software and facilities such as system integration, software experiments, custom application development and maintenance (CADM), Network and IT services and solutions, the country's IT-BPO industry expanded by 12% during the fiscal year 2009 and attained aggregate returns of US$71.6 billion. Software exports from India have increased and account for about 60% of India's total software revenue. Today, the software industry is viewed as one of the most promising industry segments and one holding tremendous future potential.

Recession notwithstanding, the demand for software is ever increasing. This appetite for software has spurred a dramatic interest in software development and management of processes related to software development. Software project management is by far the most important factor in project execution, one that has a major impact on how efficiently software development projects are executed and how successful the projects are. Many times software projects fail or are not completely successful or fail to meet expectations. This is largely because of shortcomings in managing and steering a software development initiative to its local end.

Software development projects are time bound and must meet the schedule of delivery as agreed and negotiated with the customer. The rate at which a developer organization services its customer would be dependent on the productivity of the developer organization. A reduction in the schedule to deliver through increased productivity for these software development projects would go a long way in enhancing the developer organization's profitability. Thus, it is important to understand the factors that impact the process(es) of software development so that these influencing factors can be monitored and controlled to improve productivity without affecting the quality of the deliverables. This is where software project management plays a vital role.

The importance of software project management can be gauged by the fact that frameworks such as capability maturity model (CMM) and capability maturity model integrated (CMMI) have been developed by Software Engineering Institute at Carnegie Mellon University so that best practices from different geographies can be shared with each other. These two frameworks help in implementing sound project management practices to make the project management process predictive, systematic, and be able to meet the project goals and customer requirements as well.

This book has been written in most user-friendly manner and is designed to help both practitioners and students. Its content has been drawn up keeping in view the MBA and MCA courses offered by most of universities in India. Its discussion of the topics in a learn-through-examples approach makes it equally useful to undergraduate students pursuing software engineering, systems engineering, and IT and management information related courses. Case studies discussed at the end of chapters are real-life case studies and give insight into the intricacies involved in software project management.

The book encompasses 12 chapters and some annexures.

Chapter 1 introduces the definition of software projects and their types along with the activities involved for the successful completion of software projects. It also throws light on various software development models available.

Chapter 2 deals with the project planning stage in software project management.

Chapter 3 presents different metrics that govern the execution of software projects. These metrics are quantitative measures for measuring project performance.

Chapter 4 elucidates the different processes and activities that are carried out for control and monitoring using the project management plan and statistical tools.

Chapter 5 covers configuration management (CM)—an important aspect of software project management. CM plays an important role in ensuring that correct versions of all the programs and other work products are delivered.

Chapter 6 concentrates on process definition process and process audit process—the two aspects of the software industry that are important from the process maturity point of view.

Chapter 7 is devoted to the general concepts of risk management, which include risk identification, risk mitigation, and process to manage risk.

Chapter 8 introduces the concept of request for proposals (RFP) to contract that helps in understanding the nuances involved in business development activities in the IT industry.

Chapter 9 discusses, through case studies, assessments of benchmarking practices that have been critically appraised to find their suitability for software development projects.

Chapter 10 deals with the concept of CMMI framework that helps users understand different process areas required for project management activities.

Chapter 11 discusses the lifecycle of a maintenance project consisting of project planning, scheduling, tracking, risk analysis, and release management process. The chapter also discusses how to set goals that are in line with the objectives of the customer.

Chapter 12 introduces the concept of software product management, which describes the processes dealing with the inception stage of a product until delivery to the customer.

The chapters in the book follow the lifecycle activities in project management. For example, in the project management cycle, activities start with planning followed by goal setting and monitoring and control. By arranging the chapters in the same sequence, readers of the book get a flavour of the real-life project management cycle. For each chapter instructor's manual has been provided for facilitating preparation for the class. Please contact local representative of the publisher to get the manual.

I hope that the book will be well received by both practitioners and students.

Readers' views, criticisms, or comments on this book will be gratefully appreciated and will go a long way in further improvement of the book apart from the continuous updating at author's end.

Sanjay Mohapatra

ACKNOWLEDGEMENTS

This book has been possible with contributions from my well wishers, students, family members, and colleagues in IT industry. It is not be possible to name each and every one.

I would want to thank Prof. Umesh H. Rao and Prof. Sunil Kumar Agarwal—both have rich and varied experience in IT industry. Their thought processes and contributions have enriched the content of this book. I would also like to acknowledge the contribution from Nirup Sahoo in XIM, Bhubaneswar. They all have gone out of their way in helping me to prepare and consolidate the literature for the book.

This book is a collection of best practices followed in the IT industry in India and abroad. The best practices have been highlighted in the book without disclosing confidential information from these companies. I am proud that I got the opportunity to work in such illustrious and reputed organizations where learning while working was the success mantra. Each day was a new learning for me as these organizations allowed me freehand to experiment, which made my working a challenging, knowledge-oriented, fun-filled, memorable, and pleasant experience. I would like to thank the management of these companies for making me what I am today.

I thank the editorial staff at Cengage Learning India for their encouragement, patience, and enthusiasm, which were crucial in making this book a reality.

Last but not the least, I would like to thank my family members, each working in a different industry, for meaningful and critical discussions that gave me diverse perspectives in project management. Bharati, Sandeep, Reena, Santosh, Sasmita, Niyati, Pratap, and Suniti have played variety of roles in their organizations and their viewpoints have helped me in conceptualizing the project management principles in a holistic manner. I wish them all success in their life and career.

Sanjay Mohapatra

CONTENTS

1

SOFTWARE PROJECTS

LEARNING OBJECTIVES

In this chapter, the students would learn:

- Definition of software projects
- Types of software projects
- Definition of software products
- Activities involved in project and products

UNDERSTANDING SOFTWARE PROJECTS

A project, in general, is understood to be a group of activities that are carried out to achieve a certain outcome. Each project, thus, will have well-defined objectives, which would measure success or failure of the project. Construction of house, bridge, apartment complex, airport construction as well as renovation of existing airports are some examples of projects. Making a movie, starting a new organization, and revamping the exiting organization to achieve better results would also be considered projects. In IT industry, software projects involve the implementation of applications using new technology or improving upon the functionalities of existing applications using technology. The usage of technology for completion of application and using it for organization business purposes differentiate the software projects from general definition of projects. In essence, software projects use technology to develop or improve existing applications for meeting business requirements. In software projects, the users will have a general idea about how the application would look like and its applicability, whereas in general projects, the output is usually a standard product and is known to many stakeholders. The software projects sometimes deal with the abstract nature of the end result and get modified as time elapses. Even after installation of the application, there could be requests for changing the original requirement. In general projects such as construction projects, accommodating such changes after completion will be next to impossibility, but in software projects, the changes can be accommodated to suit the changing requirements.

Software projects should have certain activities and need to have minimum attributes for its successful completion. These attributes can be grouped under a framework as discussed below.

E—Entry point: At this point an idea is germinated for starting a project. The idea, which is at abstract level, is written down and crystallized. The idea could translate into a work order, a purchase order, or a letter of intent (LOI). The written document then is re-sent to the business groups to get budget allocation or sponsorship. Depending on the merit of the idea and perceived business benefits to be accrued from such a project, the budget is allocated. The budget ensures that the business groups provide required resources—both finance and other resources—for successful completion of the defined projects. In this phase, different stakeholders are identified and their roles and responsibilities are clearly defined. The stakeholders then prepare an initial plan that will have details of milestones and expected final output. A set of goals and objectives are also defined in this plan. The goals are usually broader in nature and will contain details of expected business benefits such as increase in productivity and reduction in cost of operations. The objectives will be precise and will contain details of delivery schedule with milestone, review points, and expected quality of the application. These goals and objectives will drive the project team for execution of project in timely manner.

In order that the project team understands the goals and objectives well and works toward achieving them, the project management should take care that these goals and objectives are well understood by them. Hence, training sessions and kick-off meetings are organized to help the team understand the purpose of the project. Deliverables are also defined so that the objectives can be met. On the basis of these objectives, testing strategy is defined, which takes care of verification and validation approach for the project. The testing strategy should enumerate how the project team is going to handle and meet the different check points of deliverables.

T—Tasks or activities that need to be carried out: Here, on the basis of the objectives, tasks or activities are defined. These activities will be designed so that on completion of these activities the desired objectives will be achieved. These tasks are well identified at the lowest granular level and the resource is allocated with expected completion of schedule and effort. During project monitoring, these detailed activities help the management to track the variance. Thus, tasks play a vital role in project control and monitoring activities.

V—Verification or validation process, which is required to review and test intermediately the progress and quality of deliverables: This process is necessary to check the quality of intermediate deliverables so that the final quality meets the objectives defined at the entry point. The process should be so defined that the quality is checked properly without being an overburden on the execution. The activities in this process should follow and be aligned with the testing strategy prepared at the entry stage.

X—Exit point: This defines the deliverables and completed outputs on production of which the project is considered to be completed. After these deliverables are made ready, the quality is determined through measurement procedures, which determine whether the deliverables confirm to the objectives laid down at the entry point. Usually, these deliverables are well defined in advance, and project monitoring chart shows the readiness of the project.

M—Measurement: This refers to the system of measuring different parameters in project management. The metrics, as it is referred to, are defined by the measurement system and are aligned with the goals and the objectives of the project. Measurement system thus includes metrics, data collection procedure, interval of data collection, person or role responsible for data collection, and sample template for data collection. Metrics can be of two types—primary metrics and secondary metrics. Primary metrics talk about metrics derived from primary data such as effort, schedule, and defect/issues, and secondary metrics are derived by using primary metrics such as productivity, cost of quality, effort variation, schedule variation, and defect density. Secondary metrics are used to take managerial decision related to project management.

F— Feedback mechanism at periodic intervals as well as at the end of the completion of project is designed to give continuous feedback to the project management. Feedback can be both quantitative and qualitative. Quantitative feedback includes review comments, testing bugs, etc., which are recorded and can be quantified. However, there will be qualitative feedback where look and feel of the application, usability, etc., are given for further improvement.

In summary, a software project that is executed with this framework will have higher probability of being termed as a successful project. The criteria of successful project are defined at the entry stage. At the entry stage, objectives need to be well stated and should be made known to all stakeholders. The objectives should include timeline of delivery, and a project will be considered whether it can be delivered within the stipulated timeframe. There are other criteria for considering a project as a success. One of them is adherence to the allocated budget; a variance with respect to budget means cost over-run and will have cascading impact on related business decisions. With both schedule and budget being adhered to, the quality of deliverables cannot be ignored. The project should be able to deliver an application that would be able to perform as per agreed specifications from the end users.

Software Project Management

The essence of project management is to make sure that all the agreed objectives are accepted, executed, and shared among all the stakeholders. An effective project management will ensure that all the stakeholders are identified at the initial stage itself and then "buy in" the objectives. This makes sure that the stakeholders are involved in the decision-making process and understand their role in achieving the objectives. In order to achieve these, the first step in project management would be to start planning for all these. It is said that the more effort that we spend in planning, the better result we can get. A detailed planning will help identify minute details and plan for these details at that granular level. Even planning should include the control and monitoring aspect of the project and should have details such as when to control, who should review the progress, what should be the quality of intermediary deliverables, and so forth. Even escalation and communication protocol should be well defined in the planning document. Escalation policy should include different stages of escalation and is typically associated with service level agreement. If one particular issue is not closed within a certain timeframe, then escalation policy should detail the next level of escalation with associated timeframe. Similarly, communication protocol will have details of who to communicate with whom; this helps in offshore project development activities where there is a need to communicate with onsite team members and customers as well. The protocol guides the team members to categorize issues and to set up calls with corresponding colleagues.

The success of project management is entrusted to project manager (PM). Even though there are many stakeholders, the PM shoulders the responsibility of project management. To be successful, the PM goes through training and workshops to improve his/her skills. Some of the elements that contribute to the success of project management are as follows: clearly stated and understood objectives, role and responsibilities of each team member, communication protocol, escalation process, clearly defined project organization structure, which will show process of information flow, periodic status report review, and changed management process. These elements are translated into different processes and procedures such that the control and monitoring become quantitative and predictable. Predictability is an important aspect of project management; this ensures that customers as well as team members can predict the quality and the schedule of the deliverables. The predictability of project management is enhanced through the usage of statistical tools and techniques such as Pareto chart and trend analysis. The PM must be trained on these techniques.

Software Development Cycle

Software development cycle is used to break the entire application development into a number of processes (Figure 1.1). Small and manageable processes can be better controlled and monitored. These allow a methodical and systematic approach for development. Exact number of processes will depend on the size of the projects and also varies from organization to organization. In the same organization, depending on the skill of team members, maturity of processes and the development cycle can also vary. Sometimes processes are combined to make it shorter. In all the cases, a development cycle would at least consist of the following processes:

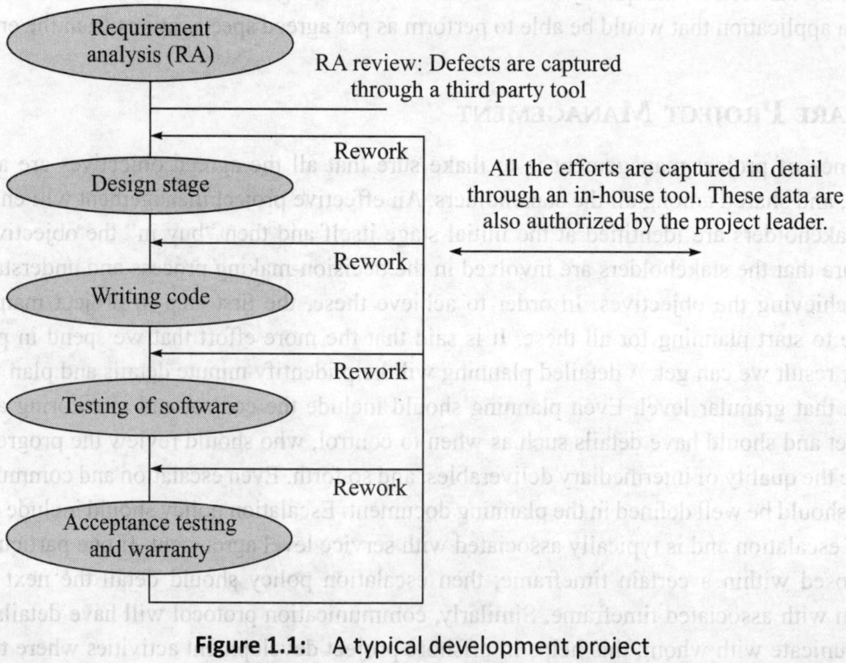

Figure 1.1: A typical development project

Pre-sales

In this process, the vendor prepares the technical and financial capabilities of the organization. The pre-sales team understands business model of the prospects and the likely area where there is a business need for developing a software application. The pre-sales team makes research in the domain as well as on the business need of the prospect, and interacts with other researching organizations such as Gartner to get valuable inputs related to their field of research. This information is then used to prepare a proposal to the prospect. Sometimes, looking at the need, the prospect may himself ask for a proposal from the vendor. This is known as "request for proposal" or RFP and is usually sent to a number of competing vendors. The proposal, in response to this RFP, will contain estimation (ball park based rough estimation), quality processes adopted in the organizations to show predictability and quality of end deliverables from the vendor, financial proposals, and past record of completing similar projects for other customers.

Requirement Analysis

Requirements from the customers are gathered and analyzed. A team from the software development team would meet the customer and would ask questions about the features and functionalities that are needed to be developed. These requirements are recorded and then reviewed again by the team along with the customer. A feasibility study is carried out to understand the viability of developing these requirements into software applications. The findings of this feasibility study are discussed with customers. Once the customer signs off this document, this process is complete. At the end of this process, the customer should give a go ahead for the application development and the project is kicked off. The formal document that is usually expected at the end of this process is a purchase order, work order, LOI, or any such document indicating that the project execution has been awarded to the vendor. It is a good practice that the customer indicates the details of quality of the deliverables with acceptable limit for defects, delivery schedule expected, and budget allocated for the project. This practice ensures that all the objectives of the project are mentioned tacitly, and the project team can follow the same during execution.

Kick Off or Initiation

Once the objectives are determined and the go ahead is obtained from the customer, the management from vendor organization should appoint a PM for execution. The PM, now, has the responsibility to successfully execute the project to completion. At this stage, when he/she has the LOI or any such document from the customer, he/she identifies all the stakeholders in this project. He/she then calls for a meeting with these stakeholders. The stakeholders could be infrastructure representative (for providing hardware and software resources required for the project), HR representative (for recruiting personnel for the project), quality representative (for setting the quality process and objectives for the team), visa representative (for arranging visa for overseas travel), technical architects (to provide technical design and assistance), training department (to provide required domain and technical training to the team members), identified team members for the project (to share and make them understand objectives of the project), etc. Depending on the nature of the project, there could be more stakeholders such as legal department representative who would apprise the team about legal points related to particular project in question. For examples, legal points related to the country where the application is to be installed and statutory need for maintaining data and back up for transactions.

Design

This stage is the next step after the requirement analysis stage. The entry criteria for this stage is the signed off requirement document from the customer. The activities in this stage are converting the functional requirements stated in the requirement document to design specifications. These specifications are arrived at by looking into hardware and software constraints, for example, if PCs with lower memory are to be used, then design needs to take care of performance-related issues. Here, the design will be made such that processing time for the CPU will be reduced. This will ensure that the final output from the application is available within performance criteria mentioned in the requirement document.

Point to be noted that during the design stage the design team usually breaks the entire requirements into manageable small modules. These modules can be developed in parallel so as to reduce the development cycle. The idea of breaking the requirements into small modules is to make manageable, independent modules that can be developed in parallel, thus, saving time.

Construction

On the basis of functional design specifications, the development team writes code, does unit self-testing, and then integrates all modules. Here, the team needs to take care that all specifications mentioned in the design documents are met. Periodic reviews are carried out to ensure that the code complies with the defined standard and also meets design specifications.

Testing

The team prepares a testing strategy. The strategy shows the type of testing that needs to be done, the stage when testing needs to be carried out, and the participants in that testing. It also explains the criteria as to when testing should be stopped. A test plan is also prepared, which will indicate all test cases and the expected results from this testing. While testing, proper environment set up (which includes test data set up, creation of IDs for testing, if required) is also done so that a proper simulated condition is created.

Acceptance Testing and Warranty

After a proper testing is done and the results are validated against the requirements, the development team would deliver the application to the customer. The customer would then test the application using the test plan that he has prepared. This testing by customer is called acceptance testing and is carried out by customer or his representatives. Once the customer is happy with the quality of the application, the development team would install the application on the customer machines. The team also supports the customer and application after acceptance testing. The period of this support/warranty will depend on the contract signed with the customer at the beginning of the project. After successfully testing the application, and migrating data to the new database, if required, the application "goes live." "Go live" implies the application is ready to be used in the production and can be used for business transactions. It also means that all the required end users are trained and well versed with the new application and can use them on regular basis.

Maintenance

This process starts after application is installed and goes to production and the warranty period is over. The project team enters into an agreement with customer to fix bugs and issues coming out of production (maintenance), enhance existing features, and add new features as well. The maintenance is usually carried out by contract.

Software Project Organization Structure

In order to get effective communication between different stakeholders in software projects, a formalized project organization structure should be defined. Figure 1.2 shows a pictorial representation of a typical project organization structure. A project organization structure has different components and roles. The structure is designed for easy flow of communication among project and customer team. The solid lines represent direct reporting, whereas the dotted lines show administrative responsibilities.

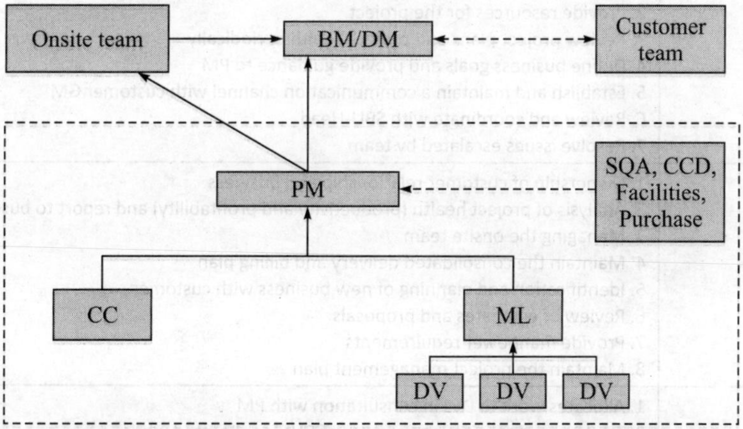

Figure 1.2: A typical software development project team

Business manager (BM) or delivery manager (DM) is the head in the structure and has the bottomline responsibility to execute the project. PM reports on the delivery status to the BM/DM on a periodic basis. This periodicity can be decided to be weekly or monthly basis depending on the complexity and criticality of the application.

PM is supported by module leaders (ML) who take care of individual modules. The MLs are typically technical leads who are expert in technology as well as in domain knowledge. They help developers (DV) who write the design and code documents. In the project team, configuration controller (CC) takes care of giving proper access to different groups. For example, the PM will have read/write access in all the folders, whereas the developers will have write access in their work area only. These are taken care by CC.

Typical Software Project Roles and Responsibilities

In order that the above organization structure is effective, responsibilities of each role needs to be defined. Table 1.1 shows an illustrative role and responsibility matrix.

Table 1.1: Roles and responsibilities in a development project

S. no.	Role	Responsibilities
1	Customer	1. Specify current and future project requirements (delivery schedules/sequence) 2. Review project schedules and issues periodically 3. Resolution of all issues (technical, operational, and business) 4. Review and sign off design packages and prototypes 5. Review and accept proposals 6. Review and accept delivered systems
2	BM	1. Provide resources for the project 2. Review project plans and project health periodically 3. Define business goals and provide guidance to PM 4. Establish and maintain a communication channel with customer GM 5. Review and coordination with SBU-head 6. Resolve issues escalated by team
3	DM	1. Take bottomline responsibility for all project issues with the customer 2. Provide resources for the project 3. Review project plans and project health periodically 4. Define business goals and provide guidance to PM 5. Establish and maintain a communication channel with customer GM 6. Review and coordinate with SBU-Head 7. Resolve issues escalated by team
4	PM	1. Ownership of customer relationship and business 2. Analysis of project health (productivity and profitability) and report to business manager 3. Managing the onsite team 4. Maintain the consolidated delivery and billing plan 5. Identification and planning of new business with customer 6. Review of estimates and proposals 7. Provide manpower requirements 8. Maintain the project management plan
5	ML	1. Allocates work to DVs in consultation with PM 2. Tracking and monitoring progress of DVs for allocated work 3. Manage the delivery plan for his team 4. Resolve technical issues with onsite coordinator and customer
6	DV	1. Develop detailed design 2. Develop test plan 3. Coding of program 4. Self-testing 5. Code reviews 6. Unit testing 7. Integration testing 8. Communicate with onsite contact
7	CC	1. Develop/maintain configuration management plan 2. Implement configuration management plan 3. Conduct configuration audits 4. Publish results to PL and MLs and create an entry in RADAR 5. Provide assistance to ML/team in implementing configuration standards

8	SQA	1. Review implementation of quality processes in modules 2. Review implementation of project plans 3. Review metrics and analyze against quality targets 4. Assist PL/MLs in implementing project plan and processes 5. Coordinate internal and external audits 6. Follow up closure of NCRs and observations 7. Escalate issues to BM, whenever necessary

Note: BM, business manager; DM, delivery manager; PM, project manager; SQA, software quality advisor; CCD, computer communication department; CC, configuration controller; ML, module leader; DV, developer.

Constituents of Software Project Management

All projects have different constituents that behave differently under different conditions and hence are unpredictable. As a result, it becomes difficult to exercise control over them. At the start of the project, these constituents are not fully known and hence add to the woes of project management. For example, initial requirement analysis and gathering would have detailed out the needs of the end users. However, as the project progresses, a lot of changes happen to these requirements. The business model of the customer might change resulting in change in requirements; change of end users, that is, a separate set of end users would definitely like to change the requirements of their predecessors, thus making it difficult to proceed in project execution as it was planned earlier. These changes have cascading effect on the next processes such as design and construction testing. Whatever would have been planned based on initial requirement analysis would have to be changed to accommodate the new changes. As a result, initial estimation for effort, schedule, and objectives have to be revisited, which result in cost overrun. Many times these changes lead to customer dissatisfaction and new elements of behavioral aspects come into play.

For project management, control and monitoring of the projects are quite important. To manage this, the project is usually broken into smaller manageable granular levels of work. These granular work help in tracking these work to completion. It has been observed that no two projects will have similar granular level details as the projects will differ from each other in terms of their objective. As a result, one project structure will not be effective for another project. This is evident from the fact that in smaller projects, higher level design and lower level design can be combined to make one design stage, whereas in larger projects, these can be separated so that databases can be effectively designed and used. In smaller projects, there could be one testing stage, which will be a combination of integration testing and system testing, whereas in larger projects, there could be more than on system testing stage. An effective project management must ensure that all these stages are well defined and at the completion of the stage, the deliverables are reviewed, corrected or modified and rework completed. It is advisable to have a formal sign off so that the team can move to the next process.

The PM must take into account different characteristics of the project that are peculiar to that project. The understandings of these characteristics allow the manager to tailor standard processes to accommodate these unique characteristics of the project. This also helps to reduce risks associated with the project. In essence, this ensures that even though the overall project management process is same, still unique characteristics are well controlled. For example, in offshore environment, it will make a lot of economic sense to station designers at offshore locations and have one onsite representative who will remain near the customer. Any issue or doubts raised by the design team will be discussed with the customer and then carried back to the team. In smaller projects, certain elements of project management can be tailored to reduce any unnecessary bureaucratic procedures.

In summary, project management process has the following constituents that need to be understood well for better control and monitoring. These are estimation, monitoring and control, defect management, change management, risk management, verification and validation process, and project organization structure. Detailed discussion on these constituents will be done in Chapter 2.

SOFTWARE DEVELOPMENT MODELS—A REVIEW

Software engineering projects follow different lifecycle models. These models are waterfall model, iterative model, spiral model, agile software development model, prototype model, chaos model, and rapid action development (RAD) model. These models can be used for developing software products.

Waterfall Model

Royce (1970) proposed waterfall model in which software development follows a sequential order of lifecycle stages. These lifecycle stages are as follows: requirement specification, design, construction, integration, testing, installation, and maintenance. However, this model is flawed as in the real world of software development, there is a need for flexibility to accommodate any change in requirement and thus in following the stages sequentially such accommodation may not be possible.

Iterative Model

Royce (1970), Boehm (1970), and Mills (1973) came up with a model called iterative model, which can be used for developing applications for customers who are not clear about their requirements. In this model, the project team goes back to earlier stage from the present stage repeatedly till the design specifications match with changes made in the requirements by the customer. The model can be used for building large projects for which domain competency is not adequate with the customer as well as with the development team.

Agile Methodology

Aydin (2005), Abraham (2003), Scrum (1986), and Curt Sampson have proposed agile methodology as a model for software development. In this method, the entire project team necessary for completing the project including customers is located in bullpen, and face-to-face communication is encouraged for discussion instead of depending on written documents. The bullpen[1] also includes testers, designers, managers, and technical writers. This method involves preference for face-to-face communication

[1] Most agile teams are located in a single open office, sometimes referred to as a bullpen. At a minimum, this includes programmers and their "customers" (customers define the product; they may be product managers, business analysts, or the clients). The office may include testers, interaction designers, technical writers, and managers.

and very little written documentation relative to other methods. Therefore, the method is criticized as lacking discipline. Also, this model is difficult to use in large projects and cannot be used where offshore development is preferred to take advantage of highly skilled and low-cost professionals. One of the well-known agile methodologies is extreme programming (XP) (Blanc, Cunningham, and Ron, 1996; McBreen, 2003) in which software is developed in small packets and lot of importance is given to testing and writing test cases even before coding. This method has a lacuna that it can be used only at customer site and for small applications and cannot be off shored.

Prototype Model

In prototype model (Haag et al., 2006), a prototype or working model is developed first to check the design and the feature aspects of the application to be developed and to get user feedback so that risk and cost associated with the final application are reduced. Prototyping is the part of design process and after incorporating the feedback the product is ready for production. However, performance related to stability and reliability of the final production cannot be tested in prototype, as the prototype may not be scalable at all times. This again can be used for small-size to medium-size applications and is not feasible with large production requirement.

Spiral Model

Spiral model (Belz, 1986; Boehm, 1988; Livary, 1987) combines prototype and waterfall models. This model is favored for large projects. In spiral model, requirements are gathered in details and a prototype is developed after preliminary design. Feedback is obtained from customers on this prototype and if required a second prototype is developed, which would be an improved version of the first prototype. In this approach, risk factors would include development cost overruns, operating cost miscalculation, or any other factor that could, in the customer's judgment, result in a less-than-satisfactory final product. Hence, this is used for mission-critical applications (for defense applications) and will be overkilled for software development.

Chaos Model and RAD Model

There are also other development models such as chaos model (Raccoon, 1995) and RAD model (James, 1980; McConnell, 1996;). In chaos model, projects can be thought of in pieces. Nobody writes tens of thousands of lines of code in one sitting. They write small pieces, one line at a time, verifying that the small pieces work. Then they build up from there. The behavior of a complex system emerges from the combined behavior of the smaller building blocks. RAD projects are typically staffed with small integrated teams comprising developers, end users, and IT technical resources, which are combined with short iterative development cycles that optimizes speed, unity of vision and purpose, effective informal communication, and simple project management. An important fundamental principle of RAD is that each iteration delivers a functional version of the final system. These models are used for developing applications where requirements are fairly stable, and the size of the application is small. Also, handling complex applications and change requests during development lifecycle becomes difficult in both these models.

A comparative analysis of these models is given in Table 1.2.

Table 1.2: Comparison of different software models

Model name / Model feature	Waterfall model	Interactive	Prototype	Spiral	Agile	Chaos	RAD
Description of model	Each stage follows the previous one	Revisiting the earlier stage repeatedly Rigorous review in each state	Prototype is developed first Acceptance from the customer is taken on prototype before further development	Prototype and waterfall combined Requirements are gathered and prototype is developed better preliminary design Second prototype may be made of requirement	Bullpen method Stress on use of face-to-face communication Customer site only	Lines of codes are written and then tested immediately	RAD projects are staffed with small integrated teams of developers, end users, and IT technical resources Developments are carried out in small iterative cycle
Assumption of the model	Requirements are processed Skill set required is available with the team	Timelines are flexible Requirements need to be captured through interactions	Requirements are frozen Performance in terms of response time can be similar with final development			Projects are combination of small pieces	A small application can be scaled up to a large application Each iteration delivers a functional version of the final system
Application	Complexity is low Risks associated with projects are low	Complex application Requirements are not clear and not frozen	Scientific application development Small-sized application	Mission–critical application Defense application	No off shoring Small application Test planning and testing are the most critical stages	Small-sized application	Scientific and research software applications

Strengths of the model	Can work for development and maintenance Good for small and medium projects where risk is low	Can accommodate change requirement Can be used when domain competency is not available with project team Requirements are not clear Can be used for complex application	Design aspects are well taken care of Chances of failure at the end are less	Robust product Can take care of complex application	Better test plans Structured testing Analyst, development and customer involvement in test planning Defects are captured at early stages	Less scope for error during implementation	Customer requirements are well taken care of
Weaknesses of the model	Testing late in the development cycle Narrow scope for testing Minimal test planning Deadlines to take priority of over quality	Timelines are missed Difficult for software application	Performance in terms of response time cannot be predicted when there is a large user base in need time May not be scalable all the time Cannot be used for large application Cannot accommodate change requests after prototype is built	High development cost Overkill for application	Expensive Coordination among all stakeholders could be difficult Large application development is not easy Change requests accommodate after development is difficult as availabilities of team members at a time are difficult	Cannot be used in medium and large-sized application development Cannot be used for change requests	Time-consuming Effort is quite high

Reliable Iterative Testing Environment (RITE)—Software Product Development Model

RITE model against other software development models lays emphasis on iterative testing. This means that packets[2] are tested even during requirement phase. As the project progresses in its lifecycle phase the testing of packets continues till the products are delivered to the customer. Using this methodology, products are developed in "packets." After building these packets, not only each packet is tested thoroughly but also these are integrated, and testing is carried out for each new product. The entire product is developed and delivered through an "integrated team" approach. The methodology has four phases. In phase 1, contract is signed with the customer and based on the contract an integrated team is developed. Contract is quite significant in RITE model as the entire scope is determined at this stage. Even though change requests are accommodated later on, this helps to track extra effort required to develop these change requests. This also helps in billing accurately to the customer. After contract is signed and purchase order is received, requirement gathering and analysis of requirements are carried out. In phase 2, detailed design specifications and test scripts are written based on requirement analysis. Phase 3 primarily takes care of packets development and testing. And finally, installation, user training, user acceptance testing, and transition to support happen in phase 4. Each of these phases is described here and a schematic diagram is given in Figure 1.3.

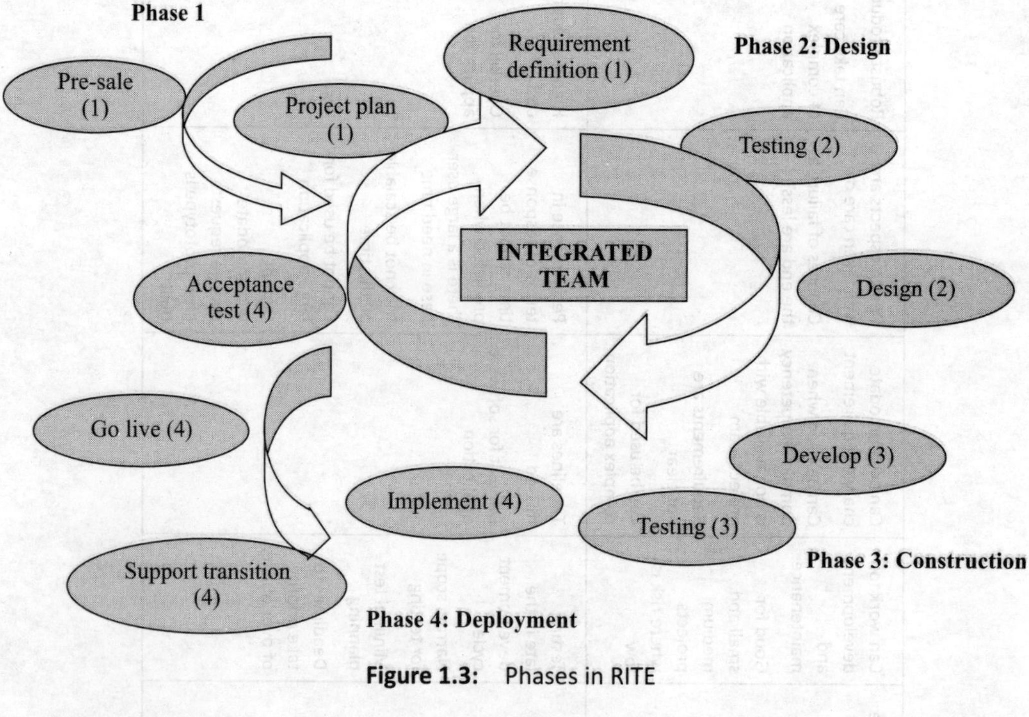

Figure 1.3: Phases in RITE

[2] A packet consists of already developed functionalities that have been tested and ready to be used. These packets are designed and developed in such a manner that they are independent of each other. Similar requirements received from different customers are grouped together and formed into these packets. This helps in reducing time required to develop these requirements again.

The RITE methodology framework also addresses how a project team is put together to deliver a product. This concept is called the integrated project team approach. The integrated team consists of project committee, product committee, product team (all these are based at onsite, near the customer), and project team based at offshore location. Project committee works with marketing team in pre-sales activities; it helps the marketing team to clarify any doubts that a prospect will raise during the initial discussion period. Once a prospect is turned into customer, it is the responsibility of the product committee to provide a detailed estimation, negotiate with the customer, and then enter into a detailed contract. The contract, apart from other things, will highlight scope, timeline of delivery, and the total effort that would be spent while executing the project. The offshore project team reports to this committee. The project committee reports to solution director who has the overall responsibility for providing the products to the customer.

The product committee largely consists of domain experts who based on market research, interaction with customers, and industry experts would design different "packets." The packets, as explained earlier, will be independent to each other and would be integrated by offshore project team. These integrated packets would be delivered to the customer. The product committee would also define what is known as road map for each product. The road map for products consists of timeline for developing different features. These features would be the part of the packets and would be developed by the product team. The product team directly reports to this product committee. Both product committee and product teams are based onsite.

Project offshore team has a primary responsibility of integrating packets, iterative testing, and delivering the final integrated products to the customers. The team has expertise in testing and integration of packets. A schematic organization structure is shown in Figure 1.4.

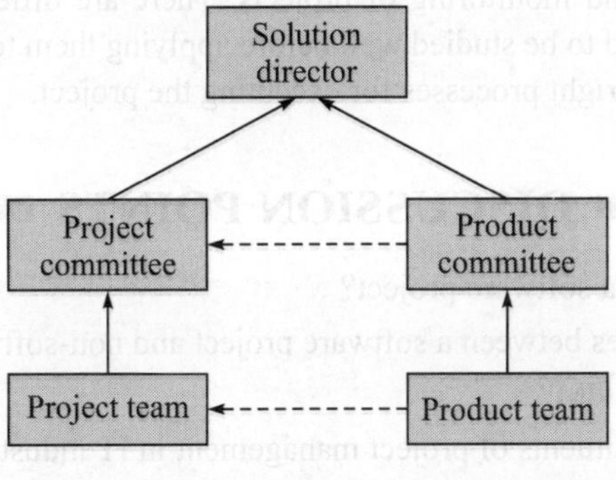

Figure 1.4: Integrated team structure

Each lifecycle stage in RITE model has defined deliverables. These deliverables ensure that proper and effective documentation is carried out without making these activities as overhead. Quality system documentation (QSD), an internal system that details all the procedures and processes, is used as reference while developing software using RITE model. QSD is internal to organization and is used as induction training material to new entrants at all levels. This ensures that employees at all levels are familiar with deliverables expected out of them. Table 1.3 lists key deliverables in RITE model.

Table 1.3: List of deliverables from RITE model

Life stages in RITE	Required deliverables
At contract/project initiation	Statement of work/contract
Project startup, ongoing revisions to the project plan	Project plan and iteration plan
Client sign off on RD	Requirements definition
Following RD delivery	Detail design document
Logical day test plan at project initiation, test scripts at design	Test plan and scripts
Upon completion of each iteration	Test results
Ongoing throughout the testing process	Issues list
Upon client delivery	Training materials
Upon client delivery	Customer/user documentation
Upon transition to support	Project transition documentation Lessons learnt documentation

SUMMARY

Software projects are different from non-IT projects in that they have many constituents that are different. Understanding these constituents will help in better understanding of risks, uncertainties, and process followed in these projects. Also, understanding lifecycle processes followed by these software projects will help in breaking the projects into granular level of work. The detailed granular work helps in controlling and monitoring of projects. There are different software development models available, which need to be studied well before applying them to a certain project. A correct model will help in choosing right processes for executing the project.

DISCUSSION POINTS

1. What do you mean by a software project?
2. What are the differences between a software project and non-software project?
3. What are the roles of a PM?
4. Explain different constituents of project management in IT industry.
5. What are differences between a software project development cycle and a software product development cycle?

CASE STUDY

Mahindras have a good reputation as IT service provider. They are known for their ability to understand the needs of their customers and develop software applications accordingly. They have successfully executed a number of projects at offshore locations (India) and have current strength of 5000 employees. Their domain knowledge has been developed over the years by working in different domains such as retail, utilities, supply chain management, and insurance sectors.

Recently, they want to enter into telecommunications domain. After making a number of attempts, they got a project in telecommunications (telecomm, in short) domain in Australia. This was a major breakthrough for the company as they not only entered telecomm domain but also made a foray into a new geography—Australia. They wanted to put together a new team and selected Gopinath as the PM. Gopinath had extensively worked in retail and supply chain domain and had handled more than 10 large projects in his 7 years career with the company. He had a good knowledge in COBOL and was considered as a good technical reviewer of code written in COBOL. He also had good understanding of customers in the United States, where all of his projects had been implemented.

Quality processes in Mahindras were matured and have stabilized over the years. However, these processes are related to domains other than that of telecomm; also, it is well known that relationship with customers in the United States will require an approach different from that of customers in Australia. This means communication protocol will require a different approach. Regulatory conditions in the United States are also different from that in Australia and these needs to be well understood by the team. Traveling to Australia was easier as there was no need to plan for H1B visas (like that for the United States) well in advance.

Questions:

1. How should Gopinath go about executing this project?
2. What are the constituents of project management that need to be stressed?
3. What kind of development model is to be followed for this project and why?

2

PROJECT PLANNING

LEARNING OBJECTIVES

In this chapter, the students would learn:

- Planning process
- Process definition and tailoring
- Process capability baseline
- Software metrics
- Quality planning and setting objectives for quality
- Estimation techniques
- Risk management
- Plan template

PROJECT PLANNING PROCESS

Project planning starts at the initial stage, after getting the "go ahead" from the customer. The "go ahead" can be in the form of letter of intent, purchase order, work order, or any such formal document. This document authorizes the vendor organization, which is engaged in developing applications, to start executing the project as per the terms and conditions of the order. This is the starting point for project planning. The vendor organization management appoints a project manager who is responsible for executing the project successfully.

A software project has two aspects—one aspect dealing with software engineering lifecycle, which is used to develop the application, and the other aspect that manages this software engineering lifecycle. Each aspect is important as the lack of good and stable engineering lifecycle will not result in good quality output, and the lack of good project management will result in unsuccessful execution of the projects even with good technically sound project team. The project management assumes importance as an effective project management practice will help in getting the resources aligned toward the goals and objectives of the project, resulting in harmony of resources, optimum utilization of the resources, and meeting the customer needs. It acts as a thread that binds different software engineering processes in one direction. Each software engineering process has procedures, activities, and is assigned to team members. These processes could have dependency on each other and tasks contained in them may require many resources. Project management aims to control and monitor these processes and achieve the desired results.

Project planning stage also includes looking at the terms and conditions mentioned in the purchase order and setting project goals and objectives accordingly. In order to achieve the contractual obligations, the project has to set goals and objectives that are either similar to or stringent than that mentioned in the purchase order. The contract mentions the specification limits and the project management sets acceptable limits, where acceptable limits are more stringent than specified limits. On the basis of these specified limits and the software engineering processes involved, a project plan is prepared. The project plan involves defining a lifecycle that needs to be followed in the project, doing activities and tasks at granular level for each of these processes, and estimating effort required for each of these granular levels of task. Apart from engineering activities, the plan also includes activities such as milestone review, quality audit, training, configuration management, peer review, and risk management.

The project manager also identifies all the stakeholders for the project and calls for a meeting. In this meeting, known usually as "kick-off" meeting, the manager shares all the relevant objectives of the project and asks for commitment from them. Issues related to hardware, software, personnel recruitment, technical architecture, and so forth are discussed in detail. The project manager, being appointed as the sole person to be accountable for project execution, reports to the management regarding outcome of the "kick-off" meeting. In case there is a gap between objectives and commitment from stakeholders, the same is apprised by the project manager to the management for suitable action.

For any project to succeed, it is essential to identify all the stakeholders and make an explicit effort to understand what the different stakeholders need in order to have a "win–win" situation for all stakeholders. In order to achieve that it is necessary to call for a kick-off meeting well in advance (as mentioned in Chapter 1), discuss the objectives of the project with them, and find out whether or not there are any conflicting interests. After that it is the responsibility of the project manager to negotiate and remove any conflict among the stakeholders so as to achieve cohesiveness among them.

Identifying Stakeholders

Stakeholders are not always the persons reflected in the official organization hierarchy, or people who have a direct connection to the project. Some of the typical stakeholders could be information system department of customers' managers of the team, end users of the application from customer organization, team that is going to maintain the application later on, project team members, visa department for visa application, travel department for making necessary travel arrangements, HR department for recruitment, training department for providing training to team members, architect group for helping on architecture-related issues, business analysts to help explain and provide resolutions for any issues raised by team members during the application development stage, etc. There can also be times when either superiors or subordinates of persons identified at the customer site as the project owner can have a vested interest in the project. When these persons are not identified and not considered, there are chances that at the end of the project they can sufficiently influence the downfall of the project simply for the fact that they were not consulted on the project.

A list of stakeholders and their objectives are mentioned in Table 2.1. However, these objectives may vary depending on the project.

Table 2.1: List of stakeholders and possible objectives

Stakeholders	Objectives
Customer business manager	Quick schedule, low budget
Vendor organization business manager	No effort overrun, no defects during implementation, no schedule variation, high profitability
Team members	Interesting work, well-planned work, no scope changes, no midnight oil burning
Customer information system department manager	Maintainability, performance, no bugs, and issues while in production
End users of the application	High security, easy to use, performance

In order that the above organization structure is effective, responsibilities of each role need to be defined. Table 2.2 shows an illustrative role and responsibility matrix. By defining roles and responsibility matrix, accountability is identified well in advance. The clear-cut explanation of expectation from different roles does not leave any room for duplication and misunderstanding. On this basis, role-specific training can be designed, which will help them to perform their roles well. For recruitment of personnel for these roles, the descriptions can act as job description, which will make it easier for HR department to look for suitable candidates. As discussed in team composition section, there should be an optimum mix of employees in different roles. Even though resource mix in one project may not be possible to duplicate in another project, still, based on experience, a role mix can be recommended. This recommended role mix has been found to be good for development projects with around 20 team members. The ratio between developer and module leader is 3:1, which means for every three developers there should be a module leader. Similarly, there should be one project manager for three module leaders.

Table 2.2: Roles and responsibilities in a development project

S. no.	Roles	Responsibilities
1	Customer	1. Specify current and future project requirements (delivery schedules/sequence) 2. Review project schedules and issues periodically 3. Resolution of all issues (technical, operational, and business) 4. Review and sign off design packages and prototypes 5. Review and accept proposals 6. Review and accept delivered systems

2	BM	1. Provide resources for the project 2. Review project plans and project health periodically 3. Define business goals and provide guidance to PM 4. Establish and maintain a communication channel with customer GM 5. Review and coordinate with SBU-Head 6. Resolve issues escalated by team
3	DM	1. Take bottom-line responsibility for all project issues with the customer 2. Provide resources for the project 3. Review project plans and project health periodically 4. Define business goals and provide guidance to PM 5. Establish and maintain a communication channel with the customer GM 6. Review and coordinate with SBU-Head 7. Resolve issues escalated by team
4	PM	1. Ownership of customer relationship and business 2. Analysis of project health (productivity and profitability) and report to business manager 3. Managing the onsite team 4. Maintain the consolidated delivery and billing plan 5. Identification and planning of new business with the customer 6. Review of estimates and proposals 7. Provide manpower requirements 8. Maintain the project management plan
5	ML	1. Allocates work to DVs in consultation with PM 2. Tracking and monitoring progress of DVs for allocated work 3. Manage the delivery plan for his/her team 4. Resolve technical issues with the onsite coordinator and the customer
6	DV	1. Develop detailed design 2. Develop test plan 3. Coding of program 4. Self testing 5. Code reviews 6. Unit testing 7. Integration testing 8. Communicate with onsite contact
7	CC	1. Develop/maintain configuration management plan 2. Implement configuration management plan 3. Conduct configuration audits 4. Publish results to PL and MLs and create an entry in RADAR 5. Provide assistance to ML/team in implementing configuration standards
8	SQA	1. Review implementation of quality processes in modules 2. Review implementation of project plans 3. Review metrics and analyze against quality targets 4. Assist PL/MLs in implementing project plan and processes 5. Coordinate internal and external audits 6. Follow up closure of NCRs and observations 7. Escalate issues to BM, whenever necessary

Note: BM, business manager; DM, delivery manager; PM, project manager; SQA, software quality advisor; CCD, computer communication department; CC, configuration controller; ML, module leader; DV, developer.

Identifying Objectives

After all the stakeholders are identified, it is critical to identify what each stakeholder expects to gain from the project. For instance, for an end user it might be that they are expecting a very user-friendly and robust software with a number of features, while for a maintainer it is the quality of the documentation and the modifiability of the system that are important. A manager would not want any overruns to the schedule, while the person who approves the budget might expect a low-budget project. By identifying each of the stakeholders' "win" condition, the project's objectives are clear from the start. In the negotiation with the customer, these objectives should be reinforced and documented. Refer to Annexure for the format of the documentation.

Steps to identify the objectives are as follows:

1. Understand how people will benefit from the project
2. Prioritize objectives for the project
3. Establish reasonable expectations on the parts of all the stakeholders
4. Transform these objectives into project activities
5. Identify and manage the risks
6. Keep people involved. Keep senior management and the customer aware of the status of the project at all times

Process Definition and Tailoring

A process is defined as one where there are inputs that are converted to outputs. A process will have certain characteristics; a process can be divided into procedures, each procedure is divided into tasks. Each procedure is allocated to a role, which would be accountable for completion of that procedure. A software project also follows a set of processes. These processes can be exclusively defined for the project or are adopted from organization-wide process repository. An organization-wide process is defined after executing a number of projects following similar project lifecycles over a period of time. For example, the organization would have executed a number of development projects for different customers. Each project would have carried out different activities and processes. These processes are usually similar in one organization. Over weeks, months, and years of following these processes, the processes will be similar and a standard process can be defined for development projects. As a result, any new development project can follow this standard process without having to define a new one. This new standard process can be accompanied by guidelines for executing these processes. An organization-wide standard process thus describes the manner in which different activities and tasks in a project will be completed. If a new project follows this standard process and guidelines, then the performance of projects in terms of quality, delivery schedule, and time required (effort in terms of man hours) can be very well predicted. The variations will be reduced and will definitely help the customers in having faith in the project processes. It has been observed that the customers usually feel more comfortable while dealing with vendors following a standard process.

For any organization, it is important to define standard processes and guidelines. This means an organization should have separate standard processes with guidelines for development projects as well as for maintenance and products. Standard processes help to reduce variations in the performance of different projects in different aspects such as productivity, cost of quality, schedule-adherence capability, and so on. In the absence of standard guidelines and processes, different projects follow different processes, which result in poor predictability in the aspects mentioned above. Lack of standard processes means past data are not used for taking decisions, which result in no or weak correlation between past, present, and future performances. In such situations, past data cannot be used for estimating new or future projects; this means all the learning from previous projects go waste and is not a desirable situation for a matured organization. A matured organization uses past data, learning, and best practices to improve continuously. Hence, standard processes need to be defined to help improve predictability of project performance, accurate estimating capability, and for continuous improvement. However, it is not possible to have standard processes for all projects as different customers have different and specific requirements. These specific nature leads to specific characteristics, which are different for different projects. In order to execute these different characteristics, the defined standard processes need to be tweaked a bit for each project. Thus, while we have general processes that help in defining and executing processes, there is a provision to tweak or "tailor" particular processes to meet specific characteristics of each project. This process is known as tailoring and is the part of project process definition. The tailoring process allows taking care of specific characteristics of each project while following standard processes. For this, tailoring guidelines need to be framed and made available during process definition. The catch is that, with these tailoring guidelines, the type of tailoring processes that can be used for the projects are limited and only approved variations are allowed to be tailored for a new project. This is an important and necessary activity in process definition.

Examples of Process Tailoring in Development Projects

Development projects use the processes for gathering and analyzing the customer requirements, and then develope that into a software application(s). The processes followed will take care of requirements, design, development, testing, implementation, and warranty support for the project. Different literature and survey of practices indicate that there are different models available for development projects. Some of these models are waterfall, iterative, spiral, prototyping, RITE, and so forth; explanation of these models is given in Chapter 1. The most used model is iterative or spiral model and traditional stages are broken into smaller processes so that parallel execution of the processes can take place without losing sight of the customer needs. After choosing the standard processes (which are already defined by the organization based on the past experience in executing similar development projects), a tailoring process from previously defined tailoring guidelines is selected. This way, the project gets flexibility but in a restricted manner and at high level. It essentially prepares subgroups among standard development processes. On the basis of need, a project manager can choose one or more of these subprocesses.

Tailoring processes is a way of adjusting standard processes of the organization so that suitable effective process can be defined for a project. This tailored process will help in meeting business needs and technical specifications of the project. The tailored process is arrived at either by adding, deleting, or modifying the defined standard process such that the final process is best suited for achieving objectives of the project. A decision is taken during the tailoring process as to what level of tailoring is allowed in process definition. Unlimited tailoring will imply that it is free for all and there is no standard process available. Tailoring guidelines are issued to control this level of deviation from standard processes. These set of guidelines are nothing but a combination of permissible rules for modifying rules. Thus, one can explain that the tailoring guidelines are a set of permissible deviations of the organization-wide defined standard processes so that the best, effective, and optimum process can be defined for a new project. For example, let us look at the construction or code-writing phase of a development project. As per the standard process, there is a code review process for each and every line of code being written. Code review is an essential process for a development project because, before sending the code for testing, any defect related to specifications in design phase will be detected in the code review process. Also, code review detects any discrepancy with respect to code-writing standards that needs to be followed while writing codes. Thus, the process adds a lot of value for quality for all deliverables. But sometimes the code review process is time-consuming and may not add value to the quality already existing in the code. This could be because code could have been written by an experienced and skilled team member or the code could have been generated using a code generator. In these circumstances, code review becomes a burden to the project as it increases total project effort and affects the schedule of delivery. Also, the review can be done by a single person or a peer group. In these cases, tailoring guidelines can help to fine-tune standard process and define an optimum process such that both high quality and productivity can be achieved. Tailoring guidelines can suggest that a project can do code review for complex and difficult programs while simple and easier programs can be reviewed by the developer himself. The guidelines can also suggest that a complex program can be group reviewed in which a group of team members will review the code and detect any anomalies with respect to design specifications.

Tailoring guidelines also records experience and knowledge of team members who have executed similar projects in the past. These team members, who have used similar tailoring guidelines, share their experience, and these are recorded in process repository. Using these experiences, new project members can decide as to which processes need to be tailored so that optimum results can be achieved. Steps involved in tailoring process are as follows: (1) identify standard process that needs to be applied, (2) identify unique characteristics of the project, (3) discuss among team members and experienced personnel (often from quality department) to decide which tailoring guidelines need to be applied, (4) take approval from senior management, (5) record the tailored processes in project plan document, and (6) share this plan with all the team members.

What Are the Various Processes That Can Be Tailored?

Some of the most common examples of processes that can be tailored are shown in Table 2.3.

Table 2.3: Various processes that can be tailored

Processes	Will this activity be performed?
Documentation	Will the output of an activity be documented formally?
Reviewer	Who should review an output?
Periodicity	How frequently will this activity be performed?
Composition of system testing team	When to have a separate system team?

If we consider the example taken here, then tailored processes are for an activity called "code walk-thru," either perform group review only for complex programs, or carry out one-person review for medium programs, or there is no need to review simple programs, and so on. A project manager after discussion with quality department and senior management can decide whether to implement the process element as per guidelines or remove the process element or replace the process element with a new process or add a new process element. These changes must be highlighted in project plan as deviations. For situations where the customer processes are to be followed, related tailoring guidelines should be mandatorily followed and noted in the project plan as tailored processes. For example, a project team can have a tailored process where they have to name integration testing as "staging" and there will be three to four stages of staging (nomenclature for testing) rather than one stage of integration testing as suggested in standard process. Such modifications need to be well accepted in the kick-off meeting itself and accepted by all stakeholders. These need to be recorded as deviations in the project plan. This is also an example of tailoring guidelines because of contractual obligation to follow the customer's process.

Some other examples of tailoring guidelines are shown in Table 2.4 for testing phase.

Table 2.4: Examples of tailoring

Lifecycle stage: testing					
Review integration plan	Tailorable	**Reviewer**	Do group review	Always	
Do integration test	Tailorable	**Requirements coverage %**	At least 90%	When the application criticality is high	
			At least 75%	When the application criticality is low	
Conduct independent unit test	Tailorable	**Execution**	Perform this activity	For all complex/critical/external interface programs; or for first few programs of each type (online, batch, report) when skill level of DVs is low	
Review unit test plan	Tailorable	**Reviewer**	Do group review	For all complex/critical/external interface programs; or for the first few programs of each type (online, batch, report) when the skill level of the DVs are low	Between unit test plan and code for a program, at least one should follow the review procedures suggested here
Write unit test plan	Tailorable	**Execution**	Perform this activity	For all complex/medium/critical/external interface programs; or for first few programs of each type (online, batch, report) when the skill level of the DVs are low, till comfort level is high	

Process tailoring	Added/modified/deleted	Remarks
Detailed design phase has been merged with the high level design	Modified	Schedule is tight and this process will not add any value to the project
System test planning and system testing	Deleted	To be done at onsite; to follow the customer standard for system testing
Acceptance and installation	Deleted	To be done at onsite; to follow the customer standard for system testing

Estimating

In the previous section, we discussed the stage of process definition in project planning. In this stage, the process needs to be defined such that we get optimum results from a combination of standard and tailored processes. The next stage involves estimating process. Estimating effort is one of the most difficult tasks in software project management but is a critical factor in determining success of the project. In estimating, both the schedule and the effort need to be estimated. During the award of contract, the customer would have set the project implementation date for vendor. The customer decides this date by considering his/her own business needs. The business needs decide when the application should be implemented so that all the benefits associated with the software can be reaped by the customer. This is usually a strategic decision and the decision is taken at the top level of management in the customer organization. The decision also takes care of factors such as competitive advantage from installation of such applications and unique selling proposition obtained from such installations. Hence, in reality, the schedule is decided well in advance by the customer and there is not much of flexibility available to the vendor. Hence, the focus in software estimation is on effort estimation. Without effort estimation, time (schedule) and effort required to complete the project will not be available; this is essential for effective control and monitoring in project management. The basic need for effective project planning is to be able to accurately estimate effort required to complete the project and schedule of delivery for the deliverables. This estimation helps the manager to have a baseline for finding out whether the project activities are on track or late.

Estimating process in project planning is also essential for the vendor organization for its own business needs. Estimating effort will have impact on resources for the vendor organization. The estimation decides the number of hours to be spent for project execution as well as the number of team members needed for timely completion of the project. The estimation also decides whether new resources need to be recruited for the project and also whether investment is needed for arranging training sessions to upgrade skills of the team members for smooth execution of the project. An underestimated effort will impact the vendor financially; project margin as well as financial health of the project will be in jeopardy. Sometimes the vendor does an underestimation to bag the contract; this is done to make inroads to a new customer or to a new domain or to gain an entry into a new geography. However, these are exceptions and are done for short-term benefits. This approach of underestimating is not sustainable and this book will deal with situations wherein an effort is made for estimating process to be as accurate as possible. In the same light of discussion an overestimation is not desirable either. Overestimating means the customer has to pay extra for the effort and does not get value for money. In subsequent projects, the vendor might lose out to competitors if this type of overestimating continues. Thus, it is important that accurate estimating process is adopted as this is only sustainable in the long run.

As discussed earlier, there is always a need for estimation before the start of a project. The process needs to be accurate as well as formal. The formality of process helps in seriousness with which the management entrusts accountability to the project manager. Different tools and techniques are also encouraged to be developed to help increase the level of accuracy and consistency. The effort that is calculated at the end of the process is then converted to monetary terms by multiplying the hours with hourly rate of the team members. While tracking and monitoring, estimated hours are used as basis against which actual values are compared. Once an estimation of effort is made, estimating schedule becomes easier. Thus, one can argue that without good and accurate effort estimation, effective planning of a software project is not possible. Usage of past data is very important here and as more and more projects are executed it is expected that past data would be used for estimation.

Effort Estimation Models

As is with any process, there is an input and output to estimating process. For estimating effort, one of the inputs is getting to know the functional requirements and characteristics of the project. This helps to convert these functional requirements to hours using available models. If these functional requirements are not known at the initial stage of the project, then estimated hours is usually termed as "ball park figure," where the final output can be quite off the target as that of a ball being thrown aimlessly in a park. The functionalities will determine whether the application will be a complex or simple one and also will determine the size of the application. The larger the size of the application, the higher the effort required to complete it. When the project is being conceived the functionalities are not well known, and hence the size cannot be measured accurately. Hence, it is a general practice to gather all the required functionalities and then use these requirements to arrive at the size of the project. In other words, this approach reduces effort estimation to size estimation problem. The next section explains how size measurement is used for converting this estimation of effort.

While measuring the size of an application, there are two approaches that are used—top down or bottom up. Using both the approaches, a simple equation-based model is used for converting size to overall effort. Once overall effort is known, the efforts for different activities are calculated. The effort for each of these activities is determined as percentage of total efforts. This is known as top-down approach for estimation, as the overall effort is determined first and then using this overall effort detailed level of efforts are determined. There are many models available for top-down approach such as function point, use cases model, consensus-based top-down model, object-based estimation technique, and Delphi model. In the following section a short description of each of the models is given with detailed description of function point methodology.

Size Measurement Using Top-Down Approach

There are two different ways of measuring the size of software applications (as accepted at international forums, e.g., IFPUG and IEEE standards). The size of software applications is measured in terms of (1) lines of code (Robert, 1992; used for development) or (2) function point [www.ifpug.org (2002)]. In the first method of measuring the size through lines of code, after the programs are written and tested, the number of lines of code are counted physically. The number of lines thus counted is an indication of the size of the program. The problem with this method is that different technology has different syntax or format to be followed. Hence, the same functionalities may require higher number of lines of code in one technology, whereas in another technology the same functionality can be developed by writing less number of codes. Also, depending on the skill level of the programmer, the number of lines of code may vary.

Function points (FPs) are a measure of the functionality that the user requests and receives independent of the technology used for implementation. FP is a metric that comprises the weighted totals of the inputs, outputs, inquires, logical files or user data groups, and interfaces belonging to an application. For the purpose of FP analysis, a system is divided into two large classes, viz., data functions and transaction functions to capture the functionality. Data functions capture the data elements of the application. These are further classified as internal logical files and external interface files. Transaction functions capture the processing of data. These are further subdivided into external inputs, external outputs, and external inquires.

Function Point Methodology

In the late 1970, IBM felt the need to develop a language-independent approach to estimating software development effort. It assigned one of its employees, Allan Albrecht, with developing this approach in 1979. The result was the FP technique. FPs are a measure of the size of computer applications that are being built. The size is measured from a functional, or user, point of view. It is independent of the computer language, development methodology, technology, or capability of the project team used to develop the application.

Functional size estimation uses the number of functionalities to be made available in the application and is a top-down technique used for estimating summary-level activity first and then breaking it into lower level activities. After collecting requirements from the customer, the project team would count number of FPs by using different methodologies available. When using FPs (Albrecht, 1979; IFPUG, 1999) or cosmic functional size units (CFSU) (Abran, Symons, and Oligny, 2001), the estimator needs to understand the required functionalities, and then use either of the above-mentioned methodologies to count FPs. But all these methodologies would give accurate results for large size new application development. In order to make a reliable estimate for (new) development project, the size should be over 200 FP or 100 CFSU. Most of the upgrade projects are smaller-sized applications and hence cannot use these methodologies. Capers Jones (1986) published a method based closely on that of Albrecht, called "feature points." This method aims to extend functional size methodology to scientific algorithms. Charles Symons (1988) modified Albrecht's (1979) FP and developed the "MkII function point method" that aimed to take care of complexity of business application software, which are "data rich." However, it was difficult to measure and classify complexity related to data requirements in business application software, and hence this method could not be used for upgrade projects in commercial software development.

Using Albrecht's (1979) approach, Whitmire (1992) developed "3D function points" for estimating the size of scientific and real-time software. The three dimensions in 3D FPs are data, function, and control. The data dimension is similar to Albrecht's FPs. The function dimension adds transformations, which are similar to the algorithms, and the control dimension adds transitions, which explains changes in application state. This approach was a proprietary of Boeing and not widely used because it is not easy to use for counting FPs and, compared with feature points, it does not help in counting FPs for algorithms in scientific software. NESMA (1997) developed its own variant for counting FPs. The variations from IFPUG method of counting FP were related to "further data processing" and data display, which is also known as "implicit enquiry." This approach also does not take care of complexities involved in the algorithm and mostly used for development projects. For smaller size of the applications, this method is not suitable. The University of Québec, Montréal, and others published the "full function point method" in 1997 that used the IFPUG rules for business application software and added extra components for sizing real-time software; however, this has not been accepted by practitioners for commercial software projects because this method can be accurate for large-sized application development only.

What is Function Point Analysis?

Function point analysis (FPA) has been proven as a reliable method for measuring the size of computer software. In addition to measuring output, FPA is extremely useful in estimating projects, managing change of scope, measuring productivity, and communicating functional requirements.

One of the initial design criteria for FPs was to provide a mechanism that both software developers and users could utilize to define functional requirements. It was determined that the best way to gain an understanding of the users' needs was to approach their problem from the perspective of how they view the results that an automated system produces. Therefore, one of the primary goals of FPA is to evaluate a system's capabilities from a user's point of view. In order to achieve this goal, the analysis is based on the different ways users interact with computerized systems. From a user's perspective a system assists them in doing their job by providing five basic functions. Two of these address the data requirements of an end user and are referred to as data functions. The remaining three address the user's need to access data and are referred to as transactional functions.

The five components of FPs are as follows:

Data functions

1. Internal logical files
2. External interface files

Transactional functions

3. External inputs
4. External outputs
5. External inquiries

Internal logical files (ILFs)—The first data function allows users to utilize data they are responsible for maintaining. For example, a pilot may enter navigational data through a display in the cockpit prior to departure. The data is stored in a file for use and can be modified during the mission. Therefore, the pilot is responsible for maintaining the file that contains the navigational information. Logical groupings of data in a system, maintained by an end user, are referred to as ILFs.

External interface files (EIFs)—The second data function a system provides to an end user is also related to logical groupings of data. In this case, the user is not responsible for maintaining the data. The data resides in another system and is maintained by another user or system. The user of the system being counted requires this data for reference purposes only. For example, it may be necessary for a pilot to reference position data from a satellite or ground-based facility during flight. The pilot does not have the responsibility for updating data at these sites but must reference it during the flight. Groupings of data from another system that are used only for reference purposes are defined as EIFs.

The remaining functions address the user's capability to access the data contained in ILFs and EIFs. This capability includes maintaining, inquiring, and outputting of data. These are referred to as transactional functions.

External inputs (EI)—The first transactional function allows a user to maintain ILFs through the ability to add, change, and delete the data. For example, a pilot can add, change, and delete navigational information prior to and during the mission. In this case, the pilot is utilizing a transaction referred to as an external input (EI). An EI gives the user the capability to maintain the data in ILFs through adding, changing, and deleting its contents.

External outputs (EO)—The next transactional function gives the user the ability to produce outputs. For example, a pilot has the ability to separately display ground speed, true air speed, and calibrated air speed. The results displayed are derived using data that are maintained and data that are referenced. In FP terminology the resulting display is called an external output (EO).

External inquiries (EQ)—The final capability provided to users through a computerized system addresses the requirement to select and display specific data from files. In order to accomplish this, a user inputs selection information that is used to retrieve data that meets the specific criteria. In this situation, there is no manipulation of the data. It is a direct retrieval of information contained on the files. For example, if a pilot displays terrain clearance data that was previously set, the resulting output is the direct retrieval of stored information. These transactions are referred to as external inquiries.

In addition to the five functional components described above there are two adjustment factors that need to be considered in FPA.

Functional complexity—The first adjustment factor considers the functional complexity for each unique function. Functional complexity is determined based on the combination of data groupings and data elements of a particular function. The number of data elements and unique groupings are counted and compared with a complexity matrix that will rate the function as low, average, or high complexity. Each of the five functional components (ILF, EIF, EI, EO, and EQ) has its own unique complexity matrix. Table 2.5 shows the complexity matrix for EOs.

Table 2.5: Complexity matrix

	1–5 DETs	6–19 DETs	20+ DETs
0 or 1 FTRs	L	L	A
2 or 3 FTRs	L	A	H
4+ FTRs	A	H	H

Complexity	UFP
L (low)	4
A (average)	5
H (high)	7

Using the examples given above and their appropriate complexity matrices, the FP count for these functions would be as shown in Table 2.6.

Table 2.6: Function point count using complexity matrix

Function name	Function type	Record element type	Data element type	File types referenced	Unadjusted FPs
Navigational data	ILF	3	36	n/a	10
Positional data	EIF	1	3	n/a	5
Navigational data–add	EI	n/a	36	1	4
Navigational data–change	EI	n/a	36	1	4
Navigational data–delete	EI	n/a	3	1	3
Ground speed display	EO	n/a	20	3	7
Air speed display	EO	n/a	20	3	7
Calibrated air speed display	EO	n/a	20	3	7
Terrain clearance display	EQ	n/a	1	1	3
Total unadjusted count					**50 UFPs**

All of the functional components are analyzed in this way and are added together to derive an UFP count.

Value Adjustment Factor—The UFP count is multiplied by the second adjustment factor called the value adjustment factor. This factor considers the system's technical and operational characteristics and is calculated by answering 14 questions. The questions are related to the following:

1. **Data communications** The data and control information used in the application are sent or received over communication facilities.
2. **Distributed data processing** Distributed data or processing functions are a characteristic of the application within the application boundary.
3. **Performance** Application performance objectives, stated or approved by the user, in either response or throughput, influence (or will influence) the design, development, installation, and support of the application.
4. **Heavily used configuration** A heavily used operational configuration, requiring special design considerations, is a characteristic of the application.
5. **Transaction rate** The transaction rate is high and influences the design, development, installation, and support.
6. **Online data entry** Online data entry and control information functions are provided in the application.
7. **End-user efficiency** The online functions provided emphasize a design for end-user efficiency.
8. **Online update** The application provides online update for the ILFs.
9. **Complex processing** Complex processing is a characteristic of the application.
10. **Reusability** The application and the code in the application have been specifically designed, developed, and supported to be usable in other applications.
11. **Installation ease** Conversion and installation ease are characteristics of the application. A conversion and installation plan and/or conversion tools were provided and tested during the system test phase.
12. **Operational ease** Operational ease is a characteristic of the application. Effective startup, backup, and recovery procedures were provided and tested during the system test phase.
13. **Multiple sites** The application has been specifically designed, developed, and supported to be installed at multiple sites for multiple organizations.
14. **Facilitate change** The application has been specifically designed, developed, and supported to facilitate change.

Each of these factors is scored based on their influence on the system being counted. The resulting score will increase or decrease the UFP count by 35%. This calculation provides us with the adjusted FP count. A detailed explanation can be found at www.ifpug.org.

Use Cases Model

Jacobson Ivar (1986) came up with a top-down approach for sizing software applications using "use cases." However, the approach had following demerits: (1) It cannot be used for measuring nonfunctional requirements (such as platform, performance, timing, or safety-critical aspects). Also, complex algorithms and mathematical requirements cannot be captured through use cases. (2) Use cases depend on individual skill to define templates, which brings inconsistency to estimation.

(3) It becomes difficult to visualize the level of complexity involved in user interface. In upgrade projects, any requirement for improvement on the performance aspects (nonfunctional requirement) or improvement on the look and feel (user interface) cannot be measured using use cases.

Consensus-based Estimation Technique

Consensus-based estimation technique (http://www.sei.cmu.edu/intro/process/technqs/q_estm.htm#14) uses the method of getting a small group of people to decide estimation required for an activity. In this method, the group is unanimous in deciding on the value for an activity. However, sometimes it becomes difficult to get the entire group to arrive at consensus and this technique is best used in a workshop and is not suitable for commercial upgrade projects. It will not be a viable option all the time because of lack of consensus and lack of continuity of same group members for all development projects.

Object-based Estimation Technique

Object-based estimation technique is a bottom-up estimation technique (Armstrong, 2006; Jacobson, 1994) in which an application is broken into different objects. Estimation for each object is then found out, and then effort is summarized at the aggregate level. The estimation depends on the identification of number of objects, and effort required for each object is calculated based on experience. The technique gives good results if all the objects are well known at the start of the project. For a new development project, an initial estimate based on object-oriented approach should be refined as the project progresses. With the progress of project, clarity is obtained with respect to objects; thus, for an upgrade project this technique cannot be used because upgrade projects are usually for relatively small duration (starting from few hours to 4–6 weeks maximum) and also initial estimate for the available application must have been done using object-oriented approach.

Other available estimating techniques are Weighted Average (WAVE) and Quickest (http://www.sei.cmu.edu/intro/process/technqs), and these two techniques are not popular as they do not provide accuracy, consistency, and predictability for estimation in upgrade projects. COCOMO (Boehm, 1981) is a popular technique used for software estimation. This technique was further refined as COCOMO II. This refined technique considers a set of four "cost driver attributes," namely, (1) product attributes, (2) hardware attributes, (3) personnel attributes, and (4) project attributes. Each of these four factors is given a rating on a six-point scale, and these ratings are added up using a multiplier to arrive at final "effort adjustment factor." For upgrade projects, which are for small durations, usually delivery schedule expected range from 1 day to 3 weeks, and it will be an overkill to consider all "cost driver attributes" and arrive at effort adjustment factor using COCOMO II for upgrade projects.

Delphi Method

In 1969, the RAND Corporation developed the Delphi method, which is essentially a group decision process about the likelihood that certain events will occur. It can also be used for environmental, marketing, and sales forecasting. It is a structured process for collating knowledge from a group of experts by administering questionnaires (Adler and Ziglio, 1996). Usually, all participants maintain anonymity, which does not allow them to dominate using their authority or personality, minimizes the "bandwagon effect" or "halo effect" and allows them to freely express their opinions and encourages open critique and admitting errors by revising earlier estimation. Problems associated with Delphi are as follows: (1) its inability to make complex forecasts with multiple factors, (2) future outcomes were usually considered as if they had no effect on each other, and (3) future developments are not always predicted correctly by iterative consensus of experts. A flowchart is given in Figure 2.1 to show the steps involved in Delphi method.

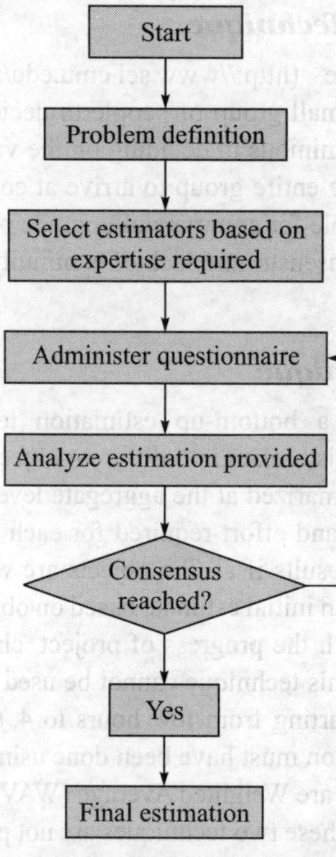

Figure 2.1: Steps involved in Delphi method

The models described above are top-down models that can be useful even if some of the detailed activities are not known in the initial stages. This is also useful when detailed functionalities are known and also when interfaces with other existing applications are well known.

Size Measurement Using Bottom-Up Approach

This approach is best suited when requirement analysis has been completed and the feasibility study has been carried out. This means details about the functionalities and details of the activities are well understood. This approach is also used when past data for similar projects are not known; projects in new domain and projects for a new customer can use this approach. This approach will be useful for estimation in organizations where development projects are executed with different processes. In this approach, the application to be developed is broken into modules. These modules represent logical units of the entire functionality requirements of the customer and can be developed independently. Usually, this division is decided in consultation with the customer and is frozen in the requirement analysis stage itself. These modules are the lowest level of granularity that can be possible logically. Based on the number of functionalities required to be developed and the number of database interfaces, these modules are classified as simple, medium, or complex. One of the criteria for deciding complexity will depend on the number of navigating windows that need to be developed in the module. The other criteria are the number of times data need to be fetched from database, the number of reports to be generated from the module, the amount of data that need to be passed to other modules, the number of times other existing applications would interact with the module, and so on.

Once the complexity at the module level is determined, the module is then again broken into programs. These programs, combined together, will form a module. Each program is then classified as either complex, medium, or simple depending on the criteria discussed above. The classification is usually abbreviated as SMC (simple, medium, complex) classification. This classification helps in understanding the number of programs that need to be written in each category. For each classification, there is a recommended average effort for writing code and self testing (usually known as build phase) that has been accepted in the organization. This average effort depends on the past experience and projects that have completed; the average effort also is modified as the organization matures in its process definition and project execution. The average effort is the time that a team member will spend in writing and self-testing the classified program. There could be variation in the actual average effort planned for the program than the recommended average effort. This variation will be dependent on the program manager, who, considering skill level of the team member, knowledge in the domain, criticality of the application to be developed, will decide the final average effort for each classified program. Once effort for each program is decided, the total effort for build phase (i.e., including effort for code writing and self-testing) of the project is calculated. So, in essence, this bottom-up approach determines how much time will be required for the build phase.

Here, the effort for build phase can be estimated using past data also. For example, if similar projects in the same domain technology were executed earlier, then actual hours spent for completing the activity can be used as recommended average effort. This helps in higher accuracy as estimation is based on similar conditions. Thus, the approach has an advantage that it can use past data for estimation and in the absence of it, because programs are small, designers and programmers can estimate the effort needed to code them directly. Bottom-up approach has been pictorially represented in Figure 2.2.

Once the effort for build phase is known through bottom-up approach, the effort required for other phases and activities of other lifecycle phases are calculated as percentage of build effort. The distribution is usually found in process capability baseline. Using these efforts, total effort for the project is calculated. One advantage of the approach is that it has the flexibility for using experience and past data, and if past data are not available, then using project manager's judgment capability build effort can be determined. The approach also helps if we do not have details at the beginning of the project, but we know that they will consume time and effort, then the estimation will add average effort to the build phase. By referring to Figure 2.2, the steps for bottom-up approach can be written in following steps:

1. Gather system requirements and do feasibility analysis.
2. Based on functionalities to be developed, the application is divided into the number of independent modules.
3. These modules are again broken into lowest level—programs that need to be coded.
4. These programs are classified as SMC. If similar projects (i.e., in same domain and technology) have been executed, then use actual effort spent in those projects as recommended average effort for writing code and self-testing.

5. Add all these effort to find total effort for the build phase.
6. Use process capability baseline to determine effort distribution percentage for each phase with respect to total effort for the project. Using these distributions, find total effort from the estimated total build effort. This becomes the final estimation value for the project.
7. As the project progresses, based on reviews, effort for each program can be fine tuned and accordingly total effort changes.

A typical project estimation has been given in Annexure A.

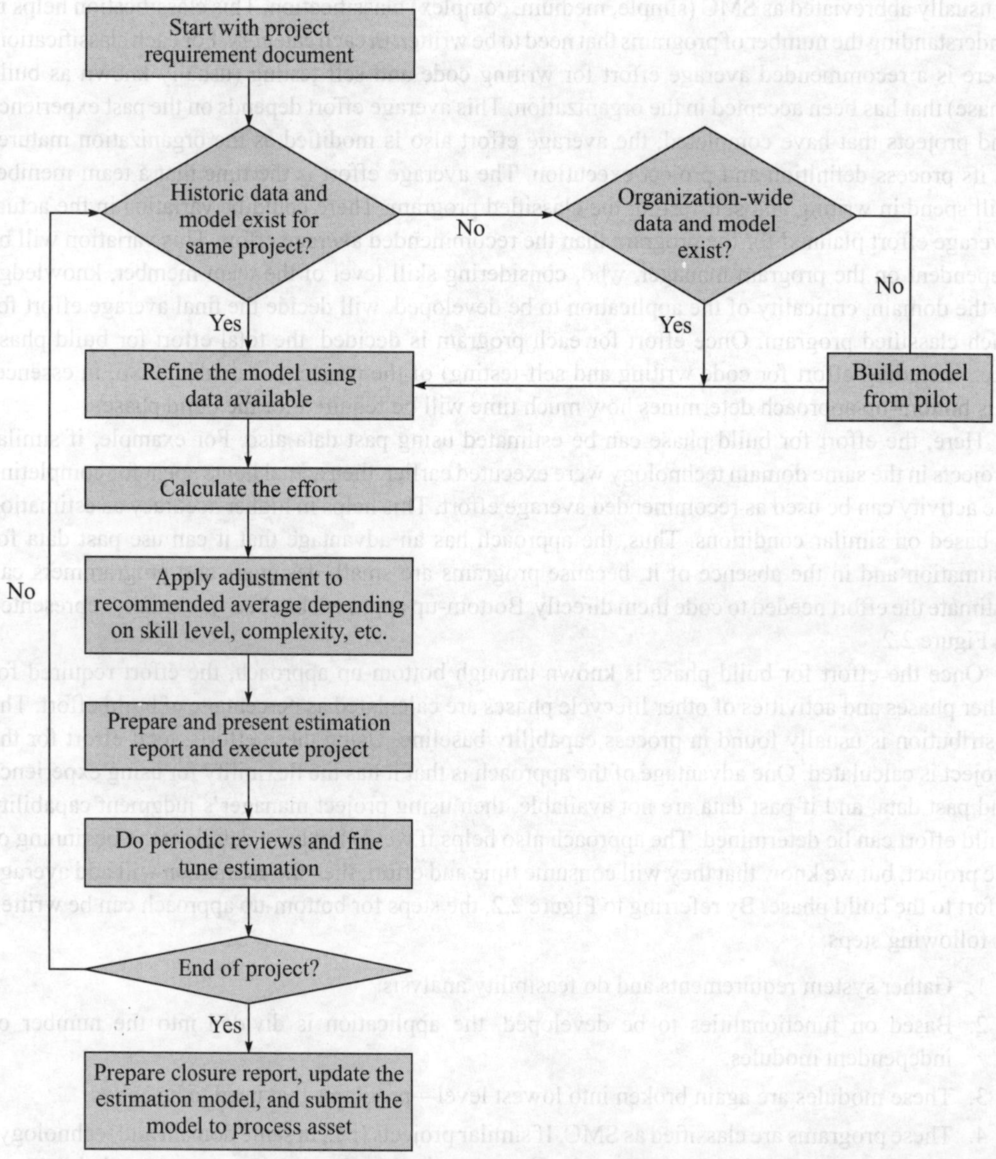

Figure 2.2: Bottom-up approach

Tips for Effective Estimation

Estimation is a technique that needs to be mastered over years of project execution. Knowledge and learning from previous projects and discussion with senior members of the organizations help in getting insight into this technique. Seniors not only can train members in estimation but can also share best practices as well as minute techniques that otherwise cannot be recorded or documented anywhere. Below some of these tips and techniques are shared.

(a) In the project plan, mini milestones need to be identified to increase the visibility into schedule changes. The plan should be such that at granular level the lowest task should have a maximum duration of 3 days. This helps the developer or team member as well as the project manager to effectively control and monitor the activity. For activities of longer duration, it becomes difficult to find percentage completion accurately; this results to perception and hence tracking the activities objectively is not possible. In case it is not possible to break the activities to smaller duration tasks, then a stage-wise breakup of work to be completed and within a stage multiple logical tracking points could be identified and tracked.

(b) Prioritization of work: It is sometimes necessary to prioritize the modules so that some of the modules are delivered earlier than the others. This situation arises (i) when there is resource crunch in the team (which in reality is the case for many organizations), (ii) the customer changes his/her priority to accommodate business needs, and (iii) there are scope changes and new set of requirements are needed to be delivered within *the same schedule as decided earlier.* Based on experience, some tips are given below, which would help in prioritizing the development schedule for different modules.

- If there are market pressures to deliver certain modules, which will help the customer to increase his/her share of business such as automation of a certain activity by a timeline to meet certain events. For example, an e-commerce web site would probably like to get the site up before Thanksgiving and Christmas because this is the time when people buy a lot of things in the United States. Hence, it will be necessary to prioritize and develop these modules first.
- The modules that will put basic stuff, which are required to be put into production. These basic modules will help to compose a workable solution reflecting the functionality of the entire application to be developed.
- The modules that will immediately help to improve most acute problems with the current system, for example, performance issues, GUI, stability issues, etc. Development and delivery of these modules will help in gaining confidence of the customers and will also help project team members in understanding whether there are any issues related to the design of architecture, database, and performance of the application to be finally delivered.
- Also, it will be prudent to prioritize development of modules that will be interacting with some third-party software, which is being upgraded by a certain date. This prioritization gives ample time to third-party vendors to iron out any issues related to interfacing with their software.

(c) Identify critical modules that can be developed in parallel. This can be achieved as mentioned below.

- Identify modules that could be developed independently. For example, help functions, error handling, etc.

- Identify modules that can be tested independent of other modules using dummy/stub functions.

This type of prioritization technique helps in keeping the project's focus on the most important features. The most essential features are developed first, and then the less essential features are developed if time permits (these could get added for the next iteration). This approach could be used in five scenarios: (i) in an ongoing project where releases are planned in an iterative mode and (ii) in a project that has a lot of impact on business models of the customer, (iii) it has to be used in projects where scope definition for application is under the control of development team, (iv) management and customer's willingness to cut the features rather than stretching the schedule, and (v) there is complete involvement from end users of the application; they are also known as business users. Also, continuous reviews of work product and progress are a must. This approach is best suited for development projects where rapid-development languages or case tools or code generators are used and also for in-house business software. Steps involved in this technique are as follows:

- Breaking the project scope into different modules, which are again broken into programs to be developed.
- Prioritize the list by identifying the most critical and less-critical features or programs for which requirement clarity is high.
- Identify the impact of the absence of less-critical programs in the product/application.
- Initiate the lifecycle stage with the most critical features and perform less-critical features, if time permits.

The estimation process accordingly needs to take cognizance of such prioritization. Benefits accrued from such approach are manyfold:

- It emphasizes the priority of schedule as timeframe is absolutely fixed.
- It clarifies feature priorities as most important features only could be addressed.
- It limits experimentation by development team and helps in avoiding possible time-stretching activities.
- It controls feature creep. Since development time is shortened, the amount of time people have to lobby for new features is reduced and feature changes due to changes in market conditions or operational environment are also reduced.
- It helps in increasing the motivation level of software engineers and end users as people feel they are doing important or critical task and sense of contribution will be high.

Planning Testing Strategy

For development projects, especially web-based projects, there are many more different types of testing that need to be carried out other than the typical unit, integration, and system testing. This decision is to be taken during the planning stage itself; a risk analysis should be carried out and a strategy should be in place for the types of testing that will take place. For instance, for web-based systems, performance and browser compatibility are big issues for certain technologies. As a result typically testing is planned for only a couple of browsers. However, if this is a site that is to cater to people who do not have those browsers, there is a risk that the system might not behave as expected on their browsers. During project planning stage, these decisions need to be taken and recorded in testing strategy document. Testing strategy will also cover details such as test bed requirement, type of data to be made available for different test cases, etc. This type of planning is necessary as in the absence of it the entire testing will get delayed and thus will result in effort and schedule overrun. The situation will be still worse if there is less time made available to the team for testing as bad untested code will be delivered to the customer. It is recommended that all test cases are reviewed and accepted by end users in the initial stage itself.

A typical testing strategy would contain details as shown in Table 2.7.

Table 2.7: Testing strategy example

	Front end	Middle tier	Backend
Functional testing	Required in all cases; could also include random testing other than unit and integration testing	Required in all cases; could also include random testing other than unit and integration testing	Required in all cases; could also include random testing other than unit and integration testing
Usability testing	This is required if any special set of users is targeted. Otherwise these inputs will occur as part of the first deployed iteration	NA	NA
Load testing	NA	Very essential when expecting number of hits more than 200 per hour	Essential when database is subject to handling large number of requests
Stress testing	NA	Essential when reliability is important	Essential when reliability is important
Security testing	Can be used to check user authentication and authorization	Used to check firewall scenarios	Used to check access to database in a secure environment
Regression testing	Necessary after the first iteration to ensure that the older functionality has not broken in the process of making changes or bug fixes	Necessary after the first iteration to ensure that the older functionality has not broken in the process of making changes or bug fixes	Necessary after the first iteration to ensure that the older functionality has not broken in the process of making changes or bug fixes

Planning for Team Members

It is important to plan for team members; what is more important is that the composition of team members should be optimum. The right mix of team requires that there should be skilled, experienced persons along with less-experienced persons. One may question the prudence of having less-experienced team members, but it is known that skill and experience will bring faster and better results. With higher skill and experience, productivity is higher as application can be developed faster; rework cost is less as defects or issues injected will be less during project execution. The same may not be true for less-experienced persons. In addition to that there will be cost related to training and skill upgrading of these less-experienced team members so that they can perform and deliver, and hence objectives of the project can be met. But in reality, the management always takes lots of pain to form a team where there will be a right mix of experience and new team members. The driving factor for this decision is always the business need of the vendor organization, where reducing the cost of project execution without affecting the quality of the deliverables is a prime concern. With experienced persons, their salary costs also increase; this also affects the total cost as it is arrived at by multiplying effort in hours with hourly rate (for experienced persons, this rate is higher than that of inexperienced persons). Based on experience, it is recommended that the ratio between experienced to inexperienced persons in team should be 1:4. Further, it is also recommended that a project should have different roles that are well defined during project planning stage. Table 2.8 defines roles that are usually found in development projects. The table explains roles and responsibilities that are defined in the project plan during planning stage.

Table 2.8: Roles and responsibilities matrix

Roles	Responsibilities
Project management	Ability to manage the project, which includes tracking, managing the customer, and risks. Familiarity with requirements of short duration project management is mandatory.
Requirements analyst	Ability to capture requirements in a manner that is easily understandable for both the development team and the customer.
Architects	Good understanding of technology required to come up with a best-fit solution for a given application. Knowledge of some of the products that solve business problems such as tax calculation, shipping and handling, credit card payments, etc., is necessary. Ability to address parameters such as functionality, usability, performance, scalability, fault tolerance, and perform architectural analysis; and ability to identify the architecture framework is essential. Architects would need to have software development experience, domain, technical experience, and be good communicators. He/she should be aware of various technical language and platforms and associated capabilities and drawbacks, and should be able to recommend multiple alternatives.
Database designers	Good understanding of what it takes to design very large databases (VLDB).
Web designers	Ability to make the web site appealing and usable.
Application designers	Ability to create the application in the blueprint given by the architects.
Security experts	Good understanding of security-related issues for web applications. Knowledge of how a web site can be hacked, threatened, etc., is required as well as details on the ways of implementing application security as well.
Network experts	Ability to help deploy the application successfully. Good knowledge of some of the network products that help in this.
Domain experts	Good understanding of the specific business domain targeted by the application.
Tools experts	Good understanding of different types of tools. This could include domain level tools or other tools that help improve quality and productivity.
Application developers	Developers who will actually build the system.
Application designers	Ability to take a framework and design the application within the framework.

In Table 2.8 we can see that all roles are not used in all the stages of the project. Different stages require different roles to take accountability. A project manager should understand this well and should allocate team members accordingly. This ensures that the roles will be available for other projects, and these persons can be released after their contributions are completed. Table 2.9 explains involvement of different roles in different stages of the project. This table helps in optimum utilization of resources with project profitability as objective.

Table 2.9: Association of roles with stages in development cycle

Profiles	Activities					
	Proposal	Requirements	Design	Build	Test	Installation
Project managers	X	X	X	X	X	X
Domain experts	X	X			X	
Requirements analyst		X			X	
Architects	X	X	X		X	
Database designers			X		X	
Web designers		X	X		X	
Application designers		X	X		X	
Application developers				X	X	

On the basis of the requirements that multiple profiles of people might be required at any one time and that tasks might have to be done in parallel to complete in a short duration, the team organization has to be planned to be able to reach this goal. Separate testing team, defect prevention team, build and smoke test team, and requirements team help in reducing the duration of a project. However, based on the individual characteristics of each project, the team organization and composition should be decided. Division of work between onsite and offshore should also be planned so that there is minimum overhead.

For an IT project, another factor for success is how cohesive the team is. It is important that the team shares the objectives of the project, understands their importance, and work toward achieving them. There could be individual brilliance, but the success of the team will depend on the overall performance of the team. It is said that the lowest performer decides the overall performance of the team. Hence, it is necessary that all the team members work in cohesion and help each other in producing results. In order to help achieve this cohesiveness, team building exercise should be taken up before the official kick off of the project. Through team outings, good relationship should be encouraged (as, for example, during weekends or during the period when there is relatively less workload, team should go for lunch or dinner together). If there is sufficient time, an offsite meeting can be planned to build cohesiveness in the team. A mock project in the technology, using the process with the team just before the actual project, would also help iron out any potential issues. This can be a 1–2 week kind of project.

Typical Project Organization Structure

In order to get effective communication between different stakeholders in software projects, a formalized project organization structure should be defined. For a typical project organization structure, please refer to Figure 2.3. A project organization structure has different components and roles. The structure is designed for easy flow of communication among project team and the customer. The solid lines represent direct reporting, whereas the dotted lines show administrative responsibilities.

Business manager (BM) or delivery manager (DM) is the head in the structure and has the bottom-line responsibility to execute the project. The project manager (PM) reports on the delivery status to the BM/DM on a periodic basis. This periodicity can be decided to be weekly or monthly basis depending on the complexity and criticality of the application. The PM is supported by module leaders (ML) who take care of individual modules. The MLs are typically technical leads who are expert in technology as well as in domain knowledge. They help developers (DV) who write the design and code documents. In the project team, configuration controller (CC) takes care of giving proper access to different groups. For example, the PM will have read/write access in all the folders, whereas developers will have write access in their work area only. These are taken care by CC.

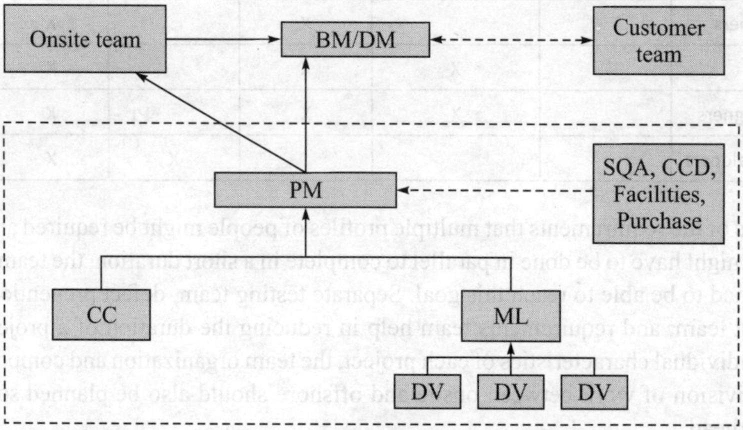

Figure 2.3: A typical software development project team organization structure

Note: BM, business manager; DM, delivery manager; PM, project manager; SQA, software quality advisor; CCD, computer communication department; CC, configuration controller; ML, module leader; DV, developer.

Planning for Onsite Travel

In offshore project management, where projects are developed offshore, planning for onsite travel well in advance is quite necessary. Depending on the needs of the project, plan for onsite travel by applying for visa well in advance. If the travel is to the United States, then additional planning is needed for applying H1 visas as there are number of regulations that need to be complied with. The time to obtain an H1 or L1 can be a minimum of 2 months and longer in the case of an H1 if the cap for the year has been reached. There might be issues in getting B1 visa, for instance, lateral entrants cannot apply for a B1 till they have completed 3 months in an organization (this is necessary as per regulations from the US visa department) and in such cases, this can become a risk for the project. It is also necessary to plan and obtain all related documents and make them available to the travel department for fast processing of visa applications. Based on experience, it is also recommended that these planning be made transparent to all team members so that criteria for selection can be well shared with the team members. This way, any issues related to perceived nepotism and favorism to some team members can be removed. This also helps in forming the required trust and bond among the team members.

Process Database

An organization always has a going concern. It means it existed in the past, continues its transactions in the present, and will strive to survive in the future. This has significant meaning in that in order to continue to exist the organization has to use past data, experience, and best practices. These play key roles in improvement and management. Any learning organization will learn from the past success as well as failures. The key factor in this learning process is how effectively the past experience has been captured, shared, and disseminated in different forums. It has been observed that the learning process can be very effective if there is a systematic way of collecting data and information, deriving the requisite knowledge from that and then sharing with others in a manner that is easy, rewarding, and also can be customizable for the project in question. The systematic way of gathering and recording data is done in process database. Based on this database, a capability baseline is formed.

Process database captures the experience of previous projects and a number of data related to these projects. These data collection is done through a systematic approach. The approach has been explained here: first, objectives are set for a project. Based on the objectives, metrics are defined. By measuring values of these metrics periodically, project manager can check the progress toward achieving the set objectives. In order to measure these metrics, variables are defined, and as the project progresses, data for these variables are collected periodically. Mechanisms for data collection are well defined and tools are employed to collect data. By employing tools for data collection, consistency and data integrity are achieved. The tools help in collecting data, which are recorded in process database. These data are used as learning for new projects. For project planning, these process databases provide vital inputs for estimating as well as for project management.

Templates are defined to collect these data. These templates capture data at different stages and then at the end of the project execution, that is, after all deliverables are completed, these data are entered into the database. A sample template is shown in Annexure B, which helps in recording data from projects. Figure 2.4 explains the systematic approach taken in one of software major for data collection and entry into PDB.

Process Capability Baseline

Process capability baseline represents the capability of the processes in quantitative terms. The capability explains the range of performance values that can be expected from a process. This means, for the processes followed in a project, process capability would explain the range of outcomes that can be expected from these processes. Hence, capability baseline has two important aspects—processes and outcomes measured quantitatively. Hence, first there is a need to determine processes that need to be considered for capability baseline. The choice of processes to be considered is based on the needs of the organization. The processes that are critical for business sustenance are to be selected. The criticality will also depend on the needs of the customer. The processes that have direct impact on the customer need to be selected for baseline also. Once these processes are selected, then measurement techniques for these processes are also defined. The measurement techniques include metrics for measuring processes, variables that will help in measuring these metrics, and periodicity of data collection. Some of the metrics that are measured are delivered quality, productivity, schedule variation, effort distribution across lifecycle stages, effort variation, defect injection rate, defect removal efficiency, defect distribution across lifecycle stages, etc.

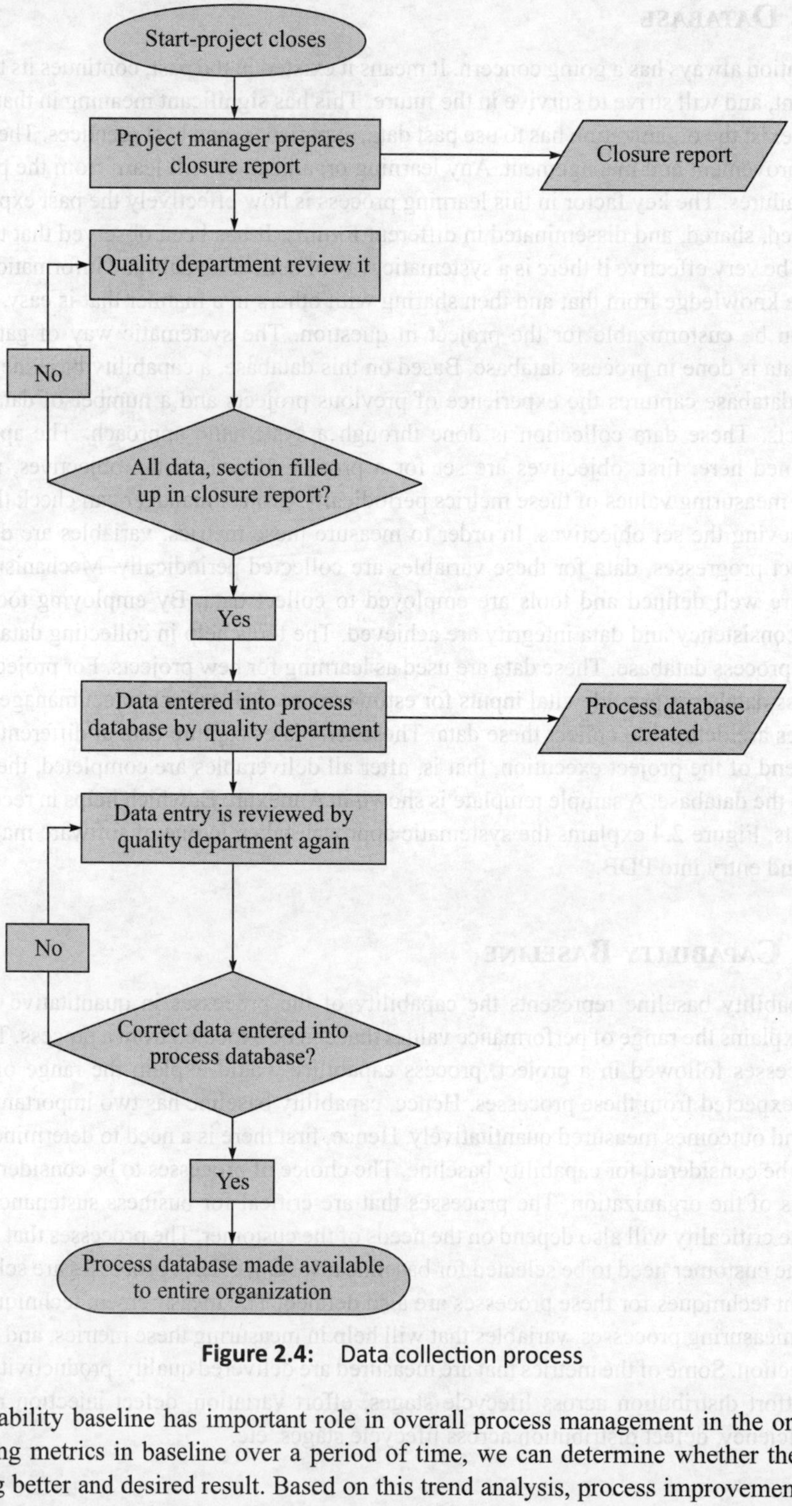

Figure 2.4: Data collection process

The capability baseline has important role in overall process management in the organization. By analyzing metrics in baseline over a period of time, we can determine whether the processes are yielding better and desired result. Based on this trend analysis, process improvement plans can be made. Operational strategies are made based on these improvement plans. The analysis also indicates whether the processes are stable. The variations in performance of processes, as recorded in capability baseline over a period of time, will indicate stability. High volatility in performance is not a good indicator; this indicates that the plans need to be put in place for stabilizing the processes. Training should be provided to improve compliance with the defined processes. Rewards and recognitions need to be defined to improve motivation for complying with processes.

As a baseline indicates the capability of a process, each process should have separate baseline. Thus, depending on the number of processes that an organization would have, there will be that many numbers of baselines. For an IT service organization, there will be a separate baseline for development processes, maintenance processes, and reengineering processes. Even these processes are at quite high level and have many subprocesses. If projects of one type are executed frequently, then capability baseline for each type of project is created. This type of approach will give specific baseline for each process and correct range of expected outcomes will be known.

Calculation of Capability Baseline

The broad objective of calculating capability baseline with regard to development projects was to identify comparable projects executed by the company in recent past, measure their productivity, and use statistical analysis to find average benchmark value as explained below.

Let the size for each project be S_i, where $i = 1$ to n, and n represents the total number of projects. Thus, $S_1, S_2, S_3, \cdots, S_n$ represent the size of the projects in the organization. Let effort in man hours for each project be T_i, where $i = 1$ to n, and n represents the total number of projects.

Thus, we obtain the average value as follows:

$$X_{\text{avg}} = \frac{(S_1 + S_2 + S_3 + \cdots S_n)}{(T_1 + T_2 + T_3 + \cdots T_n)}$$

Symbolically, it is represented as $X_{\text{avg}} = (\Sigma S / \Sigma T)_{i,\, i = 1 \text{ to } n}$.

Using statistical formulae, the upper critical limit (UCL) and the lower critical limit (LCL) are defined as

$\text{UCL} = X_{\text{avg}} + 3 \times \text{S.D.}$

$\text{LCL} = X_{\text{avg}} - 3 \times \text{S.D.}$

where S.D. is the standard deviation.

All the productivity values measured for each project were plotted, and using control limit approach, extreme values, which were outside the upper critical limit values and thus were of special cause in nature, were removed. After removing extreme data, out of the remaining data based on performance, top 50% of projects were selected and an average was calculated. Such average was used as benchmark value for productivity. As the 50% high-end performance data were taken the average also tended to be higher and the norm established on such average therefore had built into it an element of challenge. Besides, since such average of benchmark was based on actual achievements, it could be projected as achievable benchmark and this helped in developing a commitment toward such benchmark.

Ordinarily, while competitive information from other companies were not available, there was no such constraint in obtaining internal data. Internal benchmarking, therefore, could benefit from sensitive data available with the company. Besides, there was also an important advantage of internal benchmarking because the quality of analysis based on internal data was likely to be far better than in case of external data. As the internal employees were generally available for discussion and providing insights in case of internal benchmarking, the practice provided the benefits of discussion with people involved.

Figure 2.5 summarizes estimation approach by using past data from process database and process capability baseline.

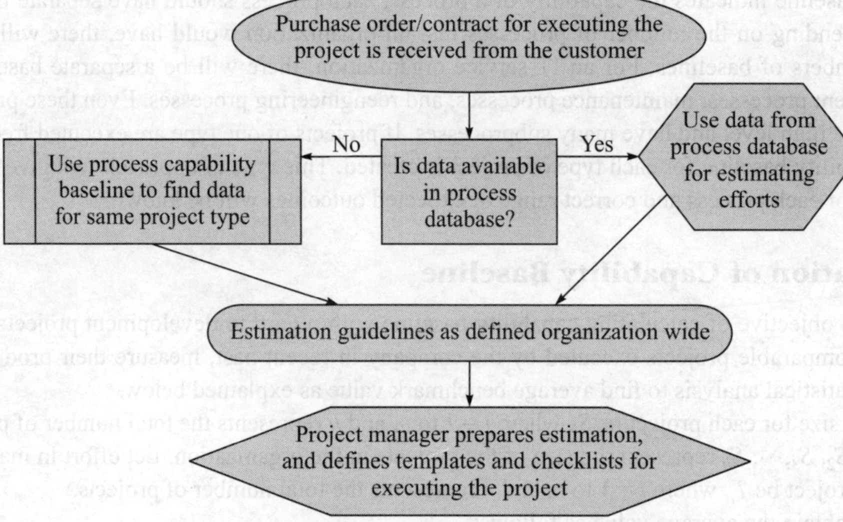

Figure 2.5: Estimation approach

Setting Quality Objectives

While setting quality goals, the PM should be able to estimate issues that would be likely injected at the end of each lifecycle stage. These are then set as quality goals for executing the project. In order to understand the process of setting quality goals, it is necessary to know the following two terms—process database (PDB) and process capability baseline (PCB). PDB contains all data from projects executed earlier. After a project is declared closed, after installing the software at the customer's site, all related data are captured through a closure report and after proper review this data is entered into PDB. Some data that are recommended to be captured through closure report are as follows: productivity achieved by the project, issues found at the end of each lifecycle stage, effort spent for each stage of the lifecycle stage, and effort spent for review and rework activities of all deliverables. An organization can choose to gather more data if it wants, but the authors recommend that above data must be collected to make quantitative project management a success. Applying statistical analysis techniques, organization-wide capability is derived and is published in PCB.

As explained earlier, all data related to the project are collected and stored in PDB from which metrics related to a project can be derived. PDB also captures qualitative comments from the product manager (PM) that are shared with the entire organization. Thus, PDB becomes a knowledge repository for new projects, which can use the experience of PM of past projects and manage the new project quantitatively with ability to predict its performance accurately. A new project can set a goal at a higher or lower than the quality level achieved earlier in similar projects. Procedure for setting goals is given below with examples.

EXAMPLE 1

Setting goal for delivered issues:

From PDB—If similar project was executed in the past and data are available in PDB, then the value of delivered issues from this project should be used for goal setting. In case there is more than one project that is similar in nature, the project with most similar characteristics in technology and domain should be used for reference. The authors would recommend that the PM should take this decision for deciding the reference project.

$$\text{Estimate for delivered issues} = \frac{\text{(number of delivered issues from a reference project in PDB)} \times \text{(effort estimated for the new project)}}{\text{(actual efforts spent for reference project)}}$$

In case, similar projects were not executed in the past and no data are available in PDB, then PM should use PCB as reference for setting goal.

From PCB—If PCB norms are used, then

Estimate for delivered issues = (average value of the delivered issues per effort for development project from PCB) × (estimated effort for the new project)

EXAMPLE 2

Setting goal for number of issues likely to be injected in each lifecycle stage:

The number of issues that a project can expect to capture during project execution can be predicted by using data from similar past projects available in PDB.

From PDB—If data are being taken from a similar project from PDB (say from project ABC) and the PM wants to set goal for issue injection for coding stage, then

$$\text{Predicted issues for coding stage for the new project} = \frac{\text{(number of issues recorded for project ABC for coding stage)} \times \text{(effort estimated for coding stage in the new project)}}{\text{(total efforts spent for project ABC)}}$$

In case data are not available from PDB, PCB should be used as reference for setting the goal.

From PCB—If PCB norms are used, then

Predicted issues for coding stage for the new project = (Average value of the delivered issues per effort) × (estimated efforts for the stage for new project)

EXAMPLE 3

Setting goal for productivity:

From PDB—If similar project was executed in the past and data are available in PDB, then the value of productivity from this project should be used for goal setting. If there is more than one project, which is similar to the existing project, then the PM should use his/her judgment for selecting a past project for reference.

From PDB—If data are being taken from a similar project from PDB (say from project ABC) and the PM wants to set goal for productivity, then

$$\text{Estimated productivity for the new project} = \frac{\text{(productivity recorded for project ABC)} \times \text{(effort estimated for the new project)}}{\text{(total efforts spent for project ABC)}}$$

In case data are not available in PDB, then PCB can be used for reference.

From PCB—If PCB norms are used, then

Estimate for productivity = (average value of productivity for development project) × (estimated efforts for the new project)

Figure 2.6 summarizes quality goal setting process using past data.

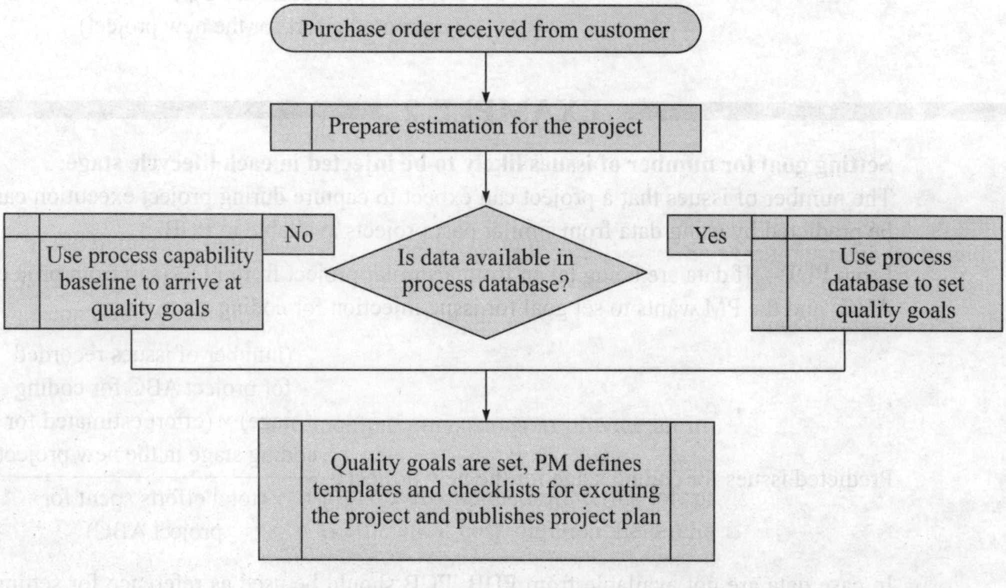

Figure 2.6: Quality goal setting process

Planning for Defect Prevention

The purpose of defect prevention is to identify root causes, that is, the causes that cause defects to be injected into work products (such as spec, code, etc.), taking action to eliminate these causes so that defects are prevented from being injected in future. This chapter deals with defect prevention done at project level.

Generally, defect prevention activities involve identification of defects that have occurred in the past, prioritization, performing analysis to find why these were injected in the first place, identifying solutions, piloting these solutions to verify the effectiveness, and implementing the identified solutions.

We will now identify various lifecycle (LC) stages in a development project where defects get injected. We will also find out through a case study how defects were prevented through prediction of the defects.

Defect injection during project lifecycle stages

Defects get injected right from the initial stage of a project. For a development project, the initial stage of defect injection starts with requirement analysis (RA). Figure 2.7 depicts a typical development lifecycle stages.

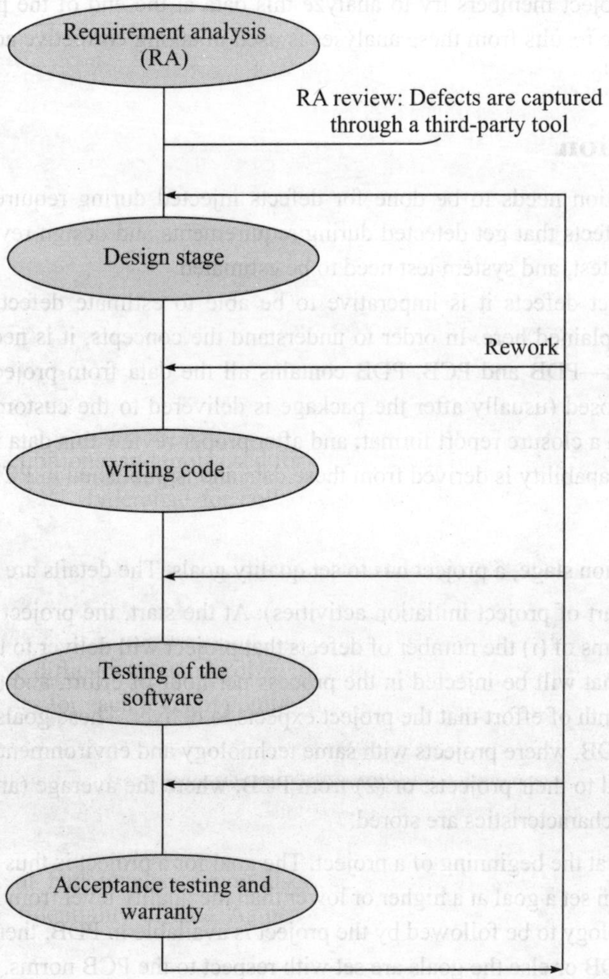

Figure 2.7: A typical development project

The figure depicts the various lifecycle stages that constitute a typical development project lifecycle. The activities considered are as explained earlier. It shows that at each stage of project lifecycle, defects are detected and these defects are rectified by going back to the start of that stage again. Here, the defects are rectified and then the next stage starts. As is evident each time, this kind of rework happens; it again involves extra time and efforts and it means more cost to the software development team and also it means delivery time committed to the customer is under pressure. That is if the team continues carrying out a lot of rework to the work product that they have completed, then there could be chances that the delivery date and schedule committed to the customer might get delayed.

As is seen here there are number of reviews where defects are captured after the work products are developed. These defects are captured through a third-party tool, and these defects are fixed or rectified before moving on to the next stage. Defect analysis consists of finding defects by type, severity, etc. The project members try to analyze this data at the end of the project or at various milestone stages. The results from these analyses is used in taking corrective action for later stages in the project lifecycle.

Defect Prediction

In a project, estimation needs to be done for defects injected during requirements, design, and coding. Also, the defects that get detected during requirements and design reviews, code reviews, unit test, integration test, and system test need to be estimated.

In order to predict defects it is imperative to be able to estimate defects at various stages. The procedure is explained here. In order to understand the concepts, it is necessary to know the following two terms—PDB and PCB. PDB contains all the data from projects executed earlier. After a project is closed (usually after the package is delivered to the customer), all related data are captured through a closure report format; and after proper review this data is entered into PDB. Organization-wide capability is derived from these data and is published in PCB.

Setting Goals

At the project initiation stage, a project has to set quality goals. The details are enumerated below:

Setting the goals (part of project initiation activities): At the start, the project has to set its goals. The goal is set in terms of (i) the number of defects that project will deliver to the customer, (ii) the number of defects that will be injected in the process per hour of effort, and (iii) the productivity in FP per person month of effort that the project expects to deliver. These goals are taken from two sources: (1) From PDB, where projects with same technology and environment in the past have put in defect data related to their projects, or (2) from PCB, where the average (and also the range of) value of all process characteristics are stored.

Project goals are set at the beginning of a project. The goal for a project is thus set either from PDB or PCB. A project can set a goal at a higher or lower than the quality level from PDB or PCB. If data similar to the technology to be followed by the project is available in PDB, then the projects collect information from PDB or else the goals are set with respect to the PCB norms.

EXAMPLE 4

Delivered defects:

From PDB—If data is being taken from similar projects from PDB, then

$$\text{Estimate for delivered defects} = \frac{\text{(number of delivered defects)} \times \text{(effort estimated for the new project)}}{\text{(actual efforts spent for that project)}}$$

From PCB—If PCB norms are used, then

Estimate for delivered defects = (average value of the delivered defects/efforts) × (estimated efforts for the new project).

EXAMPLE 5

Setting goal for number of defects to be injected:

From PDB

(Defects detected/efforts spent) × (efforts estimated for the project)

From PCB

(Defect injected density × efforts estimated)

EXAMPLE 6

Productivity:

From PDB—Take the exact figure from PDB and set that as a productivity goal.

From PCB—Take the PCB norm and set that as a project goal.

Predicting defects:

The number of defects that a project can expect to capture during project execution can be predicted by using the data on past projects. Either data on similar projects from the PDB or data from PCB can be used.

From PDB—If data is being taken from similar projects from PDB (say from project ABC), then

$$\text{Predicted defects for LC stage for the new project} = \frac{\text{(number of defects recorded for project ABC for that LC stage)} \times \text{(effort estimated for that LC stage in the new project)}}{\text{(total efforts spent for project ABC)}}$$

From PCB—If PCB norms are used, then

Predicted defects for LC stage for the new project = (Average value of the delivered defects/efforts) × (estimated efforts for the stage for new project).

This procedure can be used for estimating the defects for any LC stage. When using the process database to get information about related projects, either averages or information about a project can be used. The estimates obtained using this procedure can be refined keeping project-specific factors in mind.

- Once the defects are predicted for different LC stages, the project defines a strategy for preventing defects and estimate the percentage of defects that are likely to be prevented.
- Re-estimate the total number of defects injected taking into consideration the strategy to prevent defects.
- Estimate the number of defects injected at each lifecycle stage using organization-wide distribution for defect injection given in PCB.

Project Management Plan

So far we have discussed processes for estimating size, effort and schedule, setting goals, and kick off for any project. These processes are part of project planning and one leads to the next. The next process to be done for project planning is to prepare project management plan. The plan is a document where outputs from planning activities are recorded. This document is used as a guide for many stakeholders. This document is usually not shared with the customer, and hence all stakeholders do not use it. This is prepared by the project manager and is usually used by team members, and approved by business manager and delivery manger who use this as a baseline document for review, finding performance of the project, and to decide if any action needs to be taken. The plan also provides an overall view to senior managers as to how the project is going to be managed, the resource requirement (including hardware, software, and team members), and hence the cost involved in executing the project. The plan explains the assumptions based on which estimation has been done and commitments are made to the customer based on these assumptions. These aspects are taken into consideration during periodic review by senior management.

The plan is also used by team members to understand the shared objectives of the project. It helps them to understand the nature of the project, their roles and responsibilities, communication and escalation process, and key contact details from the customer's side as well as from vendor's side. These key contact details are needed to escalate any matter that is not resolved within specified time limits. They also understand commitments made to the customer and related milestone-based deliverables to be delivered. Also, the quality objectives for each lifecycle stage are set in the plan. This helps team members to understand the quality of output that is expected out of them.

The plan is also shared with other stakeholders such as training department, human resources (HR) department, and infrastructure department. HR has to look into staffing plan and providing team members with requisite skills. Given the lead time that is associated with recruitment, HR has to advertise, recruit, and then provide necessary team members to the team. Training department also has to understand the training requirements and arrange such training sessions for upgrading skills for better performance in the projects. Infrastructure department has to understand hardware and software requirements of the team and provide such needs to the team.

A typical project plan template has been provided in Annexure C.

SUMMARY

This chapter dealt with project planning stage in software project management. Software project management starts with the organization getting a work order or contract from the customer asking it (vendor) to develop an application(s) for *him*. Every project has a number of stakeholders, and it is important that these stakeholders are identified at the beginning of the project. In a common forum, these stakeholders are shared with objectives of the project. The purpose behind this sharing is to align each and every stakeholder toward project objectives. If there is any conflict, then it is ironed out at this stage. As a part of project planning, it is important to define process that the project has to follow. Along with standard process, the project also customizes some of the standard processes based on tailoring guidelines. This combination of standard and tailored processes allows the project to cater to the unique needs of the customer as well as to reap benefits from past experience in executing similar projects. Estimation process has two approaches—top down and bottom up. In top-down approach, size is measured and then that is converted to effort and schedule estimation. In bottom-up approach, application is broken into programs, which are the lowest granular level of work. Effort is then estimated for each of these programs and then aggregated to find total effort for build phase of the application. Using process capability baseline, this build effort is then converted into overall project effort.

Project planning also has processes for planning for resources—hardware, software, and team members. Roles and responsibilities are defined at this stage so that accountability for each activity is made known to different team members well in advance. Planning for travel to the customer site, applying for visa, and providing requisite training to team members are done at this stage. Quality objectives, which are aligned with the objectives of the project, are set for each lifecycle stage of the project. All these planning processes are documented in project management plan and are shared with many stakeholders.

DISCUSSION POINTS

1. Who are stakeholders in software projects?
2. Why projects should do tailoring of the processes? What is the need to define standard processes in an organization?
3. What are the different types of estimation approach available? What is the difference between top-down and bottom-up approaches?
4. How do you measure size of an application? What is the need to measure size of software to be developed?
5. How do you plan testing for a project? What are the elements that a project manager should take care of while planning for testing?
6. What is the need for communication protocol?
7. What is the difference between process database and process capability baseline? What is their usefulness?
8. How do you set quality objectives?
9. What are the minimum sections required in project management plan?

CASE STUDY

(A) ASL Software Inc. is a leader in providing software applications in remittance and payment processing area in banking industry and has been in existence for the last 25 years. The organization had revolutionized the image-based payment processing industry by providing simple-to-install and easy-to-maintain software applications that are capable of meeting specific customer needs. These products are developed using the software development model that allows the organization to meet change in requirements with optimized cost. The customer profile includes organizations from regional and money-center banks, insurance companies and mutual funds, credit card and student loan processors, telecom, utilities, government, and non-profit and commercial organizations.

Recently, ASL has bagged project A, which is an object oriented project using C++ and running on Windows. The application has been estimated to have the total effort of 400 person days. The project manager scanned through process database and found that another project B (500 person days) using C++ on UNIX platform had delivered 10 acceptance defects. The process capability baseline indicates ratio of effort for different stages as follows:

Requirement analysis:design:build:testing = 2:2.75:4.5:1.5.

How will the project manager estimate effort for each stage using bottom-up approach?

(B) Effort estimation for different stages is given in Table 2.10.

Table 2.10: Effort for different stages

Stage	Person hours
Requirement analysis	300
Coding	290
Code review	20
Unit test	64
Integration and system testing	140
Project management	90
Training	20

Other factors that are known are as follows:

- Defect injection rate in coding as per process capability baseline for development project is 10.7 defects/100 person hours.
- Defect injection distribution as per capability baseline is: requirement analysis = 28% and coding = 72%.
- As per commitment made to the customer, the project has to show an improvement of 5% on its present capability baseline.

Question:

1. Estimate defects in different stages.

3

Software Quality and Metrics

LEARNING OBJECTIVES

This chapter deals with metrics related to software projects. In this chapter, students would learn:

- Different metrics in software projects
- Need for metrics
- Decisions being taken from these metrics

Understanding Software Metrics

Software quality is primarily concerned with defects that are injected into different lifecycle stages. These defects can be injected right from the requirement analysis stage to the testing stage. These defects are injected because of many reasons. These reasons could vary from lack of knowledge to lack of complete understanding of customer requirements to error in design specifications, and so forth. These defects are then detected and removed during the execution stage. An application is always measured for its quality in terms of defect injection and defect removal rate. This is an important concept in software project management and is one of the aspects that needs to be controlled and monitored during the lifecycle of project execution. This is because of the fact that software development is a highly people-intensive activity and "to err is human." Defects can be injected and detected at any stage. Thus, defects can be injected in requirement analysis, design, and coding stages. These are the stages where requirements are converted to deliverables to the customer (such as design specification, code, etc.).

As discussed earlier, defects are injected at all stages of development lifecycle, and hence they need to be detected and removed. The removals in requirement analysis and design stages are done through review of their deliverables, whereas in coding stage, both review and testing will help in removing defects. A project is considered successful if these defects are removed in all these stages and application is delivered with no or less defects. The project management process has to plan for activities such that these are removed at the appropriate stage; defect injected in the initial stages has a cascading effect on defects downstream. This is because defects at early stages will inject new defects and time and cost involved in removing these defects, if not removed early, become higher and higher. Thus, it is imperative that the project management process should be matured enough to detect and remove the defects immediately. This is however easier said than done. The project manager has to plan for activities such as reviews of all deliverables from requirement, design, and coding stages and also has to decide testing strategy for codes written during the lifecycle stages.

Software metrics deal with the measurement of the software product and the process by which it is developed. The software product should be viewed as an abstract object that evolves from an initial statement of need to finished software system, including source and object code and different forms of documentation produced during development. Ordinarily, these measurements of the software process and product are studied and developed for use in modeling the software development process. These metrics and models are then used to estimate/predict product costs and schedules and to measure productivity and product quality. Information gained from the metrics and the model can then be used in manage and control of the development process, leading to, one hopes, improve results.

Jalote (2000) feels that good metrics should facilitate the development of models that are capable of predicting process or product parameters, not just describing them. As per Jalote (2001), ideal metrics should be

- Simple, precisely definable so that it is clear how the metric can be evaluated.
- Objective, to the greatest extent possible.
- Easily obtainable (that is, at reasonable cost).
- Valid—the metric should measure what it is intended to measure.
- Robust—relatively insensitive to insignificant changes in the process or product.

In addition, for maximum utility in analytical studies and statistical analyses, metrics should have data values that belong to appropriate measurement scales.
Hence, the objectives of software project measurement are as follows:

- Ensure that software projects operate at the desired quality and productivity levels. Quality also covers attributes such as reliability, usability, stability, and performance, as applicable.
- Ensure that projects meet the service level agreements (SLAs).
- Ensure that processes operate within the defined bounds and look for opportunities for improvement.
- Ensure that project meets the commitments made to the customer in terms of delivery schedule and other parameters, as applicable.

Mapping between business goals and measures are given in Table 3.1.

Table 3.1: Mapping between business goals and measures

Business goal	Measurement objective	Measures
Increase in productivity	Ensure that project operates at the desired quality and productivity levels; Measure process performance	Size, effort, review effectiveness, rework effort percentage
Improvement in delivered quality	Ensure that project operates at the desired quality and productivity levels; Meeting SLAs; Ensure customer satisfaction	Delivered defects, defects detected at all stages, turnaround time, service levels (as applicable)
Adherence to schedule	On-time delivery; Meeting SLAs	Elapsed days, schedule adherence percentage

Definitions of Metrics

Software Engineering Institute at Carnegie Mellon University (www.sei.cmu.edu) has stated that broadly the metrics can be classified into basic and derived metrics. Basic metrics are collected as a result of direct measurement of the process or product characteristics. The typical basic metrics collected are as follows:

Effort—This is the amount of time spent for an activity and is measured in person hours or person days.

Defects—This represents noncompliance to requirements and is measured in numbers.

Size—It is the size of the application being developed and is measured in function points or lines of code.

Elapsed time—This is the time spent between the start and the end of an activity and is measured in days.

Requirements count—This is the number of requirements given by the customer and is measured in numbers.

Number of requirement changes—This represents the number of times the customer has changed his/her mind resulting in changes in the original requirements. It is usually measured in numbers.

Number of requests (maintenance projects)—This represents the number of requests received from the customer to be fixed. It is measured in numbers only.

Derived metrics are quality indicators that are calculated using basic measures in order to gain insight into process and product quality characteristics. Some of the derived metrics are as follows:

- Productivity
- Delivered quality
- Defect injection rate (DIR)
- Defect detection rate
- Review/test effectiveness
- Review/test efficiency

- Cost of quality (COQ)
- Average turnaround time
- Age of bug fixes

ATTRIBUTES OF MEASURES

Productivity in a software development project is substantially different from productivity in manufacturing industries. In the manufacturing industry, productivity is the result of capital, technology, human resource, competence, and skill of management. In software development, capital and equipment play a very nominal role. In software development, no raw material or bought-out component is used. However, in manufacturing industry, these two components form a very significant part and these determine, to a great extent, the productivity. Given this kind of difference, a study for productivity in the manufacturing industry cannot be straightaway applied to the software industry. If one takes a precise view of the software industry, one observes that the key factor determining productivity in this industry is the human resource. Hence, in this chapter measuring the software output in relation to manpower deployed has been considered for measuring productivity. Further, while dozens of studies are available in manufacturing industries, there is hardly any study on productivity in software industry.

In early 1990s, IT industry, which includes both hardware and software, was considered as a sunrise industry. After mid-1990s it became clear that this industry was going to occupy a prominent place and the impetus for this industry's growth was coming from revolutionary changes in telecommunications, supply chain management, utilities, insurance and banking sector, greater use of satellites, etc. With increasing competition and rising cost of skilled manpower, attention to productivity was becoming inevitable in such industry. While in early 1990s hardware had the pre-eminence over software, in late 1990s and early 2000 software has taken a pre-eminent place. In view of these changes, the need for efficiency has been increasingly felt in software industry. This need has become essentially the driving force for the present study.

High productivity implies that given the number of function points in a project, it has consumed less man months. However, it is possible that with less man month being spent, the project may be completed in a hurry and may result in high delivered defects, which can create customer dissatisfaction. It is therefore important that while less effort is spent, no relaxation should be made on the final quality of the deliverable. In other words, while a higher value of productivity is maintained, better quality software with less or no delivered defects should be guaranteed. Such guarantee can help in increasing efficiency and eventually result in higher profitability and higher return on investment. In this chapter, a detailed approach for measuring metrics has been provided.

Table 3.2 gives an overview of basic measures, their typical attributes, and data capture mechanism. The list of tools given in Table 3.2 is used for capturing data during the project execution. At the completion of a project, data related to all lifecycle stages are summarized and captured. For an ongoing maintenance project, usually these data are captured at the end of a defined period of time (e.g., data for maintenance project can be captured at the end of 3 months and then metrics is derived).

Table 3.2: Typical attributes of measures

S. no.	Measure	Unit	Typical attributes of measures	Mechanism for capturing data
1	Effort	Person hours or person months[a]	Actual and estimated task, review, rework effort for each LC stage; Preparation effort for reviews	Time sheet
2	Size[b]	LOC/FP for source code; Number of pages for documents; S/M/C count for programs; Feature points/use case points/ object points in special cases where size is not captured in LOC; Number of test cases for test plans	Size of modules; Size of application	LOC[c] counters if available; FP count using IFPUG (International Function Point User Group) method
3	Defects	Number of defects	Stage injected; Stage detected; Defect type; Severity; Root cause; Status	Defect tracking tool
4	Schedule	Elapsed days		MSP or Excel
5	Requirements count	Number of requirements	Initial number of requirements; Total number of requirements	None
6	Number of requirement changes	Number of changes	None	Requirement tracker
7	Number of requests	Number	Type of request	Project-specific tracker

[a] A person month constitutes 168 person hours of effort. This is arrived at using the standard working hours per day, 8.0 hours and 21 days a month.

[b] The size can also be measured directly in terms of FP using IFPUG (International Function Point User Group) method (www.ifpug.com, 2006).

[c] LOC can be either non-commented, non-blank source statements (NCSS) or physical lines of code (PLOC). In the case of PLOC, it is necessary to include a note on how NCSS can be estimated, e.g., 70% of PLOC = NCSS.

Metrics for Different Types of Projects

Different types of projects will have different measurement approaches. Because the very nature of their lifecycles are different, the metrics will also be different (Demarco, 1982, www.sei.cmu.edu).

Development Projects

Basic Metrics

Effort

Effort spent on all lifecycle activities and management activities.

The typical lifecycle activities are as follows:

Requirements
Design
Coding
Testing

Typical management activities are as follows:

Project management
Configuration management

The estimated and actual efforts are captured for the task, review and rework involved during these activities.

Effort is measured in person hours.

Defect

Defects detected during reviews and testing, details such as stage injected, stage detected, severity, defect type, etc., are captured for all defects.

Size

Size of any software work product going through all lifecycle activities is measured as follows:

LOC or FPs

Wherever it is not feasible to capture size in LOC or FP, use other measures such as feature points, use case points, object points, as appropriate [for detailed definition of use case points and object points, please refer to www.ifpug.com (2006)].

For documents (design docs, requirements doc): number of pages.

For test plans: number of test cases.

In some cases the size is measured in terms of number of simple, medium, and complex programs.

Schedule

The number of calendar days taken for a particular activity per lifecycle stage, including holidays.

Requirements count

The number of initial requirements and the number of total requirements.

The number of requirement changes and the number of added or deleted or modified requirements.

Derived Metrics

Productivity

Productivity = Size of the delivered product in FP/total effort person months.

Delivered quality

Delivered quality (in terms of delivered defects per FP) = total number of delivered defects found during acceptance testing and warranty/size of the software delivered in FP.

Delivered quality (in terms of delivered defects per person hours) = total number of delivered defects found during acceptance testing and warranty/total effort for the project in person hours.

Requirement stability

(A) Overall requirement stability (%) = (Number of initial requirements × 100)/total number of requirements, where, the total number of requirements = number of initial requirements + number of added, modified, or deleted requirements.

For example, number of initial requirements = 90 and number of total requirements = 125.

So, overall requirement stability = 72%.

Overall requirements stability is computed at the end of the project.

(B) Requirements stability for a given period (%) = number of added, modified, or deleted requirements in a given period/cumulative requirement changes up to that period.

Re-engineering

All metrics are the same as development metrics except productivity, the definition of which is as follows:

Productivity (size in FP per person months) = total size added, modified, or deleted from the application/total effort in person months.

For re-engineering projects, the project has to capture LOC added, modified, or deleted in the existing application. This is converted to FP and is used for calculating productivity.

Maintenance

Maintenance projects are characterized by six kinds of requests:

- Bug fixes
- Minor enhancements
- Major enhancements
- Production support
- Analysis/R&D
- Testing

For each request type serviced, the actual and estimated efforts, the actual number of programs added, the number of programs modified, the LOC added/modified/deleted, and the equivalent FP are to be captured.

Basic Metrics

Size

For enhancements:

The unit of measure of size is the number of LOC (as in most cases) that have been added, deleted, and modified. The size can also be measured in FP using the IFPUG method.

For bug fixes:

Capture the number of bugs that are fixed.

Also, for maintenance projects, the number of each type of request should be captured.

Effort

Estimated and actual efforts are captured separately for each type of request.

For major enhancements, capture the management and lifecycle efforts as detailed under the development project metrics described earlier.

For minor enhancements, bug fixes and analysis/R&D requests the lifecycle-related effort should to be captured.

Defects

Same as development project.

Schedule

The number of calendar days taken for servicing the request, including holidays.

Derived Metrics

Productivity

For bug fix:

Productivity = total number of bug fixes/total effort spent in person months for servicing bug fix requests.

For enhancements (major and minor):

Productivity = size in FP/total effort in person months.

For system appreciation:

Productivity for system appreciation would be collected at the end of the SA phase of the project.

Productivity = size in FP analyzed/total effort in person months, or

For analysis/R&D:

Productivity = size in FP analyzed/total effort in person months or person days.

Note: FP is calculated as (LOC of added programs + LOC of added or modified or deleted programs)/conversion factor for LOC to FP conversion. This conversion factor is taken from Caper Jones conversion factor. This factor is a proprietary item and cannot be obtained or published without permission from the publisher.

Delivered quality

For bug fix:

Delivered quality = rejected (during acceptance testing or warranty) bug fixes/total number of bugs fixed during that period.

For enhancements (major and minor):

Delivered quality = delivered defects (number of defects detected during acceptance testing and warranty)/FP

= Delivered defects (number of defects detected during acceptance testing and warranty)/[(total LOC added/modified/deleted)/(conversion factor)].

For analysis/R&D:

Requests requiring predominantly analysis and comparatively little code change:

Delivered quality = delivered defects/FP.

Totally analysis type of request:

Delivered quality: not applicable

Turnaround time (TAT) for a request

The unit of measurement is hours.

TAT (hours) = time and date of delivery of the request to the customer – time and date of receipt of the request from the customer.

This is applicable for bug fixes and production support requests.

Age of open request:

Age of open request (hours) = current time and date – time and date of receipt of request.

Age of open request (days) = current date – date of receipt of request.

Average turnaround time:

Average turnaround time = total turnaround time in hours/total number of requests serviced.

This is applicable for bug fixes and production support requests.

Testing Projects

Basic Metrics

Size

Size is measured in terms of number of test cases. The unit of measure is the number of test cases.

Effort

Same as development project.

Derived Metrics

Productivity

For manual or regression testing/automated testing:

Productivity = number of test cases executed/total effort spent on testing in person hours.

For test automation:

Productivity = number of scripted test cases/total effort on automation of test cases.

Delivered quality

For manual or regression testing:

Delivered quality = number of defects raised by the customer/total number of test cases executed.

For automated test cases:

Delivered quality = number of defects raised by the customer/total number of test cases executed.

For test automation:

Delivered quality = number of test cases (scripts) rejected by customer/total number of test cases automated (scripted).

Metrics common to all processes

Review effectiveness:

Review effectiveness = (number of defects detected in reviews at a given stage)/(sum of defect injected in that stage + number of defects slipped from earlier stages). An example is given in Table 3.3.

Table 3.3 Calculation of review effectiveness

Injected stage	Number of bugs injected	Detected stage	Number of bugs detected	Review effectiveness	Remarks
Requirements	150	Requirements review	75	50% (requirement review effectiveness)	
		Design review			
		Code review			
		Testing			
Design coding	50 125	Design review Code review	40 90	32% (design review effectiveness) 42.9% (code review effectiveness)	Design review: Number of bugs injected in design = 50 + number of bugs slipped from requirements = 75 (total number of bugs present in the system is 125), out of which only 40 detected Code review: Number of bugs injected in coding = 125 + number of bugs slipped from requirements and design (125 – 40 = 85) totaling to 210 defects, out of which only 90 detected

Review efficiency

Efficiency is measured to check whether the time taken to review any work product is worth the effort.

Review efficiency = number of defects detected in a review stage/review effort.

DIR in coding

DIR in coding = number of defect injected during coding/task and rework effort of coding.

Schedule adherence

Schedule adherence % = 100 – schedule deviation % (in case of positive deviation).

Schedule deviation % = [(Actual delivery date – planned delivery date) × 100]/(planned elapsed days).

A negative schedule deviation % indicates that the project delivery was within the planned date of delivery, and schedule adherence is 100%.

Deviations

Negative deviation in delivered quality and process performance parameters is indicative of better performance. In case of % deviation calculation, numerator is always estimated value.

Effort deviation (%) = (actual – estimated)/estimated × 100

Delivered quality deviation = actual – estimated.
COQ deviation = actual – estimated.
DIR deviation = actual – estimated.
Defects deviation = actual – estimated.
Productivity deviation = estimated – actual.
Overall defect removal effectiveness = Estimated – actual.
Overall defect detection effectiveness

Overall defect detection effectiveness % = [(number of defects detected in all internal reviews and testing) × 100]/[total number of defects detected in the system (including acceptance defects)].

Group review coverage rate

It is defined as pages divided by elapsed hour of review for documents and LOC per elapsed hour of review for code.

COQ

The COQ consists of two factors: cost of conformance (prevention and appraisal) and cost of nonconformance (failure).

COQ includes the following:

Cost of prevention—includes training, defect prevention, and process improvement activities.

Cost of appraisal—includes reviews divided by inspection effort, testing, audits, etc.

Cost of failure—includes any rework caused by delivering bugs to customer plus any rework after internal reviews and testing.

Cost of rework, reviews, prevention, and training can be considered as directly proportional to effort. The effort data can be captured through time sheet and group review (inspection) summary reports. The COQ can then be expressed as the sum of appraisal, prevention, and failure cost as a percentage of total effort for lifecycle activities. Thus,
COQ% = [(review effort + test effort + training effort + rework effort + effort for prevention activities) × 100]/[total effort (for the project for development projects; for major enhancement for maintenance projects)].

Software reliability

Mean time between failure (MTBF) is a basic measure of reliability for repairable items. It can be described as the number of hours that pass before a component, assembly, or system fails. It is a commonly used variable in reliability and maintainability analyses. MTBF can be calculated as the inverse of the failure rate for constant failure rate systems. For example, if a system has a failure rate of two failures per million hours of usage, the MTBF would be the inverse of that failure rate.

MTBF = 1,000,000 hours/2 failures = 500,000 hours.

Mean time to failure (MTTF) is defined as average of elapsed time between the ith (e.g., 5, 6,…) and the $(i-1)^{th}$ (e.g., 4, 5,…) of failure in the system.
Mean time to repair (MTTR) is defined as average time to implement a change or to fix a bug and restore the system to working order.
MTBF = MTTF + MTTR.

System availability

System availability is the probability that a program is operating according to the requirements at a given point of time and is defined as

$$\text{System availability} = \frac{\text{MTTF}}{(\text{MTTF} + \text{MTTR}) \times 100}$$

Other measures are as follows:

Percentage of customization required or number of modules modified to implement at customer site.

This is mainly applicable to product development scenario where software products are developed; here, the requirements of a larger customer base are catered to rather than servicing a single customer.

Software usability

Usability or user friendliness of a software is the extent to which the product is convenient and practical to use. This means the probability that the operator of a system will not experience any user interface problem during a given period of operation under a given operational profile. Evidence of good usability includes:

Well-structured manuals or documentation or help functions.

Informative error message, consistent interfaces, and good use of menus and graphs

Some quantitative measures are as follows:

Ease with which users can learn to use the system (in person days)

Number of defect raised during acceptance testing because of user misunderstandings

Number of usability defects recorded during testing and support

Data Collection and Usage

Data at the project level are used for process control, process performance monitoring, and improvements. At the organization level, data are used for organization-wide performance measurements, identification of improvement areas, setting improvement goals and to define the process capability baseline. The following section defines how data are used at the project and organization levels.

At the project level

The data to be collected at the project level depends on many factors such as

Project goals and objectives

Project's defined software process

LC stages to be monitored and controlled

The project's SLAs with the customer

Using Metrics for Decision Making

In their research papers, Mohapatra and Mohanty (2003) have shown that the output from software projects can meet customer satisfaction if they use quantitative project management. In quantitative project management, metrics is used as the basis for making decisions. Thus, results from decisions made based on metrics can be predictable and can meet customer satisfaction as the project manager can take corrective actions accurately. As we saw earlier, there are a number of metrics defined for measuring different parameters. These parameters are obtained at all stages of lifecycle of software projects. Each metrics has a different interpretation and is used at different stages of project lifecycle. Based on the goals that have been set for the projects, the values of these metrics would indicate whether the project is in a good position or any improvement or, for example, if the metrics value review effectiveness at requirement stage is 80% against a goal of 90%, then the project manager has to carry out an analysis and has to take a decision on all improvements that should be brought into the project. The project manager can decide to review requirements again and plug the gaps in requirement analysis. In Table 3.4, based on prior experience, we have suggested some of the metrics as well as statistical tools that can be used to measure these metrics in all lifecycle stages.

Table 3.4 Statistical tools for metrics measurement

S. no.	Measurement	Statistical tools suggested	Applicable LC stage	Remarks
1	Delivered quality	Run chart Scatter diagrams	After AT	This is more appropriate for maintenance projects
2	Productivity	Run chart Scatter diagram	After AT	This is more appropriate for maintenance projects
3	Requirement stability	Run chart	Requirements analysis	
4	Review effectiveness	Bar chart (for comparing review effectiveness of all stages)	Requirement Design Build	
5	Defect injection rate	Control chart	Requirements analysis Design Build	
6	Effort deviation	Control chart	Design Build	SPC tool available for build phase
7	Turnaround time	Run chart	NA	For maintenance projects

SUMMARY

This chapter dealt with different metrics that are used in software projects. For different types of software projects, different metrics are defined. These metrics are quantitative measures for measuring project performance. Different tools are used for collecting data so that data integrity is maintained. By using well-defined guidelines for collecting data, metrics can be robust, valid, easily and consistently obtainable, and reliable. The entire measurement system becomes sustainable if there is a proper mapping of business goals and metrics.

DISCUSSION POINTS

1. **Draw a mapping between business goals and metrics.**
2. **What do you mean by typical attributes of measures? Explain with respect to productivity.**
3. **What is the difference between basic and derived metrics? Take example of maintenance project and explain this difference.**
4. **What are the metrics that are common to all processes?**
5. **How do you calculate review effectiveness for development projects?**

CASE STUDY

ZFT PLC is a multinational company with more than 15,000 employees operating in 27 countries. It has an office in Chennai, India, where it develops software for exports. ZFT specializes in developing software application in banking industry. It has provided banking software to more than 8000 organization in 27 countries in both private and public sectors for managing customer information and driving improvement in banking services. It focuses on innovative banking software solution using latest technology and is a leader in the Internet banking domain in the United Kingdom. Being a new development center in India, it did not have past data for estimating the effort required for developing these applications. In addition, the technology used for developing the applications was new. The current case is about an application to be developed for Internet banking in banking industry in the United Kingdoms. The size of the application was of 14,000 function points and the management team in Chennai wanted to benchmark productivity for its development team. Hence, to get benchmark productivity, external benchmarking practice was adopted. Similar applications were earlier developed in UK development center of the same organization; however, the data available from earlier development activities could not be used as there was a difference in the level of available skill. In addition, domain knowledge of the resources and technology was new.

Questions:

1. What are the business goals for an offshore-onsite project that is being developed in Java?
2. What are the metrics that should be defined for the above new project, which is being developed in Java technology?

4

PROJECT MONITORING AND CONTROL

LEARNING OBJECTIVES

In this chapter, the students would learn:

- Monitoring activities that consist of monitoring performance of the processes, identifying variances, and taking corrective actions
- Milestone analysis
- Resetting goals if required
- Defect prevention (DP) activities

INTRODUCTION

The chapter on project planning described different planning activities that are carried out at the initial stage. The chapter also discussed how goals are set to be inline with the objectives of the project. It also explained the need for process capability baseline and process database, and how to use historical data for estimating size, effort, and schedule. These aspects of planning are documented in the project management plan, and this plan is used as a baseline document for monitoring. This chapter deals with the different processes and activities that are carried out for control and monitoring using the project management plan and statistical tools.

Project Control and Management Processes

The processes involved in project execution ensure that the project continues to move along a path that will lead to successful completion. The criteria for successful completion are set well in advance. The criteria include the following:

(i) Delivering the project within the budgeted estimates and schedule,
(ii) Number of defects in the final products less than or at least equal to the acceptable limits,
(iii) Providing all technical features that are required by the customer, and
(iv) Seamless integration with existing applications and systems available at the customer site so that business transactions are not hampered for the end users of the application.

In order to achieve these success criteria, the project has to move along a defined path that will lead to achieving these targets. But it is important for a project manager to know whether the project is following its desired path or not. This can only be known when the project manager has the visibility about the status of the project execution path. The difference between manufacturing or any non-IT project and a software project is with respect to the abstract nature of the deliverables. In non-IT projects, deliverables are concrete in nature and hence can be measured to determine its percentage completion, whereas in software projects, because of its abstract nature, the completion percentages cannot be measured. Hence, the degree of completion of software projects is measured through intermittent results such as defects, cost of quality, effort spent on rework, etc. Hence, by measuring these intermittent results accurately, we will be able to get the correct status of the progress of the project.

As discussed earlier, accurate measurement of intermittent effects is critical for monitoring. Thus, project management has two aspects: (i) collection of data and information about different parameters of the current state of the project and (ii) taking corrective actions through control mechanism to bring the project back into track. The value of these parameters would indicate whether or not the desired state has been achieved. Achieving desired state will imply that the project is moving along the planned path; monitoring in this case suggests that the execution of the project is moving as planned. If, however, these parameters exhibit values that are not as desired, then the health of the project is weak and it needs to be brought back to the desired state. This can happen by taking some corrective actions. This implies that after monitoring the progress, control mechanisms need to be applied for bringing back the project to its desired state. In essence, the monitoring and control mechanism is the foundation for sound project management principles. Different processes involved in this sound project management principle are as follows:

1. Preparing a plan for the project to follow;
2. Measuring values of parameters as defined in the plan;
3. Monitoring progress against parameters as defined in the plan;
4. Comparing actual versus planned results of these defined parameters and finding variations;
5. Using control mechanism to correct the variations; and
6. Repeating processes (2) to (5) .

The starting point for project management is the measurement of parameters in the above cycle for knowing the correct status of the project. To measure these accurately, software metrics are defined and measured for different stages of the project lifecycle. As discussed in Chapter 3, metrics are different for different lifecycle stages as well as for different processes. By using the values of these metrics, the project status is monitored and variances are found out. These variances, if negative, are then controlled to bring the project back into its desired path. In the next section, we discuss data collection activities. Raw data that need to be collected for control and monitoring are effort data, defect data, and size data.

Effort Data Collection

As discussed earlier, the foundation of monitoring and control in project management process is data collection at different lifecycle stages. After data collection, models and business rules would help in analyzing and interpreting data for taking meaningful decision. In order to get effective meaning out of these data, the fundamental principle is to define metrics correctly that will help in gathering required data. These data and usage of models and business rules will help in arriving at the correct status of the project. However, the collection of these data has many challenges. These challenges are as follows: (i) willingness of team members to provide accurate data about their activities, as they would fear that the data can be used for appraising their performance and hence impact their career. (ii) At the initial stages of data collection, team members are not habituated to provide data. Hence, unintentionally they delay in providing data related to their daily activities and make errors. For example, a team member who has not provided details of his/her effort on Monday and Tuesday will not remember finer details of his/her work-related data on Wednesday. So, when he is asked to submit his/her data for Monday and Tuesday, he/she would definitely make errors while submitting these data on Wednesday. (iii) For each team member data need to be collected under correct buckets for consolidation at the project level. By collecting data in proper buckets (category), error in consolidation is avoided. However, the problem would arise if there are incorrect and different interpretations of these buckets, leading to data collection in wrong buckets. This will lead to error in consolidation and subsequent error in the interpretation of this information. (iv) Data collection has to be done using tools. If different parts of an organization use different types of tools for data collection, this would lead to incorrect interpretation as well as inaccurate consolidation at aggregate level.

Data for software metrics are primarily data related to effort, which team members spend for each activity. This determines the cost of the project and is mentioned in the contract between the customer and the vendor. In project planning, effort is used for estimating size. Clearly, tracking of effort is a key activity during control and monitoring in project management process. By monitoring effort, we know whether the project is being executed within allocated budget. The collection of data related to effort is done at each activity level in all lifecycle stages and then analyzed at predefined milestones. In order to take care of such collection, tools are used in organizations where individual team members are expected to enter their own effort data for each and every activity that they spend for project execution. A sample template for the collection of effort is shown in Annexure B (template for data collection).

Defect Data Collection

Another raw data that needs to be collected is defect data. This data is of considerable importance as it has direct relationship with the final quality of deliverables. A defect is considered to be a mismatch between what was expected in a work product or deliverable and what actually is found in it. These defects, if not removed, will adversely affect the performance of the application and the project will not achieve its objectives. This section deals with the need for defect data collection and procedures associated with it.

Defect Closure Lifecycle

By very definition, defects are not acceptable at any stage of projects. These defects are injected at all stages of lifecycle. Defects are found either during the review of deliverables or during testing stages. A defect once found is recorded and logged in "defect tracking" tool. The defect is then considered to be in submitted stage. The person who does the review or testing usually records these defects and assigns it to the person who has authored the original document. In case of testing, the developer who has written the code is assigned with this responsibility. The person who has been assigned the defect does the debugging or fixing of the defects, and the defect is considered to be in fixed stage. By fixed stage, it does not mean that defect is in closed stage. Usually, the person who has done the initial submission of defects verifies that the defect has been fixed and then is marked as closed. In case the submitter is not happy with the quality of defect fixing, then he/she would again mark it as open and the cycle of submit, fixed, and closed follows. If finally a defect is not closed, then it is called open defect. A typical defect collection of metrics is shown in Annexure B (template for data collection).

Data Collection for Size

Size is another primary data that is collected. This measurement helps in normalizing different applications, and the measurement can be used to compare and normalize different applications. While measuring productivity, the metrics used is size per unit of effort; this measure helps in normalizing a big and small team performance, which only effort would not have helped. Similarly, there are other metrics that use size for comparison, such as defect per size of the application. These metrics are used for process capability baseline preparation and also can be used not only for monitoring and controlling but also for setting quality goals. Thus, by collecting data with respect to size and using it for measurement, it helps in benchmarking process performance. For example, if the productivity of a project is found to be *x* function per unit of effort and process capability baseline shows a value of *y*, where *y* is greater than *x*, then the productivity of the present project is lower and corrective actions need to be taken to improve productivity. Clearly, only the number of total defects and total efforts cannot be used for estimating or for predicting performance for another project. By using size measurements, past data can be used for predicting performance of a new project. Also, by measuring size, benchmarking exercise can be carried out.

Measurement of size in software has three approaches: (i) measuring the number of programs of similar complexities, (ii) measuring the number of uncommented lines of code in an application, and (iii) function point. The first two measures have problems while normalizing across different programs written in different technology. For example, even though there is a guideline for defining complexity, still there could be errors while deciding complexity. Similarly, using the number of uncommented lines of code for size measurement has its own pitfalls. For example, one programmer could write less number lines of code for same feature while another could write in explicit manner, and one technology could require less number of code for developing a feature while another technology could require more number of lines of code. Hence, function point is usually used for size measure.

Monitoring and Control

As discussed earlier, monitoring implies monitoring progress of executing projects with respect to the objectives set. By monitoring, the project manager would know whether the health of the project deliverables are good or need to be improved. This is so, as IT projects are nonvisible projects compared with manufacturing or non-IT projects, where one can see the progress in concrete form. That is why the status of intermediate deliverables in IT projects is used as a basis for monitoring. At each predefined milestone, the project manager checks the status of defects, productivity, cost of quality, schedule variation, effort variation, etc., for the deliverables. These metrics are already defined in the project management plan and are used for monitoring the progress. However, how does a project manager know the degree of percentage completion of a deliverable (such as a design document or a program)? Difficulties arise because these deliverables are partially complete during milestone analysis and, based on completion percentage, effort and schedule variations need to be calculated. Even if a program is broken into smaller components, still it becomes difficult for calculating percentages of completion. The other alternative could be to discuss with team members and assess the percentage completion, which may lead to erroneous results. This is because even if a program seems to be complete still it could take long time to debug and remove the final defect present in the program. In addition to this, the quality of deliverables needs to be monitored. This monitoring has three aspects: (i) monitoring with respect to customer specifications and requirements, (ii) monitoring with respect to the scope of deliverables, and (iii) monitoring with respect to compliance with standards set in the project plan. As the project progresses, it has been seen that the amount of scope increases and new requirements are added or present requirements are modified. These posses a challenge while monitoring, as additional human resources would be required leading to changes in project objectives in terms of effort and schedule timelines. Thus, a task might seem to have been completed, but poor quality of end deliverables implies that the activity has to be reworked and percentage completion (which is used for monitoring) is brought back to zero.

Another problem in monitoring comes with respect to usage of resources, which are primarily human resources. These resources are usually overheads or employees and not similar to direct expenses encountered in non-IT projects such as raw materials. The monitoring problem of these human resources becomes more pronounced when these resources are permanent employees of a service provider and hence do not contribute to the hourly expenses. This situation is more prevalent in third world countries where software vendors provide services to their overseas clients.

Monitoring Process

There are formal and informal methods for monitoring, and they need to be used judiciously. Many a times, tailoring guidelines are used during the project planning stage, which will decide the type of method to be adopted. For example, the tailoring guideline can suggest that complex programs should go through a formal method while simple programs can be monitored through an informal method. This saves time and adds value to the project management; productivity increases without sacrificing the quality of end deliverables. The formal method involves the usage of mails, recordings minutes of meeting, progress reports, etc., for future reference. This helps in knowledge management and sharing of best practices across team members as well as across projects. Here, a process can be established so that people can commit themselves to the monitoring process. This way, their schedule are booked and made available for the purpose. The disadvantage is that time spent for documentation and waiting for all the members to be made available for meeting (because of other commitments) can be seen as wastage of time. Some examples of formal method are group review (where a work product is reviewed by several peer members), customer review of design specification, etc.

In the informal method, documentation may not be a must, but work products are reviewed by peers and defects are closed. In small teams and simple programs, this method works the best. Some examples are one-to-one informal discussion, discussion during team outings, etc. This method does not yield data that can be used in future projects and is best suited for experts working in small-size projects that have less chance of being repeated. This type is not very much recommended for software projects.

Control Process

Monitoring can be successful only if effective control process is being used. Based on results from monitoring, control mechanisms need to be applied for getting the desired result. For example, monitoring process would indicate that there are deviations in the effort spent till design phase; this means that actual effort spent till design phase is more than the planned effort till that phase. To remedy the deviation, control process would implement some of the activities that would reduce cumulative deviation in the subsequent phases so that by the end of the project, the total effort deviation is reduced to zero or is kept under control. A list of these action items are discussed in detail in section "Monitoring Process—An Example."

During project planning phase, the project manager plans for review activities and milestone analysis. In project plan a clear mention of the role or person responsible for reviewing different work products are mentioned. This not only makes the control process formal but also makes it focused and the reviewers are committed to the monitoring and control process. Reviewers' calendars are booked and made available for these activities. The frequency and the persons who would get the reports of the monitoring and control should also find mention in the communication protocol defined in project management plan. Project organization structure also determines the communication protocol for these reports.

Status Reporting

Status reporting is a key to control processes. Through status reporting all the stakeholders are apprised of status or project health. Inputs to status report are the results of monitoring process. This means variations and deviations found during monitoring process are made as input to the status report. Results of the review process and milestone analysis are recorded in the status report. The status report also has inputs related to the action items that have been taken by the team and the persons responsible for carrying out these action items. These action items are the result of the control processes. In essence, the status report has outputs of both monitoring and control processes and serves as the health report of a project at the reporting time. Two sample reports have been provided in Annexure D.

Status reports to different stakeholders should be different. This is because different stakeholders have different objectives. For example, internal issues related to team should not be reported to customers, rather they should be reported to senior management. The status report by the project manager to the customer and business manager should contain the following minimum fields:

Report to the customer

- Milestones achieved this week
- Milestones missed this week and the reasons for them
- Milestones planned for the next week

- Issues requiring clarifications
- Escalation, if any

Report to the BM (a sample status report for senior management is shown in Annexure D)

- Customer complaints
- Milestones achieved this week
- Milestones missed this week and the reasons for them
- Milestones planned for the next week
- Issues requiring clarifications/attention
- Escalation, if any
- Estimated work versus available time by milestone
- Number of requirement changes and effort estimate
- Major changes from plan

Quantitative Techniques in Monitoring and Control Processes

For effective quantitative management, there are a number of statistical tools that are used for taking decisions. Some of them have been discussed in this section.

1. Check sheet
2. Histogram
3. Pareto chart
4. Run chart
5. Control chart
6. Scatter plot

Check Sheet

A check sheet is a form used to gather and record data of events or occurrences in an organized manner. This tool records the frequency of an event by recording the number of occurrences over a specified interval of time. The data are recorded to support or objectively validate the significance of the event. This tool is usually used in conjunction with Pareto analysis or cause-and-effect diagram. The output of this tool is used for validating a problem, or it may be used to build Pareto charts or histograms. A sample checklist is shown in Table 4.1.

Table 4.1: A sample checklist

Daily system failures	Week of dd/mm/yy					
	Day 1	Day 2	Day 3	Day 4	Day 5	Total

Check sheets can be used to record the following types of information:

- Defects found or review results of work products, stage detected, stage injected, etc.
- Documentation defects by type or frequency
- Turnaround time for bug fixing
- Nonconformance to GUI or coding standards
- Defects and issues found after implementation of an application
- Late deliveries

Advantages of check sheets are that they predefine areas to gather data, decide the scope, and provide a consistent, organized, and documented approach.

Questions on check sheets should be organized by topic and tested prior to use. A response of "I don't know" should be allowed and bias should be avoided. The person using the check sheet should understand the reason for the questions and be able to anticipate a response. The disadvantage of using a check sheet is its applicability of using it for questions not mentioned.

Histogram

A histogram (or frequency distribution chart) is a graph that groups data by predetermined intervals. This can be used to show frequency of the data set. It provides a way to measure and analyze data collected about a process or problem as well as a way to prioritize problem areas. Histograms are also useful for displaying information such as defects by type or source, productivity or number of employees with experience or skill levels. Figure 4.1 shows a sample histogram.

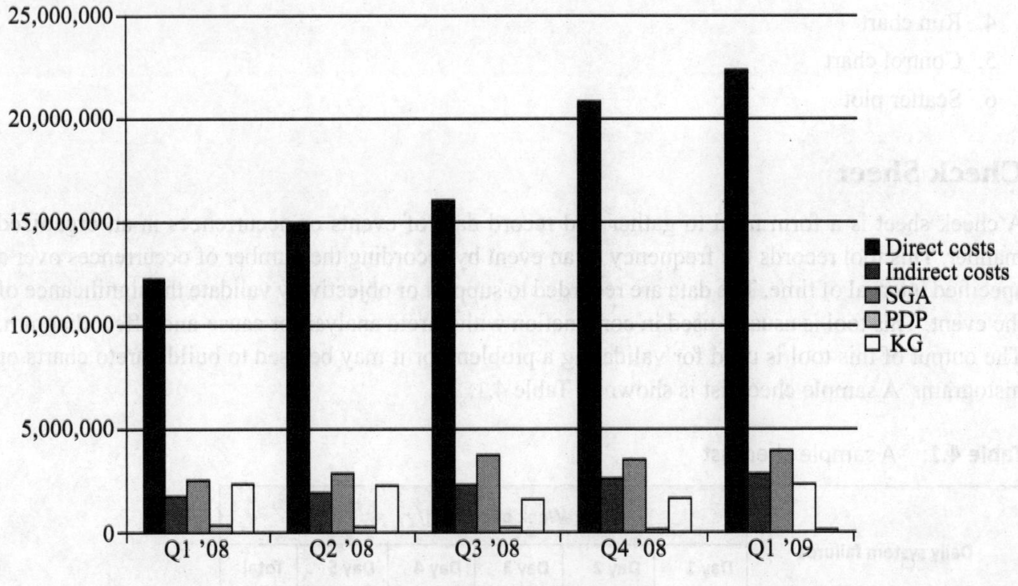

Figure 4.1: Histogram

A histogram requires some understanding of the data set being measured to consolidate or condense it into a meaningful display. To create a histogram, perform the following steps:

1. Gather data and organize it from lowest to highest values.
2. Calculate the range, which is the largest value–smallest value.
3. Sort the data or observations into their respective cells.
4. Count the data points of each cell (frequency) to determine the height of the interval, and create a frequency table.
5. Plot the results.

The distribution is normally a bell-shaped curve.

Pareto Chart

Pareto chart is used on the basis of 80-20 rule. The inventor, Pareto, said that 80% of wealth is accumulated with 20% of population. This concept is extended to quantitative techniques to find the problem areas that need to be tackled first. The Pareto chart is a special type of histogram used to view causes of a problem in order of their severity. It is a simple statistical tool that graphically shows the 20-80 rule where 20% of the sources cause 80% of the problems. This is also used for separating "vital few" from the "trivial many."

A Pareto chart is typically used early in the continuous improvement process when there is a need to order or rank problems or causes by frequency. The vital few problems and their respective root causes can be focused on. The steps used for software project management are as follows:

1. Use brainstorming, affinity diagrams, or cause-and-effect diagrams to define the problem clearly.
2. Collect a sufficient sample size (at least 30 occurrences) of data over the specified time, or use historical data, if available.
3. Categorize defects such as critical, major, minor, etc.
4. Group them to find the maximum to minimum by first drawing a histogram and then sorting it from maximum to minimum.
5. Identify the causes or characteristics that contribute most to a problem.
6. Decide basic causes of a problem to work on first.

Sample problems for Pareto analysis include the following:

- Problem solving for the vital few causes or characteristics
- Defect analysis at the customer site
- Analysis of defect types
- Employee satisfaction/dissatisfaction

Run Chart

A run chart, as shown in Figure 4.2, is a graph of data in chronological order that displays changes and trends of a particular parameter such as occurrence of defects over a period of time. This chart can help in understanding whether there is an inherent problem or a specific instance for occurrence of defects in the lifecycle. Thus, run charts can be used as input for establishing control charts.

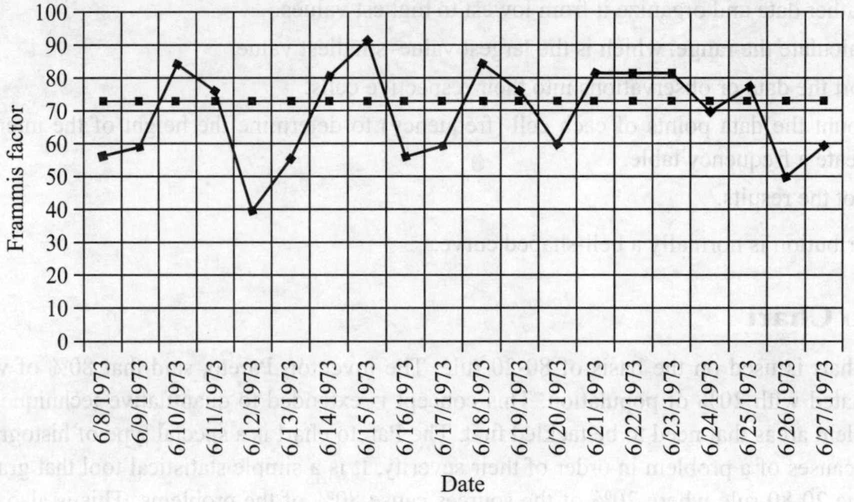

Figure 4.2: Run chart

Run charts can track events such as

- Defects in each lifecycle stage over a period of time
- Defects across lifecycle stages
- Customer complaint levels
- End user satisfaction levels
- Productivity across the organization over a period of time
- Response time to customer complaints

The steps for developing a run chart are as follows:

1. Decide which parameter of a process is to be measured.
2. Plot the individual measurements over time (plotting the data chronologically).
3. Use an Excel sheet to plot the trend line by using features available in the Excel sheet; any other tool can be used to develop similar trend line.
4. Monitor the data points for any obvious trend, which could explain regular inherent problem or any specific cause.

Control Chart

Control charts are used for finding deviation from defined path. They provide a way of objectively defining expected progress of a process and variation observed in practice. These help in establishing measures on a process, improving process analysis, and allow process improvements to be used based on facts. The intent of a control chart is to determine if a process is statistically stable and then to monitor the variation of stable process where activities are repetitive. There are two types of variation:

- Common or random causes of variation

These are inherent in every system over time and are a part of the natural operation of the system. If we have to resolve common causes that lead to variation, then it requires a process change. This means as long as process is stable, the output of the process will remain the same. Any change in the output requires process to be redefined.

- Special causes of variation

  If a process experiences environments that are not expected in normal circumstances, then special variations are experienced. For example, in software projects, a sudden attrition of experienced team members will lead to more defects being injected by inexperienced team members. This phenomenon is not part of the system all the time. They result from some special circumstances and require changes outside the process for resolution.

Common causes of variation are typically due to many small random sources of variation. The sum of these sources of variation determines the magnitude of the processes-inherent variation due to common causes. From the sum, the process control limits and current process capability can be determined. If a process exhibits common causes of variations only, then it is considered stable; this implies that for a stable process, performance predictability increases. For a stable development project process, we can predict productivity and schedule variation accurately. However, if a process contains both special as well as common causes of variation, then it is considered to be unstable. From the above discussion we understand that the special cause always falls outside of the control limits of the unstable process. Control charts also require that upper critical and lower critical limits are calculated. The upper critical limit represents the maximum upper range that can be expected as output from a process and the lower limit indicates the least value that can be expected from a process. Statistically, the upper critical limit is calculated by the formula average plus three times standard deviation. Similarly, the lower critical limit is calculated by average minus three times standard deviation.

Control charts are suitable for tracking items such as

- Defects, bugs, and any production failures
- Defects by lifecycle phase
- Turnaround time for new requests
- Response time to complaints/failure by application/software
- Response time to change request
- Productivity of a team over a period of time

Steps involved in using a control chart are as follows:

1. From the initial evaluation, identify the parameters/metrics of the process to monitor, such as defects, cycle times, productivity, failures, cost, or maintenance.
2. Select the appropriate type of control chart based on the characteristic to monitor; data that is variable (measured and plotted on a continuous scale such as time, cost, figure, etc.) may require different charts.
3. Determine the methods for sampling, such as how many or over what time frame.
4. Collect sample data; check sheets can be used to gather data.
5. Analyze and calculate the sample statistics: average, standard deviation, upper control limit, and lower control limit.
6. Construct the control chart based on the statistics.

7. Monitor the process for common and special causes of variation; the process is in control when observations fall within the control limits.

While trying to find whether a process has common variation or specific variation, some rules are used. If observed, the process needs to be evaluated and analyzed for causes related to the situation. The rules constituting a special cause are as follows:

- Any point outside the upper or lower control limit.
- Any run of eight or more data points above or below the average value (center line), indicating the average has changed.
- Six or more consecutive data points, which are increasing (trend up) or decreasing (trend down).
- Two out of three consecutive points in the outer one-third control unit.
- Fifteen consecutive points between the center line and inner one-third of the chart.

Scatter Plot

In quantitative project management, a scatter plot is used as a problem-solving tool that helps explain cause-and-effect relationships. It shows whether a relationship exists between two variables, by testing how one variable influences the response (other variable). Using regression coefficient, these relationships are explained. Some of the variables that can be used are as follows:

- Defect density versus productivity
- Defects density versus skill levels (training)
- Change response versus people availability
- Defect cost versus review effectiveness
- Preventive cost versus failure cost

The steps for creating scatter plots are as follows:

1. Select the variables whose relationships need to be determined; define independent and dependent variables.
2. Gather data on the variables.
3. Plot the data; determine the appropriate scale to plot the relationship.
4. The pattern of the plots will suggest correlation: positive, negative, random, linear, curvilinear, cluster, etc.; use features available in the Excel sheet or any such tool for plotting scatter diagrams.

Figure 4.3 shows a typical relationship between productivity and skill by using scatter plot.

Monitoring Process—An Example

During project execution, the goals set by the project for defect injection are closely monitored with respect to the actual number of defects to enable control. The project compares the actual number of defects found in a project LC stage with the predicted number of defects. Various inputs for enabling this control are efforts, number of defects captured, and predicted number of defects. The actual number of defects detected is checked against the number of defects estimated for each LC stage. If there are deviations, the reasons for deviations must be investigated and suitable corrective actions should be taken. Possible reason and actions to consider are discussed later in this chapter.

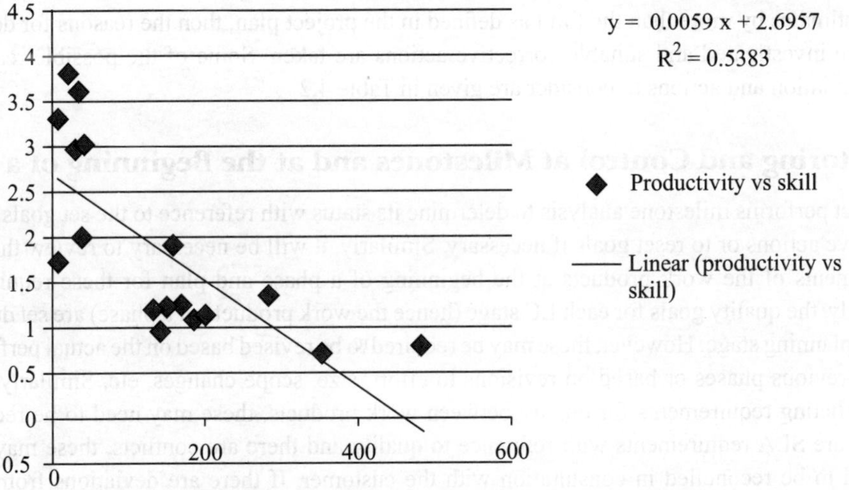

Figure 4.3: Scatter plot for productivity vs skill

For Code, Code Reviews, and Unit Testing

- For code reviews

  Following steps are followed for tracking:

  1. Coding effort for each program/unit as well as the number of defects injected for each program is found out.
  2. Efforts as well as defects captured for all such programs are found out by summing them up; actual defect injection rate = (number of summed defects/actual efforts spent on code).
  3. This rate of defect injection is compared with the initial goal set at the project initiation stage. If there is a deviation found, then corrective action is proposed by the project team in separate defect prevention (DP) meeting. An example of corrective actions to be followed for various symptoms when there is a deviation from the set goals is given in Table 4.2).

- For unit testing

  The effectiveness of unit testing is tracked at the program level. Following steps are followed for tracking:

  1. The rate of defect injection is compared with the initial goal set at the project initiation stage. If there is a deviation found, then corrective action is proposed by the project team in separate DP meeting. An example of corrective actions to be followed for various symptoms when there is a deviation from the set goals is given in Table 4.2. If there is a deviation from the predicted injection rate, then possible reasons are discussed and suitable actions are taken in a separate DP meeting.

- For integration testing/system testing

  Here, the actual number of defects detected during integration and system testing is compared with the estimated number of defects. If the actual number of defects differs from the estimates by more than the limit as defined in the project plan, then the reasons for deviations are investigated and suitable corrective actions are taken. Some of the possible reasons for deviation and actions to consider are given in Table 4.2.

Monitoring and Control at Milestones and at the Beginning of a Phase

A project performs milestone analysis to determine its status with reference to the set goals and take corrective actions or to reset goals if necessary. Similarly, it will be necessary to review the quality requirements of the work products at the beginning of a phase and plan for these requirements. Generally, the quality goals for each LC stage (hence the work products of a phase) are set during the project planning stage. However, these may be required to be revised based on the actual performance of the previous phases or based on revisions to effort, size, scope changes, etc. Similarly, if there are conflicting requirements for quality between work products, these may need to be reconciled. If there are SLA requirements with reference to quality and there are conflicts, these may also be required to be reconciled in consultation with the customer. If there are deviations from desired results, then actions need to be taken as part of project management activities. Table 4.2 shows a list of corrective actions that need to be taken for different deviations.

Possible Actions When Deviations Are Beyond Limits

For Reviews

Table 4.2: Possible actions for correcting deviations

Symptom	Possible reason	Actions to consider
If defects found are less than limits	Work product was very simple	• Convert group reviews of similar work products to one person reviews (refer tailoring guidelines) • Combine reviews (refer tailoring guidelines)
	Reviews may not be thorough	• Check coverage rate; if too low, reschedule a review, perhaps with a different team
	Reviewers do not have sufficient training on group reviews or experience with the reviewed material	• Schedule or conduct group review training • Re-review with a different team
	Work product is of very good quality	• Confirm this by coverage rate, experience of the author, reviewers, etc.; see if this can be duplicated in other parts of the project • Revise defect prediction in downstream activities; see if there are general process improvement lessons
If defects found are more than limits	Work product is of low quality	• Examine training needs for author • Consider reassigning future tasks (i.e., assign easier tasks only to the author)

	Work product is very complex	• Ensure good review or testing downstream (refer tailoring guidelines) • Increase estimates for system testing • Break the work product into smaller components
	Too many minor defects (and too few major defects)	• Identify cause of minor defects; correct for future by suitably enhancing checklists and making authors aware of the common causes
	Reference document against which review was done is not precise and clear	• Get the reference document reviewed and approved
	Reviewed modules are the first ones in the project	• Analyze the defects, update review checklist, and inform developers • Schedule training

Monitoring Defect Prevention Activities at Project Level

DP at the project level is done by

- Studying the DP measures of similar kind of projects.
- DP measures at the organization level.
- Analyzing the project data at appropriate stages during the course of project execution and taking preventive actions.

Before DP activities are started in a project, it is necessary to take inputs from organization-wide DP activities and from the DP activities of similar kind of projects. This is generally done in a kick-off meeting. Also, DP activities are carried out on an ongoing basis using project data at appropriate intervals during project execution.
Following are the steps for DP activities at the project level:

- Identify existing solutions
- Plan for defect prevention
- Do defect prevention
- Capture learning

DP team within the project is identified and their roles are defined. A kick-off meeting is organized and existing solutions are identified; this is done by collating organization-wide DP information. Appropriate checklists, tools, templates, etc., available in organization are identified to be used in the project; project goals are set/revised.

Defect Prevention Planning

A kick-off meeting with all project members is organized and DP activities are explained. Simultaneously identify training requirements for team members and provide them detailed training on technical knowledge as well as on project management. The DP team is trained on causal analysis. Moreover, define the frequency at which DP activities will be carried out (it is preferable that these activities are carried out after coding, code review, and unit testing a few programs; 20% of the programs and 50% of the programs).

Defect Prevention Activities

At defined milestone intervals as planned during project initiation, defects data are collated and most common types of defects are identified by doing Pareto analysis. For each defect, causes are identified through a brainstorming session (see Table 4.2). Then, root-cause analysis is carried out to identify the root causes/common causes and these causes are prioritized. A causal analysis report is prepared. Solutions for common causes/root causes (such as tools, updating of checklists/templates/standards/guidelines, introduction of tools, process changes, and training) are developed and implemented. At project milestone the status and benefits of DP activities are reviewed with the senior management.

Pareto Analysis

A sample Pareto analysis from a project is shown in Figure 4.4. As can be seen in the figure, GUI defects alone contribute to 50% of total defects. GUI and logic defects put together contribute to 85% of total defects. Hence, if we address GUI and logic defects, 85% of problems would get addressed.

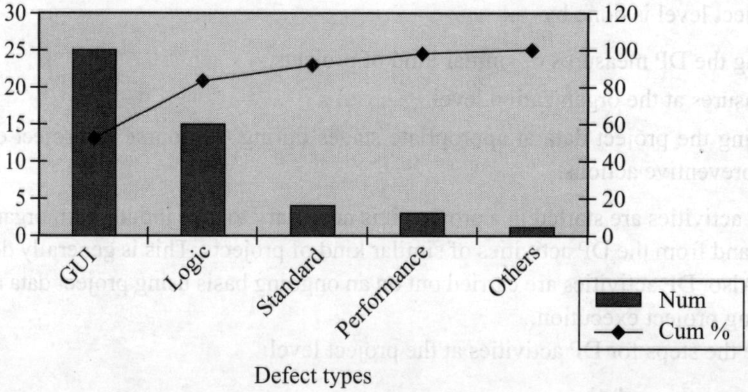

Figure 4.4: Defect analysis

In summary, the DP activities follow PDCA cycle, that is, plan, do, check, and act. Monitoring and controlling processes are implemented, and then based on periodic feedback, they are further improved so that there can be better performance.

Tools and Techniques Used in Quantitative Project Management—An Example

Quantitative techniques used in the project predict values of different parameters at different stages of the project. These parameters are decided such that by controlling these parameters we can not only control the quality level but also predict the quality standard of the end product. The prediction of quality is done using actual data from the projects or based on past experience from similar projects. As a result at any point of time we can predict whether the concerned project follows process as defined at the start of the project. Thus, we can not only crosscheck deviations from the defined process at various stages but also ensure that we get maximum benefits by following predefined process.

There are several techniques for quantitative measurement, for example, Pareto analysis, statistical process control activity, causal analysis, milestone analysis, to name a few. These techniques are applied throughout the project at defined intervals to check various parameters. These parameters are used for comparison with benchmarked values. These benchmarked values are quality goals that are set by the project at the initial stage. These goals in turn are derived from defect patterns observed in similar projects executed in the past.

As is evident, the techniques described above become effective depending on how well can we set the quality goals and hence be able to predict the outcome. Hence, the collection of defects data is a very important activity. These defect data is not only used to find the pattern at every stage but also used to predict the pattern at a future stage and is also used to set quality goals for similar projects later on. Various tools are used to collect these data and stored in a databank for easy accessibility across the organization.

Forms/Tools/Checklists

Checklists, standards, and forms are defined at the execution time to smoothen the development process. These forms are either picked up from the existing database of these forms stored from previous projects or modified to suit the project requirements. An example of such a form is given in Table 4.3.

Table 4.3: Checklist

S. no.	Description	Remarks
1.	File name should be <program name>.tp	
2.	Program type should contain add service, add service manager, trandriver, dispatcher, etc.	
3.	The expected result column should contain the output that can be seen	
4.	All branches of the program should be covered in the test cases	
5.	The order of the test cases should be such that the first test condition corresponds to the first possible exit in the program and the second corresponds to the next exit and so on	
6.	There should be sufficient test conditions to test the boundary conditions	
7.	Detail SQL (corresponding to each test case) to be specified to check the output	
8.	Follow the template \css\quality\tpchk.doc	
9.	The points that are not relevant for the test plan should not be deleted but instead should be specified as N/A	

Defect Prevention Through Defect Pattern Analysis

In order to achieve the quality goals that have been set, the process is tuned to achieve the desired goals. The team uses the existing templates and checklists for various stages of project. These checklists are also continuously updated to suit the project needs. Review stages are defined and scheduled at various check points. These reviews would highlight project health as would analyze actual results against planned.

A typical milestone report will be used in these reviews. Defects detected during the process are identified and the pattern is analyzed. A typical defect analysis by defect type would look like as shown in Figure 4.5.

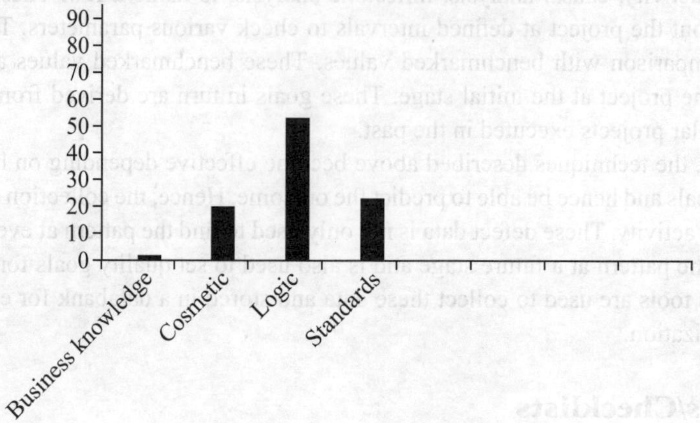

Figure 4.5: Defects by type

The graph can be used to decide the corrective actions needed to keep the project under control. By looking at the chart, a PL can analyze defect type that occurs most. This will help him/her prioritize his/her actions so that the occurrence of such defects (which occur most of the time) can be minimized. These two graphs are adopted from a project using PL/1 and VB5.0 language.

Causal Analysis

A causal analysis is done when the project team tries to find the root cause of defects (after they analyze defect pattern and defect severity—Figure 4.3) and try to come up with solutions. Usually, a team is formed—called DP team. The members would have identified the defects that occur most of the time. This identification is done after they have analyzed defect pattern at the milestone analysis level. A meeting is convened where all the DP team members are invited. The project manager usually coordinates this meeting. A brainstorming session follows where the team comes up with various action items against these defects as shown in Table 4.4. These action items are then piloted in the project and if found to be successful, the project will adopt these guidelines. Impact and cost are measured on a 0–1 scale. For impact, the larger the number, the higher the impact, and the larger the number, the lesser the cost and is easier to implement.

Table 4.4: Action items

S. no.	Root cause	Preventive action	Impact (*I*)	Cost (*C*)	Rating ($I \times C$)
1.	No template available for test planning	Identify a template for test planning	0.25	0.2	0.0500
2.	Unplanned execution of tasks	Scheduling and tracking to be done using MS project	0.15	0.15	0.0225

3.	Improper knowledge management	Develop and maintain BOKs; Organize regular seminars	0.1	0.1	0.0100
4.	Initiative and attitude problems	Mentoring, identify mentors for all team members	0.05	0.15	0.0075
5.	Poor communication skills	Training on communication skills	0.15	0.05	0.0075
6.	Lack of business knowledge	Training on business domain	0.1	0.05	0.0050
7.	Improper estimation	Estimates/schedules to be verified before accepting	0.1	0.1	0.0100
8.	LC process not followed	Process should be strictly followed	0.15	0.2	0.0300

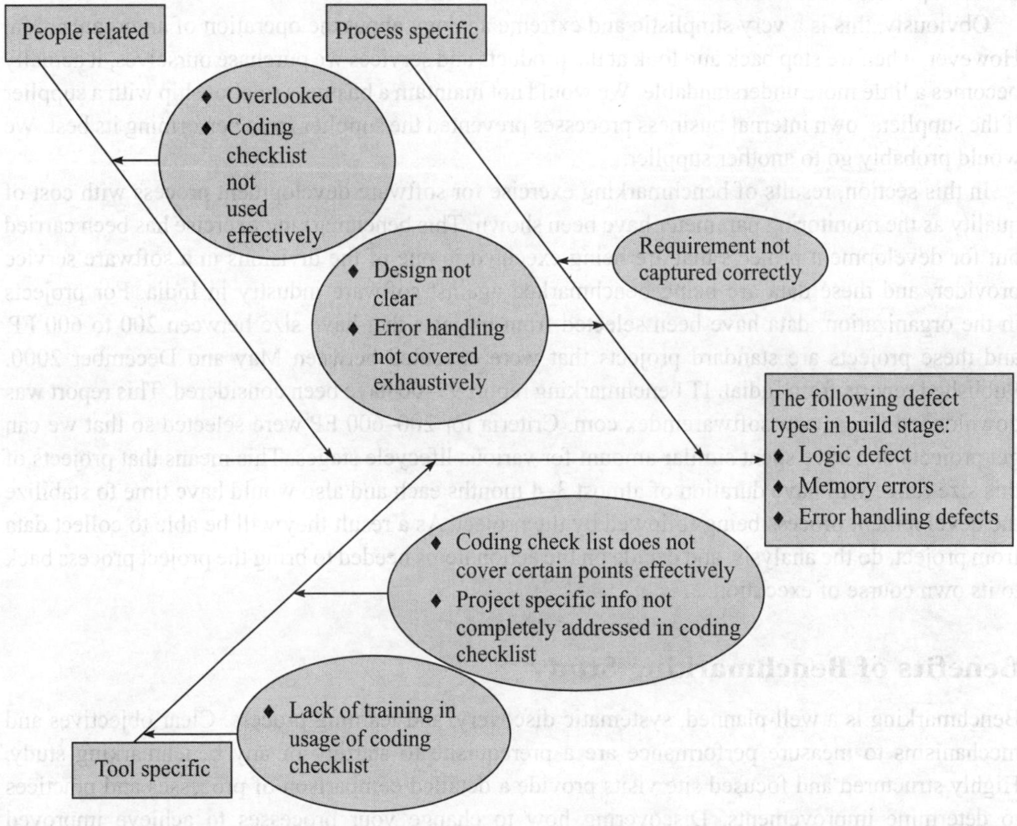

Figure 4.6: Root-cause analysis

An Example of Monitoring Through Benchmarking Exercise

Benchmarking is a tool that helps us improve our business processes. Any business process can be benchmarked. A benchmarking exercise can be done within an industry as well as across industries.

It is easier to understand the dynamics of one's own industry and hence sometimes an organization stops at benchmarking exercise inside the industry. But then who should carry out this exercise – the leader in an industry or someone who aspires to be a leader in an industry?

Business Process

A business process is best defined as a function within an organization that enables the organization to successfully deliver its products and services. A simple analogy would be to look at an organization as a wheel and the individual business processes as spokes of the wheel. The spoke is the individual process that makes up our organization. Having loose spokes can make a wheel roll out of balance. The longer a wheel runs out of balance, the more damaging the effect to the wheel. When the wheel becomes so unstable that its primary function fails, we could simply replace the wheel. Obviously, an organization cannot simply replace itself; but our customer can and will replace the wheel if it does not perform to the customers' needs and expectations.

Obviously, this is a very simplistic and extreme analogy about the operation of an organization. However, when we step back and look at the products and services we purchase ourselves, it actually becomes a little more understandable. We would not maintain a business relationship with a supplier if the suppliers' own internal business processes prevented the supplier from performing its best. We would probably go to another supplier.

In this section, results of benchmarking exercise for software development process with cost of quality as the monitoring parameter have been shown. This benchmarking exercise has been carried out for development projects that are being executed in one of the divisions in a software service provider, and these data are being benchmarked against software industry in India. For projects in the organization, data have been selected from projects that have size between 200 to 600 FP, and these projects are standard projects that were executed between May and December 2000. Published reports from Indian IT benchmarking report 99–00 have been considered. This report was downloaded from www.softwareindex.com. Criteria for 200–600 FP were selected so that we can get projects that have spent similar amount for various lifecycle stages. This means that projects of this size range will have duration of almost 3–4 months each and also would have time to stabilize the development process being followed by the project. As a result they will be able to collect data from project, do the analysis, and decide on the action items needed to bring the project process back to its own course of execution.

Benefits of Benchmarking Study

Benchmarking is a well-planned, systematic discovery, and learning process. Clear objectives and mechanisms to measure performance are a prerequisite to starting of any benchmarking study. Highly structured and focused site visits provide a detailed comparison of processes and practices to determine improvements. Discovering how to change your processes to achieve improved performance is one of the strengths of the benchmarking process.

Benchmarking not only tells you how good your business needs to be but also tells you how to change your processes to get there. Benchmarking can be carried out internally between different business units within an organization, between organizations within an industry sector, or between organizations across industry sectors. The most powerful results are likely to be achieved across industry sectors because this encourages thinking outside normal industry paradigms. Out of industry benchmarking can assist organizations to leap ahead of their competitors.

Benchmarking is best done by small teams of people working in various aspects of a particular practice or process. However, benchmarking also requires overall strategic guidance to ensure that the right processes and practices are being improved for the most overall benefit to the organization.

Benchmarking falls into five categories as described by McNair and Liebfried:

1. Internal benchmarking identifies cost drivers and non-value-added activities and is performed before comparing performance with external service providers.
2. Competitive benchmarking is a one-to-one comparison with other service providers or competitors that assesses relative performance.
3. Industry benchmarking identifies trends in baseline performance among categories of similar service providers.
4. Best-in-class benchmarking identifies breakthrough performance across various classes within an industry or field of operations.
5. "Benchmarking outside-the-box" is learning from processes in other industries to improve your own. For those who are used to thinking of benchmarking as a secret process of comparing one's performance to competitors, this shift in thinking requires new levels of openness and creativity.

On the basis of this a definition of benchmarking could be:

> The process of identifying, understanding, and adapting outstanding practices and processes from organizations anywhere in the world to help your organization improve its performance.

Practices and processes range from customer service to human resources, and from warehousing and distribution to leadership. Even industry-specific processes, such as claims processing in insurance, are candidates for learning from any organization that processes "orders" rapidly, including mail order houses and banks.

Speed is critical, if for no other reason than to overcome the enormous inertia of the status quo. As Jack Welch at GE has said, "Incremental change doesn't work very well in the type of transformation GE has gone through. If your change isn't big enough, or revolutionary enough, the bureaucracy can beat you." They benchmarked and found it would take 18% to merely catch up, and much more to stay ahead. Benchmarking outside the industry can legitimize stretch goals. Goals picked out of thin air and from off-the-wall guesses rarely inspire anyone. Numbers from competitors analyzed in a black box are equally suspect, and ignored, by most managers. But stretch goals based on believable external evidence, not only of results but also of the process that produced those results, are believable and give people a model from which to work.

In this section, we have tried to explain details of a development project lifecycle and define various parameters for the project. These parameters are used to measure and quantify a development project and are also used to help the project team to manage a project. One such parameter is development productivity. This parameter is used to measure the size of the development project, and it is the desire of this author to make a study on benchmarking development productivity in software industry.

What Does It Take to Successfully Benchmark Outside Your Industry?

- Knowledge of your own process and problems to see the underlying characteristics and spot analogies across other industries.

- Ability to look for common themes without having them spoon-fed to you.
- Information about outstanding companies in other industries. This information needs to be organized by process and not only by industry.
- Language that is common to all. One of the barriers to sharing across industries is finding a common language that describes processes regardless of industry. For example, the medical center had to equate its admissions process with hotel registration in order to see the analogy and potential transfer. With our members' assistance, we have developed a process classification scheme that identifies generic processes from other industries and contexts.

Methodology Adopted for Benchmarking

Task definition

We will benchmark against each other on the following metrics:

1. Size metrics
2. Cost of quality metrics

On the basis of comparative metrics, we would be able to decide on action items for further improvement.

Objective

1. Gain practical experience in result-based benchmarking.
2. Capture best practices from the benchmarking effort.

Exit criteria

1. Generate a set of best practices.
2. Define action items to improve project practices being followed.

DATA COLLECTION

Internal Data Collection

During the period between May and December 2000, there were number of projects (development) executed in a development center. However, as defined earlier, projects with size 200–600 (measured by function point unit) were considered for data collection and analysis.

The formula used to calculate cost of quality was based on following principle:

$$\text{Cost of quality} = \frac{[\text{efforts spent for (training + review + testing + rework)}]}{(\text{total efforts for the project})}$$

Hence, the cost of quality was determined as a percentage figure. A table was prepared, which had three columns, namely, name of project, size delivered (in terms of function points), and cost of quality. All these details are taken from metrics analysis report for the corresponding project. As per Infosys process methodology, each project needs to prepare a metrics analysis report that captures details of all measurable data. Data like efforts spent for each activity for the project, defects injected and detected in the projects, and so forth, are captured. These data are captured through various tools developed either in-house or purchased from the third party. These data are validated by the project manager as well by the software quality advisor.

Results

In the period defined for collecting data, data from 13 projects were available. These data were then segregated for the defined criteria and then average figure for these projects were calculated. As was decided earlier, the cost of quality was decided for benchmarking and was the factor for considering a project for data analysis. Table 4.5 shows figures for various projects selected.

Table 4.5: Figures for various project selected

Projects	Size	Cost of quality
Project 1	258	25.37
Project 2	535	44.22
Project 3	567	33.11
Project 4	221	34.61
Project 5	281	57.44
Project 6	232	31.21
Project 7	335	29.58
Project 8	450	27.46
Project 9	572	28.65
Average		**34.63**

External Data Collection

External data were collected from www.softwareindex.com, which had published data for Indian Industry. These data were analyzed to find the cost of quality metrics that we were looking for. From the published report for Indian Industry, it was found that industry-wide cost of quality figure stands at 32%.

Gap Analysis and Action Items

As is evident here, benchmarking tells us as to where we are right now. The gap between the industry average and that of Infosys seems to be marginal 10%. On the basis of a brainstorming session, we have decided the following action items for beating the industry average:

1. Each project should identify its technological needs at the time of signing contract with the customer. This will ensure sufficient time for training department to arrange training sessions with the help of volunteers/experts.
2. Arrange for a boot camp for each project at the start of offshore project; this will ensure adequate business and domain expertise.
3. Ensure to have self-review checklist for detail design and coding; this will reduce the occurrence of defect injection, which will ensure less efforts for review, rework, and testing.

Based on the analysis of data, brainstorming sessions were conducted to gauge the problem and to identify plausible solutions. Categorized root causes and corresponding action items are listed below. They are listed as per priority in Table 4.6.

Table 4.6: Action items

S. no.	Action item	Action by
1	Sensitization project folks on COQ	SQA
2	Plan for test in advance	PM
3	Publish review comments to the team	PM
4	Proactive domain knowledge transfer	PM, SQA
5	Reusing test results, test queries, and test script	Project team
6	Mentor project members on process	GPM, SQA
7	Review of test cases and test plans	PA, PM
8	Knowledge of test data set up	Test expert
9	Traceability of requirement to program	PM
10	Involve everybody in the team in resolving issue	PM, project team
11	Make a resource pool for reviewers	DM
12	Use tools for code generation and automating testing	PM, SQA
13	Train resources to be good testers	PM
14	COQ calculation at each milestone stage	PM, SQA
15	Create a resource pool for testing	DM
16	Surprise check on time sheet	SQA

PILOTING

Solutions identified in the brainstorming sessions were piloted in development projects. Identification of projects for piloting was done after defining a process for such identification. The criteria for the project selection were as follows:

(i) The project should be following Infosys development process.
(ii) The project should have a scheduled duration of at least 3 months.
(iii) Total efforts for the project should be more than 15 person months.

Once projects were identified, top 10 action items (as applicable), which were generated from brainstorming session, were piloted in these projects.

The implementations of these action items were planned right from the initiation stages in all the pilot projects. The progress of the projects with respect to the action items was tracked at every milestone.

Project 1

The customer is one of the largest players in the insurance sector in the United States. The project had planned for testing (UT, ST) for its work products. The lifecycle stages included testing by the project team (UT) and ST by a separate independent testing group. All the testing efforts have been captured for arriving at COQ.

After implementing the action items, the figure came down to as follows:

1. COQ 40.20%
2. Defect injection rate/person hour 0.097
3. Delivered defect 0
4. Review effectiveness 100%

The action items implemented were as follows:

1. Sensitize project folks on COQ; presentation on COQ at account level
2. Proactive domain knowledge transfer
   - Design quizzes and question and answer sessions to measure effectiveness of knowledge transfer.
   - Redesign training materials based on feedback from participants.
   - Ask the new resources to give presentation to the team on their understanding on the application knowledge.
3. Review of design documents; review all the design work products through offline group review approach

Project 2

The customer is a major player in the insurance sector in the United States. The project is a standard re-engineering project in field force area in that account. This was assessed at level 4 in process compliance check. At the time of closure, effort related to onsite and independent test teams for testing were collected. The action items implemented were as follows:

1. Publish review comments to the team; share this with onsite team as well
2. Proactive domain knowledge transfer
   - Design quizzes and question and answer sessions to measure effectiveness of knowledge transfer.
   - Redesign training materials based on feedback from participants.
   - Ask the new resources to give presentation to the team on their understanding on the application knowledge.
3. Review of design documents; review all the design work products through offline group review approach
4. Random check on time sheet
5. COQ calculation and monitoring at milestone stage

Results of implementation:

1. COQ 39.08%
2. Defect injection rate/person hour 0.034
3. Review effectiveness 100%
4. Delivered defect 0

Project 3

This is a project from logistics domain. This application offers global supply chain management for manufacturers and merchandisers and provides logistics solutions that go beyond the physical movement of goods. In the present project, the scope was to replace mainframe legacy systems with a more flexible and responsive application to better support the current operation, varying business practices as well as the expansion of business. In addition, it will also supplement the current functionality with a new customer-based rules-driven approach, enabling the legacy systems to more easily customize and to proactively trap customer exceptions. The action items implemented were as follows:

1. Publish review comments to the team; share this with onsite team as well
2. Review of design documents; review all the design work products through offline group review approach
3. Random check on time sheet

Results from this pilot are as follows:

1.	COQ	34.70%
2.	Defect injection rate/person hour	0.013
3.	Delivered defect	0
4.	Review effectiveness	100%

Results at the end of project completion are tabulated in Table 4.7.

Table 4.7: Results from piloting

Project code	Reduction in COQ (%)	Defect detection efficiency	Delivered quality
Project 1	5.04	100	0
Project 2	7.08	100	0
Project 3	11.36	100	0

The results of the pilot show that the action items implemented resulted in decreasing cost of quality for the projects and also improving other parameters. Defect detection efficiency is calculated by dividing the total number of defects being detected through all internal reviews and testing by the total number of defects found in the system, including defects delivered to the customer. This parameter suggests the effectiveness of review and testing procedure adopted by the project at various lifecycle stages.

Effective peer reviews, adherence to code coverage norms, and work product-based checklists helped in the reduction of COQ. Aided by tools, extensive defect leakage analyses were conducted with phase-wise defect-containment effectiveness and root-cause analyses. Total review effectiveness (defect detection effectiveness) is further ensured by a management-review of the data at milestones. Special attention is paid to usage of control charts to predict trend in defects and taking actions to rectify them.

As COQ is monitored and controlled, we see benefits in terms of reduced project effort for delivering the work products. The benefits can be manifested in terms of reduced actual effort (while comparing with estimated effort), reduction in schedule deviation (from initial negotiated schedule), or no deviation at all. In real terms, these benefits can mean release of critical resources from projects and are available for allocation to other projects. This will substantially increase revenue-earning capacity for the organization by redeploying these critical resources in other projects.

A reduction in cost/efforts in attaining desired quality would help improve profit margin at project level. An aggregate of this sum will again achieve the revenue target that the organization would have targeted for. This approach will thus validate the business model that a software service provider has adopted.

The entire exercise has proved to be beneficial as there is a lot to gain in terms of efforts, time, and margins by implementing these piloted action items. And from customer's point of view there is a gain in terms of quality of product/service delivered and cost of production. Operating at optimizing level, the organization has to optimize its resources. Also, these benefits can be passed on to the customers while competitive services can be offered to the customers.

Conclusion

Quality-aware learning organizations tend to embrace benchmarking as a matter of course. The concept of best practice benchmarking gives a wider choice of the process to be benchmarked, focuses on identification and sharing of best practices and their underlying enabling factors with selected partners, and, finally, results in the implementation of the findings. The best practice benchmarking goes beyond mere standards and measurement against them. Furthermore, as the best practice benchmarking focuses on processes, it gives the opportunity to extend the search for best practices beyond the higher education sector. In the struggle for customers and profitability in a global economy, learning organizations will increasingly respond to rapid change with greater resilience and evolve winning strategies and practices more effectively. As the Malcom Baldrige criteria recognize, benchmarking importance will only grow in the years to come.

Benchmarking adds value not only by improving a given process but also by helping companies evolve more quickly and effectively into learning organizations and facilitate the transition to a total quality culture. Thus, it is imperative that our organization has embarked on such an activity. If cost of quality can be reduced by 10%, this will also result in reducing efforts for the entire project. In a fixed price environment, this will result in higher productivity and this can be translated to better value for the customer.

SUMMARY

Software project management has an important aspect called monitoring and control of project status. For this to be successful, project plan becomes the input to the monitoring process. Due to different factors, such as unforeseen factors that were not taken care of during planning stage, deviations occur. These deviations are noted and recorded during the monitoring process, and then control mechanisms are applied to bring the project back into its desired status. The basic monitoring activity involves tracking completeness of activities that are scheduled in the project management plan. Also, defects that are found and recorded during the execution need to be tracked to completion. The chapter also dealt with examples of tracking progress through different parameters by comparing actual values with respect to planned values and how to carry out the benchmarking exercise. The chapter also discussed the lifecycle for closing an open defect.

DISCUSSION POINTS

1. What is meant by monitoring? How do you achieve this?
2. What are the activities of controlling deviations?
3. Please explain statistical tools used for quantitative project monitoring.
4. Why do you need status report?
5. What are the inputs to status report?
6. What is milestone analysis? When do you plan for milestone analysis?

CASE STUDY

Background

In 1973, Excel Inc. decided to hive off its consulting division into two—**Excel Inc**. remained as the parent consulting division and Quantas was formed, which would provide IT solution to its present customers as well as can grow on its own by acquiring new customers. The split was made with the agreement that the parent division would fund the spin-off division and help it grow by using its consulting expertise; this would be also logical vertical extension for Excel where the parent division would extend its services into IT solution development area through Quantas. The management will be the same to draw benefits from rich experience from consulting knowledge. It was decided that Quantas would be started in Bangalore to take advantage of low-cost skill available in India.

Quantas India and Global Delivery Network

Quantas considers India as one of its largest developing markets. In India, Quantas works for 7 of the top 10 business groups—6 of the top 10 companies (based on sales). India is also an integral part of Quantas's global delivery model, which enables the company to provide clients with seamless delivery of services from multiple geographic locations, with 24/7 coverage.

The Quantas delivery centers in India enable Quantas to extend its global reach and provide deep technology, outsourcing and industry skills, and a proven delivery approach. Driving this capability through the India delivery centers helps Quantas deliver quality services at competitive prices that enhance a client's business performance. The India delivery centers provide a wide variety of services, including application development and maintenance, as well as various business process outsourcing capabilities, such as call center, human resources, and finance and administration functions.

Quantas's delivery centers in India are one node among many in its global delivery model—a global network of more than 45 integrated delivery centers (including 10 in India) in over 30 countries that provide a seamless set of offerings and capabilities to meet each client's unique priorities. These facilities are strategically located wherever they can tap an expansive pool of talented knowledge workers, and wherever their clients need specific language skills and geographic proximity to key global or regional markets. In fact, the global delivery network (GDN) consisting of well-networked delivery centers sets Quantas apart from many other outsourcing companies by significantly reducing implementation risk and rapidly realizing benefits. The GDN harnesses industry expertise and deep technology and outsourcing skills to provide cost-effective business solutions and improved business performance. Through Quantas's GDN, the clients have access to a number of services: system integration, application development and outsourcing, infrastructure outsourcing, and business process outsourcing. Quantas delivery centers form the backbone of their approach to delivering excellence in technology and outsourcing.

Today's Situation

Quantas started executing its global delivery model in early 2001. The entire management was confident that with its huge domain expertise it would very soon become one of the top players in solution developing industry. They had presumed that with high-ending consulting that the company has had experienced, it would be easy to understand the requirements of the customer. This way, Quantas had forecast that there would be tremendous rise in the customer base.

Employees Turnover

Quantas started its operation in Bangalore in the year 2001. To start with, it decided to recruit the best of breed people from the industry. The strategy adopted as to recruit the best in the industry who have experience in global delivery model and they would do the rest. To attract the best pool of resources, it decided to target tier 1 company in India and headhunt the best talent from these companies. The goal was to offer a steep rise on their present salary and lure them to Quantas. As Quantas was new to India and the brand equity was low, it would be easy to recruit people by offering them the maximum possible salary. With a high monthly salary, it wanted to create a barrier for its own employees. At the end of the first year, this proved to be wrong. The attrition level was 23% and most of the time Quantas was losing its employees to other companies where they joined at less-than-present salary.

Training

It established a training department. Training was vital to the growth and this was identified as a crucial factor in the initial stage. A separate training department was formed and a head was recruited from a well-established company. The training head had worked in IT training institute and was familiar with all technical training needed for the company. Thus, it was thought that the training head would be able to increase requisite technical skills for smooth functioning of the development center.

Leveraging Consulting Experience

Chief operating officer Mr. White was brought in from parent division as he would establish the company culture in India. This would help in propagating vision of the company at every level and would provide direction to the employees. Mr. White was with the parent division for 25 years and has mostly served out of the United States. He has tremendous domain knowledge and consulting experience and would be the requisite person to provide guidance for IT solution development. As IT solution development was a low-end job compared with consulting, it was thought to be a good strategic move.

To help Mr. White, a delivery head, Mr. Green, was appointed from parent division who would control and monitor all the project managers and team members and set on the growth path. However, it soon became apparent that Mr. Green had problems in coping with the teams. Mr. Green would easily get upset because many team members would arrive late for meetings. Deadlines accepted by the project managers were missed many times. When a new project would arrive, a number of problems would be experienced. In one instance, when dot net was the technology requirement, resources with that skill set were not available in the company. Mr. Green wanted to hire dot net skill sets as part-time employees since the forecast for such projects was not encouraging. But his HR team informed that it would be difficult to get such employees into the organization as the candidates would be more interested in full-time opportunities rather than part-time jobs (even though offered salary was three times than their normal salary).

Mr. Green wanted to use resources efficiently and thus reduce the cost of operations. He also wanted to use "factory model" where an expert resource pool would be created based on their competency. Thus, he created dot net pool where all resource with dot net competency would be available and these resources would be loaned to each and every project. The training department was geared up for training resources in the identified skill set. This sometimes created problems when the customer wanted to have resources with skill set not available in the factory model. Green was in dilemma whether to accept these projects or to reject them. This seriously undermined the brand equity in solution development market where the customers did not see the company as one-stop solution provider for all their needs.

Consulting assignments in the parent division were highly profitable. The rates charged by the parent division were always at premium and the brand equity was at the high end. The same pricing was to be followed for GDM and Mr. Green was keen on creating that image. He even had directed that any project with less than 45% net margin will not be executed through GDM. This created uneasiness among the employees as a lot of projects were not executed after initial proposals were accepted by the customers.

Reducing Cost of Operation

Every month the status report from Bangalore would include the number of persons on "bench," that is, those who are not being allocated to projects. There was a constant endeavor to reduce this bench strength, as this "bench" was not a healthy sign and would eat into the bottom line. The campaign "lean force" was started to find out such persons who are not allocated to projects and then to ask them to leave. Each project manager was asked to identify persons under them and a combined list was prepared. However, when the final list was prepared, it was observed that the number of resources on "bench" was far less than perceived and HR department had no clue as to who is actually not being utilized in projects. This process of identifying unutilized resources had an impact on the employees; they understood that there was a need to reduce workforce and they started looking for opportunities elsewhere. As HR head put it "it was a boon in disguise; we suspected there was a manipulation by the project managers in identifying the unutilized resources. But I am happy that the total number of employees has reduced." But who left the company? Good resources or bad resources—as Mr. Sridhar, a PM, put it "Good guys would always get jobs, only the unwanted ones are left out." The attrition rate shot to 27% that quarter.

Quality Issues

Quantas had bagged a number of projects by showcasing its consulting capability. However, customer complaints were many. The customer complained that even though there was evidence that requirements have been captured [System Requirement Study (SRS) had captured all the necessary requirements], still the delivered applications did not have the required functionalities. The team that prepared SRS was based out of the United States and blamed it squarely on the offshore development team.

The code delivered also had bugs in it, making it unsuitable for immediate roll out. Immediate fall out of this was that a quality head was appointed and was given the goal to improve the quality level over a period of 4 months. He was explained that his role was very important and he has to ensure that all the applications delivered were acceptable to the customers.

Customer complained about communication skills of Quantas employees. The major grievance of the customer was that Quantas employees do not understand their culture and also tend to agree everything that the customer says but are not able to deliver as per the timeline agreed upon. They also complained that many times Quantas employees agree with many points during meetings and discussions but would not complete the action items agreed during the meetings and discussions. This was new to Mr. Green as these complaints were not expected from highly skilled personnel that Quantas had employed.

Estimation Issues

After a gap of 4 months, it was found that it was difficult to meet the schedule as negotiated with the customer, as quality took front stage. Customers were unhappy, as a delay in the negotiated delivery timeline was not acceptable to end users; they also complained that such delays were not discussed with them. It was becoming a hard decision—whether to meet quality or miss the schedule of delivery. The delivery schedule was proposed based on the initial estimation and the management started doubting if the estimation process needs to be looked into.

One such case was a project in utilities vertical. The organization bagged a development project, which had to be developed in VC++ in the utilities segment. The project manager had worked in the vertical earlier but did not have exposure to VC++ in his earlier projects. Using his experience, he estimated stagewise effort as percentage of total effort as follows:

Design: 15%

Code and unit testing: 60%

Integration and system testing: 15%

Acceptance testing and implementation: 10%

The project was to be delivered in 4 months time. However, after completing the project, it was found that even though the project was delivered with 5% schedule variation, still there was 65% effort overrun. Almost all the project team members worked till late night for 3 months. The project manager had to spend almost 18 hours a day; he was exhausted and so also his team members. Clearly, the estimation has gone wrong somewhere.

During several discussions it was found that the domain knowledge obtained from the consulting assignments was with the parent division and the offshore development team lacks this knowledge. This lack of knowledge was attributed as the root cause for lack of understanding requirements as written down in SRS. In order to increase this knowledge base in offshore, several visits were made by domain experts from the parent division, which increased the cost of operation and bottom line declined.

The management was quite worried and wanted to get to the bottom of the problem. The questions that the management had were as follows:

1. Was there a problem in global delivery model?
2. Was there a problem with recruitment strategy or training approach?
3. Can you suggest improvement in estimation process?

Solution to the Case

Global Delivery Model

Quantas was a spin-off from the consulting firm Excel Inc. Most of the top management at Quantas was from Excel, which brought in the Excel's strategy to Quantas. But Quantas being in India, the management style needed to be attuned to the Indian environment.

The global delivery model of Quantas was based on the consulting experience gained at Excel. The premise that the high-ending consulting experience would lead to easy understanding of the requirements from the customer was inappropriate. There were many flaws in this model. The following fish-bone representation states the causes of GDM's failure.

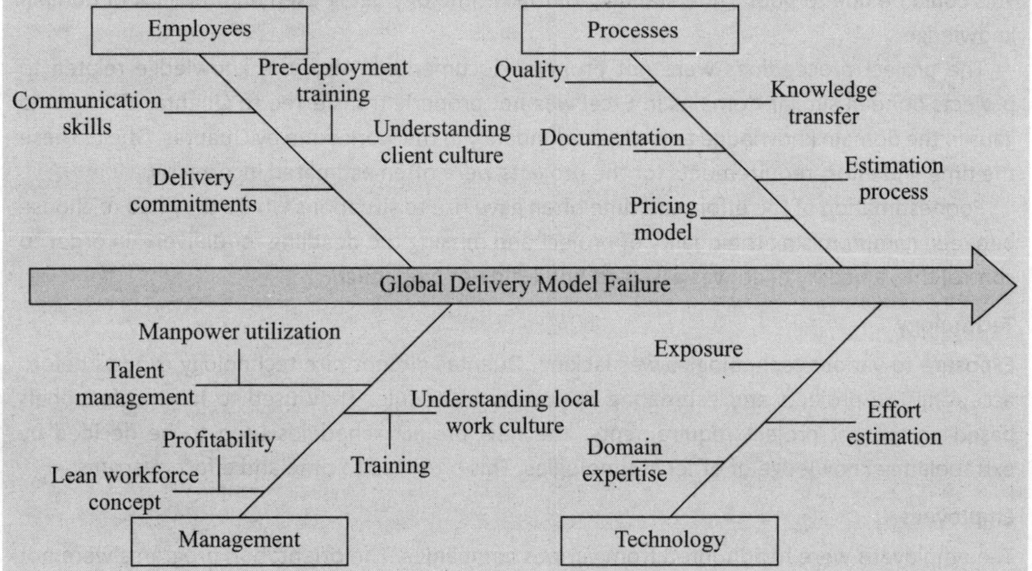

Management

The top management was mostly from Excel. Excel being an organization based in the United States, it had different work ethics from those followed in India. During the policy formation, Quantas maintained its focus on plush monetary benefits of the job, while sidelining critical parameters such as job satisfaction, job enrichment, etc.

In order to improve the bottom line of the organization, they decided to implement *lean workforce policy*. But this led to the employees believing that the organization was downsizing. Hence, attrition rates increased.

The top management tried to replicate the US work culture in the Indian setup. For example, they tried to hire part-time professionals on project basis. But in India people prioritize job security over monetary benefits. Hence, the part-time recruitment idea did not look feasible.

The management was not sensitized to the work culture in the India. The US work culture is fiercely competitive and highly professional. But in case of Quantas, the HR did not enforce the policies leading to notions that deadlines are generally stretchable, hard bargaining is nonexistent, over promising, etc. The talent acquisition process at Quantas was questionable. One of the reasons could be mismatch of employee aspirations with the organization expectations. The organization picked up its workforce primarily through headhunting from competitors. The HR team did not select the right kind of people. This led to a sustained high attrition rate despite the compensation levels being on the higher side.

Processes

Quantas borrowed most of its processes from its parent organization Excel. It was expected that the best practices followed at Excel could be easily replicated in Quantas. Contrary to the expectations, there were huge gaps in the processes.

The effort and time estimation process was largely off the mark as mentioned in the case. This could be due to poor understanding of the technology being used and the lack of domain knowledge.

The project proceedings were not properly documented. Also, the knowledge related to projects done in similar domains in Excel was not properly transferred to Quantas. This led to gaps in the domain knowledge as well as redundancy in the work done by Quantas. Due to these the time and effort requirements for the projects were often estimated incorrectly.

Poor estimation of the effort and time often gave rise to situations where they had to choose between compromising the quality of project and missing the deadline for delivery. In order to control this, a quality head was assigned but it did not help much.

Technology

Exposure to various technologies was lacking. Quantas did not hire technology experts before accepting the projects and estimating the project schedule. They used to hire professionals based on current project requirements. The new project schedules used to be decided by extrapolating knowledge of other technologies. This often led to time and effort overruns.

Employees

The employees were headhunted from various companies. The orientation programs were not effective. The employees did not understand the importance of delivering on commitments in a timely manner.

The employees' communication skills were also not up to the mark. Quantas being a global organization had clients from all over the world. The employees were not sensitized about the various cultural differences in these countries. This led to misunderstandings on the deliverables and their deadlines.

Proposed Solutions

HR policies

The talent acquisition process needs to be revamped. There should be a match between the aspirations of the employees and the organization's expectations from them. Their individual goals should be aligned with those of the organization. The job description should be stated before hiring any professional. Also, there should be two rounds of interviews that will test the technical as well as communication skills. The HR team should look to place the right people with the right set of skills in the right post.

Revisit the *lean workforce* concept. It should be modified in order to accommodate an acceptable level of reserve workforce. These employees on the *bench* should be trained in new technologies during this phase.

Professionals with expertise in one technology should be trained in other technologies to improve cross-domain exposure to various technologies. Also, training in improving communication skills and other soft skills should be imparted.

Estimation process

The organization should improve the estimation process by doing the following:

- Establish a thorough set of metrics to measure various processes.
- Document processes, thereby aiding in performing internal benchmarking.
- Take assistance from external benchmarking forums like SPIN, MetaGroup, etc., to understand the trends in the industry.
- Improve knowledge transfer between Excel and Quantas.

5

CONFIGURATION MANAGEMENT

LEARNING OBJECTIVES

In this chapter, the students would learn:

- Need for configuration management
- Configuration management process
- Configuration audit process

INTRODUCTION

As discussed in Chapters 1 and 2, a software project starts with planning and objectives to be achieved for the project. During planning stage, a lot of assumptions are made and accordingly a project management plan is prepared. However, during the course of project execution, these assumptions may change. For example, often scope as defined, recorded, and accepted by both customer and vendor organization may change. The scope is used as input for estimating size, effort, and schedule for delivery. Hence, any change in the scope adversely affects planned effort and schedule. This "scope creep" results in variations and the project manager is forced to re-plan the entire project. As we know, a software project can have a number of work products during project execution. Some of them are programs, specification and design documents, data, and user and training manuals. Unlike non-IT projects, output from software projects can be changed. This is a unique advantage of software projects that provides flexibility to the project process. But this can be used by the customer to demand and change anything and everything at any point during project execution. This adds to the complexity in project management and needs to be well monitored through effective process management. In order to manage the scope changes, there should be a well-defined process that will control and manage these changes. This process is known as configuration management (CM) process, which helps in systematically controlling any changes in the project.

Software CM process is a systematic process of controlling and organizing different procedures and activities so that work products can accommodate the changes and be in sync with the scope and objectives of the project. This helps in delivering good quality end products as planned during the project planning stage. These end products are specification documents, source codes, library of all executables, and any related document. These end products would have undergone many changes and revisions during the course of project execution. In fact, there will be more than one version of each document at the final stage. For maintaining quality and consistency of these deliverables, all these versions should be tracked properly so that the correct version of each document should be delivered. As we know, a project is broken into smaller modules and work progresses in parallel with many teams working together. As the project progresses, changes to the scope and requirements happen; these changes are done because of many reasons. One of the reasons would be business needs of the end users of the application, who would like to use certain modules of the software at the earliest; this changes the priority of delivery schedule and leads to changes in the work products. This implies that project team has to ensure that correct version of the end products containing the prioritized delivery schedule be delivered. This process of delivering correct version of the end products is ensured by the CM process.

Need for CM process comes from the fact that the development models in software engineering cannot accommodate any changes to the scope during the execution cycle. Models such as iterative and spiral have provisions to go back to their previous lifecycle stages and compare work products with respect to the requirements, but they do not have provisions for allowing any changes to the scope. In reality, changes to the scope happen as the customer changes his/her mind, and not acceding to these changes will not be prudent from business point of view. The software has to be produced while accommodating these changes and still objectives of the project should be met. This definitely requires a proper and effective process, and the CM process helps in achieving proper version control of different software units.

Configuration Management Process

As discussed already, CM has to manage the configuration of deliverables of the software application to be delivered. An effective process will define the sequence of activities that need to be performed. The first stage in the CM process is planning, that is, identifying work products that need to be under the CM process. These work products are called configuration items. During the CM planning stage, not only these configuration items are identified but also it needs to be planned as to where to store these documents, what would be the procedure for change control, and so on. The second stage in the CM process is the execution of these defined processes and carrying out a compliance check with the defined process (also known as CM audit).

Configuration Management Planning

The first stage in CM process is planning; it involves identifying configuration items and specifying procedures to be used for controlling and monitoring these procedures. This is a basic activity to be carried out by all projects. Team members should be made aware of configuration items so that they can track the changes as required. In a typical project, contract from the customer, system requirement specification, testing strategy document, design documents, source code, test plans, test scripts (for automation in testing), test data, GUI standards, coding standards and any such standard used in the project, user manual, project management plan, and CM plan are examples of configuration items. If there is a third-party software that needs to be integrated with the application for delivery, then that software also becomes configurable item. Also, if customer has supplied a hardware or software for integration with the final delivery, then they should be controlled through CM as well. However, if any new work product, which is not mentioned during the planning stage, needs to be controlled, then that can also be identified and controlled after suitable approval process.

After choosing the configuration items, they should be named as per naming convention. This naming convention needs to be decided in the planning stage as well. In addition to naming convention, version numbering process should also be decided. Whether a version should be incremented by 1 or 0.01, should be decided at this point of time. Version control will also decide whether a baseline document should be named as 1.0 or 0.0. This process should be followed uniformly for the entire project. This is done because when a configuration item is changed the old item is not replaced, rather a new one is created while keeping the old one as well. This results in multiple versions of the same work product being available at the same time. It is important that these work products be numbered in a manner so that there is no ambiguity about the version to be used for delivery. It is not required to deliver the latest version to the customer always; it might so happen that the earlier version of a particular work product be delivered rather than the current version. Hence, numbering scheme is quite important. The next section suggests numbering scheme that can be adopted with modifications, as required.

Numbering Scheme

The following numbering scheme is suggested for documents that come under document control. This scheme enables easy storage and retrieval of documents. In cases where the numbering scheme is not adequate or appropriate, a specific numbering scheme may be defined and documented (in the CM plan). The numbering scheme on electronic media could be such that the path of the document file should uniquely identify the document and the document number could be the same as the disk file reference. In case a different file numbering scheme is required, a cross-reference between the document number and the file number should be maintained.

Documents are numbered as DDDD/XXX/YYY/nn, where

DDDD: project/department code

XXX: system/process/function code

YYY: extension as necessary

nn: unique number assigned sequentially for a given project/process/type combination. Use Arabic numerals.

Document Type Numbering

The following document type may be used. Additional types may be defined in the document master list/CM plan and used.

PLN: plan documents

PRC: procedural documents

REC: records
RR: review records
F: forms
STD: standards
TCH: techniques
SMP: sample documents
DOC: any other documents
MAN: manuals (user manuals, operations guide, etc.)

Folder Numbering

Folder numbers should be unique. Folders are numbered sequentially as 1, 2, 3, and so on. The department/project to which it belongs should be clearly indicated on it. In case multiple folders are required for storage of related documents, these folders may be numbered as 1, 1.1, 1.2, and so on. All folders could have user friendly labels denoting the contents in the folder. All communication folders with continuation folders could have start dates indicated on it, for easy location of a document within it.

The document numbers of all documents in a folder must be clearly indicated on the cover of the folder. In the case of folders having several records, which require to be retrieved quickly, indexing may be used. If separators are used, index could be maintained on them. Indexing with dates and retrieval/return information is advisable. The suggested contents of the index are serial number, document name, document number, version number, description, soft copy location, etc.

The CM process must plan for keeping different versions of the work products in different folders as required. During planning, it must be decided as to how to move one version of a work product to another version. This is done by defining different folders for different versions of the work products. All work products of same versions then would be stored in one folder (such as work folder and review folder). When the versions of the work products change, they move from one folder to another folder. There are tools available that can be used for defining and storing in the folders. All these planning are done by the project manager and configuration control board (CCB). CCB usually starts CM planning after the project is kicked off and the system requirement specification document is base-lined. All these planning activities are done in a document known as CM plan. The sections that a CM plan should have are as follows: list of configuration items, naming and numbering scheme, folder structure for the project, change control procedure, etc. A sample CM plan is provided in Annexure E.

Configuration Control Board

The CM plan is authored by the CCB. The plan has different sections as indicated in the sample CM plan in Annexure E. The CCB is responsible for implementation of CM process in the project. The CCB, for a small project, is usually a part-time role, where he/she carries out other responsibilities as well. However, for large projects, the CCB can be a full-time role. In either case, the CCB has to manage release, archive the previous releases, and has the permission to retrieve and release appropriate versions. For large teams or when the development is taking place simultaneously at more than one location, the CCB will have representation from different development teams. This is required because each team has to declare the list of configuration items and required folder structure. The team members also have to provide access permissions that need to be given to the respective team members. The CCB of this nature will have one configuration controller (CC) who will head the CCB and will be responsible for the implementation of CM processes in all the teams. For example, CC will provide access to change and modify programs to senior members in the team and not to all team members.

The CCB also defines policies and procedures for change control in CM plan. For example, changes made to a program for fixing a bug, which has been reported by customer, need to be incorporated in the code that has already been baselined. Although production jobs have to continue, these fixes need to be applied to the previous code and then should be reconciled with the code that is running in production. Another example could be that a change request for changing scope of the project has impact on many programs, which have already been reviewed, tested, and baselined. An impact analysis will be done to find out the programs that will be impacted. Once these "impacted programs" are identified, CM process will help in properly implementing these changes. In these examples, CM process ensures that different programs have been modified properly and that they have gone through review, testing stages, and is baselined and reconciled with other programs. After the reconciliation, the programs are released.

There are situations when concurrent updates to a program are to be carried out. In that case a strict reconciliation process needs to be applied. For example, let us take an instance wherein a critical bug fix is being carried out and a change request also has to be accommodated. Both have high-priority business needs and hence need to be completed. For such situations, which happen quite frequently, reconciliation process is needed. One option for reconciliation would be to examine the differences between original version and the new version and these differences would be merged with original code and tested for all relevant interphase. If the changes are in different parts of the original program, then merging is straightforward, otherwise the team has to review the overlap and then accommodate the changes.

Configuration Management Execution

After CM planning is finished, the execution of the defined process starts. The execution deals with the version control of documents and managing change requests. Managing version control implies that different work products are moved from one directory to another and creating versions when change requests come in. For each change request, new versions will be made for all work products and these work products go through their lifecycle as well. CM ensures that these work products comply with the process of completing all the lifecycle stages and be ready for delivery and is stored in baseline directory. Once all the work products are in baseline, the software is ready for delivery. These activities are best performed with CM tools as they provide consistence, easier to use, and business rules can be defined as per the project's objectives. Table 5.1 provides comparison of some of the open sources CM tools available*. These tools employ check in and check out procedures for controlling the access and handling version control. By using check in feature, the work product is considered to be in controlled environment and the document cannot be modified. Authorization is required to check the document out from the server and then modify the document. This feature ensures that the modification trail is maintained by the tool and can be used for audit later on. By checking out, a copy of the original document is made while keeping the original version in tact. When a work product is checked out, all the team members are made aware of this by tool and there will be no attempt to modify the document in between. In case a work product requires that there would be simultaneous modifications, then after making modifications, reconciliation process should be adopted.

* The matter has been taken from Wikipedia.

Table 5.1 Comparison of open source CM tools

	Language	License	Mutual authentication	Encrypts	First release	Latest stable release
Arusha Project (ARK)	Python	BSD	Yes	Yes	2001-07-21	2005-04-19 20050419
Bcfg2	Python	BSD	Yes	Yes	2004-08-11	2008-11-13 0.9.6
Cfengine	C	GPL, FAL	Yes	Yes	1993	2009-04-26 3.0.1
Chef	Ruby	Apache	Yes	Partial	2009-01-15 0.5.0	2009-02-13 0.5.4
ISconf	Python	GPL	Yes	No	1998	2006-08-13 4.2.8.233
LCFG	Perl	GPL	Partial	Partial	1994	2007-02-19 2007021901c
OCS Inventory NG with GLPI	Perl, PHP, C++	GPL	No	Yes	2003	2007
opsi (open pc server integration)	Python, Delphi	GPL	No	Yes	2004	2008-11-07 3.3
PCfengine	Python	GPL	No	No		
PIKT	C	GPL	Yes	Yes	1998	2007-09-10 1.19.0
Puppet	Ruby	GPL	Yes	Yes	2005-08-30	2009-02-28 0.24.8
Quattor	Perl	EDG	Yes	Yes	2005-04-01	2007-12-12 1.3-2
Radmind	C	BSD	Yes	Yes	2002-03-26	2008-10-8 1.13.0
SmartFrog	Java	LGPL	Yes	Yes	2004-02-11	2008-01-21 3.12.018
STAF	C++	CPL	No	Partial	1998-02-16	2008-02-27 3.2.5

Source: http://en.wikipedia.org/wiki/Comparison_of_open_source_configuration_management_software

Not all tools have the same goal and the same feature set. To help distinguish between all of these software packages, here is a short description of each one.

Arusha Project (ARK): Manage package and configuration specification of hosts via a custom XML description language. It can be used as a front end for Cfengine or PIKT. It provides some collaboration features between administration "teams." The last commit dates from April 2007.

Bcfg2: Software to manage the configuration of a large number of computers using a central configuration model and the client–server paradigm. The system enables reconciliation between clients' state and the central configuration specification. Detailed reports provide a way to identify unmanaged configuration on hosts. Generators enable code or template-based generation of configuration files from a central data repository.

Cfengine: Manages configuration of a large number of computers using the client–server paradigm. The server has the authoritative version of configuration: any client state that is different from the server is always reverted to the authoritative version. Configuration state is specified via a declarative language.

Chef: Chef is a configuration management tool written in Ruby and uses a pure Ruby DSL for writing configuration "recipes." Chef can be used as a client–server tool, or used in "solo" mode.

ISconf: Tool to execute commands and replicate files on all nodes. The nodes do not need to be up; the commands will be executed when they boot. The system has no central server so commands can be launched from any node and they will replicate to all nodes. It implements many of the ideas in "Why Order Matters: Turing Equivalence in Automated Systems Administration."

LCFG: LCFG manages the configuration with a central description language in XML, specifying resources, aspects, and profiles. Configuration is deployed using the client–server paradigm. Appropriate scripts on clients (called "components") transcribe the resources into configuration files and restart services as needed.

OCS Inventory NG with GLPI: OCS Inventory NG, when integrated with GLPI, provides inventory and asset management scans/database, package deployment, distributed script execution, and via plugins permissions management and other CM functions.

opsi (open pc server integration): opsi is a desktop management software for Windows clients based on Linux servers. It provides automatic software deployment (distribution), unattended OS installation, patch management, hardware and software inventory as well as administrative tasks for the CM.

PCfengine: This tool aims to be a better Cfengine written in Python. It uses Python directly as a language to describe configuration files. In contrast to Cfengine, it determines automatically the order in which actions are applied in the client.

PIKT: PIKT is foremost a monitoring system that also does configuration management. "PIKT consists of a sophisticated, feature-rich file preprocessor; an innovative scripting language with unique labor-saving features; a flexible, centrally directed process scheduler; a customizing file installer; a collection of powerful command-line extensions; and other useful tools."

Puppet: Puppet consists of a custom declarative language to describe system configuration, distributed using the client–server paradigm (using XML–RPC protocol), and a library to realize the configuration. The resource abstraction layer enables administrators to describe the configuration in high-level terms, such as users, services, and packages.

Quattor: "The quattor information model is based on the distinction between the desired state and the actual state. The desired state is registered in a fabric-wide configuration database (CDB), using a specially designed configuration language for expressing and validating configurations, composed out of reusable hierarchical building blocks called templates. Configurations are propagated to and cached on the managed nodes."

Radmind: Radmind manages hosts configuration at the file system level. In a similar way to Tripwire (and other CM tools), it can detect external changes to managed configuration, and can optionally reverse the changes. Radmind does not have higher level configuration element (services, packages) abstraction. A graphical interface is available (only) for Mac OS X.

SmartFrog: Java-based tool to deploy and configure applications distributed across multiple machines. There is no central server; one can deploy a .SF configuration file to any node and have it distributed to peer nodes according to the distribution information contained inside the deployment descriptor itself.

STAF: "The software testing automation framework (STAF) is an open source, multi-platform, multi-language framework designed around the idea of reusable components called services (such as process invocation, resource management, logging, and monitoring)." There are STAF plugins to perform a variety of common CM functions, such as distributed scheduling, execution, and file copying.

Change Request Management

CEO of a software service provider said to his employees: "we get paid because customer changes his minds"; that very well sums up the amount of scope changes that are part of software industry itself. The processes need to be defined to take care of scope changes and deliver software with additional features rather than avoiding or postponing any scope change. A change request is considered to be addition, deletion, or modification to the scope as was defined in the contract. A change request usually results in change in baselined plan. A baselined plan consists of (i) negotiated scope, (ii) quality of work products, (iii) effort and cost for the project, and (iv) timeline for delivery. So any change request will have impact on some of these elements in baselined plan.

When customer sends a change request, asking for additional/modified features for the application, or asking in schedule changes, a change request is logged. Usually, a unique number is given to this request and logged by the project manager. An impact analysis is done to determine the impact of change request on configuration items. A list of impacted configuration items is prepared. These configuration items include programs as well as documents that need to be modified to take care of change request. Along with these, cost effort and schedule impact are also analyzed.

Change request management has two important processes: (i) negotiation with the customer after the impact analysis and (ii) executing change request process. Once impact analysis has been done, customer has to be shared with information related to extra cost, schedule, and work products that need to be changed (some of these work products could have been delivered earlier). These changes are given in the form of a proposal for getting customer's approval and also project management plan is reflected with these changes. All these are usually authorized by the project manager as he/she is answerable to the top management for meeting project objectives (such as schedule, effort, quality, etc.). The change request is recorded so that in future reference can be given for the same. A sample change request template is shown in Annexure F. The steps involved in change request logging are as follows: log the change request in a standard template, carry out impact analysis, find impact on effort and schedule, get approval from customer for extra cost and modified schedule of deliveries, and then start working on the change request.

A change request log is maintained to keep track of each change request. The tracker uses unique change request number to track change requests. A simple tracker is shown in Table 5.2. However, each project can modify this to suit its needs.

Table 5.2 Sample change request tracker

S. no.	Tracker number	Impacted work products	Impacted hours	Received date	Assigned to	Planned end date	Present status	Actual end date	Remarks

Some organizations have a rule that if impacted hours do not go beyond a threshold value, then the effort and cost are not charged from the customer. If there are a number of change requests and cumulative impacted hours go beyond the threshold value, then the project effort is renegotiated and charged from the customer.

Once the change request has been accepted and negotiation with customer for effort and schedule is completed, execution starts. The CCB will check out impacted work products from server; the project manager then allocates these documents to different team members. Once the work products go through development, review, or testing, as the case may be, these are again checked into servers and base-lined for future delivery.

Roles and Responsibilities

In change management, it is important to understand the roles and responsibilities of different players. Table 5.3 elaborates the roles that each player has to play.

Table 5.3 Roles and responsibilities in change management

Project manager	• Ensures that all requests are recorded and handled properly • Makes sure that customers have correct expectations of change delivery • Control the scope of change requests • Records any informal change requests also, as they are important for customer satisfaction • Responsible for maintaining change request log • Conducts feasible study for all change requests
Change requester	• This role is played by customer, who gives details of changes that are required to be done
Change control board	• Review all the change requests in detail • Facilitates impact study • Approves or rejects each change request based on impact study • Resolves any conflict for change requests • Communicates with project manager and team members for deciding schedule, effort, and cost

Configuration Management Audit

CM audit is an activity that ensures that each configurable item goes through its lifecycle stages, and all defects that have been detected are either closed or if in open stage then proper communication is made to customer during delivery. CM audit acts as a check point for the deliverables to make sure that the deliverables are in proper state before being delivered. Each work product has to go through different states. These states depend on the kind of work product; for example, a program has to be written, reviewed by peers so that it is in conformance with design specifications, unit tested, integration tested, and finally system tested before being delivered to customer after acceptance testing. If a deliverable misses any one of the states, then chances of defects creeping in are high. CM audit finds actual state of each of these deliverables and advises team members as to the action that needs to be taken. If a program has not been unit tested, but moved to next state, then it could cause problems later on. Let us take another example. For a change request, if an impacted program has been checked out from baseline, but changes in the code have not been reflected in final delivery, then CM audit should point that and suggest corrective actions.

CM audit also involves checking if change requests are completed. To know this, CM audit checks status of each change request. The status of change request is then compared with the desired state and any variation is reported. CM audit also checks that each change request goes through all the lifecycle stages and then baselined for the final delivery.

CM audit also checks if proper access control as defined in the CM plan is followed. Table 5.4 shows a typical checklist that is used for CM audit.

Table 5.4 CM audit checklist

	Desired result	Actual result	Remarks
(a) Has the CM plan been reviewed and approved by project manager? (b) Has it been shared with team members? (c) Have the team members been trained on CM process?			
(a) Are the roles and responsibilities of CCB clear? (b) Is the CC trained for performing CM activities?			
(a) Is the configuration items list complete and up to date?			
(a) Is the movement of configuration items through the identified states of review, test, and baseline areas happening as stated in the CM plan?			
(a) Are all the configuration items identified in the CM plan under CM tool? (this includes software units, tools, and documents.) (b) Are the identified naming conventions being practiced? (c) Is the version numbering scheme identified in the CM plan being followed? (d) Is the access to the storage areas controlled as stated in the CM plan? (e) Are there multiple versions of the sources lying outside baseline area? (f) Are there any multiple copies within the baseline? (g) Are changes to baseline controlled? (h) Are documents that are linked from another document under version control?			
(a) Are changes to a configuration items controlled through approved change requests? (b) Are simultaneous modifications made at more than one place controlled?			
(a) Is the current status of the configuration items known? (b) Is each action taken on a configuration item being recorded in sufficient detail so that the status is known? (c) Record of change requests and their approval (d) Record of reconciliation of different versions of the same program			
(a) Are configuration audit reports available? (b) Are the backups being retrieved and checked? (c) Is the procedure identified for archival being followed?			
(a) Have all the items in the work product been identified?			
(a) Are the right versions being released?			
(a) Does the work product satisfy requirements?			
(a) Are all open defects identified and listed in the release note?			
(a) Have the backups been taken? (b) Have these backups been retrieved and tested?			
(a) Is the release checklist prepared? (b) Is the release list as per the contract signed with customer?			

SUMMARY

This chapter discussed an important aspect of software project management—configuration management (CM). This is important because of the very nature of this industry. One of the characteristics of the industry is to accommodate changes all the time and hence CM plays an important role in ensuring that correct versions of all the programs and other work products are delivered. CM starts with planning; CM is usually planned by the CCB in a project team and is headed by the CC. CM planning takes care of deciding access control, folder structure, naming convention, and version control mechanism. This approach ensures consistency and correctness while delivering right versions of the products.

Work products go through different states during their lifecycle stages. If a work product does not go through any of these states, then it could lead to defective output later on. CM ensures that work products go through desired states before being made ready for the final delivery. This is achieved by conducting CM audit.

DISCUSSION POINTS

1. What do you understand by CCB? What is the role played by CCB?
2. What is change management process?
3. Give an example of numbering process that can be followed for documents in a project.
4. Why CM audits need to be carried out?

CASE STUDY

PSL has bagged a new project called INFTIME. This is a time and material project. The customer is a highly technical person and does not believe too much in following a process. The interaction between the customer and the project team is highly informal. The customer requests for changes are very common and the project team always incorporates them. At the end of the release the project team could not meet the scheduled release date and the product testing stage revealed many bugs. Surprisingly, the customer blamed the project team entirely for the delay and the poor quality. The project team felt that the customer was unreasonable since the delay was mainly due to incorporating the changes requested by the customer. As the customer was not particular about the quality processes, the team had skipped most of them, which attributed to poor quality. But it was their words against the customer and in the end the customer is always right.

Questions:

1. What could have been done to prevent this?
2. What should the project manager do now?

6

SOFTWARE PROJECT AUDIT

LEARNING OBJECTIVES

In this chapter, the students would learn:

- Definitions of quality
- Principles of quality
- Quality assurance and quality control
- Quality audit practices—planning, auditing, and follow up in audits

INTRODUCTION

The quality language is the way quality professionals describe the principles, concepts, and approaches used for improving quality. Until the vocabulary is learned and its use is encouraged in an organization, a program for achieving quality becomes difficult to implement. Thus, it is essential that the quality concept is learnt by everyone in the organization, and there is a common wavelength of industry about the quality. For example, when the term "quality" or "defect" is used, there must be a common understanding of what is meant by those words.

Operationally, quality refers to the state of products or services. A product is a quality product if it is defect free. Thus, quality and defects are interrelated. The higher the quality, the lesser will be the defects and vice versa. To the producer, a product is a quality product if it meets or conforms to the statement of requirements that define the product. This statement is usually shortened to "quality means meeting customer requirement." To the customer, a product is a quality product if it meets the customer's needs, regardless of whether the producer's requirements are met. This is referred to as "fitness for use" or even more than fitness. Hence, even though we define quality as meeting the requirements, there are two views of quality that are used by professionals. They are producer's view and customer's view as explained below. These two views are not contradictory, rather they are complementary to each other. In an ideal situation the two may be identical.

Quality Definitions

The dictionary has many definitions of "quality." Definitions from various dictionaries have been shown in Table 6.1.

Table 6.1: Definitions of quality

Chamber's Twentieth Century Dictionary published by Allied Publishers Pvt. Ltd., 1969	That which make things what it is; grade of goodness, excellence
Random House Compact Unabridged Dictionary	• An essential or distinctive characteristics, property, or attribute • Character with respect to fitness or grade of excellence • A personality or character trait • An accomplishment or attainment • The superiority or distinction associated with high social status • Logic—the character of a proposition as affirmative or negative • Providing or producing products or services of high quality or merit which satisfies the customers
The Concise Oxford Thesaurus	• Degree of excellence, standard, grade, feature, attribute, characteristics, excellence, superiority, merit

A short definition that has achieved acceptance is: *quality is customer satisfaction*. "Fitness for use" is an alternative short definition. Although such a brief definition has a focus, it must be further developed to provide a basis for future action. Unfolding this definition starts with defining the word "customer." A customer is anyone who is impacted by the product or process:

1. External customers include not only ultimate users but also intermediate processors as well as merchants. Other customers are not purchasers but have some connection to the product, for example, government regulatory bodies.
2. Internal customers include not only the other divisions of a company that are provided with components for an assembly but also others that are affected, for example, purchasing department that receives an engineering specification for procurement.

Conventionally, products and services are different. Product refers to tangible objects, whereas services mean intangible benefits provided by the supplier. However, more recently services are becoming more and more productized through scope of service definition and specifications. For example, banking services are now being referred to as products, such as housing loan, vehicle loan, personal loan, etc.

A "product" is the output of any process. It means goods, software, or services. These three categories can be identified as follows:

- Goods, for example, automobiles, circuit boards, and reagent chemicals.

- Software, for example, a computer program, a report, and an instruction.
- Service, for example, banking, insurance, and transportation. Service also includes support activities within companies, for example, employee benefits, plant maintenance, and secretarial support.

We now need to define "customer satisfaction." Customer satisfaction is defined as meeting the customer-expressed and latent needs. The customer may or may not express his requirements clearly and explicitly. But it is important for the producer to understand both the explicit and tacit requirements of the customer and deliver the product or service, which would meet both these requirements. This is achieved through two components: product features and freedom from deficiencies. Examples of the main categories of these components are shown in Table 6.2. We can see dramatic differences between manufacturing and services in terms of features.

Table 6.2: Two components of quality

Component one: product features	
Manufacturing industries	**Service industries**
Performance	Accuracy
Reliability	Timeliness
Durability	Completeness
Ease of use	Friendliness and courtesy
Serviceability	Anticipating customer needs
Aesthetics	Knowledge of server
Availability of options and expandability	Aesthetics
Reputation	Reputation
Component two: freedom from deficiencies	
Product free of defects and errors at delivery, during use, and during servicing	Service free of errors during original and future service transactions
Sales, billing, and other business processes free of errors	Sales, billing, and other business processes free of error

A closer examination will provide further insights.

1. *Product features* have a major effect on sales income (through market share, premium prices, etc.). In many industries, the total external customer population can be segmented by the level or "grade" of quality desired. Thus, the spectrum of customers leads to a demand for luxury hotels and budget hotels and also leads to a demand for refrigerators with many special features as well as for those with basic coding capabilities. Product features refer to the *quality of design*. Increasing the quality of the design generally leads to *higher* costs.
2. *Freedom from deficiencies* has a major effect on *costs* through reduction in scrap, rework, complaints, and other results of deficiencies. "Deficiencies" are stated in different units, for example, errors, defects, failures, and off-specification. Freedom from deficiencies refers to the *quality of conformance*. Increasing the quality of conformance usually results in *lower* costs. In addition, higher conformance means fewer complaints and therefore increased customer satisfaction.

To summarize, quality means external and internal customer satisfaction. While external customer implies that these entities are outside the organization boundary, and they want to buy company's products and services, internal customers are those who are within the company premises but receive the products or services internally from another department. As a result the receiving department becomes the customer of the sending department. For example, when the production department sends a requisition to stores to issue some items from its inventory, then it becomes the customer of the stores department. Product features and freedom from deficiencies are the main determinants of satisfaction. For example, an external customer of an automobile desires certain performance features along with a record of few defects and breakdowns. The manufacturing department as an internal customer of the product development department wants an engineering specification that is producible in the shop and is free of errors or omissions. Both of these customers want "the right product at right time."

Quality Pioneers

Many individuals have contributed to the quality movement. Three individuals are highlighted here because they have either organized a business to promote their concepts or have developed a set of quality principles. These three are Dr. W. Edwards Deming, Philip Crosby, and Dr. Joseph Juran. Both Dr. Deming and Dr. Juran have developed a set of quality principles. Dr. Juran is well known for his trilogy and distinction between "little Q" quality and "big Q" quality.

Dr. W. Edwards Deming's Quality Principles

Dr. Deming defined 14 principles for quality, which formed the basis for turnaround of the Japanese manufacturing industry. He believed that all the 14 principles must be used concurrently to make quality happen. The 14 principles are discussed briefly below.

1. **Create consistency of purpose in the company:** In quality-oriented companies, quality should be the cornerstone of the corporation. All the units in the organization should work toward the common goal and purposes. Within IT this can be translated to mean that the training department teaches standards, the operations department works toward the same goal as system programming, and system programming is dedicated to improve application performance. Assuring quality involves:
   (a) Innovating new approaches and allocating resources for long-term planning, such as possible new service, new skill required, training and retraining of personnel, satisfaction of the user.
   (b) Putting resources into research, education, and maintenance.
2. **Learn the new philosophy:** We are in a new economic age. We can no longer live with commonly accepted mistakes, defects materials not suited for jobs, people on the job who do not know what the job is and are afraid to ask, failure of management to understand the problems of the product in use, antiquated methods of training on the job, and inadequate and ineffective supervision. Acceptance of defective systems and poor workmanship as a way of life is one of the most effective way to roadblocks to better quality and productivity.
3. **Require statistical evidence of information technology quality:** There is no other way to know the quality that is being delivered and no other way to achieve the best economy and productivity.

Managers must learn the statistical control of quality. They must proceed under new philosophy; the right quality characteristics must be built in, without dependence on inspection.

4. **Reduce the number of vendors:** Requiring statistical evidence of quality control in the purchase of hardware and software will mean, in most companies, drastic reduction in the number of vendors with whom they deal. Companies have to consider the cost of having two or more vendors for the same item. A company will be lucky to find one vendor who can provide statistical evidence of quality. A second vendor, if they cannot furnish the statistical evidence of their quality, will have higher cost than the one that can furnish the evidence, or they have to chisel on their quality, or go out of business. A person that does not know his or her costs or whether today's distribution of quality can be repeated tomorrow is not a good business partner.
5. **Use statistical methods to find the sources of trouble:** Which are user faults? Which faults belong to IT? Put responsibility where it belongs. Do not rely on judgment because it always gives the wrong answer on the question of where the fault lies. Statistical methods make use of knowledge of the subject matter where it can be effective, but substitute it where it is a hazard.

   Constantly improve the system. This obligation never ceases. Most people in the management do not understand that the system (their responsibility) is everything not under the governance of a user.
6. **Institute modern aids to training on the job:** Training must be totally reconstructed. Statistical methods must be used to learn when training is finished, and when further training would be beneficial. A person once hired and trained and in statistical control of his/her own work, whether it be necessary or not, can do no better. Further training cannot help. If their work is not satisfactory, move them to another job and provide better training there.
7. **Improve supervision:** Supervision belongs to the system and is the responsibility of the management.
   (a) Project leaders must have more time to help people on the job.
   (b) Statistical methods are vital aids to the project leader to indicate whether the fault lies locally or in the system.
   (c) The usual procedure by which a project leader calls the worker's attention to every defect, or to the half of them, may be wrong—is certainly wrong in most of the organizations—and defeats the purpose of supervision.
8. **Drive out fear:** Most people on a job, and even in management positions, do not understand what the job is, or what is right vs wrong. Moreover, it is not clear to them how to find it out. Many of them are afraid to ask questions or to report trouble. The economic loss from fear is appalling. It is necessary for better quality and productivity that people feel secured.

   Another related aspect of the fear is the inability to serve in the best interest of the company through necessity to satisfy specified rules, or to satisfy a production quota, or to cut costs by some specified amount. One common result of fear is seen in inspection. An inspector records incorrectly the result of an inspection for fear of overdrawing the quota of allowable defectives of the work force.
9. **Break down barriers between departments:** People in user areas must learn about the problems encountered with various technologies and specifications in system design and operation. Otherwise, there will be losses in production from the necessity of reruns and from

the attempts to use the systems unsuited for the purpose. Why not have users spend time in IT department to see the problems and hear about them?

10. **Eliminate exhortations:** Eliminate numerical goals, slogans, pictures, posters urging people to increase productivity, sign their work as an autograph, etc. "zero defect (ZD)" is an example. Posters and slogans like these never helped anyone do a better job. Numerical goals have often a negative effect through frustration. These devices are management's lazy way out. They indicate management's desperation and the incompetence of the management. There is a better way.
11. **Look carefully at work standards:** Do they take account of quality, or any numbers? Do they help anyone do a better job? How old are they? Work standards are costing as much loss as poor materials and mistakes. In hundreds of companies, any day, people stand around last one hour or two waiting for the whistle to blow. They have completed their quotas for the day. Is this good for the competitive position for the company in its own industry? These workmen are unhappy doing nothing, and would rather work.
12. **Institute a massive training program for employees in simple but powerful statistical methods:** Thousands of people must learn rudimentary statistics methods. One in 500 must spend the necessary 10 years to become a statistician. This training will be a costly affair.
13. **Institute a vigorous training program for retaining people in new skills:** The program should keep up with changes in technology and methods and, if advantageous, new hardware.
14. **Create a structure in the top management that will push every day on the above 13 points:** Make the maximum use of statistical knowledge and talent in your company. The top management will require guidance from an experienced consultant, but the consultant cannot take on obligations that only the management can carry out.

Philip Crosby's Quality Principles

Philip Crosby has developed 14 steps for an organization to follow in building an effective quality program. They are as follows:

1. **Management commitment:** Clarify where management stands on quality. It is necessary to consistently produce conforming products and services at the optimum price. The device to accomplish this is the use of defect prevention techniques in the operating departments: engineering, manufacturing, quality control, purchasing, sales, and others. The management must ensure that no one is exempted.
2. **The quality improvement team:** They run the quality improvement program. As every function of an operation contributes to defect levels, every function must participate in the quality improvement effort. The degree of participation is best determined by the particular situation that exists. However, everyone has the opportunity to improve.
3. **Quality measurement:** Communicate current and potential non-conformance problems in a manner that permits objective evaluation and corrective action. Basic quality measurement data are obtained from inspection and test reports, which are broken down by operating areas of the plant. By comparing the rejection data with the input data, it is possible to know the rejection rates. As most companies have such systems, it is necessary to go into them in detail. It should be mentioned that unless these data are reported properly, they are useless. After all, their only purpose is to warn the management of serious situations. They should be used to identify specific problems needing corrective action, and the quality department should report them.

4. **The cost of quality:** Defines the ingredients of the cost of quality (COQ) and explains its use as a management tool. The COQ is the money spent beyond what it would cost to build a product right the first time. As this situation does not occur, there are costs associated with getting a defect-free product produced. There are three COQ categories:
   (a) *Prevention*: Money required to prevent errors and to do the job right the first time is considered prevention cost. The category includes money spent on establishing methods and procedures, training workers, and planning for quality. Prevention money is all spent before the product is actually built.
   (b) *Appraisal*: Appraisal cost covers the money spent to review the completed products against the requirements. Appraisal includes the cost of inspections, testing, and reviews. This money is spent after the product or subcomponents are built, but before it is shipped to the user.
   (c) *Failure*: Failure costs are all costs associated with defective products. Some failure costs involve repairing products to make them meet requirements. Others are costs generated by failures, such as the cost of operating faulty products, damage incurred by using them, and the cost incurred because the product is not available. The user or the customer of the organization may experience failure costs.
5. **Quality awareness:** Provide a method of raising the personal concern raised by all personnel in the company toward the conformance of the product or service and the quality reputation of the company. By the time a company is ready for quality awareness step, they should have a good idea about the types and expense of the problems being faced. The quality management and COQ steps will have revealed them.
6. **Corrective action:** Provide a systematic method of permanently resolving the problems that are identified through previous action steps. Problems that are identified during the acceptance operation, or by some other means, must be documented and then resolved formally.
7. **Zero defect (ZD) planning:** Examine the various activities that must be conducted in preparation for formally launching the ZD program. The quality improvement task team should list all the individual action steps that build up to ZD day in order to make the most meaningful presentation of the concept and action plan to personnel of the company. These steps, placed on a schedule and assigned to members of the team for execution, will provide a clean energy flow into an organization-wide ZD commitment. Since it is a natural step, it is not difficult, but because of the significance of it, the management must make sure that it is conducted properly.
8. **Supervisor training:** Define the type of training the supervisors need in order to actively carry out their part of the quality improvement program. The supervisor, from the board chairman down, is the key to achieving improvement goals. The supervisor gives the individual employees their attitudes and work standards, whether in engineering, sales, computer programming, or wherever. Therefore, the supervisor must be given primary consideration when laying out the program. The departmental representatives on the task team will be able to communicate much of the planning and concepts to the supervisors, but individual classes are essential to make sure that they properly understand and can implement the program.
9. **ZD day:** Create an event that will let all employees realize through personal experience that there has been a change. ZD is a revolution to all involved that they are embarking a new way of corporate life. Working under the discipline requires personal commitments and understanding. Therefore, it is necessary that all members of the company participate in an experience that will make them aware of this change.

10. **Goal setting:** Turn pledges and commitments into action by encouraging individuals to establish improvement goals for themselves and their groups. About a week after ZD day, individual supervisors should ask their people what kind of goals they should set for themselves. Try to get two goals from each area. These goals should be specific and measurable.
11. **Error-cause removal** (ECR): Give the individual employee a method of communicating with the management the situations that make it difficult for the employee to fulfill the pledge to improve. One of the most difficult problems that the employees face is their inability to communicate their problems with the management. Sometimes they are just put up with the problems because they do not consider them important enough to bother the supervisor. Sometimes the supervisor does not listen anyway. Suggestion programs are some help, but in a suggestion program the worker is required to know the problem and also propose a solution. ECR is set up on the basis that the worker needs to only recognize the problem. When the worker has stated the problem, the proper department in the plant can look into it. Studies of ECR programs show that over 90% of the items submitted are acted upon, and 75% of the problems can be acted upon at the first level of supervision. The number of ECRs that save money is extremely high, since the worker generates savings every time the job is done better or quicker.
12. **Recognition:** Appreciate those who participate—people really do not work for money. They go to work for it, but once the salary has been established their concern is their appreciation. Recognize their contribution publicly and noisily, but do not demean them by applying a price tag to everything.
13. **Quality councils:** Bring together the professional quality people for planned communication on a regular basis. It is vital for the professional quality people of an organization to meet regularly just to share their problems, feelings, and experiences with each other. Isolated even in the midst of many fellow workers, these people are primarily concerned with measurement and reporting, and it is easy for them to become influenced by the urgency of an activity in their work areas. Consistency of attitude and purpose is the essential personal characteristics of one who evaluates another's work. This is not only because of the importance of the work itself but also because those who submit their work unconsciously draw a great deal of their performance standard from the performance evaluator.
14. **Do it over again:** Emphasize that the quality improvement program never ends. There is always a great sigh of relief when the goals are reached. If care is not taken, the entire program will end at that moment. It is necessary to construct a new quality improvement team, and let them begin again and create their own communications.

Dr. Joseph Juran's Principles

Dr. Juran believed that managing for quality required the same attention that other functions typically receive. In order to ensure that adequate attention was given, he developed a trilogy consisting of interrelated, basic managerial phases and processes: quality planning, quality control, and quality improvement. These are known as "Juran trilogy" or "the quality trilogy."

- **Quality planning:** The purpose of this phase is to create a process that enables goals to be met. In developing the process, the quality planning should identify the customers and their needs, and then incorporate those needs into the product and process designs. The planning process should also attempt to avoid costly deficiencies, such as rework, and optimize the company performance. This phase occurs before the process is used to produce a product.

- **Quality control:** Quality control takes place at all levels in the organization, with everyone using the same feedback loop. Dr. Juran believed that in order to achieve control, the processes must have numerical measures and adjustment capabilities. When the products are produced from the process, there will always be some acceptable (inherent) variation, and the occasional spikes (those representing special causes of variation) should be investigated. The management should strive to give process users the capability of making the necessary adjustments to control the process. He refers to this as "self-control." When the process is being designed, control should be the part of the planning process. Typically, the quality control will be performed to prevent defects from worsening; it will not focus on the process.
- **Quality improvement:** At some point in the quality control phase, the continuous loop of product deficiencies will be traced back to the planning process, and the problems will be seen as an opportunity to improve. Improvements will be made to revise the process, and problems will become less than originally planned.

Dr. Juran believed that business processes presented a major opportunity for improvement. He developed a structured approach for improvement, which included the following list of responsibilities for the senior managers that could not be delegated:

- Create an awareness of the need and an opportunity for improvement
- Mandate quality improvement; make it a part of every job description
- Create an infrastructure: establish a quality council, select projects to improve, appoint teams, and provide facilitators
- Provide training in how to improve quality
- Review progress regularly
- Recognize winning teams
- Propagandize the results

In addition to his trilogy, Dr. Juran is also known for his distinction between "little Q" quality and "big Q quality." Prior to TQM there was only "little Q," which he called the narrow focus on quality. "Little Q" quality is considered important, but it has a limited scope and impact, such as a team of people and their manager improving a specific work process. Dr. Juran referred to "big Q" quality as the new focus on quality. An example of "big Q" quality is cross-functional teams throughout an organization working to prevent problems. Although the scope of "little Q" quality is a specific departmental mission, the scope of "big Q" quality emphasizes the coordination of various activities conducted in other functions and groups so that all the plans contribute to achieving the organization's goals for quality.

Quality in Information Technology (IT)

In today's highly automated business world, the strategies and directions of the IT department increasingly form the basis for the overall corporate strategy. Once regarded as merely a service department, the quality of IT infrastructure now influences a company's competitive position, and often dictates its ability to exploit market opportunities. For example, manufacturing firms depend on their supply chain infrastructure to respond quickly to shifting production demands, while retailers look to the intelligence built into their inventory management systems to withstand cyclical downturns. Thus, it is no surprise that executive managers are placing a greater emphasis on improving the quality of IT. Time and time again, it has been found that aligning the IT quality with the corporate objectives and discovering methods for measuring the IT quality are two of the top issues on executives' minds. Unfortunately, cost-cutting measures driven by the recent economic recession have caused many IT organizations to focus inwardly and to emphasize their own efficiency rather than the ramifications of their actions on the organization as a whole. This emphasis distracts IT from the true role it should be playing within the enterprise. An outwardly focused IT group concentrates on the effectiveness of information management, not just the efficiency of the underlying technology infrastructure.

Quality Attributes of an Information System

Quality is a multifaceted concept driven by the customer requirements. The level of quality can vary significantly from project to project and between organizations. In IT, the attributes of quality can vary significantly from project to project and between organizations. In IT, the attributes of quality are examined in order to understand the components of quality and as a basis for measuring quality. Some of the commonly accepted quality attributes are described in Table 6.3.

Table 6.3: Quality attributes

Attributes	Definitions
Correctness	The extent to which a program satisfies its specifications and fulfils the user's mission and goals
Reliability	The extent to which a program can be expected to perform its intended function with required precision
Efficiency	The amount of computing resources and code required by a program to perform a function
Integrity	The extent to which access to software or data by unauthorized persons can be controlled
Usability	The effort required for learning, operating, preparing input, and interpreting output of a program
Maintainability	The effort required for locating and fixing an error in an operational program
Testability	The effort required for testing a program to ensure that it performs its intended function
Flexibility	The effort required for modifying an operational program
Portability	The effort required for transferring a program from one hardware configuration and/or software system environment to another
Reusability	The extent to which a program can be used in other applications—related to the packaging and scope of the functions that the programs perform
Interoperability	The effort required to couple one system with another

Producer's View

Meeting requirements is a producer's view of quality. This is the view of the organization responsible for the project and processes, and the products and services acquired, developed, or maintained by these processes. Meeting requirements means that the person building the product does so in accordance with the requirements. Requirements can be very complete or they can be simple, but they must be defined in a measurable format so that it can be determined whether or not they have been met. The producer's view of quality has the following four characteristics:

- Doing the right thing
- Doing it right way
- Doing it right the first time
- Doing it on time without exceeding cost

Customer's View

Being "fit for use" is the customer's definition. The customer is the end user of the products or services. Fit for use means that the product or service meets the customer's needs regardless of the product requirements. Out of the two definitions of quality, "fit for use" is the most important. The customer's view of quality has the following characteristics:

- Receiving the right product for their use
- Being satisfied that their needs have been met
- Meeting their expectations
- Being treated with integrity, courtesy, and respect

In addition to the producer's and customer's views of quality, the organizational infrastructure also includes a provider's and a supplier's view. These views are discussed in the following section.

The Two Quality Gaps

Most IT groups have two quality gaps: the producer gap and the customer gap. The producer gap is the gap between what is specified (the documented requirements and specified standards) and what is delivered (what is actually built). The customer gap is the difference between what the producer actually delivered and what the customer wanted.

Closing these two gaps is the responsibility of the quality function. The quality function must improve the processes to the point where the producer can develop products according to the requirements received and its own internal standards. Closing the producer's gap enables the IT function to provide its customers consistency in what it can produce. This has been referred to as the "McDonald's effect"—at any McDonald's in the world, a Big Mac should taste the same. It does not mean that every customer likes the taste or that it meets everyone's needs, but rather Macdonald's has now produced consistency in its delivered product.

Closing the customer gap requires the quality function to understand the true needs of the customer. This can be done by customer surveys, joint application development (JAD) sessions, and more user involvement through the process of building information products. The processes can then be changed to close the customer gap, keeping consistency while producing products and services needed by the customer.

Quality Assurance

Quality assurance in software organizations has two aspects–process definition and process implementation. In process definition, the processes that need to be followed during project execution are defined. The objectives of the defined processes are to get maximum quality and productivity. The process definition aspect has different lifecycle stages such as identifying processes, forming a working group to define the process, piloting the process in few projects, rolling out the process throughout the organization. The second aspect deals with the implementation of these defined processes; this aspect ensures that the defined processes are followed in the entire organization. This aspect has the objective to ensure compliance with defined processes so that the projects reap benefits from the processes. The compliance with processes ensures that the capabilities of the processes are utilized to the fullest extent. Hence, for a matured organization, it is essential that the defined processes be followed in all the projects. The role of software quality assurance is to facilitate defining of these processes as well as to ensure compliance.

The difference between a non-IT process definition and an IT process definition lies in the maturity of the industry. In non-IT industry such as manufacturing industry, engineering industry, and so forth, the defined processes become the part of production line. Sometimes the entire production line is woven with the defined processes such that any change in the process would require a change in the production line itself. But this is not the case with software industry. The execution process requires quite an amount of manual involvement as intellectual needs are quite high here. Each project has some element of uniqueness, which cannot be automated. For this reason project compliance check becomes quite an important aspect in addition to process definition.

In software industry, because of its immaturity, the defined processes are not executed in assembly lines; rather the degree of automation is quite less. There are many manual interventions and people need to apply themselves to the changing requirements of the project. As there is human intervention, sometimes shortcuts are employed to increase productivity, which might lead to defects in the application. If there is a delivery deadline, this tendency of applying shortcuts is more common and during these trying periods the team members tend to skip the defined processes. Also, inexperience in team members sometimes brings in lack of compliance as they do not understand the need for complying with these processes. The processes then deem to be bureaucratic and they term it to be "overhead." The documentation process, which is required for future maintenance work, also seems to be unnecessary, and these team members might like to do away with this process. Thus, compliance with the defined process goes down giving necessary to serious project compliance and audit requirements. Only when the team gets customer complaints or spends endless hours in solving issues related to configuration management, etc., do they realize the importance of following the defined processes. Also, following the processes requires that the team members change their style of working. This means they have to forgo their earlier habits and adapt to new style. This becomes a change management issue where there is resistance to change of inertia. This change implies effort and relearning and means they leave what had been comfortable to them so far and adopt to new uncertain ways of working. This restricts their freedom that they would have found earlier, and they would try to stop the process implementation. One more reason for such resistance is the transparency that processes bring in with their implementation. This would expose them and may damage their career as well. Hence, they do everything to resist the change.

Thus, just because an organization has defined the processes will not ensure that the processes will be followed. Management effort is needed to ensure compliance with the defined processes. Quality departments are set up to help the project team members to implement the processes and make the projects compliant to the processes. They will provide training, mentor the project managers, and provide periodic assistance for improving compliance with the processes. They also define a formal method for checking regularly the level of compliance and these formal methods are "project compliance" checks or project audits. These are planned at regular intervals, may be two to three times a year.

Process Definition Lifecycle

One of the major aspects of quality assurance is to facilitate process definition process for the organization. The process definition lifecycle talks about meta process for process definition, maintaining the process, and improving the process further. This aspect is a continuous process and is based on Deming's principle of PDCA (plan–do–check–act) cycle. The cycle is represented in Figure 6.1.

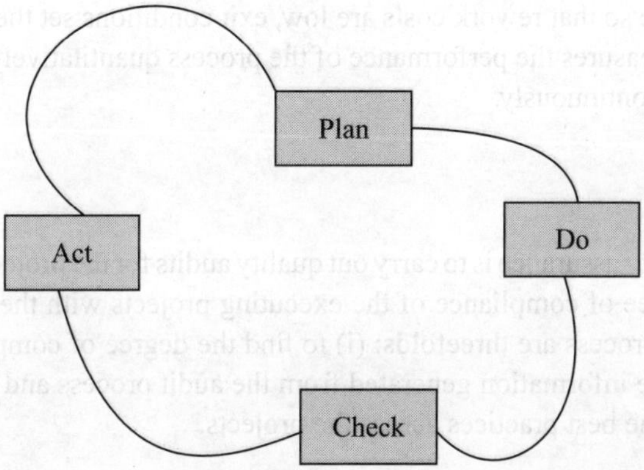

Figure 6.1: PDCA cycle

The definition of process starts with the identification of business processes. An organization will have a number of processes that are executed for its business model. However, all the processes need not be defined as some of these may not be critical and may not be followed always. Hence, the quality department along with practitioners decides the processes that need to be defined. The practitioners are involved to get their opinion about the critical processes; it also becomes easier for the implementation of these processes as the practitioners are involved in the identification stage itself. Once the processes are identified, a process definition group is defined that will have representation from quality and practitioners. The group is known as software engineering process group (SEPG) and is usually headed by a senior representative from the quality department.

Once SEPG is formed, a process is defined and is used in pilot projects. The pilot projects are usually chosen in a manner such that all the procedures and activities involved in the process are used fully. At this stage, feedback is obtained from the pilot projects regarding effectiveness and usefulness of the processes. The feedback is incorporated in the process and if the changes in the process are major ones, then the process needs to be retested again in another set of pilot projects. The objective of any process is to transform an input to a desired output. The objective of a process will be thus to achieve desired result at the least possible input value. This will ensure that the process results in higher productivity; the process should also be easy and user friendly so that it can be easily implemented with consistency.

After the feedback from pilot projects are incorporated, the processes are institutionalized and rolled out. This ensures that consistency and performance of the processes are predictable. It is expected that each and every project will follow these processes, and there should be a high degree of compliance with the process. However, there are elements of uniqueness in each project that needs to be taken care of. This uniqueness occurs because of varying customer needs and different project environment such as technology, project organization structure, etc. The institutionalized processes should be able to take care of these customization needs of the project; tailoring is provided to take care of these customization. While the standard, institutionalized processes ensure predictability and consistency, tailoring helps in managing customization. The process definition usually uses a framework; the framework helps to define the process for giving optimal results. The framework consists of ETVXMF (E, entry; T, tasks; V, verification or validation; X, exit; M, measurement; F, feedback). Entry pinpoints the conditions or environment at which the process will start, tasks are activities that are to be executed, verification and validation ensure that defects are detected well in advance so that rework costs are low, exit conditions set the correct expectation for output, measurement measures the performance of the process quantitatively, and feedback helps in improving the process continuously.

Quality Audits

The other aspect of quality assurance is to carry out quality audits for the projects. Audit is a systematic process to find the degree of compliance of the executing projects with the defined processes. The objectives of the audit process are threefolds: (i) to find the degree of compliance with the defined processes, (ii) to analyze information generated from the audit process and determine health of the project, and (iii) share the best practices across the projects.

Audit Process

Audit can be internal as well as external. Usually, it is a practice not to have simultaneous internal and external audit processes at the same time. The simultaneous occurrence is avoided so as not to strain the project machinery unnecessarily. External audit happens when auditor(s), external to the organization, conduct independent audits of the projects. Such audits happen when there is a need for statutory compliance (such as financial or regulatory compliance), certification need (such as ISO, CMMI, BS 27,000, etc.). During these audits, the processes are checked for compliance against external standards. Internal audits, on the other hand, are conducted using people from the organization. The internal audit is carried out to check compliance against organization's processes, and the auditors are considered as the representative for top management. The internal auditors are conceived as "eye and ear" of the top management because they (auditors) report the true project health to the top management. They also suggest corrective actions and track it down to closure ensuring that the project health is brought to its desired state.

Audits should be carried out regularly so that the projects would be motivated to remain compliant to the defined processes. This planning should be done in such a way that audit should cover maximum of projects that are being audited. The usual tendency is to make the projects compliant with the process during the audit time. Hence, by conducting the audits regularly (say once in three months), the degree of compliance can be improved. By covering the maximum number of projects under the audit process, the projects would be encouraged to follow the organization processes. No project should be outside the purview of the audit process, as these projects would slowly deteriorate by not using organization processes. This is quite important as the internal resources available for the audits are limited; hence, not all projects will be selected for the audit. This means either we have to do a sampling or the projects will be selected at random. Whatever may be the strategy, the audits should be carried out in a formal manner. The audits should be planned and notified to the project managers well in advance so that he/she can plan for it. All these are planned by the quality department, and the role of software quality advisor (SQA) is quite important.

SQA is responsible for planning audit for the projects as well as are the auditors. The audit plan is shared with all the stakeholders, such as project manager, quality department, top management, and administrative department (to take care of logistics). Table 6.4 shows a sample audit plan for a software services company.

The audit plan shows the level of planning required for each audit cycle. All the projects are selected and focus area of the audit is also decided. The focus area is chosen based on the lifecycle stage of the project. For example, if the project has started and is in initial stages, then planning will be the focus area. During the execution stage, where the project manager has to monitor the status of the project, metrics analysis will be the focus area for the audit. Similarly, after stabilizing the processes, defect prevention will be the focus area to ensure that the learning obtained from the execution of the organization projects are ploughed back to the project. The date and time are also fixed and the expected duration of the audit (in form of effort to be spent) is also indicated so that both the auditor and the auditee can plan their activities.

SQAs, who are the auditors, should have thorough knowledge about the processes and also be aware of current issues and challenges faced by the team. They should also have enough maturity and stature to be able to assess the health of process implementation in the projects. The auditors need to be trained in the audit process as there are behavioral issues as well as change management issues that need to be handled during the audit. The auditor should not have the motive for finding nonconformance only, rather should help the project manager in improving the degree of compliance. If an audit is conducted with this kind of positive attitude, then the auditee will be open to discuss different issues and challenges faced by him during the execution. The auditor can then share the best practices from other projects and help in resolving the problems.

Some of the best practices in audit planning are as follows:

1. Conduct audits regularly (monthly)
2. Prepare an audit strategy to cover all the projects during the audit cycle
3. Decide the focus area for the audit for each project
4. Plan well in advance and intimate all the stakeholders
5. Have a fact-finding mission rather than a fault-finding attitude during the audit
6. Share the audit reports with the stakeholders

During the audit process, it is advisable to prepare a checklist that can be used for conducting audits. A sample checklist is shown in Table 6.5.

Table 6.4: Audit plan

Project name	Project manager name	Contact details of project manager	Auditor's name and email ID	Focus area	Planned date	Effort in hours	Actual date	Remarks
				Metrics analysis	29 Oct 2003	2		
				Metrics analysis	29 Oct 2003	2		
				DP meetings	28 Oct 2003	2		
				Compliance checks	22 Oct 2003	4		This is a planned visit to Hyderabad for review of Hyderabad projects
				Independent metrics review	20 Oct 2003	3	20 Oct 2003	These are closure reports received from Chennai for authorization
				Compliance checks	16 Oct 2003	2		
				Orient, RADAR, metrics, etc.	15 Oct 2003	2		
				Compliance checks	13 Oct 2003	4	13 Oct 2003	
				Compliance checks	13 Oct 2003	2		
				Compliance checks	10 Oct 2003	2		
				Compliance checks	07 Oct 2003	2	07 Oct 2003	
				Compliance checks	07 Oct 2003	2		
				DP meetings	06 Oct 2003	4	06 Oct 2003	
				Metrics analysis	01 Oct 2003	3	10 Oct 2003	
				Total effort to be spent				

Table 6.5: Audit checklist for all lifecycle stages of a project

Quality system section	Processes	Control objective
4.2	Requirement definition	Is the process entry criteria satisfied? SM advises completion of requirement definition.
4.2	Requirement definition	Has the system analyst prepared the RDD and done walkthrough of the requirements with the customer to ensure that there are no gaps in the requirements (scope) understanding? Have the feedback been updated and the revised document sent to the PM for review?
4.2	Requirement definition	Has the PM reviewed the requirement document been reviewed using the checklist? Have the defects, if found, been fixed and sent to the SM for approval?
4.2	Requirement definition	Has the SM approved the document and sent it to the system analyst to obtain sign off?
4.2	Requirement definition	Has the system analyst obtained the customer approval on the document and communicated to the project manager?
4.3	Preliminary assessment	Is the process entry criteria satisfied? (communication received from JBB/customer to start the project based on SOW/requirements defined)
4.3.1	Validation of inputs	Has the SM reviewed the marketing collaterals for adequacy (e.g., SOW, margin sheet, pre-sales documents, etc.) and obtained clarifications, if inadequate from JBB/customer? Have PM and PL/TL been identified and updated in "resource utilization sheet"? Has consent been obtained from COO for project initiation?
4.3.2	Project kick off	Has the PM initiated PIN (project charter), prepared MOM based on initial kick-off meeting with JBB/customer, identified resource requirements for the project, and communicated the MOM to project stakeholders?
4.3.2	Project kick off	Has the SM approved PIN (project charter)?
4.3.3	System resources	Has the PM identified additional system resources and access rights for the project members, updated in SAP, and sent for SM's approval?
4.3.3	System resources	Has the SM reviewed and approved the SAP, updated the resource utilization sheet?
4.3.3	System resources	Has the PM sent the approved SAP to NSG for provision of resources and access rights?
4.3.4	Process tailoring	Has the PM prepared the process tailoring document and sent to manager-PEG for review? Have review comments been assimilated and obtained recommendations for approval from manager-PEG?
4.3.4	Process tailoring	Has the SM approved the PTD based on manager-PEG's recommendation?

4.3.5	Project risk assessment	Has the PM identified all the project risks and prepared risk management sheet incorporating the risks and mitigation plan?
4.3.5	Project risk assessment	Has the SM reviewed and approved the risk management sheet?
4.3.6	High-level project plan	Has the PM prepared a high-level plan covering the requirement phase to ensure that tasks are executed within the project effort in the margin sheet?
4.4.1	Requirement document understanding	Is the entry criteria satisfied to commence this process? (process step specified in approved PTD, and JBB/customer provides access to current system/sends enhancements over current system)
4.4.1	Requirement document understanding	Has RAD been prepared detailing the understanding of the existing system, updated the RTM, and sent for review?
4.4.1	Requirement document understanding	Has PL/TL reviewed RAD using checklist and the RTM, ensure closure of defects, if any?
4.4.1	Requirement document understanding	Has PL/TL approved RAD after ensuring closure of defects?
4.4.1	Requirement document understanding	Has the PM approved RTM after ensuring closure of defects?
4.4.2	Requirement understanding—fragmented inputs	In the case of fragmented inputs, has PL/TL prepared the system requirement specification and the requirement traceability matrix?
4.4.2	Requirement understanding—fragmented inputs	Has the technical consultant reviewed the system requirement specification and the requirement traceability matrix for adequacy, tracked feedback to closure, and recommended for approval?
4.4.2	Requirement understanding—fragmented inputs	Has the PM approved the requirement traceability matrix and system requirement specification after verifying the review results?
4.5	Requirement understanding—existing system	Has the SE prepared RAD detailing the understanding of the existing system, updated the RTM, and sent for review?
4.5	Requirement understanding—existing system	Has PL/TL reviewed RAD using checklist and the RTM, ensure closure of defects, if any?
4.5	Requirement understanding—existing system	Has PL/TL approved RAD after ensuring closure of defects?
4.5	Requirement understanding—existing system	Has the PM approved RTM after ensuring closure of defects?
4.6	Requirement presentation	Is the entry criteria satisfied to commence this process? (RTM is baselined)

4.6	Requirement presentation	Has the PM, based on the presentation session, obtained feedback and commitments? Have they been documented in MOM and communicated to participants?
4.7.1	Effort estimation	Is the entry criteria satisfied to commence this process? (RTM is baselined or project schedule received from customer/JBB)
4.7.1	Effort estimation	Has the PM prepared the estimates and validated with estimates in margin sheet or any other document specifying the agreed estimates with the customer?
4.7.1	Effort estimation	Has the peer review (PM) evaluated the estimates, given feedback, and ensured its assimilation in the estimates?
4.7.1	Effort estimation	Has the SM approved the estimates after ensuring that advisories have been closed?
4.7.2	Project schedule	Has the PM considered resource availability and capability in task assignment while preparing the project schedule?
4.7.2	Project schedule	Has the SM reviewed and approved the project schedule?
4.7.2	Project schedule	Has the PM communicated the project schedule to JBB/customer
4.8	PMP	Is the entry criteria satisfied to commence this process? (RTM is baselined)
4.8	PMP	Has the PM prepared the "project management plan"?
4.8	PMP	Has the SM reviewed for completeness and approved the document?
4.8.2	Risk management sheet—Updates	Has the PM tracked the risks, effectiveness of mitigation, new risks, etc., through the "risk management sheet"?
4.8.2	Risk management sheet—updates	Has the SM reviewed and approved new risks and its mitigation plans? Has the weekly status of risk been reported to the management along with the PSR?
4.8.3	Requirement traceability matrix—updates	Has the PL/TL updated the RTM as and when the other artifacts are developed and baselined?
4.9	Architectural design	Is the entry criteria satisfied to commence this process? (process step specified is approved PTD, and RTM baselined?)
4.9	Architectural design	Has the PL/TL prepared the ADD and presented the design to the technical team?
4.9	Architectural design	Has the technical consultant reviewed the ADD using the checklist, tracked advisories to closure, and recommend for approval?
4.9	Architectural design	Has the PM approved the ADD after ensuring that all findings have been satisfactorily closed?
4.9	Architectural design	Has the PL/TL made a demonstration of proof of concept model to validate the conceptualized design—to JBB/customer or to an in-house technical team? (prototype, vendor's publication on tool's capabilities and its limitations, design proofing by technical experts, etc.)

4.10	High-level design	Is the entry criteria satisfied to commence this process? (process step specified in approved PTD, and ADD is baselined?)
4.10	High-level design	Has the PL/TL prepared the HLD? Has the relevant guideline/review checklist been used while preparing the HLD?
4.10	High-level design	Has the technical consultant reviewed the HLD using the checklist, tracked advisories to closure, and recommend for approval? (Verify whether design maps to requirements.)
4.10	High-level design	Has the PM approved the HLD after ensuring that all findings have been satisfactorily closed?
4.11	Low-level design	Is the entry criteria satisfied to commence this process? (process step specified in approved PTD, and HLD is baselined?)
4.11	Low-level design	Has the SE prepared the LLD? Does the pseudocode specifies the high-level approach to program, essential reference to dlls/components, select statements, table names, function logic, etc.?
4.11	Low-level design	Has the technical consultant reviewed the LLD using the checklist, tracked advisories to closure, and recommend for approval? (Verify whether design maps to ADD, HLD, and requirements.)
4.11	Low-level design	Has the PL/TL approved the LLD after ensuring that all findings have been satisfactorily closed?
4.12	Design for customization projects	Is the entry criteria satisfied to commence this process? (Process step specified in approved PTD, and RTM is baselined?)
4.12	Design for customization projects	Has the SE prepared the custom design document? Does the pseudocode specifies the high-level approach to program, essential reference to dlls/components, select statements, table names, function logic, etc.?
4.12	Design for customization projects	Has the technical consultant reviewed the custom design document using the checklist, tracked advisories to closure, and recommended for approval? (Verify whether design maps to requirements.)
4.12	Design for customization projects	Has the PL/TL approved the custom design document after ensuring that all findings have been satisfactorily closed?
4.13	Integration test cases—definition	Is the entry criteria satisfied to commence this process? (HLD or custom design document is approved)
4.13	Integration test cases—definition	Has the SE prepared the integration test cases?
4.13	Integration test cases—definition	Has the technical consultant reviewed the integration test case document using the checklist, tracked advisories to closure, and recommended for approval? (Verify whether test scripts maps to design and requirements.)
4.13	Integration test cases—definition	Has the PL/TL approved the integration test case document after ensuring that all findings have been satisfactorily closed?
4.14	Development	Is the entry criteria satisfied to commence this process? (LLD or custom design document is sent for review.)

4.14	Development	Has the SE prepared unit test cases based on LLD/custom design document? Has standard test cases suite been used for coining test cases?
4.14	Development	Has the SE complied with appropriate coding standard?
4.14	Development	Has the SE ensured adequate identifiers for defect fix/changes?
4.14	Development	Has the technical consultant performed code review using checklist? (Verify whether code review has commenced after baseline of design documents.)
4.14	Development	Has the technical consultant performed UTC review after code review using checklist? (Verify whether unit test cases map to LLD/custom design/requirements and any enhancements identified during code review.)
4.14	Development	Has the PL/TL approved UTCs after ensuring adequate closure of the UTC review findings?
4.14	Development	Has the author of the code performed unit testing and recorded results? (Verify whether unit testing is done after code review.)
4.14	Development	Has the independent tester performed unit testing and recorded results? (Verify whether unit testing is done after unit testing by the author of the code. Track closure of all priority A issues.)
4.15	Integration—testing	Has the SE performed integration testing and recorded results in ITR and DTL?
4.16	Release management	Is the entry criteria satisfied to commence this process? (Criteria for release to system test are met as specified in the system test plan or release need to be made as hot fix to the customer.)
4.16	Release management	Has the PL/TL prepared release note and sent for approval? Is the approved release note sent to manager-test and release?
4.16	Release management	Has the PM reviewed and approved the release note? (Verify whether open issues in the release are consistent with the system test plan or a waiver obtained from manager-QAT.)
4.16	Release management	Has the PM evaluated the reported issue and assigned the issue for resolution as hot fix?
5.2.1	Program management—definition	Has manager-PEG reviewed the process tailoring document in the context of project risk in realizing its objectives?
5.2.1	Program management—definition	Has the SM approved after ensuring that all review comments are incorporated and authorizes the project team to implement the tailored process for the program?
5.2.2	Program management—updation	Has the PM reviewed and approved all revisions to apex level artifacts?
5.3	Effort tracking	Did the PL/TL update the project schedule with actual effort before the project review meeting?
5.3	Effort tracking	Do all the project members have access to project schedule to view the tasks?

5.4	Project review—planned	Is the entry criteria satisfied to commence this process? (Task planned in the project schedule.)
5.5	Project status report	Is the entry criteria satisfied to commence this process? (PSR required to be sent every week and ensure that the PM has reported project performance for the week and projected performance for the ensuing week.)
5.7.1	Presentation	Has the PM given presentation after closure of the project?
5.7.2	Knowledge base log	Has the KBL been updated with the learnings in the project?
5.8	Quantitative project management	Is the entry criteria satisfied to commence this process? (process commences at the end of last business day, for the reporting period.)
5.8	Quantitative project management	Has the PM prepared AOD and done the variance analysis?
5.8	Quantitative project management	Has the SM reviewed and presented the AOD in the MR meeting?
5.9	Clarification management	Has the PL/TL tracked the open issues in the query list and open issues pertaining to project management in MOM-external?
5.10	Change management	Has the PL/TL reviewed the CMR (IAR) for adequacy and approved the IAR?
5.10	Change management	Has the PM revised the project schedule based on effort in IAR? Has the approved project schedule communicated to JBB/customer?
5.10	Change management	Has SM reviewed and approved the project schedule?
5.10	Change management	Has PL/TL reviewed and approved the revised project artifacts?
5.11	Issue management	Has the PL/TL assessed the issue and the resolution proposed? Has PL/TL reviewed and approved the revised project artifacts?
5.12/5.13	Defect tracking	Has the reviewer logged the defects identified during review in the DTL? Have the defects been tracked and the status revised to "closed" in DTL?
5.12/5.13	Defect tracking	Has the PL/TL walkthrough the defect assessment and proposed resolution?
5.15	R&D process	Has the PM authorized the closure of the project after completion of the R&D activity?
5.16	Onsite implementation process	PL/TL tracks onsite activities through OAL. Review and approve revised artifacts.
		QAT
4.2	Estimation	Is the entry criteria satisfied to commence this process? (Business requirements received from project team.)
4.2	Estimation	Has test lead obtained all the relevant inputs (like customer's business requirements, clarity of queries, etc.) for preparing the testing effort estimate?
4.2	Estimation	Has the manager (test and release) approved the testing effort estimation document to the project team?

4.2	Estimation	Has the testing effort estimation given by QAT been incorporated in the project team's schedule?
4.5	System test plan	Is the entry criteria satisfied to commence this process? (Project team completes the requirement presentation to QAT.)
4.5	System test plan	Has the test lead considered the following factors for preparing the system test plan?- 2.a. Gaps in customer requirements and testability 2.b. Risks based on the production environment and testing environment 2.c. Reusability of the system test scripts 2.d. Delivery approach (e.g., phased delivery, UAT cycles, etc.)
4.5	System test plan	Has the manager (test and release) approved and sent the system test plan to the project team?
4.6	System test scripts	Is the entry criteria satisfied to commence this process? (Project team completes the requirement presentation to TL/TE.)
4.6	System test scripts	Has the TL mapped requirements/RTM to "requirement traceability and status report" and developed test scenarios? Has the test scenarios (system test scripts) been sent to test engineer to define test scripts based on test scenarios?
4.6	System test scripts	Has the PM provided acceptance of the "system test scripts" through email? Has the document been shared with customer/JBB?
4.6	System test scripts	Has the manager (test and release) approved STS after ensuring that defects, if any, are closed, and sent the document to project team/JBB/ customer?
4.7	System test ware revision	Is the entry criteria satisfied to commence this process? (Change request received from customer—STS needs revision.)
4.7	System test ware revision	Has the test lead made an impact analysis due to the change request and detailed in "change management record"?
4.7	System test ware revision	Has the manager (test and release) reviewed and approved the change management record?
4.7	System test ware revision	Has the TL revised the STP, TE revised STS and requirement traceability and status report, manager (test and release) reviewed and approved the revised documents and sent them to PM/JBB/customer?
4.9	System test scripts execution	Is the entry criteria satisfied to commence this process? (Tagged release made into the testing repository)
4.9	System test scripts execution	Has the TE executed the scripts and recorded findings in STS and defects in welms tool?
4.9	System test scripts execution	Has the TL managed new scripts assimilation, approval, and confirmed test findings, updated STP?
4.9	System test scripts execution	Has the TE published the test progress data in STM and DSR worksheet of "requirement traceability and status report"?
4.9	System test scripts execution—planned CRs	Is the entry criteria satisfied to commence this process? (Tagged release made into the testing repository)

4.9	System test scripts execution—planned CRs	Has the manager (test and release) discussed with the PM to decide whether the change request should follow this process or regression test process?
4.9	System test scripts execution—planned CRs	Has the TL documented the minimum set of scripts in STS and advised TE to proceed with the testing?
4.9	System test scripts execution—planned CRs	Has the TE performed the test and recorded results in STS and logged failed cases in welms tool? Has he tracked them to closure? Have new system test scripts or scenarios been incorporated as and when testing is carried out and findings recorded?
4.9	System test scripts execution—planned CRs	Has the TL evaluated the findings and confirmed the defects? Were new test scripts accepted by the project team and the test script version revised?
4.10	System test scripts execution—regression	Is the entry criteria satisfied to commence this process? (Tagged release made into the testing repository)
4.10	System test scripts execution—regression	Has the TL identified the test scripts that would validate the impacted area?
4.10	System test scripts execution—regression	Has the TE executed the scripts and recorded findings in STS and defects in welms tool?
4.10	System test scripts execution—regression	Has the TL managed new scripts assimilation, approval, and confirmed test findings, updated STP? Has the TL sent the STP and the STS to the PM?
4.12	Delivery—projects	Is the entry criteria satisfied to commence this process? (Delivery required to be made to the customer after QA testing.)
4.12	Delivery—projects	Has the TL verified that there are **no open defects**, prepared the release note and built the release?
4.12	Delivery—projects	Has the manager (T&R) reviewed and approved the release note, sent the release to customer/JBB with a copy of the communication to project team?
4.12	Delivery—projects	Has the manager (T&R) obtained consent from the PM to make a release under concession (i.e., **delivery with open issues for B & C only**)?
4.12	Delivery—projects	Has the TL prepared the release note incorporating the number of open issues and built the release?
4.12	Delivery—projects	Has the manager (T&R) reviewed and approved the release note, and has he/she sent the release to customer/JBB with a copy of the communication to project team?

Auditing and Reporting

As discussed earlier, auditing process will be a planned one. On the day of audit, it is advisable to be punctual and be present at the place of audit well on time. It is recommended that the auditor should have gone through the project management plan of the audit beforehand so that he is well prepared with the questions to be asked and the points to be discussed. However, the information being gathered during the audit will determine the course of audit questions. Using checklist as described in Table 6.5 or any modification of that, answers are noted down. This checklist not only helps to cover the focus areas but also reduces the total time spent by the auditor as well the auditee. By using checklists, more questions can be asked for focus areas rather than wasting time on less important areas and thus increasing return on time spent. The audit is considered complete when the audit team has asked all the questions and cross-referenced with all required artifacts. A noncompliance report (NCR) is issued if the evidence suggests that the project does not follow the defined processes. Also, if a weakness is found that could lead to the failure of the project later on, then NCR can be issued, as such a situation might lead to loss of control. A key fact in auditing (which also stresses during behavioral training for auditors) that audit should be conducted for processes and not for people. This approach will center around process-oriented approach rather than person-dependent result; this approach helps in process improvement in the long run. NCRs should always point at the deviation in the processes rather than the behavior of the auditee. Table 6.6 shows a sample NCR as reported after the audit process.

Table 6.6: Sample NCR

Project code	Quality system process	Severity	Status	Audit date	NCR description	Corrective action	Closure comments	Actual close date
	Maintenance process	Serious	Closed	28 Nov 02	Tracking not being performed in the project (a) Task tracking (and scheduling) (b) Requirements tracking	Tasks in the project will be tracked through MPP and DART Requirements will also be tracked under a requirements tracking doc which will be maintained in the project docs folder on the server	As the project is nearing completion, the data analyzed should be taken as inputs for similar project, which is in initiation phase Please plan accordingly	30 Dec 02

Follow Up NCRs

NCRs are not prepared to penalize any project manager, and hence mere submission of the report is not the end of the auditing activity. The report is the first step to ensure that the projects deploy the organization's approved processes, and the NCRs are used to make sure that the project manager incorporates the required changes in the project processes, which will address these discrepancies. Corrective steps must be taken against each NCR and also are recorded in the NCR report itself. These become objective evidence for the auditors as well as for the management to be assured that all the gaps have been addressed. The corrective actions, as recorded in the NCRs, are approved by the auditor and only on his approval that the NCRs are closed. The completed NCRs are then returned to all the stakeholders in the audit process such as audit coordinator, auditors, auditee, and senior management.

Hence, as is seen here, the NCRs are duly followed up by the audit coordinators so that they are tracked to closure. Follow up of the NCRs ensures that all the projects are executed with similar processes meaning that there is a consistency of process implementation and the predictability of process performances is high. NCR follow up is given a priority in all the organizations and many organizations tie up this follow-up activity with service level agreements. As, for example, some organizations ask their project managers to close the NCRs within a specified period of time from the NCR date. If a project manager fails to do so within the stipulated timeframe, the matter is taken up at an appropriate senior management level.

A typical NCR will contain (at the least) the following information:

- Project name
- Project manager name
- Auditor name
- Audit date
- Severity of NCR reported
- Reference to quality manual section
- Description of NCR
- Corrective action
- Preventive action Action by Action date
- Follow-up action approved by: Date Recommendation

Audit Analysis

Audit analysis is different from NCR in that in NCRs process-wise nonconformity for each project is reported whereas in audit analysis an organization-wide analysis is done by consolidating all the NCRS that have been reported. As a best practice, the first analysis in "audit analysis" consists of a number of audits conducted as a percentage of the total number of projects being executed. This analysis explains whether or not the sample taken for the audit process is a true representation of the entire project population. This gives confidence to the management that all possible process deviations have the chances of being corrected. Other sections in the analysis will tell the senior management as to percentages of different projects that are being carried out such as what is the percentage of the development projects, maintenance projects, and so on. This gives an indication to the management about the priorities that the management needs to take for putting the required resources for improving the processes. A section in the audit analysis also deals with categories of NCRs, such as what percentage of NCRs were related to the configuration management, project planning processes, risk management, etc. This analysis helps the management to pinpoint the area where further training could be required for process improvement. The highest incidence of nonconformity areas also indicates the area where there is a lack of understanding of the project processes.

Quality Assurance Vs Quality Control

In summary, the basic objectives of the software quality advisor's role are as follows:

- to assist projects implement defined processes

- to ensure project's compliance with projects planned process
- to assist in metrics analysis
- to help share best practices from different projects

Hence, the SQA does not become an active member of the project and does not take part in direct project activities as he/she is more concerned with quality assurance. The focus of SQA is process implementation in the project, data collection, and analysis. The activities of SQA are different from that of software quality control and thus reviews and testing are the part of roles of the team members. Quality assurance job is that of quality department, whereas quality control activities are that of line or project members. Quality assurance helps define points where quality control activities are to be carried out, which makes it a process oriented and happens as a systematic manner. In a matured organization, where processes have stabilized, quality assurance is done at the planning stage and is given more importance; this helps in planning quality control jobs and carrying out audits to find if these control activities have been carried out.

Quality assurance is associated with process. Once, processes are consistent, then assurance process "assures" that output from the processes are predictable in their quality in a consistent manner. Quality control is considered to be a controlling mechanism where output quality is compared with requirements and applicable standards, and the action taken to remedy if nonconformance is detected. Quality control uses reviews and testing to focus on detection and reworking on the defects before final delivery. Quality control is always a responsibility of the project team and is planned along with daily activities. Because of the definition, this is considered as police activity.

Activities of Software Quality Advisor

The SQA activities for a project can be broadly divided into three groups:

- Project initiation activities
- In-process activities, such as training, etc.
- Project audit activities

In project initiation activities, the focus is to familiarize with the project and check the various project plans for consistency with the quality system. During project initiation activities, the SQA helps in setting up of project plans and processes and participates in the project plan review and as a SEPG member authorizes deviation to process tailoring. The project folder is set up according to configuration management plan. In-process activities are performed according to the SQA plan. Audits are planned and performed at project milestones (e.g., end of a module, deliverable, lifecycle stage) or time triggered. It may also be done on special request by the project or senior management. The focus for project audit check is decided depending upon the current stage and requirement of the project. Different focus areas of compliance check are project planning, requirements management, configuration management, metrics management, reviews, and testing. The procedure or process followed for different work products of project is verified during compliance check on random sampling basis, for example, group review process followed for code review, etc. The compliance report should have a summary of noncompliance, specific focus area noncompliance with suggestion, severity of nonconformance, responsibility and expected date of closure as agreed. The review of the project status is done along with the senior managers as required. Internal audit is arranged for the project as per the stated policy. Nonconformances raised are tracked to closure. And the analysis of customer feedback is done for the project.

SQA participates in causal analysis and defect prevention meetings for the project as required. Periodic analysis of the project data is performed by the SQA and presented to the team. The period for metrics analysis is specific to the process type or as and when required by the project for customer presentation. During the closure phase of the project, the project leader prepares the closure report with the help of SQA and submits for review to the SQA and the senior management. The report is reviewed by the SQA and, based on the final review process, database is updated with the project data.

Status Reporting by Quality Department

For each project, the SQA will prepare a status report indicating project health. The following documents maintained by the SQA are deliverables to the quality department:

(A) SQA's plan for the project
(B) SQA's schedule for the project
(C) Log of risks and issues
(D) Any other enclosures and attachments
(E) Mail archive files

The SQA plan should have the following minimum information:

- Proposed frequency of interaction.
- Number and frequency of compliance checks and analyses planned.
- Any special activity planned by the advisor to do in the project, for example, orientation, training.
- Location of files, documents maintained by the SQA for the project. Directory name with complete path is recommended. This should synchronize with the overall group CM plan.

A typical status report from the SQA will look like as follows:

1. SQA plan

Project-wise activities carried out with date

Project initiation
Project plan review
Configuration management plan review
Compliance check
Metrics analysis
Audits
Project closure

Training

Training conducted by the SQA

Project-wise audits conducted with dates
(Audit reports from different projects)

2. Project-wise risks

A log of issues has to be maintained. The format would be as follows:

Date	Issue no.	Issue addressed to	Issue description	Open/closed	Review date	Remarks

3. Other deliverables

Other enclosures and attachments are as follows:

- All compliance reports
- Data analysis reports
- Survey records and reports, for example, team satisfaction survey
- Any other reports that the SQA has prepared for this project
- Filled-in checklists for project plan review, project schedule review, and CM plan review are mandatory
- Training records

Table 6.7 shows some of the SQA activities.

Table 6.7 SQA activities

Kick-off period
Provide orientation on quality system to the PM
Provide templates for project plan and CM plan
Provide necessary checklists and standards
Give orientation guidelines for estimation
Provide inputs on effort, defects, etc., from PDB and PCB
Provide inputs on checklists, standards, and other information from process assets database
Assist in project plan preparation
Assist in estimation process
Assist in risk management
Assist in process tailoring
Ensure that requirements change management process is set
Assist in establishment of traceability
Study project proposal
Assist in project plan preparation
Assist in CM plan preparation
Project plans review and project set-up activities
Arrange a group review of project management plan and CM plan
Review project plan as part of team
Review CM plan
Ensure that all issues raised during group review are addressed and closed
Discuss training gaps and training plan; arrange or provide training as required
Check compliance of project schedule with the project milestones
Ensure proper set up of data collection tools (WAR/DART and RADAR) and other required tools

Assist in proper setting of WAR/DART codes in MSP
Assist in setting up defect collection tool as per QSD guidelines
Organize group review training for those who have not attended
Prepare SQA plan and share with the PL and communicate to GPM and DM as required
Plan frequency/schedule for regular checks, metrics, and CM audits
Review SQA plan with GL
If the PM was not part of the requirements team, check whether the PM has reviewed the requirements and project scope, and negotiated with BM appropriately
Participate in DP kick-off meeting
Perform continuous activities in the project
Do planned compliance checks and other planned project meetings
Do planned metrics analysis
Check if planned CM audit are being done
Ensure that project plan, schedule, checklists, standards, program-level tracking, and other documents (like traceability doc) are updated, if required, based on the analysis and feedback
If deviation is too large, ensure that proper action is taken
Ensure causal analysis is conducted as per schedule and defect prevention action is taken as appropriate
Participate in causal analysis and DP kick-off meetings as required
Participate in project closure activities
Assist project for preparation of closure report
Ensure all best practices are collected in the closure report
Perform root-cause analysis on the deviations from quality goals
Review and analyze project metrics, submit for independent review, group leader review, and authorization; update PDB for project data and baseline the report
Review process assets submitted by projects, e.g., project management plans, schedules, standards, checklists, templates, causal analysis reports, customer feedback, etc.
Pass tools-used info to the tools coordinator, capture in closure report, and ensure BOK submission
Summarize and update SQA folder and archive as per group CM plan

SUMMARY

In software industry, two aspects are important from process maturity point of view—process definition process and process audit process. The process definition process is considered to be essential to process maturity; however, without a proper and effective audit process, effective implementation and degree of compliance cannot be guaranteed. This is because process implementation and compliance with the defined processes are not easy and have to be ensured through audit process. Different reasons have been cited for the tendency of not to follow the processes—sometimes the inertia to change from existing process becomes a deterrent to process implementation. Team members also try to take shortcuts and reduce or eliminate processes; this they believe will increase productivity. But in the end, the project lands in carrying a lot of rework while addressing customer complaints. Processes also improve transparency, which again is resisted by many team members, making process compliance a big challenge. For all these reasons, audit helps in improving the degree of compliance.

Audit process has three stages—planning, auditing and reporting, and following up for closing NCRs. Audit planning is done to see that the maximum number of projects is covered. In order to achieve this, a strategy is adopted for selecting projects for audit so that all the lifecycle stages are covered and the management gets good knowledge about the health of different projects. The process of auditing should be carried out with the intent to help in improving compliance level and share best practices from other projects rather than in fault-finding mission. If any noncompliance is found during the audit; an NCR is prepared and it is followed up to the closure. Once corrective action is taken and implemented in the project, NCR is considered to be closed.

DISCUSSION POINTS

1. What is meant by quality?
2. Why audit is necessary in software projects?
3. Describe the lifecycle for process definition.
4. Why quality assurance is important? How is it different from quality control?
5. What are the differences between internal and external audit?
6. What are the points that need to be considered while planning for audit?
7. Give examples of audit strategy.

CASE STUDY

INFPL is a software services provider in different domains such as telecom, banking, finance, insurance, and healthcare. It uses offshore development process to meet customer requirements. Recently, they bagged a project ABC0013 in banking domain. It was a 25-member team and had a schedule of 7 months for delivery. After 2 months of starting the project, it was audited by the internal auditors. Following results were recorded during the audit process:

1. The auditor was interviewing a developer. He asked to see the requirements and design specifications. He was shown the system requirement specifications (SRS) for ABC0013. The auditor noticed several handwritten amendments made in pages 3 and 7. The developer claimed that he had made the changes after being instructed by the project manager. The project manager confirmed this and said that he had raised this issue in a telephone conference call with the customer just last week and had received oral permission to go ahead with the changes. He thought it a waste of time waiting for written confirmation from the customer. However, as per the communication protocol in the project management plan, it is clearly warranted that written communications should be available for effecting any change in the code.
2. The project had elaborate training plan to train its members in domain as well as technology. As per the project plan, all the training requirements for the team members should be identified and the team members should undergo these training. The auditor asked to see the training records of the project team members. The PL explained that the records were with HRD, but profiles of the team were in the project plan. On seeing the relevant section, the auditor noticed that two people working in the project had no training in the new technology. The project manager explained that they have been nominated for the next offering of the training program. This was scheduled to be held in a couple of weeks.
3. While looking at the project schedule, the auditor noted that the request on which work was being done was marked as completed. The PL said that a simple change had come in on the same maintenance request. The auditor then asked if the schedule covered all work being done. The PL replied in the affirmative. The auditor then asked what documentation came with a request. He was shown the incoming mail log. On going through the register, the auditor observed that quite a few similar requests were not considered in the schedule.
4. During the audit, it was found that there were many software being used in the project that were not mentioned in the project management plan. He found that developers were using various software packages, including games and data manipulation software.
5. During discussion, the project manager informed that the customer is a highly technical person and does not believe too much in process. At many instances, the interactions between the customer and the project team are highly informal. The customer requests for changes are very common and the project team always incorporates them without going through detailed documentation as needed by the process. This, the project manager explained, is to reduce the time taken for delivery. But, at the end of the release the project team could not meet the scheduled release date and many bugs were reported during testing at customer site. But to the great surprise the customer blamed the project

team entirely for the delay and the poor quality. The project team felt that the customer was unreasonable since the delay was mainly due to incorporating the changes requested by the customer. As the customer was not particular about the quality processes, the team had skipped most of them, which attributed to poor quality. But it was their words against the customer and in the end the customer is always right.

As an auditor of the project, please examine all the audit results explained above and determine if these are considered as nonconformance and the reasons for the same.

Hints to case studies:

1. Yes—In the specification for ABC0013, amendments were noticed in pages 3 and 7, which should have been reflected in the master copy; however, these amendments were not incorporated in the master copy as confirmed by the project manager.
2. Yes—In the project plan it was noticed that two people in the project were assigned to tasks requiring training in Oracle. However, they had not been trained in Oracle, which was confirmed by the PL.
3. Yes—It was noticed that the current request was not in the project schedule, whereas it was required that all deliverables and tasks were to be scheduled. Examination of the project mail log showed that several similar small requests were not scheduled.
4. May be.

7

Risk Management

LEARNING OBJECTIVES

In this chapter, the students would learn:

- Identifying risks
- Quantifying risk exposures
- Mitigation plans for risks
- Risk mitigation plans
- Information security risks

Introduction

Risk is defined as any condition that will have an unfavorable impact on the desirable outcome of the project. A risk is not a certainty but a concept and denotes the probability of eventualities. This implies that any project may fail. The reasons for the failure could be myriad—such as the lack of effective project management, team members' attrition, customer changing his/her requirements quite often, and so on. Project management has to take care that the project does not fail due to poor management. Risk management tries to reduce the chances of failure for any of these reasons by planning mitigation well in advance.

In a software project, risk is not certain but has a probability of occurrence, and when the risk occurs, it will affect the desired outcome in an unfavorable manner. In other words, a risk has three elements: (1) the chances of risk occurrence (degree of probability), (2) the amount of impact it will have on the project, and (3) the equivalent amount of monetary impact to the project budget. Through risk management, these risks are identified and actions are taken to reduce their effect on the project.

Risk Management

The first step in risk management is to identify the possible risks (e.g., failure of link line to customer machines) and to assess the consequent losses in achieving the project objectives. Once risk assessment is done, a risk management plan with a detailed mitigation plan can be developed. Hence, risk management has two steps, namely, risk assessment and risk control.

1. Risk assessment involves activities such as
    - Risk identification
    - Risk categorization
    - Risk prioritization
2. Risk control involves activities such as
    - Risk management planning
    - Risk monitoring and tracking

Risk assessment activities such as risk identification, categorization, prioritization, and risk management planning are done during the project initiation and execution. Risk control activities such as risk monitoring and tracking are done during the project execution.

Risk Management Process

Risk management process, as discussed earlier, consists of activities such as identification, categorization, prioritization, planning, and tracking of risks. The entire process can be well understood from Figure 7.1.

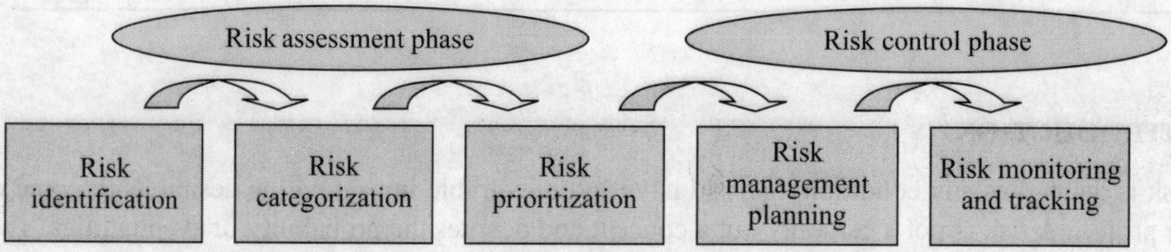

Figure 7.1: Risk management process

Risk Identification

This activity involves identification of all the risks that are applicable to the project and may hinder in achieving the project's objectives. Sources for identifying project risks can be identified both by the team internal to the project and by the team external to the project. The project team may find the list of risks for the project from different sources such as risk database available in the enterprise risk database; risks from similar projects executed in the past; risks identified in the proposal/contract/master service agreement of the project; assumptions made in the proposal, which have a likelihood of becoming a risk; risks specific to the project, that is, decisions made in the project such as design choices, choice of tools, deviations or tailoring related, etc. However, there could be sources for finding these risks from other sources as well such as during quality review, senior management review, etc.

Risk Categorization

Once risks are identified, they need to be categorized; the objective of this activity is to enable logical categorization of risks so as to identify relevant stakeholders in the project and involve them in reviewing/mitigating the risks. Categorization of risks helps in identifying the relevant stakeholders so that they can be involved in mitigation planning and implementation from the beginning. Risks are categorized as risks related to business/domain, communication, customer, environmental/natural cause, infrastructure, people/personnel/HR, project management, quality processes and technology, etc.

Risk Prioritization

This is a step that involves prioritizing the risks using quantitative techniques. The objective of this activity is to prioritize the risks identified based on risk exposure and re-prioritize them based on its impact on the project's cost, schedule, and the goals. This will enable the project team to focus the utilization of resources on the key risks that have been shortlisted for mitigation. The idea behind this approach is to make sure that the available resources are used optimally. The risk prioritization is first done to determine the probability of occurrence of risks (see Table 7.1) and its impact on the project output. This explains the severity of risks as perceived by the project team manager. Impact explains the degree to which project outputs are affected by the occurrence of each risk element.

Table 7.1: Risk probability

Probability range (%)	Severity	Impact
10–20	Low	1–3
30–60	Medium	4–7
70–90	High	8–10

Using values as indicated above, risk exposure is calculated as risk exposure = probability of the risk × impact. Using risk exposure numbers, rank the risks in descending order so that top risks are given priority and management efforts are spent in mitigating those risks. Now these prioritized risks are tabulated and cost of risk occurrence is calculated. Table 7.2 shows a sample risk prioritization plan for a software project.

Table 7.2: Sample risk prioritization plan

Lifecycle stage	Risk category	Risk description	Probability	Impact	Risk exposure	Schedule impact (person days) (*A*)	Cost impact due to schedule (₹) (*B*)	Other costs (₹) (*C*)	Cost of risk (₹) [*D*=(*B*+*C*)]	Cost of risk mitigation (₹)	Risk status/ priority (*S*)
All	People/ personnel/HR	Manpower attrition resulting in schedule impact	0.9	6	5.4	7	700	1000	1700		1
Testing	Infrastructure	Lack of infrastructure in time to simulate the business scenarios	0.4	8	3.2	10	800	800	1600		2
All	People/ personnel/HR	Low motivation to work on specific platforms	0.6	7	4.2	NA	NA	NA	NA		3

Using the cost of risk, risks are prioritized and given serial numbers, which will indicate the level of priority. Using these prioritized risks, the cost of mitigation plans is allocated to different risks. Using the cost of mitigation, a managerial decision is taken whether to stay with the risk or carry the mitigation plan. For example, if the cost of risk is ₹900 and mitigation plan is ₹1500, then the management may take a decision to stay with the risk rather than mitigate it. Sometimes the impact of risks could be higher and may not be quantifiable. For example, because of a particular risk occurrence, if there is loss of face with the customer, then it could have greater impact in future. In such cases even if the cost of mitigation plan is higher than the cost of risk, still risks are mitigated keeping in mind the relationship with the customer.

Risk Management Planning

This activity is part of risk control phase where the objective is to identify mitigation steps/ contingency plan for all the risks and to manage the risks by implementing them so that any adverse impact on the project's goals are avoided. Hence, risk mitigation steps are nothing but the plan of action to be implemented to mitigate the risks. The steps involved in this activity are identifying mitigation steps for all risks and articulate these risks clearly and plan for mitigations that would reduce the impact of risks triggering deployment of contingency plan. These risk mitigation steps can be arrived at by using the mitigation plans for similar risks in the enterprise risk database; depending on project characteristics, these can be customized and used after due changes. Then, calculate the cost of risk mitigation and prioritize and identify risks that can be accepted.

In this phase, risks are classified at each risk level or at category of risk, such as resource related, function/department related, technology related, etc. Once this classification is done, mitigation plans are detailed out with minute details. For each mitigation plan, the cost is calculated using these minute details, and then these costs are summed up to find the total cost of that mitigation plan. If the cost of mitigation plan is greater than the cost of risk, then the risk can be accepted and the team will stay with the risk. Hence, some risks are accepted and no mitigation plan is deployed. Thus, risk acceptance can be considered in situations where the total cost of mitigation for all the risks is greater than the revenue impact of the risk on the project, then some risks can be considered for acceptance. In such cases, senior management should approve the risk plan.

During the risk management planning phase, roles and responsibilities of all the stakeholders are defined so that risk mitigation steps are executed on time. The project manager is responsible for overall risk management, that is, identification of risk mitigation steps, monitoring risk, and tracking of risk. Once the risk management plan is finalized, it should be reviewed and approved by the senior management and appropriately communicated to all the team members. These responsibilities should be the part of assigned tasks in the project management plan so that detailed activities are tracked and monitored. As a best practice, these activities have to be monitored on a continuous basis as a part of milestone reviews.

Using the example in Table 7.2, a complete risk mitigation plan with proper risk mitigation plan will be similar to that of a sample shown in Table 7.3.

Table 7.3: Sample risk mitigation plan

Lifecycle stage	Risk category	Risk description	Probability	Impact	Risk exposure	Schedule impact (person days) *(A)*	Cost impact due to schedule (₹) *(B)*	Other costs (₹) *(C)*	Cost of risk (₹) *[D=(B+C)]*	Cost of risk mitigation (₹)	Risk status/ priority *(S)*	Mitigation steps *(K)*
All	People/ personnel/ HR	Manpower attrition resulting in schedule impact	0.9	6	5.4	7	700	1000	1700		1	Ensure that backup resources are available for key project areas Maintain proper documentation of individual's work.
Testing	Infrastructure	Lack of infrastructure in time to simulate the business scenarios	0.4	8	3.2	8	800	800	1600		2	Coordinate with CCD at early stages of project and get commitment. Take consultancy help from E&R on infrastructure for testing.
All	People/ personnel/ HR	Low motivation to work on specific platforms	0.6	7	4.2	NA	NA	NA	NA		3	PL to engage in active conversation with team members on technology and future prospects.

Risk Monitoring and Tracking

Risk monitoring and tracking phase deals with the monitoring of risks and tracks them to completion. The aim of this phase is to ensure that status of risks are tracked and monitored to manage current risks. During periodic review, the project manager should review the status of risks and should also find out whether the mitigation plans have been executed as per the plan. The manager will assess the effectiveness of the risk mitigation at identified milestones and appropriate actions are taken. As part of monitoring and control activities, the project manager should assess whether the risk exposure is negligible and whether the risk does not recur during downstream lifecycle stages. The manager needs to update the risk management plan as per actuals. Also, the manager needs to watch out for the risks that have been mitigated already may arise later. Hence, he/she should continue to review the status for such risks till the project closure. If there is an occurrence of additional risks, then they should be identified and risk mitigation steps need to be planned and executed accordingly. The status of risks is to be continuously tracked/reviewed using regular status reporting mechanism. This monitoring should continue till the project ends; after that risk database will be updated at enterprise level so that the next project can benefit from the experience.

Enterprise Risk Database

As a best practice, every organization should maintain risk database. This database will use learning from different projects and hence is constantly updated after the closure of a project. The database should have role-based access and should not be visible to the entire organization. The database should be maintained by an administrator who would ensure that a process is followed for downloading and uploading risk elements. The administrator, in consultation with quality and risk department, must design a process so that consistency can be maintained in categorizing risks and approach used for finding the cost of risk elements. A sample template for maintaining the risk database is given in Table 7.4.

Table 7.4: A sample template for risk database

S. no.	Risk category	Risk description	Mitigation steps suggested

SUMMARY

In this chapter, we learnt that risk is a situation that may happen during the course of project execution, but the certainty of the risk can only be forecasted, but not with entire accuracy. The risk, when it actually materializes, can adversely affect the project goals. The chapter discussed the general concepts of risk management, which included risk identification, risk mitigation, and process to manage risk. Risks are identified and then are prioritized based on the amount of impact it could have on the project goals. The amount is quantified based on the monetary impact that the risk can inflict. Risk database is created so that a new project manager does not have to reinvent the wheel and can make use of past knowledge in risk management. After identifying the risks, based on the probability and the corresponding monetary impact, the risks are listed down. The mitigation plans are then decided and a managerial decision is taken whether to mitigate the risk or let it happen. This decision is taken based on the cost of the mitigation plan vis-à-vis impact of the risk. However, many times the project management decides to mitigate the risks even if the risk impact is not high. This is done for better customer relationship management. Each and every risk should be tracked and monitored for effective project management.

DISCUSSION POINTS

1. What do you understand by risk management?
2. How do you mitigate risks?
3. Give an example of quantifying risks in terms of monetary value.
4. How do you carry out risk audits?
5. What is the usefulness of risk database?

CASE STUDY

Airosonic Travels Pvt. Ltd. (http://www.corporatetravels.in/)

Objective

The objective of Airosonic Travels Pvt. Ltd. company was to develop an e-commerce web application, which would enable the corporate customers to book air tickets, hotels, car rentals, and holiday packages online without the need of a travel agent.

Overview

For over two decades, Airosonic Travels Pvt. Ltd. brand has been synonymous with travel in the local market with an endeavor to provide the customers with specialized and immediate solutions to all travel-related innovative holiday solutions. It is established as a provider of superior quality tailor-made offerings, which have satisfied many customers across the country and overseas. With a vision to indelibly reinvent the business of corporate travel in the country, Airosonic wanted to develop online travel services, **http://www.corporatetravels.in** services that characterize the dawning of a new era, which would witness a paradigm shift in the corporate travel scenario. This could also be to meet their myriad travel requirements for employees, vendors, dealers, end users/customers, etc., that is in the form of incentives for your employees as a part of their HR package or an award to your faithful customers to boost their brand loyalty.

Airosonic was incorporated in the year 1988. The primary business is air travel ticketing, tour packages, hotels, car rentals, cruises, and leisure holidays. It has offices in Panjim (Goa), Anjuna (Goa), Mumbai, Bangalore, and Sydney (Australia). Airosonic group has tie-up with major airlines, hotels, and tour operators around the world. Airosonic has acquired the globally preferred airline reservation system Galileo with state-of-the-art computers having the latest operating system/software, round-the-clock net connectivity, facsimile facility, and up-to-date telephone system. Airosonic business deals with retail and corporate travel management services catering to domestic and international travelers, including hotels, car rentals, insurance, foreign exchange, etc. In the financial year 2008–2009, the company achieved a turnover of ₹ 24 crores.

Achievements

Airosonic has been awarded several awards by most of the leading airlines in India for the highest sales performance. Airosonic Australia was awarded the BEST CBD CORPORATE TRAVEL AGENCY by Australian Federation of Travels Agents (AFTA) in 1999. Airosonic Australia launched its out-bound tours to the Indian subcontinent with professionally tailor-made brochures and marketed India as tourist destination by networking through Australian tour operators and travel agents. In the year 2000, Airosonic by joining hands with Singapore Airlines–Silk Air and Government of India Tourist office, Sydney, marketed Kerala brochures showcasing Kerala in grand style. Airosonic has simultaneously launched brochures in India to promote Australia in the Indian travel market.

Airosonic Holidays in Mumbai has tie-ups with top 30 corporates of India for their corporate conferences, domestic as well as international. Last month Airosonic has been awarded the

"Best Tour Operator Award" by M/S Johnson & Johnson India. Airosonic Australia has close association with the media and has played a crucial role in hosting the famous Australian TV channel Channel 9's GATEWAY program about India, which was telecasted on the National Network for one full year. During this period Airosonic gained wide publicity for its packages to India. Airosonic has been retained as one of the top tour operator for DESTINATION INDIA by the Government of India.

Director's Profile

Mr. Pramod Rane, chairman/managing director, has more than two decades of airline and travel industry experience with world-renowned airlines like British Airways, Northwest Airlines, and Kenya Airways. Mr. Rane was general manager for British Airways GSA for Western India (offices in Mumbai, Ahmedabad, Baroda, Surat, Pune, and Goa) from the year 1979 to 1988. He has been awarded the highest sales performance awards in the Indian subcontinent by British Airways.

Mr. Rane was managing director for Northwest Airlines GSA for India from the year 1989 to 1997 and was managing the whole airline operation in India. He is actively involved in Australia–India Chamber of Commerce in building the business growth between Australia and India. Mr. Rane has been awarded the NATIONAL PLATONIC TOURISM AWARD for the year 2004 from Australia Tourism for the highest contribution for the nation.

Problem Definition

Develop an e-commerce web application, http://www.corporatetravels.in/, to meet the objectives of Corporate Travels.

Customer perspective:

- The website should provide information on the tourism packages available.
- The customers should be able to browse through the packages and pick and choose them.
- Provide information on the cost involved.
- Confirm the bookings by making the payments through debit or credit cards.
- Website should be up and running 24 hours with no or minimal downtime.

Administrator perspective:

- Able to update the information on existing packages
- Able to add new package information

Risks and Challenges

Airosonic had no prior experience in IT or software development. It had no IT department in the organization. If it had to develop application in-house, then it has to find the expertise in the software development and IT. Following are some of the challenges and risks identified by the organization/management for this e-commerce software project:

(a) *IT department*—starting an IT department would involve

  (a) *Recruitment of senior person*—As the company or the management had no prior experience in this field, it had to recruit a senior person who runs the IT department.

(b) *Recruitment of software programmers*—As this is a travel company, it was a **risk** finding senior software engineers and pay more money than any other IT companies to attract him/her to work for a travel company.

(b) *Location and business*—Attracting good programmers was also **challenging** because of

- *Location*—Bangalore is an IT hub and many multinational companies (MNC) are in Bangalore and pay more competitive salary/money.
- *Nature of company/business*—Bangalore software programmers' mentality preference is to work for an IT company than for a travel agency company.

(c) *Setting up IT unit on time*—As Bangalore is an IT hub, it is difficult to attract talent because of competition, and ramping up team was a challenging task within given time frame.

(d) *Managing attrition*—As attrition rate was high in Bangalore for IT, keeping the talent for 2 years continuously was a big challenge and risk.

(e) *Space and other facilities management*

- Having an IT department with another 20–30 people would require bigger space.
- Current space was not enough to accommodate the same and hence had to find another facility for IT wing, which adds to the cost.

(f) *Budget*

- Although the company had business plan with a well-defined ROI, it had budget constraints.
- Budget of setting up a new IT department within the company was becoming more expensive than the budget allocated.

Resolution

Although developing the software and launching the e-commerce web application, http://www.corporatetravels.in/ would have significant risks and costs beyond the budget, the management decided to **distribute the risks** in the following ways:

(a) Outsource software development to a third party (**ProWeb**)

- A software company was identified who are well versed with developing travel-related e-commerce web application with a cost that is well within the budget.

(b) Outsource software project management tasks to another company (**e-Infra Software Solutions**)

- As Airosonic had no prior IT experience or knowledge, it decided to outsource the project management tasks to a consulting company who have expertise in software project management.

(c) Point of contact was assigned from Airosonic Travels Ltd. for requirement clarifications, conducting progress reviews, and final acceptance testing.

Following are the assignment for each of the parties involved in developing this web application:

ProWeb—design, development, and testing

(a) Document the requirements with screen shots and get the review signed off from Airosonic
(b) Design and develop the website
(c) Provide the detailed design document
(d) Carry out the required pre-acceptance tests (both functional and performance during integration, system tests, etc.)
(e) Provide a report of bugs detected and fixed
(f) Carry out the acceptance testing as per the acceptance test plan provided by Airosonic
(g) Fix the bugs found out during the acceptance tests and get it verified by e-Infra
(h) Carry out the production setup, installation, and pre-live tests. Provide "go live" green signal
(i) Provide technical support during maintenance phase after going live (6 months)

e-Infra Software Solutions (project management)

(j) Manage software development activities
(k) Review contractual agreement
(l) Coordination of the project (design and acceptance phase)
(m) Develop the project plan with schedule for the intermediate milestones and key milestones
(n) Conduct weekly progress review meetings with ProWeb and provide status reports to the customer (Airosonic)
(o) Carry out the acceptance test and verify the bug fixes
(p) Website and production management
(q) Provide maintenance support for the live website in terms of fixes to any functional issues

Airosonic

(r) Provide single point of contact (SPOC) for the entire project
(s) Sign off on the requirements document
(t) Provide required inputs during the development, acceptance, and live (production) phases
(u) Participate in the acceptance test reviews
(v) Make available all the resources needed for production setup
(w) Monitoring the overall project progress and report to all the stakeholders

Conclusion

As the risks were distributed, it became easier for the individual parties/companies to manage their respective risks and not to worry about the overall project risks. Also, a dedicated company, e-Infra Software Solutions, was assigned for the software project management and this has significantly reduced the software management risks. However, only risk that Airosonic had to monitor and manage was to monitor and review the overall project progress. The "distribution of risk" has significantly saved time and money for Airosonic and it successfully launched its online business, http://www.corporatetravels.in/, on time and well within the budget. Now this website is fully operational and has future plans to add more international sectors and also has the vision of becoming one of the leading and prominent organizations in travel industry focusing global destinations in the tours and holiday package market.

Questions:

- It is well understood that when the company subcontracts the development activities, there is loss of revenue, margin, and control. What is the need to outsource software development activities in this case?
- Does this case throw similarities with off shoring IT development work to India by the US corporates?

8

ACQUIRING SOFTWARE PROJECTS: RFP TO CONTRACT

LEARNING OBJECTIVES

This chapter will introduce the readers with the processes and the activities involved in bidding/winning a software project and the nuances of getting into a contractual obligation for software project completion.

In this chapter, the students would learn:

- Why software development is done as projects and what are the reasons to outsource?
- Types of software projects
- Processes involved in awarding a software project contract
- Introduction to RFP, RFQ, and RFI
- An insight into writing a winning proposal for a software project
- Contract and statement of work (SOW)—a high-level understanding

WHY SOFTWARE DEVELOPMENT IS DONE AS PROJECTS AND REASONS TO OUTSOURCE?

Before getting into the details of how to select and award a software project to an IT service provider and those of writing successful proposals to win software projects, it would be very important to recap a little background on the software development lifecycle and the reasons for undertaking software development assignments as project activities versus traditional operational activities.

All software projects are always conceived as a consequence of a business or strategic demand. Be it the need for a new software application to automate a business process in an enterprise, developing a software product as a result of technological advancement, or even writing the software to manage and control a space shuttle, all software applications or products are designed and developed once and are used thereafter throughout its life as long as the business demands.

One can divide the entire life of a software application or a software product into two main parts. The first part involves the time spent in creating the software, and the second part consists of the duration within which the software is put into use until finally it is sunset by the user community. The first part of the software lifecycle can be termed as the creation phase and the second part as the maintenance phase. Maximum effort and resources are invested in the creation phase, whereas some ongoing efforts and resources are spent continuously to maintain the software. In the creation phase, the software application or the product is conceived, designed, and developed from a high-level business requirement to well-functioning software. While in the maintenance phase, the created software undergoes changes, corrections, enhancements based on new user preferences, etc., throughout its life.

As all software is developed because of a business or a strategic need, there is always a sense of urgency associated with this to complete the same within a stipulated time frame along with possible imposed cost constraints. These are known as project triple constraints in the project management parlance. The three project constraints are scope (the exact work that needs to be done), time, and cost (see Figure 8.1). There are two additional constraints, namely, quality and stakeholder satisfaction. A successful project is one which gets completed on time, within cost, meets all the quality parameters, and satisfies all the project stakeholders. All the projects and hence all the software projects are bound by constraints.

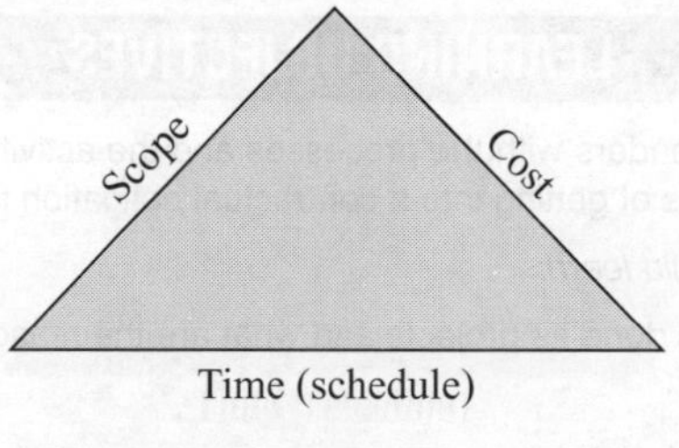

Figure 8.1: Project constraints

Outsourcing a Software Project

Typically, there are primarily two types of software projects: one developing/implementing a new software from the scratch and the second involving minor or major changes to an existing software. The organization or the user who feels the need for specific software application or product or changes to existing ones conceives the requirements and features of the software and then typically either assigns the task to a software development team within the organization or awards the assignment to an outside software development organization. Most of the business organizations prefer to focus on their core business functions and decide to outsource or entrust the job of doing all their IT and software-related activities to external and very competent IT consultancy and service provider organizations.

The various constraints (scope, time, cost, quality, etc.) associated with all software projects make it imperative for the project-awarding organization (known as purchaser or client) to carefully specify the project requirements and also diligently choose the software development team either internal or external to the same organization, typically known as a seller (of service or product). In any case, the purchaser typically follows a structured process to select and award the project to a competent internal group or an external organization. The project award is typically bound by a contract and the contract clauses in turn ensure that the project constraints are explicitly addressed and forced upon the seller. We will discuss this process in more detail in the subsequent part of the chapter.

Types of Software Projects

Software projects can be classified into different ways. One good way to look at different software projects can be based on the nature of software work involved, technology associated with the projects, and the associated business domains. Table 8.1 shows the different types of software projects.

Table 8.1: Types of software projects

Types of software development	Technologies	Domain
• Application development • Application maintenance and support • Product development • IT infrastructure support • Migration and re-engineering • Product implementation • IT strategy and roadmap	• Legacy (mainframe, AS 400) • Client server (C, C++, VC++) • Web technologies (J2EE, .Net) • ETL and OLAP tools (BI and DW) • ERP, SCM, and CRM • Embedded systems	• Banking and finance • Insurance • Retail • Energy and utility • Auto • Healthcare • Hi-tech • Aerospace

The list in Table 8.1 is only indicative and the classification described gives a fair idea about the types of software projects. Many other types can be added to the above list based on the technologies and domains.

Processes Involved in Awarding a Software Project Contract

Typically, a purchaser or a client organization adopts the following steps or processes to diligently select a qualified software services provider who can successfully undertake and complete the software project:

- Plan purchases and acquisitions (conceive and consolidate requirements)
- Plan contracting (prepare an RFI or RFP for sellers)
- Request seller responses (sellers prepare and submit their proposals)
- Select sellers (client organization evaluates proposals and selects a seller)
- Contract administration (prepare a contract and use it throughout the project cycle)
- Contract closure

As the business need to develop software originates from the purchaser or the client organization, it becomes the responsibility of the client organization to explicitly define the business need for the project, the objectives those must be met by successful project completion, the detailed features and functionality expected from the software under consideration, scope of work, time to complete, cost constraints, quality and stakeholder expectations, etc. In other words, the purchaser (client) organization must know what they want and must be able to clearly convey the above information to the seller or service-providing organization. Typically, the client organizations use various tools such as request for proposals (RFP), request for information (RFI), and request for quotations (RFQ) to convey their needs to the prospective sellers or service providers and solicit required responses from the sellers. These tools are generally known as procurement documents.

A purchaser uses an RFI when it is only looking for gathering preliminary and important information such as software development processes, available resource pool, financial statements, list of clients, and past project experiences of the seller organization. An RFI from a client will include a list of questions about the seller organization in above lines and will not contain the details of the specific project requirements. Typically, an RFI is used by the client organization to do a first-level assessment and short listing of sellers.

However, in an RFP, the client provides more detailed project requirements and solicits a much wider response from the sellers as compared with an RFI. RFPs are used by the client organizations to request detailed proposal from the service providers who would ultimately manage the software project, if awarded. As the RFP will contain all the possible information about the requirements of the software project, the business need, and the detail structure/format/questionnaire of the proposal expected from the seller, in many cases of complex software requirements the client organization may even engage another consulting organization to help them prepare the RFP document. Hence, RFP documents typically are very structured with detailed information on the expectation. While preparing an RFP document, the purchaser (client) organization faces the biggest challenge in clearly specifying the requirements and features of the software that will be created or enhanced as the part of the project. This is because of the intangible nature of the software application or product.

Many times the client organization may use another tool called RFQ to solicit specific commercial rates such as the cost of a software product, rates of skilled IT resources, etc., as may be required for a project. Generally, any procurement document must have information on (i) relevant SOW, (ii) description of the desired format of the response, (iii) required contractual obligations, (iv) relevant dates and deadlines, and hence forth. The SOW provides details of the work to be done as a part of this project assignment.

The purchaser or the client organization manages the entire procurement activities, starting from consolidating their business and software requirements to floating tenders and inviting proposals from interested sellers to finally awarding a contract to the selected seller, as a set of coordinated project activities. Figure 8.2 depicts this aspect by showing that there is planning, executing, controlling, and closing activities in the entire process.

Typically, the purchaser organization floats RFI, RFP, or RFQ document and solicits responses from interested bidders. The purchaser may use a combination of these documents as well. The purchaser structures these documents to facilitate an accurate and complete response from each prospective seller and also to facilitate easy evaluation of bids submitted by the sellers. The complexity and the level of detail of the procurement documents should be consistent with the value of, and the risk associated with, the planned purchase or acquisition. Procurement documents are rigorous enough to ensure consistent, comparable responses from the sellers but flexible enough to allow considerations of seller recommendations for better ways to satisfy the requirements.

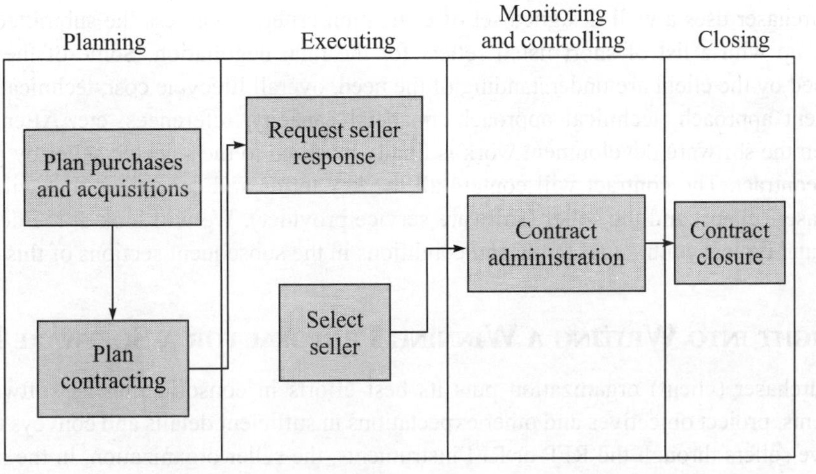

Figure 8.2: Different phases in RFP process

The purchaser (also known as buyer) organization formally issues request to potential sellers to submit a proposal or a bid by floating tenders or notifications in newspapers, magazines, on Internet, and by using some of the above-mentioned procurement documents. These documents will list the important dates by which the proposals have to be submitted. The purchaser organization also organizes something known as bidder's conferences before the final proposal/bid submission date in order to formally invite all the sellers and clarify any queries pertaining to the proposal raised by the sellers. The idea is to provide all clarifications so as to facilitate the sellers to provide most apt proposal addressing the buyer's needs.

Figure 8.3 depicts the flow and relationships between the activities followed by a client organization to source and select a competent software development organization.

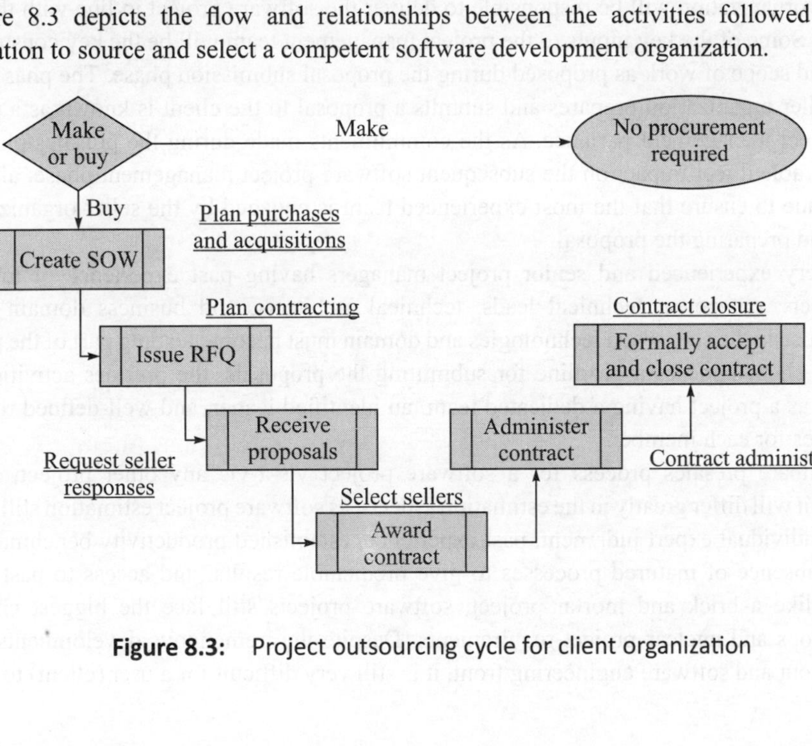

Figure 8.3: Project outsourcing cycle for client organization

The purchaser uses a well-designed set of evaluation criteria to assess the submitted proposals and come up with a list of short listed sellers for the final negotiation. Some of the evaluation criteria used by the client are understanding of the need, overall lifecycle cost, technical capability, management approach, technical approach, financial capacity, references, etc. After successful negotiation the software development work is finally awarded to the selected seller by getting into a formal contract. The contract will contain all the key terms and conditions that will bind both the purchaser (client) and the seller (software service provider). We will look at the details of the contracts and typical contractual terms and conditions in the subsequent sections of this chapter.

An Insight into Writing a Winning Proposal for a Software Project

As the purchaser (client) organization puts its best efforts in consolidating its software project requirements, project objectives and other expectations in sufficient details and conveys the same to prospective sellers through the RFP or RFI instruments, the seller organization, in the same spirit, has to put its best resources and efforts to understand the client's requirements and prepare a proposal addressing all the project needs.

The seller (software services providing organization) complies with the purchaser's requests (RFP, RFI, RFQ) by carefully understanding the requirements and expectations of the client and by suitably providing proposals, quotations, and necessary information addressing the needs of the purchaser. The seller organization, if selected by the client, will ultimately do the software development by managing the whole activities of a project; the seller organization has to take utmost care while preparing the proposal. The time, cost, and other performance-related commitments proposed by the seller organization will then become binding to them during the project execution phase.

The seller organization will be responsible to deliver the software project in line with the client expectations. Some of the key inputs to the project management team will be the key constraints of time, cost, and scope of work as proposed during the proposal submission phase. The phase during which the seller organization prepares and submits a proposal to the client is known as a presales phase in project management parlance. As the commitments made during the presales phase will have considerable direct impact on the subsequent software project management phase, all efforts should be made to ensure that the most experienced team is engaged by the seller organization in estimating and preparing the proposal.

Ideally, very experienced and senior project managers having past experience of managing similar projects, competent technical leads, technical architects, and business domain experts having expertise in the concerned technologies and domain must become leading part of the presales team. As the client imposes a deadline for submitting the proposals, the presales activities itself are managed as a project having a dedicated team, an identified leader, and well-defined roles and responsibilities for each member.

If we compare presales process for a software project vis-à-vis any other project, such as construction, it will differ greatly in the estimation aspects, as software project estimation still heavily depends on individual expert judgment, past experience, established productivity benchmarks, the presence or absence of matured processes to give predictable results, and access to past project histories. Unlike a brick and mortar project, software projects still face the biggest challenge from ambiguous and unclear project requirements. Despite the tremendous developments on the technology front and software engineering front, it is still very difficult for a user (client) to exactly articulate and define the requirements of a software application or product that they want. The onus thus passes to the service provider's presales and software project management team to extract and clearly understand the requirements before making any proposition. The difficulties in clearly stating the software requirements can make it tricky for the bidding organization to estimate the efforts accurately and stand by the same. Furthermore, these days most of the clients ask for something called fixed bids for the entire project development and even topped with penalty clauses in case of any delay or failure. This really adds tremendous amount of responsibility and accountability on the presales team to ensure that they do not overestimate to minimize risks and also do not underestimate in their zeal to win business at any cost.

Once the appointed presales team receives the tender documents, the most important thing they need to do is to very quickly come up with a bid/no-bid decision. The presales team must carefully evaluate the RFP document and assess if their organization have the necessary expertise, resources, and past experience to successfully take up such a software development project. Looking at the long-term impacts, it may be very important to say "NO" to bid for a project, if the presales team will feel so. More important will be to convey the decision for not bidding to all stakeholders, once taken by the team. In reality, it has been observed that many times the presales team end up bidding and finally taking up some projects, while they should have said "NO," mainly because of organizational pressures. The organization culture should be open enough to encourage honest assessment and decisions.

Once decided to bid to an RFP, the presales team then gets into a project management mode to prepare the proposal itself. At this stage, the team may further acquire additional resources to help them to address the RFP. Typically, the entire team addressing an RFP and preparing a proposal work in a collocated and very coherent manner. A project plan is prepared with detailed activities and their completion dates. The activities are assigned to different members of the presales team. Typically, proposal preparation happens under very tight schedule pressures. It is at this stage where the seller organization will be preparing and making a commitment for future software project completion on time and within cost.

As mentioned earlier, the absence of clear software requirements can really make the presales activities very tricky and challenging. If the tender documents do not provide all project information clearly, the presales team then must ask all possible relevant questions to the client to bring the required clarity and understanding of the project requirements and expectations. Most of the clients or purchasers have a provision in their RFP schedule for a bidders conference to address and clarify all queries pertaining to the RFP requirements.

Typically, a proposal will be a detailed and well-structured document containing responses to each and every questions and requirements of the client as mentioned in the RFP document. The format and details of a proposal will directly depend on the size and complexity of the requested software project. Irrespective of the type of software project under consideration in the RFP, generally the proposal format can be as mentioned below.

The main sections of a proposal should have the following:

- **Executive summary**: This is the first and the most important section of the proposal. This section gives a bird's eye view of the important aspects of the proposal such as timelines, cost with references to specific sections, and henceforth. The objective is to provide the most senior executives with a quick summary of the proposal.

- **Introduction**: This section is generally used to provide all relevant information about the seller organization.
- **Scope of work**: This is the most important section of the proposal. This section enlists the understanding of the project requirements, the scope boundaries, what is included in the scope, and what are excluded from the scope to bring all clarity. This section also provides the client with an idea about what the selling/bidding organization has understood about the requirements.
- **Proposed technical solutions**: This section depicts the details of the recommended technical solution. This will include the proposed technologies, tools, and the technical architecture for the solution to be used for the project.
- **Major deliverables**: This section enlists the project deliverables at the end of each project phase. This is very important to measure the work in progress of the project and shows the client different project milestones.
- **Project schedule and resource plan**: This is typically a Gantt chart showing the start and finish of various project phases and milestones. This section may also provide a resource matrix by aligning the project phases with resource requirement at each phase.
- **Project costs**: This section provides the overall commercials for undertaking the project. This also includes high-level terms and conditions related to the pricing and payments.
- **Assumptions and dependencies**: This is one of the most critical sections of the proposal and requires great attention by the proposal writing team. In many cases, in the absence of clarity in specifying the exact requirements by the client organization, the proposal team has to make suitable assumptions for arriving at the proposed solution, time, and cost. There may be many dependencies, which will have direct impact on the project's schedule and cost. All such assumptions and dependencies must be very carefully articulated and enlisted in the proposal.
- **Project risks and constraints**: Risks come from uncertainty, imposed constraints, assumptions, and dependencies. Risks in any project are bound to be there. It is very important to identify these risks very early and assess their impact on the project's schedule and cost. The impacts of these risks should be appropriately factored in the proposed project schedule and cost. At this stage, the intention of the presales team would also be to convey the client that they are well equipped to successfully handle these risks, if they occur.
- **Development strategy and approach**: This section specifies the proposed software development methodology and project phases that will be adopted for this project. This also includes the organizational processes (CMM or CMMI), which will be followed for the development phase. The proposed development approach should address the mitigation of any risks related to technology and development process.
- **Project management approach**: Adopting a structured project management will be crucial for successfully completing the project. Gradually the project environments are becoming more and more complex. The project teams, which will include the client members also, are geographically spread out and work from multiple locations. Some of the important aspects addressed here are project team structure, roles and responsibilities (of client and seller organization), communication and escalation mechanism, project control mechanisms, change management procedures, status reporting procedures, and document formats.

- **Project handover**: Post development and implementation of the developed software, the developed code, documents, training manuals, etc., need to be handed over to the client organization. This section also addresses the training needs, if any, for the users of client organization, who will ultimately be using and maintaining the developed software.
- **Appendices**: The specific details about the seller organization such as financial statements, customer references, history of past project experiences, sample formats of the tools, and templates to be used during the project are added as a part of the annexure.

There is a great deal of relationship between the proposal document as prepared above and the detailed project management plan, which is subsequently prepared after winning the project. Both the documents mention about the scope, cost, time, management approach, and henceforth. But the major difference is the fact that the amount of information available regarding scope at RFP stage is very high level and minimal, whereas in a project management plan, the scope is sufficiently elaborated. If the proposal is accepted by the client organization, then the presales team will hand over the proposal to the project management team to carry forward and execute the project. The high-level estimates of time and cost submitted by the presales team during the bidding phase has to be reasonably accepted by the software project management team for subsequent execution. The software management team has to comply with the commitments made during the presales phase with minor and reasonable adjustments based on the clauses of the proposal. This very fact demonstrates the seriousness and need of expert judgment and proven estimation and project management experience to be used during the presales phase.

Most of the matured software services providers such as Infosys, TCS, Wipro, Accenture, and EDS will have well-defined processes to guide the presales team in every stage of proposal preparation. These processes typically will establish various guidelines, templates, and checklists to be used across the organization during the proposal preparation phase in order to adopt a standard approach, standard proposal structure, and also to ensure predictability of successfully winning the submitted business proposals. Most of the matured organizations also maintain a repository of all RFPs received and the proposal responses submitted with an analysis of win/loss for each RFP and reasons thereof. Hence, the organization's process and proposal repository become a very critical reference for successful proposal preparation.

Best Practices in Writing a Winning Proposal

It is extremely important to understand the mindset and the psychology of the client with regards to their expectations while evaluating a proposal submitted by a prospective seller. The client, while assessing a proposal, typically will look for the following from the seller:

- Responsiveness (am I getting what I need?)
- Competence (can they really do it?)
- Cost factors (does the pricing represent good value?)

Hence, the presales team while preparing a proposal must focus on providing:

- a clear evidence of understanding the client's requirements,
- a recommendation for specific solution,
- an evidence of their competence to deliver on time and within budget, and
- compelling reasons to choose their recommendation over any others.

It is believed that every client requirement is unique and hence deserves unique proposition to be made. An unambiguous and well-documented section of "our understanding of your requirements" in the proposal response provides the first and the most comfort feeling and confidence to the prospective client while assessing a proposal. More so because the proposed solution, project timelines, and approach will only become successful and credible if the understanding of the requirements were very clear. The proposal team hence should seek all possible clarifications by sending relevant questions pertaining to the requirements from the client. Rest of the response in the proposal will automatically fall in place if the bidding organization has the right resources and experience to handle such projects.

Following is a list of sacred best practices proposed by Tom Sant for preparing a winning proposal:

1. **Never title your proposal "Proposal"**: As one never titles a book "Book," the same philosophy applies here. A title should be stating a benefit to the client.
2. **Focus on your client's business needs or mission objectives first**: Mirror what you have heard from the client before offering a solution. This shows that you have listened and understood their needs and pain areas and you have considered the client's interests before proposing a solution.
3. **Avoid lengthy corporate histories**: No one is interested!
4. **Eliminate jargon**: Avoid using technical jargons as the proposal may be evaluated by many senior executives who may not be conversant with the lower lever technical jargons and may only be interested in the solution fit and return on investment (ROI). If at all required, one can use the jargons commonly used and referred by the client members.
5. **Keep your proposal as short as possible**: Control the temptation to throw anything and everything into the proposal that might be of interest, because in reality the decision makers won't read all of this. They will generally skim through this. A short proposal is more likely to be read first. And other proposals will be read in comparison to this. One of the winning proposals from a leading IT services company had less than 15 pages in its main body with a deal value of $ 150 million.
6. **Highlight your key points**: As the decision makers like to skim through the proposal, it will be a great idea to highlight the main ideas and make the document "skimmable." Use bullets, headings, boldface type, color, border, graphics and any thing else that will make key points to come out very visibly.
7. **Quantify your benefits and pay back**: It is always a winning idea to show the tangible benefits such as monetary savings, increase in productivity, etc., which the client organization will derive by acceding to implementing this project and accepting your proposed solution. Effort should be made to show the ROI for the client.
8. **Prioritize your organization's unique differentiators**: List and prioritize your competitive advantages by specifying your organization's strengths and if possible tie them to ROI.
9. **Ghost the competition**: The competitors must be very well known. Their strengths and weaknesses must be well researched by the presales team. If you know about the weaknesses of your competitors, raise issues in your proposal that will strike their weak points. Do not take their names. For example, if you know that their processes have failed to protect the IP rights of a client, then make a fuss about how important it is to protect IP rights and how your organization has a clean record on this.

10. **Ask for their business**: Ask for it in the cover letter, in the executive summary, and when you deliver or present the proposal. Being passive does not work. You have to ask for the business.

Every proposal is unique. The more RFPs one addresses and more proposals one writes, he/she will gradually develop the art of writing winning proposals. As already mentioned, it is always a team consisting of various experts, who can successfully prepare great proposals.

Contracts and SOW—A High-Level Understanding

Each RFP will contain a section that is typically referred to as a contract statement of work (SOW). A contract SOW defines in sufficient detail the scope of the entire software project or a specific portion of the project scope, as the case may be. The information provided in an SOW is provided in a structured and detailed fashion so as to allow each prospective seller to determine if they are capable of providing the requested project item or service. An SOW may include information such as software functional specifications, technical performance specifications, quality levels, performance data, period of performance, work location, service level agreements (SLAs), etc.

A contract SOW is written clear, complete, and concise. The contract SOW can be revised and refined as it moves through the procurement process until incorporated into a signed contract. The changes in the SOW can be proposed by the client or the seller during the process to bring in more and more clarity.

A contract is awarded to each selected service provider who will carry out the requested software development on behalf of the client.

There are various types of contracts to be chosen based on the business need, culture, and the risk-taking abilities of both the purchaser (client) and the seller (service provider). Some of the broad categories of contracts are as follows:

- Firm fixed price
- Fixed price with economic adjustment
- Cost reimbursable contracts
- Cost plus incentive fee
- Cost plus fixed fee
- Time and material contract

Figure 8.4 illustrates the risk spectrum involved for both buyers and sellers in contracts.

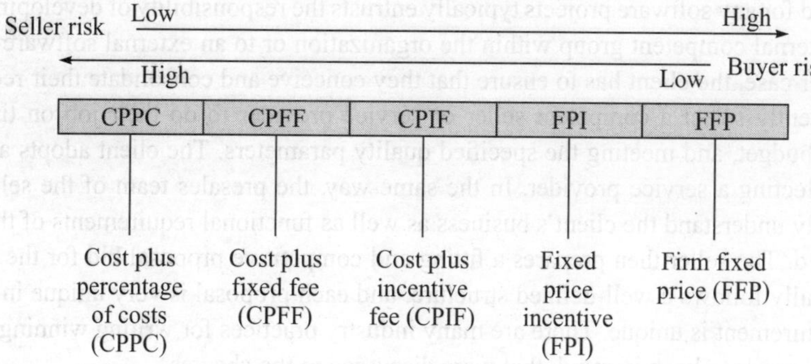

Figure 8.4: Risk spectrum in contracts

Structure of a Contract

Most of the contract documents will have various sections, which will be generic. The content and clauses of the contract document will be a reflection of the client requirements given in the RFP and the terms proposed by the seller in the proposal. Following are some key sections, which will be integral to any contract document:

- Scope of work
- Project deliverables
- Schedules of deliverables and agreed upon milestones
- Project progress reporting and project status review mechanisms
- Communication and escalation mechanism
- Change management process
- Acceptance criteria
- SLA, if any
- Nondisclosure agreement (NDA), if any
- Penalties for late delivery
- Project cost
- Payment terms, payment schedule, credit period, etc.
- Warranty clauses
- Termination clauses

A contract is a mutually binding legal agreement that obligates the seller to provide the specified software product, services, or results and obligates the buyer (client) to pay the seller. A contract is a legal relationship subject to remedy in the court in case of any disagreement or dispute. A contract document will generally include the SOW, schedule with important milestone dates, period of performance, roles and responsibilities, pricing and payment conditions, inflation adjustments, if any, acceptance criteria, warranty, product support, SLAs, limitation of liability, fees, penalties, incentives, insurance, performance bond, change request handling mechanism, termination and dispute handling mechanism, and hence forth.

SUMMARY

Software development activities are carried out as projects. The business organization (client) having the need for any software projects typically entrusts the responsibility of developing the same either to an internal competent group within the organization or to an external software consulting house. In either case, the client has to ensure that they conceive and consolidate their requirements and very diligently select a competent seller or service provider to do their job on time, within the stipulated budget, and meeting the specified quality parameters. The client adopts a structured process for selecting a service provider. In the same way, the presales team of the seller ensures that they clearly understand the client's business as well as functional requirements of the software to be developed. The seller then prepares a fitting and competitive proposal bid for the client. The proposal typically follows a well-defined structure, and each proposal is very unique in its content since each requirement is unique. There are many industry practices for writing winning proposals, which a bidder needs to keep in mind, that were discussed in the chapter.

DISCUSSION POINTS

1. When should you outsource?
2. What are different types of software projects?
3. Describe the process of awarding a software project.
4. What are different phases in RFP process?
5. What are the main sections in an RFP?
6. What is the significance of SOW?
7. What are best practices in writing a proposal?

CASE STUDY

Background

XYZ Corporation, which is a leading IT services provider, receives an RFP from ABC Corporation to submit a proposal for their new software development needs.

The Department of Ports, Department of Customs, and the Department of Free Trade Zone of the government of a developed nation got merged as per a new government notification to provide business benefits and integrated services to the community of Cargo and Transportation Industry of the nation. The new merged entity is known as ABC Corporation. ABC Corporation has multiple business portals to serve its customer community consisting of a wide range of importers/exporters, shipping agents, freight forwarder, clearing agents (brokers), and free zone licensees. As per earlier provisions, each business unit (port, customs, and free zone) has its own business portals to serve its customers. To present a unified service to the customer community, ABC is planning to merge its multiple business portals to a consolidated corporate portal. The current requirement of ABC is to consolidate a corporate portal to make it an e-hub to combine all the services offered in the current business portals and to establish itself as an e-service provider for the trade and transportation industry. ABC provides the below information as part of an RFP and seeks a proposal from software development and consulting organizations to satisfy their needs.

Present scenario in ABC Corporation

ABC at present is providing services to their different customer segments through the existing portals, which in turn uses the various backend application and utilities. Following are the few limitations of the present systems infrastructure that needs to be addressed in order for ABC (as the new single entity) to provide better services to its customers:

- Existence of multiple independent portals and multiple websites for business units with very limited interfaces between portals and websites.
- In current scenario, there is no mechanism to have unified customer identification across the business units, and also there is no uniform customer access mechanism.
- A very basic content management tool for the portals and websites is available, which is restricted to uploading and publishing through a Microsoft Access database for direct HTML pages.
- No uniform security measure due to heterogeneous underlying application systems (OS, database, web architecture, web servers, etc.).
- There is no consolidated bill presentment facility.
- Payment gateway facility is not available currently with the existing portals.

Current system details and technologies are shown in Table 8.2. The individual portals are developed using different middleware/application servers such as .Net and J2EE and having difference databases such as Sybase, SQL Server, and Oracle.

Table 8.2: System details and technology

Component	Free zone portal	Port authority portal	Portals for agents	Customs portal
Presentation layer	JSP 0.9, HTML	JSP 0.9, HTML	ASP (VB Script, Javascript), HTML	ASP (VB Script, Java Script), HTML
Web server	Netscape Enterprise Server 4.0	Netscape Enterprise Server 4.0	IIS 4.0	IIS 4.0
Business layer	EJB 1.0, Servlets 2.1, Netscape Application Server 4.0	EJB 1.0, Servlets 2.1, Netscape Application Server 4.0	VB DLLs on MTS	VB DLLs on MTS
Databases	Oracle 8i, Sybase 11.5	Oracle 8i	SQL Server 7.0	SQL Server 7.0
Authentication	LDAP	LDAP	NT Domain Authentication	NT Domain Authentication
Operating system	Open VMS 7.2.1, Solaris 5.7	Open VMS 7.2.1, Solaris 5.7	NT 4.0	NT 4.0
Development tool	JDK 1.1.7, Netscape Application Builder Dreamweaver 3.0	JDK 1.1.7, Netscape Application Builder Dreamweaver 3.0	Microsoft Development Studio	Microsoft Development Studio
Messaging	None	MQ Series 2.0	None	MQ Series 2.0

ABC corporation's new functional requirements

To build a corporate portal for consolidating the existing business community and customer segments so that the company can achieve better focus on customer needs, highest level of customer satisfaction and improving the efficiency of the services provided by ABC Corporation. In order to achieve these, the corporate portal must have the ability to move business data between the portals, websites, and multiple business applications. To achieve the above business objectives, ABC Corporation, as the merged single entity, is looking to have the following functionalities in the corporate portal:

- Unified customer access (single sign-on to all portals and underlying backend applications)
- Profiling (role-based profile for internal and external users)
- Bilingual support for user interfaces, data entry, and reports
- Robust content management tools of state-of-the-art technology
- Consolidation of bill presentment
- Incorporating a payment gateway
- Providing EDI interfaces migration to the new corporate portal
- Scalability and flexibility in terms of collaboration with other portals (specialized transportation industry standard portals such as INTTRA, horizontal e-market places like Tejari, and other local e-government portals)

Scope of work

ABC Corporation currently requires an efficient and experienced vendor such as XYZ Corporation to undertake an extensive study to understand their requirements and propose a cost-effective and efficient solution roadmap to build the proposed corporate portal.

ABC Corporation is expecting the following work products as deliverables from the proposed study:

- System requirement analysis document (URD)
- System delivery specification document (SRS)
- System technical design document (HLDD)
- System technical architecture diagram with suggested integration technology platform
- Implementation plan (A detailed plan with schedule to implement the corporate portal based on the above technology platform and the above-mentioned software documents such as URD, SRS, HLDD, etc.)

Proposal content to be submitted

A detailed commercial proposal is to be submitted addressing all the above need as mentioned in the scope of work section. The proposal should provide a fixed-bid pricing to complete the work as mentioned above excluding the actual implementation of the corporate portal.

XYZ Corporation, who is a renowned IT services provider, submits its proposal for the above RFP and wins the contract for the project.

Questions:

1. What should be an ideal presales team structure for addressing a complex software development RFP like the one mentioned in the above case from ABC Corporation?
2. Prepare your understanding of the work (scope) that needs to be done under this RFP.
3. Why estimation becomes a challenge during the course of addressing an RFP from a client?
4. What are the challenges the presales team will face while addressing the above RFP and how should the team handle such challenges?
5. What should be the solution approach (both technical and management) for the above RFP?
6. What kind of contract should ABC Corporation choose if they are not sure of what exactly is required?
7. What kind of contract the client should choose when they know very clearly what they want as a part of the software assignment and are also technically internally capable?
8. Which contracts are most risky for a seller? Which type is most rewarding? What contract type should XYZ Corporation choose for the above requirements of ABC Corporation?
9. What approach XYZ Corporation should take to address this RFP?
10. Enlist the different sections of the proposal to be prepared for the above RFP.

9

Case Studies on Benchmarking Practices on Productivity

LEARNING OBJECTIVES

In this chapter, the students would learn:

- Internal benchmarking practices
- External benchmarking practices
- Assessment of these practices

Understanding Benchmarking

External benchmarking initially was driven by the need to improve efficiency by learning from competitors. In manufacturing sector, such benchmarking exercise was systematically used in 1940s, 1950s, and later. However, organizations ordinarily were not willing to provide data to their direct competitors but were not hesitant to provide such data to an industry association if they could get similar data from such associations about their competitors. Such industry association could be used to collect data from the competitors. In doing so, they perceived mutual benefit or win–win situation between themselves and their competitors through exchange of data.

In software industry, instead of industry association, independent forums do this job of data collection and provide such data to their members. Three such forums that are active in data collection are as follows: Metagroup (www.metagroup.com), SPIN (Software Process Improvement Network) Hyderabad (www.hydspin.org, 2005), and SPIN Bangalore (www.bspin.org, 2005).

External Benchmarking Using Metagroup Data

Metagroup was set up in 1979. The objective of the group was to provide benchmark data for different industries such as manufacturing, retail, information technology (software), and telecom. In 1979, Metagroup was taken over by Gartner Inc. (www.gartner.com, 2005), a renowned research firm that has interests in carrying out benchmarking through original research and publishing results from different studies. Metagroup and Gartner together offer the combined brainpower of more than 1200 research analysts and consultants who advise executives in 75 countries everyday. They publish results of original research annually and answer more than 215,000 client questions every year. As of March 2005, they have more than 10,000 customers worldwide.

Many software companies use data from Metagroup for benchmarking their performance. Metagroup maintained data on different software companies with domain-wise classification such as banking, insurance, and finance and project-wise classification such as development, maintenance, and product. Data were compiled by Metagroup based on different metrics such as productivity, schedule variation, and effort variation. In the present case, Metagroup data consisted of 107 software development projects in banking and financial sector, which were collected from organizations in different countries such as the United States (59 projects), the United Kingdom (19 projects), India (29 projects), and so on. Metagroup also collected data on 98 maintenance and 63 products but these were not used, as the present study was only on software development projects.

These data were taken as representative of development projects in general as there was a fair amount of representation from different organizations. Productivity was measured as the ratio of function point to person month. Domain-wise productivity for these domains culled from such data has been shown in Table 9.1.

Table 9.1: Domain-wise productivity for software development projects

Domain area	Development productivity in FP/person month
Banking, finance, and insurance	12.40
Telecom	10.74
Retail	14.55

External Benchmarking by SPIN Bangalore

One of the forums for providing benchmark data is SPIN Bangalore. This forum was formed when some of the IT organizations in Bangalore came forward to share their metrics data such as productivity, effort variation, schedule variation, and so on, through a common independent forum. Their objective was to benchmark their performance against the best performance in the industry. SPIN Bangalore had 10 benchmarking partners, namely, MindTree, Motorola, Lucent, Philips, Honeywell, Novel, HP, HPS, Wipro, and Logica. These companies provided their data related to size, defects, cycle time, effort distribution, productivity, and cost of quality (COQ) from 53 software projects completed in 2003.

As the scope of the project was to collect data for development projects only, the report published by SPIN Bangalore on development projects was considered. In collecting data, the following criteria were used by SPIN Bangalore:

1. The data were for development projects that had a schedule of 190 days with a variation within 10%.

2. Projects that used only C, C++, Java, VB, and VC++ technologies were considered.

Only those projects that provided detailed data on all the phases were considered for this practice. Results of benchmarking obtained from SPIN Bangalore are represented in Table 9.2.

Table 9.2: Results of SPIN Bangalore benchmark data

Metrics	Development
Productivity (LOC/staff day)	72
Defect density (defects/KLOC)	6.5

External Benchmarking by SPIN Hyderabad

Hyderabad SPIN is a nonprofit professional group and is a part of International Software and Systems Process Improvement Network (www.sei.cmu.edu, 2005). Hyderabad SPIN (www.hydspin.org, 2005) has been founded by a group of practicing software professionals in the second half of 1995. The group organizes knowledge-sharing lectures, newsletters, e-groups, presentations, and discussions, thus contributing to software process improvement. The knowledge is shared by the professionals from the software development organizations in the Hyderabad city and by eminent people during their visit to Hyderabad from other cities and countries. The participating members are from different software development organizations in the Cyber City in Hyderabad. The member participating organizations are from software industry located in Hyderabad, such as Wipro, Satyam, Motorola, Intergraph, Orbitech, Tanning, Baan, Visual Soft, CETE, Danlaw, Divine, Softpro, CMC, Sierra Optima, Duncan Infotech, and so forth. These companies have their head office or development center in Hyderabad. It also has academicians representing ESCI, IPE, Osmania University.

In 2002, Hyderabad SPIN conducted a benchmarking study at industry level. The objective of this benchmarking study was to derive industry benchmarks for the software industry, gather the best practices, and help organizations in their process improvement efforts. The organizations that participated in the exercise were Baan Info Systems India Ltd., Divine India Ltd., Duncan Infotech, Infotech Enterprises, Motorola India Electronics Ltd., Orbitech Solutions Ltd., Satyam Computer Services Ltd., Sierra Atlantic, Softpro Systems Ltd., Tanning Technologies Ltd., and Wipro Technologies Ltd. The scope for this benchmarking study was to benchmark productivity levels, defect rates, COQ, and effort distribution. Definitions of these variables are given in Table 9.3.

Table 9.3: Variable definitions by SPIN Hyderabad

Size	KLOC (non-commented, non-blank statements)
Defects	From system test, integration test, reviews (requirements, design, code) From self-unit test not counted; defect density is measured as defects per KLOC
COQ	Sum of prevention cost, appraisal cost, and failure cost, where Prevention cost is the sum of training and planning efforts Appraisal cost is the sum of review/inspection and testing efforts Failure cost is the sum of rework, re-review, and re-test efforts (Unit of COQ is expressed as percentage of total project effort)

Productivity	Expressed as LOC/person day
Total project effort	Includes efforts on requirements, analysis, design, coding, testing, project management, configuration management, and reviews and project-specific trainings
Cycle time	Elapsed time from project kick-off to release; expressed in calendar days

Benchmarking Approach

Eleven companies participated in benchmarking exercise and provided data for 50 projects. These projects were categorized as web applications development, embedded systems, and client server based. To maintain consistency in data collection, questionnaires with guidelines for filling and definitions of variables were also sent to these respondents. It took 17 person days to collect data from different project managers and again 12 person days to analyze the data collected. All selected projects were categorized into three categories. The first category was web-based projects that used Java, ASP, JSP, and HTML languages. The second category of projects was embedded software projects, which were developed using special hardware or where combinations of both hardware and software were used for development. The third category of projects was client server category in which client and server components are clearly visible, with predominantly data processing focus; projects were developed using SQL, Oracle, distributed processing methodology, or any other RDBMS. Results obtained from SPIN Hyderabad are presented in Table 9.4.

Table 9.4: Summary of SPIN Hyderabad benchmark data

Metrics	Web applications	Embedded systems	Client server
Overall productivity (LOC per day)	33	54	196
Defect density per KLOC	6.2	6.0	3.0
COQ (percentage of total effort)	41%	47%	35%

Appraisal of Benchmarking Practices in External Forums

1. The benchmarking partners had apprehension that confidential data related to their projects may be leaked out to the outside world. As each benchmarking partner was legally bound to its respective customers for maintaining confidentiality, it took quite some time for the independent benchmarking forum to collect project-related data. Data were finally provided by benchmarking partners without disclosing sensitive information related to the project.
2. It was a time-consuming affair for collecting data in external forum and required a great amount of persuasion to supply data.
3. Different partners used different technology for developing applications. This became a problem for standardization of size, which was measured in terms of lines of code. To address this problem, Caper Jones' table (www.ifpug,org, 2003) was used for converting LOC-based productivity to function-point-based productivity.
4. Forums differ from each other in providing data for different metrics. In SPIN Hyderabad, data on COQ, defect density, and productivity were available, whereas in SPIN Bangalore, COQ data were not available. In Metagroup, only productivity data were available. It is observed that same comparable metrics are not available in all the forums, which made it difficult for companies to use the data from forums for benchmarking.

External Benchmarking Practice in JNV Software

JNV Software Inc. is a leader in providing software applications in remittance and payment processing area in banking industry and has been in existence for the last 25 years. The organization had revolutionized the image-based payment processing industry by providing simple-to-install and easy-to-maintain software applications that are capable of meeting specific customer needs. These products are developed using the software development model that allows the organization to meet change in requirements with optimized cost. The customer profile includes organizations from regional and money-center banks, insurance companies and mutual funds, credit card and student loan processors, telecom, utilities, government, and nonprofit and commercial organizations.

In the remittance and payment industry area in banking domain, in 2005, JNV had 75% market share in the United States. There are five other organizations, although small in size, which also develop similar products. JNV developed about 50 software applications that had more than 1200 functionalities, which are also known as "features." An example for feature is sort pattern or extracts, which are used by the end users for business transactions. For estimating the effort required to develop these features, the organization used past data from the completed projects. However, for the features for which the organization did not have prior experience, it depended on outside data and followed external benchmarking practice. Here, one such case of external benchmarking is presented. In this case, the software to be developed was a recognition engine application in image-based payment processing area. The size of the application to be developed was of 3700 function points and 24 features, and the target customers were in image processing industry such as banks, passport office, retail industry, and so forth.

External Benchmarking Approach

With regard to benchmarking, the organization selected five competing organizations in the remittance and payment area, and the head of operations in each organization was contacted. After obtaining the willingness from these organizations to participate in benchmarking practice, separate non-disclosure agreements (NDAs) were signed. A task force was set up with the head of quality, the head of operations, and the head of computer department as members. This committee explained all the 24 features as stated in the last paragraph to each of these five organizations. Table 9.5 shows the details of these features and explanations. The names of five organizations have been withheld to maintain confidentiality.

Table 9.5: Guidelines for defining level of complexities in features

S. no.	Required features	Complexity level				
		1	2	3	4	5
1	Sort pattern—total number of modes (each mode has to be classified based on the complexity level as per the guidelines)	Singles EO COW SO Page Works	Image Page Works Multiples Standard Modes with custom data entry, custom stagers	Image Page Works with ICR Recognition Standard modes with custom data entry and custom stagers	Image Page Works with ICR and form recognition	Not applicable

2	Sort pattern—total number of work sources	Standard flow	Number of data entry formats ≤ 2	Number of data entry formats > 2 and ≤ 4	Number of data entry formats > 4 and ≤ 6	No of data entry formats > 6 and ≤ 8
3	Sort pattern—customization (custSpg changes)	Custom CDV changes	Creation of new functions to be used in sort pattern	Not applicable	Not applicable	Not applicable
4	Extracts (porting ExtGen)	Simply extract with standard database fields output	Output from custom fields like the user data fields, look ups	With custom coding	With field map, sorting	With field map, sorting and grouping
5	Extracts (new ExtGen)					
6	Extracts (porting Dextract)	Direct porting without any modification	Code has to be re-looked or optimized	With sorting	With sorting and grouping	Not applicable
7	Extracts (new Dextract)	Simple extract requirement	Transaction-based requirements	With sorting	With sorting and grouping	Not applicable
8	Custom coding (porting for data entry modules)	An entry for each function point. Custom hooks already exists, code can be ported without any changes and a good understanding of the requirement	An entry for each function point. New custom hooks has to be created	An entry for each function point. Code has to be re-looked or optimized	Not applicable	Not applicable
9	Custom coding (new for data entry modules)	Already existing custom hooks	New custom hooks have to be created	Complex routines with transaction processing logic	Not applicable	Not applicable
10	Exports (porting)	Simple with direct porting	Custom image handling requirements	Custom image handling requirements as a service instead of an application	Not applicable	Not applicable
11	Exports (New)	Simple	Custom image handling requirements	Custom image handling requirements as a service instead of an application	Not applicable	Not applicable

12	PRF reports (Porting)	Simple direct porting	With sorting	With sorting and grouping	Not applicable	Not applicable
13	Crystal reports (New)	Simple	With sorting	With sorting, grouping and subtotal	Complex reports with image printing requirements	Not applicable
14	Data entry application (porting)	Simple direct porting	Different data entry formats, conditions and validations, coding has to be rewritten or optimized	Complex image handling requirements	Multiple screens, complex image and transaction-based data entry requirements	Not applicable
15	Data entry application (New)	Simple direct coding	Different data entry formats, conditions, and validations	Complex image handling requirements	Multiple screens, complex image, and transaction-based data Entry requirements	Not applicable
16	Custom stager (porting)	Simple direct porting	Code has to be re-looked or optimized	New code has to be written in addition to porting to cater to the requirements	Complex logic like transaction processing, applying balancing logic from variance spg, print, merge stager	Not applicable
17	Custom stagers (new)	Simple direct coding	Performance-based stagers	New code has to be written in addition to porting to cater to the requirements	Complex logic like transaction processing, applying balancing logic from variance spg, print, merge stager	Not applicable
18	Track driver changes (porting)	Simple direct porting	Code has to be re-looked or optimized	New code has to be written in addition to porting to cater to the requirements	Complex logic like pocket sorting, auto batching	Not applicable

19	Track driver changes (new)	Simple direct coding	Performance-based coding	Complex logic like pocket sorting, auto batching	Not applicable	Not applicable
20	Custom modules (porting)	Simple direct porting	Code has to be re-looked or optimized	New code has to be written in addition to porting to cater to the requirements	Complex processing logic, service application	Not applicable
21	Mark sense (new)	Number of zones for one sort pattern ≤ 4 (the units has to be specified based on the number of sort patterns)	Number of zones > 4 and ≤ 6	Number of zones > 6 and ≤ 8	Number of zones > 8 and ≤ 10	Number of zones > 10 and ≤ 12
22	Custom module (new)	Simple direct coding	Performance-based coding	Complex processing logic, service application	Not applicable	Not applicable
23	ARC Integration	Only forward flow	Both forward and returns flow		Not applicable	Not applicable
24	Check 21 – IQA, IUA	Only C21 extract	C21 extract with IQA\IUA	C21 extract with IQA, IUA	Not applicable	Not applicable

Each feature was categorized on a scale of 1–5 based on the level of its complexity. Category 1 represents the least complex situation, whereas category 5 represents the most complex situation. Table 9.5 describes conditions or activities that determined the level of complexities in each feature. For example, in item no. 12, the required feature (PRF reports, porting) was taken as complexity level 1 when development team needed to carry out only simple data porting, whereas if PRF reports (porting) requires sorting and grouping, then complexity level was taken as 3. There were no categories 4 and 5 for this required feature since no scenario could be visualized in which complexity could be categorized as 4 and 5. However, for the "feature" for which the development team was quite confident that there could be scenarios with all levels of complexities [for example, feature extracts (porting ExtGen) and extracts (new ExtGen) as in item nos. 4 and 5], then scenario for all levels of complexities are described.

Table 9.6 lists the effort required for each unit of these levels of complexity for company 1 and is used in conjunction with guidelines explained in Table 9.5. All these efforts are given in person hours and vary depending on the level of complexity. For example, for the feature "PRF reports (porting)" (item no. 12), simple direct porting (see Table 9.6, item no. 12) has been categorized at complexity level 1 and would take Y121 hours to complete this. If there is more than one porting required, then this number would be multiplied with Y121 to arrive at the estimation for the required feature. This process of estimation is done for the entire required feature, and the total is arrived at the end using the mathematical model as shown below:

Total effort in person hours, E1, for company 1 for developing this application is $\Sigma X_{mn} \times Y_{mn}$ person hours (for $m = 1$ to 24, $n = 1$ to 5)

where X stands for serial number of feature required at different complexity level and Y stands for person hours required to complete the required feature at the corresponding complexity level. This estimation in person hours is the effort required for all the features for company 1.

Table 9.6: Effort estimation table for company 1

S. no.	Required features	Number of features (X_{mn})					Effort required at complexity level in hours (Y_{mn})				
		1	2	3	4	5	1	2	3	4	5
1	Sort pattern—total number of modes	X11	X12	X13	X14	X15	Y11	Y12	Y13	Y14	Y15
2	Sort pattern—total number of work sources	X21	X22	X23	X24	X25	Y21	Y22	Y23	Y24	Y25
3	Sort pattern—customization (custSpg changes)	X31	X32	X33	X34	X35	Y31	Y32	Y33	Y34	Y35
4	Extracts (porting ExtGen)	X41	X42	X43	X44	X45	Y41	Y42	Y43	Y44	Y45
5	Extracts (new ExtGen)	X51	X52	X53	X54	X55	Y51	Y52	Y53	Y54	Y55
6	Extracts (porting Dextract)	X61	X62	X63	X64	X65	Y61	Y62	Y63	Y64	Y65
7	Extracts (new Dextract)	X71	X72	X73	X74	X75	Y71	Y72	Y73	Y74	Y75
8	Custom coding (porting)	X81	X82	X83	X84	X85	Y81	Y82	Y83	Y84	Y85
9	Custom coding (new)	X91	X92	X93	X94	X95	Y91	Y92	Y93	Y94	Y95
10	Exports (porting)	X101	X102	X103	X104	X105	Y101	Y102	Y103	Y104	Y105
11	Exports (new)	X111	X112	X113	X114	X115	Y111	Y112	Y113	Y114	Y115
12	PRF reports (porting)	X121	X122	X123	X124	X125	Y121	Y122	Y123	Y124	Y125
13	Crystal reports (new)	X131	X132	X133	X134	X135	Y131	Y132	Y133	Y134	Y135
14	Data entry application (porting)	X141	X142	X143	X144	X145	Y141	Y142	Y143	Y144	Y145
15	Data entry application (new)	X151	X152	X153	X154	X155	Y151	Y152	Y153	Y154	Y155
16	Custom stager (porting)	X161	X162	X163	X164	X165	Y161	Y162	Y163	Y164	Y165
17	Custom stagers (new)	X171	X172	X173	X174	X175	Y171	Y172	Y173	Y174	Y175
18	Track driver changes (porting)	X181	X182	X183	X184	X185	Y181	Y182	Y183	Y184	Y185
19	Track driver changes (new)	X191	X192	X193	X194	X195	Y191	Y192	Y193	Y194	Y195
20	Custom modules (porting)	X201	X202	X203	X204	X205	Y201	Y202	Y203	Y204	Y205
21	Mark sense (new)	X211	X212	X213	X214	X215	Y211	Y212	Y213	Y214	Y215
22	Custom module (new)	X221	X222	X223	X224	X225	Y221	Y222	Y223	Y224	Y225

23	ARC integration	X231	X232	X233	X234	X235	Y231	Y232	Y233	Y234	Y235
24	Check 21 – IQA, IUA	X241	X242	X243	X244	X245	Y241	Y242	Y243	Y244	Y245
Total effort E1 = $\Sigma X_{mn} \times Y_{mn}$, *m* = 1 to 24 and *n* = 1 to 5											

The same practice was used for the other four organizations that had participated in external benchmarking. For company 1, the total estimated effort, E1, came to be 67,134.02 person hours or 381.443 person months (i.e., 67,134.02 person hours divided by 176 person hours per month, which was calculated as 22 working days per month multiplied by 8 working hours per day). The productivity for company 1 was calculated as 3700 FP divided by 381.443, which came to be 9.7 FP per person month. Similarly, productivities for all other four companies were calculated and benchmarked as shown in Table 9.7.

Table 9.7: Results obtained from benchmarking productivity

Company no.	Productivity value in FP per person month	Remarks
1	9.7	The best benchmark value
2	7.8	
3	6.7	
4	8.9	
5	8.6	

JNV wanted to maintain its leadership in the image processing industry and decided to use the best benchmark value of 9.7 FP per person month. Using this value, the productivity goal of 10.6 FP per person month was set, which was 10% more than the best benchmark value. This helped JNV to be competitive in the industry. However, JNV decided that after executing few projects the exact amount of effort required for each feature could be assessed afresh. Nonetheless, this external benchmarking practice provided a good check against the industry standard.

Assessment of External Benchmarking Practices in JNV

1. In the initial stages, the partners were unwilling to share their data. But when they were assured of confidentiality and exchange of data for mutual benefits, the partners signed the NDA (non-disclosure agreement) and shared their benchmark data.
2. The researcher defined the complexity levels for each of the features but these complexity levels were on different dimensions, and on all these dimensions the answer instead of being "yes" or "no" could vary in terms of degree or extent. To that extent, the replies were based on their own perception of the weight on those dimensions. This could distort the data.
3. Benchmarks are useful when they provide the detailed course of action. In these cases, the overall productivity was calculated for all the 125 features together and not for the 125 items separately. In these circumstances, there existed hardly any scope of improvement on each feature.
4. Benchmarking is generally done by the lifecycle stages such as requirement analysis, design, coding, integration testing, acceptance testing, etc. In these cases, the features were not

classified on the basis of lifecycle. Therefore, it was not possible to identify the productivity benchmark on the basis of the stages of the lifecycle.

5. The aggregate productivity data could not be obtained from five companies. They provided the data only for the 24 features. For the remaining 101 features, benchmarks were based on the internal data. There was no way of finding out whether external benchmark was more efficient than the internal benchmark or not, since external benchmarks dealt with different features from internal features. Further, the internal data were based on the reality prevalent inside the organization and therefore were readily agreed as benchmark, the software engineers were reluctant to accept the external data as benchmarks.
6. As per the systems followed, only the lowest effort company or, in other words, the best benchmark was finally accepted for adaptation. Such benchmarks are likely to be very high and in certain cases were not achievable. There was no clear indication as to how such nonachievable benchmarks were reconciled and made achievable.
7. The external data were always in aggregate form and therefore did not have the potential for providing detailed insight into the processes. Internal data based benchmarks clearly had an advantage on these fronts over the external data.
8. After completing the practice, there were certain doubts related to data collected and clarification was sought from the partners. The clarification was provided after a long wait. Because of this, there were question marks on the reliability of data that led to low acceptability among employees.
9. The amount of time and effort required to collect these data from benchmarking partners were quite high; hence, the management decided not to conduct this practice at frequent intervals.

External Benchmarking Practice in ZFT PLC

ZFT PLC is a multinational company with more than 15,000 employees and operating in 27 countries. It has an office in India in Chennai, where it develops software for exports. ZFT specializes in developing software application for banking industry. It has provided banking software to more than 8000 organization in 27 countries in both private and public sectors for managing customer information and driving improvement in banking services. It focuses on innovative banking software solution using the latest technology and is a leader in the Internet banking domain in the United Kingdom. Being a new development center in India, it did not have past data for estimating the effort required for developing these applications. Besides, the technology used for developing the applications was new. The current case is about an application to be developed for Internet banking in UK's banking industry. The size of the application was of 14,000 function points, and the management team in Chennai wanted to benchmark productivity for its development team. Hence to get benchmark productivity, external benchmarking practice was adopted. Similar applications were earlier developed in UK development center of the same organization; however, the data available from the earlier development activities could not be used as there was a difference in the level of available skill. Besides, domain knowledge of the resources and technology was new.

Benchmarking Approach

The management team in ZFT wanted to use data available from different benchmarking forums. The available forums from which external benchmarking data could have been used were Metagroup,

SPIN Bangalore, and SPIN Hyderabad. Metagroup had data from several countries and hence could not represent true Indian performance. This forced the management to look for forums in India. SPIN Bangalore had already published an external benchmarking report, which was 4 years old, whereas SPIN Hyderabad had carried out an external benchmarking practice only 6 months ago and had benchmark data for technology in which ZFT wanted to develop its application (web-based technology). Hence, the management team decided to use SPIN Hyderabad report as it seemed to represent the latest performance benchmarks in the industry in web-based technology.

ZFT applied to SPIN Hyderabad for membership and became a member of the forum. An NDA was signed to ensure that ZFT would not share this information with any other organization. The NDA also provided that data obtained from SPIN Hyderabad should have limited access by employees and these should not be stored in public domain. Table 9.8 shows the summary of such data obtained from SPIN Hyderabad. As ZFT PLC was engaged in developing web-based application, values for web-based projects were used.

Table 9.8: Summary of benchmark values from SPIN Hyderabad

Metric	Unit of measurement	2003 values
Productivity	LOC/PD	33
Defect density	Defects/KLOC	5
Effect profile		**As percentage of total project effort**
Training		2.6%
Requirement		12.4%
Design		19.6%
Coding and unit testing		45.4%
Testing		20.0%
	Total effort	**100%**

It may be noted that ZFT had decided to use function point per person month as the unit for productivity and the number of defects per function point for defect density. As the unit of measurement in SPIN Hyderabad was different, it was decided to convert productivity value in LOC per person day to FP per person month. This was achieved by using Caper Jones (2005) conversion factor. As per Caper Jones' table, for web technology, where ASP is used as technology for programming, it is found that one function point is equivalent to 14 lines of code. Assuming 5 days work per week and 20 working days in a month, productivity value of 33 LOC per person day amounted to 47.14 FP per person month as productivity value.

It was felt that because of new technology and not so experienced development team, the team was operating only at an efficiency of 85% vis-à-vis SPIN Hyderabad benchmark. However, in order to make the goal challenging, the company decided to achieve 100% efficiency. For requirement analysis, which is the first stage of software development lifecycle, the company found that for the web-based projects, the recorded hours for the stage was 8250 person hours. As the development team was aiming at 100% efficiency, the benchmark was calculated as 8250 multiplied by 0.85, which was equal to 7012.5 person hours. Further, as per SPIN Hyderabad, requirement analysis was 12.4% of total project effort (Table 9.8). Thus, the total project effort came to be 56,552.5

person hours (this was obtained by multiplying 7012.5 with 100 and then dividing by 12.4). Using benchmarking effort profile from SPIN Hyderabad, the efforts for other stages of lifecycle were found in the similar fashion and these are shown in Table 9.9.

Table 9.9: Effort distribution

Benchmark value in percentage	Estimation based on benchmark and efficiency factor in person hours	Remarks
Requirement	7012.5	Equivalent of 100% efficiency for actual hours spent by the team
Training (2.60%)	1470.4	Calculated using effort profile
Design (19.6%)	11,084.3	
Coding and unit testing (45.4%)	25,674.8	
Testing (IT, ST, etc.) (20.0%)	11,310.5	
Total effort	56,552.5	

The software was then estimated to have involved 14,000 FP (the size of the application to be developed). As it involved 56,552.5 person hours, it accounted to 0.248 FP per person hour. Based on 20 working days in a month and 8 hours per day, the benchmark was set at 39.6 FP per person month.

Assessment of External Benchmarking Practice in ZFT

1. There existed major gaps in data in terms of unit of measurement, standardization of measurement definitions, and tools used for collecting data.
2. Tools used by SPIN Hyderabad for collecting data were different from that used by ZFT. This resulted in data being presented in different templates, which were not acceptable to employees. To circumvent this, templates for data collection were standardized and then used for benchmarking.
3. The understanding of levels of complexities was different for different companies, which initially made it difficult to standardize. To adjust the issue of complexities, ZFT had to provide guidelines for each level of complexity.
4. Collecting data from external forums requires enormous amount of time, effort, and management initiatives. Also, the cost for collecting these data was high. Because of this, the periodicity of collecting data from external forums is high, and management from ZFT had decided to collect data from forums after 5 years.
5. The management had to sign a non-disclosure agreement with the external forums for maintaining confidentiality of data. As per the agreement, the collected data were not to be stored in public domain, which restricted access to all the employees.
6. As there was no involvement of employees from ZFT in collecting data, the reliability of data was perceived to be less. This resulted in suspicion to some extent about the quality of data. The management had to take initiatives to assure employees that data were reliable and can be accepted for benchmarking.

The practice has helped ZFT to have a basis for benchmarking productivity for web-based technology for which the organization did not have prior experience in the technology. The practice also used industry benchmark values (SPIN Hyderabad), which helped the development team to perform close to industry standard.

Internal Benchmarking Practice in ISL

Internal benchmarking is the process of identifying the best practices followed in different business units of an organization and sharing it across the units so that everyone can learn from these best practices. Through internal benchmarking, norms and standards can be formulated and based on these norms, targets and goals can be set for each business unit so that these are realistic and achievable. The following paragraphs explain the procedures adopted for internal benchmarking at ISL.

The broad objective of internal benchmarking in ISL with regard to development projects was to identify comparable projects executed by the company in recent past, measure their productivity, and use statistical analysis to find average benchmark value as explained below.

Let the size for each project be as S_i, where $i = 1$ to n, and n represents the total number of projects. Thus, $S_1, S_2, S_3, \ldots, S_n$ represent the size of the projects in the organization. Let effort in person hours for each project be T_i, where $i = 1$ to n, and n represents the total number of projects. Thus,

$$\text{average value } (X_{\text{avg}}) = \frac{(S_1 + S_2 + S_3 + \cdots + S_n)}{(T_1 + T_2 + T_3 + \cdots + T_n)}$$

Symbolically, it is represented as $X_{\text{avg}} = (\Sigma S/\Sigma T)_{i,\, i = 1 \text{ to } n.}$

Using statistical formulae, the upper critical limit and the lower critical limit (LCL) are defined as

$\text{UCL} = X_{\text{avg}} + 3 \times \text{S.D.}$ and $\text{LCL} = X_{\text{avg}} - 3 \times \text{S.D.}$

where S.D. = standard deviation.

All the productivity values measured for each project were plotted and using control limit approach extreme values, which were outside the upper critical limit values and thus were of special cause in nature were removed. After removing extreme data, out of the remaining data based on performance, top 50% of projects were selected and an average was calculated. Such average was used as benchmark value for productivity. As the 50% high-end performance data were taken, the average also tended to be higher and norm established on such average therefore had built into it an element of challenge. Besides, since such average of benchmark was based on actual achievements, it could be projected as achievable benchmark, and this helped in developing a commitment toward such benchmark.

Ordinarily, while competitive information from other companies was not available, there was no such constraint in obtaining internal data. Internal benchmarking, therefore, could benefit from sensitive data available with the company. Besides, there was also an important advantage of internal benchmarking on account of the fact that the quality of analysis based on internal data was likely to be far better than in case of external data. As the internal employees were generally available for discussion and for providing insights into the case of internal benchmarking, the practice provided the benefits of discussion with people involved.

Steps for Internal Benchmarking

ISL is a leading Indian multinational in providing customized solution to customers. It has over 50,000 employees worldwide and uses onsite–offshore model to service its customers in more than 35 countries. The organization bagged its first project in banking industry, which was worth 100 million dollars to be executed over a period of 2 years. This is the first time that the organization was awarded such a big project, and the management wanted to set appropriate goals for productivity. The goals for productivity were set by using current performance capability in other projects.

In this case, a sample of 36 projects was chosen and the steps involved in internal benchmarking were as follows:

1. The company found that in banking domain, 74 projects were completed during 5 years ending in April 2003. Out of these 41 were development projects and the rest were maintenance projects and products. These were compiled and listed. This ensured that workload pressure was similar for the organization as a whole and time differences did not create any additional factor, which could distort the results.
2. Out of these projects, for choosing projects for benchmarking study, the following criteria were used:
   (a) The projects should have been executed in its local development center at Bhubaneswar where data could be easily accessible. This criterion was to ensure that differences in environment and location did not distort the comparability.
   (b) The projects should have been fairly large and the size of the application developed should have been more than 2000 function points. This criterion was essential to ensure that projects were characteristically similar so that those were handled in the same way (not in the way mega or mini projects were handled). Thus, the differential features of mega or mini projects making differences in productivity and in defect density were unlikely.
3. A core team consisting of key project managers and process improvement specialists were selected to carry out the initiatives. The core team consisted of five project managers (who had worked as project managers in at least five projects) and two process consultants from quality department and was headed by the head of quality in the local development center of the organization. These five project managers were chosen in such a way that each one of them represented a business unit and could impress on other project managers to participate in the study. Having worked in at least five projects, their presence lent credibility to the study and instilled confidence among other participating project managers.
4. Boundary conditions including cost, schedule, deliverables, roles and responsibilities of core team members as well as for participating projects were defined for the benchmarking exercise.
   (a) Roles and responsibilities: (1) The project manager was to assist in data collection in his business unit. The researcher would approach the project manager of the selected project with prior appointment for personal interviews for data collection. The process consultant would assist him during these interviews. (2) The process consultant was from the quality department and would design the data sheet and templates for collecting data. He also would decide the criteria for selecting projects and was empowered to select the final list of the projects selected for the study. (3) The head of quality would

chair the kick-off meeting and decide the final benchmarked data for presentation to the top management. He would liaison between the top management and the core team for communicating objectives, for resource allocation, and was empowered to solve any problem or issues related to the study. These issues could be related to data or behavior.

5. Time and effort required for core team members and other employees were specified during kick-off presentation.
6. Methodologies for gathering data, conducting interviews, post interview confirmation, and data validation ensuring that there were at least 30 data points to properly study the trend after removing outliers were decided.
7. Projects that were incomplete or were canceled prematurely were not included in the study.
8. During intensive personal interviews, enough chance was given to each project manager to narrate his or her own story regarding size, team, effort, and defects. The project managers were supported by one or two key developers. A process improvement specialist was also invited.
9. Quantitative measures such as project size, time, defects, efforts and qualitative measurement such as application complexity, team experience in development domain and technology, availability of modules, and availability of testing tools were defined.
10. It was decided to transform wherever required SLOC (source lines of codes) measures to function point measures using IFPUG (International Function Point User Group; www.ifpug.org, 2003) methodology as the management felt that IFPUG provided better accuracy compared to Caper Jones conversion factors.
11. Data were aligned in terms of phases of development such as requirement study, function design, coding, and testing.
12. Core measures were defined. These were size, number of defects, effort spent for each stage, and number of months of experience for team members.
13. Through data classification and measurement system and creation of uniform database, consistency in data collection was ensured.
14. Validations of data were done through cross checking and scrutinizing by quality department consultants.
15. Data were stratified into multiple dimensions to provide an in-depth analysis from various angles.
16. Positive and negative aspects were studied in terms of percentage improvement and decrease of metrics, such as efficiency, cost, duration, field reliability, team size, scope, staff turnover, experience in application being developed, customer issues, and development tool capabilities.
17. Estimation models modified to generate accurate results in forecasting.

Assessment of Internal Benchmarking Practice

During the study, the researcher faced several issues. Some of these are as follows:

1. Each project had to use time sheets for capturing data, but different projects used different activity categorization, thus affecting data compatibility. However, this was overcome by re-categorizing some of the activities.

2. At the initial stage, measurements followed by all the projects were not same. Therefore, the data needed conversion to a common metrics. However, after discussion with the project managers, this nonuniformity was removed and all the projects had similar measurement systems.
3. There was an apprehension about the correctness of data. The time recorded in time sheet, more often were not accurate. To overcome this problem, a number of awareness sessions were conducted for the project team members to ensure proper time keeping.
4. During the tenure of study, a number of project team members and project management staff left the organization. This turnover of project manager staff and project team members came as stumbling blocks during the internal benchmarking exercise. To overcome this, the new members were given awareness sessions so that continuity in data collection as well as the correct understanding of the measurement systems could be ensured.
5. Many times the transfer of project managers or their staff led to the loss of qualitative information, particularly that information which were not recorded and kept in files. To overcome this problem, a project document library was created where qualitative information were formally recorded and stored.
6. A software development project starts with a kick-off meeting. The definition of measurement systems and data collection would start after these kick-off meetings. But in many projects, which were selected for the study, activities were stalled after the kick-off meeting as the customers would stall requirement gathering process. Thus, there were several false starts of the development projects.
7. The mode of data collection for internal benchmarking was through intensive personal interview, and during the discussions, the project manager shared many of the best practices that were recorded otherwise. These practices were then shared across different projects in different forums such as best practice sharing, knowledge management sessions, etc. Best practices of requirements management, project planning, staff training, and metrics collection were shared in these sessions so that other project members learnt these and practice them in their projects.
8. Need for future benchmarking practice: On the basis of benefits obtained from internal benchmarking, the project manager and senior management planned to carry out new initiatives that would improve productivity while keeping defect density low. The management wanted to know the results of these initiatives, and it was decided that internal benchmarking should be carried out with annual frequency. It was also decided that external benchmarking should be carried out in parallel to internal benchmarking to keep abreast of industry trends.

Internal Benchmarking Practice in PSL

PSL is a multinational software development organization, which has headquarters in Chennai with a total of 13 development centers in India. Out of these, six are in Chennai, three in Mumbai, two in Hyderabad, one in Gurgaon, and one in Bangalore. It has offices in 13 other countries and more than 7500 employees in India alone. It provides solutions to banking and financial institutions and uses state of the architecture called service-oriented architecture (SOA) to develop software. During the last two decades of its existence, it has grown to become a leader in providing solutions to a number of Fortune 500 companies. Relationship management with its customers is one of the best in industry, as this relationship is based on providing a cost advantage to customers with quality and reliability with the flexibility of meeting delivery schedule while being able to incorporate any change requests.

The software developed by PSL helped in boundaryless banking with robust security features. Using SOA architecture, the solution helped the customers to bank anytime, anywhere, and on any platform. This has reduced the cost of ownership for this software for its customers as the customers did not have to invest in upgrading their platform. In the 15th year of operation, the organization bagged its first project in Australia. As this was a new customer account, the organization wanted to decide the productivity rate at which the development team for the new customer account was to perform. In order to decide on this value, which was to be competitive and should provide good operating profit, the organization wanted to know the productivity rate used in different development centers and decided to follow internal benchmarking.

Internal Benchmarking Practice

The objective of this practice was to find productivity rates for each development center and to find the increase in the productivity rates over a year. A template was designed for collecting data from each development center as shown in Table 9.10. The managing director of PSL called a meeting of all heads of development centers and asked for this information. He explained the reasons for collecting such data. A task force consisting of the head of quality, the senior most head of development center, and the head of finance was set up. All the requested data were collected.

Table 9.10: Results of benchmarking productivity

Development centers	Number of projects	Present productivity in FP/person month	Last year productivity in FP/person month	Increase in productivity over the last year (%)
1	53	2.7	2.4	13
2	37	2.8	2.5	12
3	42	2.6	2.3	13
4	29	2.4	2.2	9
5	33	2.9	2.6	12
6	38	2.6	2.3	13
7	42	2.7	2.4	13
8	22	2.6	2.3	13
9	37	2.5	2.3	9
10	41	2.6	2.3	13
11	25	2.4	2.1	14
12	27	2.6	2.3	13
13	21	2.7	2.4	13

It was observed that the maximum productivity benchmark was 2.9 FP per person month and minimum was 2.4 FP per person month. As it was the first project in Australia, the management decided to go for the highest productivity benchmark of 2.9 FP per person month as an entry strategy in a new territory. It was also decided to go for an increase of 14% in productivity in the subsequent year (from Table 9.10, this is the highest increase in productivity rate over a year). These values were put in the contract signed with the customer.

Assessment of Internal Benchmarking Practice at PSL

1. This practice ensured that the productivity rate was targeted to be consistent with the best in the organization. As both development centers 4 and 11 were operating at this rate and were still able to generate healthy operating profit and retain customers, the management team decided to use this value as the benchmark.
2. Using 14% as the increase for next year and putting that into contract ensured that the customer was happy, and it resulted in more number of projects in the next few months.
3. Time consumed for this practice was only 8 days. As the managing director had given the directive to follow this practice, the collection of data was fast. Thus, the practice was less time-consuming.
4. The unit for measuring productivity was same for all projects and so benchmarking was easier.
5. Tools used for collecting data from projects were same in all development centers, which made data collection easier.

Critical Assessment of Benchmarking Practices

In the previous sections four case studies were discussed, two related to external and two related to internal benchmarking practices were presented. Based on the practices followed by these organizations, critical appraisal had been done.

1. **Time requirement:** External benchmarking practice consumes time and money and requires "enormous" amount of initiative. In contrast, internal benchmarking practice takes less time, as it is conducted within the organization.
2. **Confidentiality and NDA:** The data collected during internal benchmarking practice are not shared outside the organization, and therefore the confidentiality is maintained. In external benchmarking, data collected are shared in a forum, and therefore the chances of information leakage are high. This problem is partly addressed by signing non-disclosure agreements (NDAs) with the member organizations to maintain confidentiality about data.
3. **Reliability:** Data collection, aggregation, and subsequent analysis become difficult in external benchmarking practice. In addition, reliability of data sometimes is low as accuracy of data is questioned. This is so because each organization follows different templates and measurement units for data collection. Hence, before the start of the practice, detailed guidelines are given to the participating members. This is not required in internal benchmarking as same measurement unit and data collection tools and templates are used in different units of the organization. As there is control over the collection procedure and quality of data, reliability is high.
4. **Participation of employees and acceptability:** Many times, after the collection of data, there are situations in which clarifications are needed for refinement. In external benchmarking, as there is hardly any participation from the members (other than supplying data), acceptability

of data is low. To address this problem, the management has to take initiatives to explain to the employees about the need for such practice and encourage them to use the data for benchmarking.

5. **Source of mandate for data:** Directions from the top management set the initiative for following the internal benchmarking practice. This makes sure that employees are involved and they accept the practice. In external benchmarking, however, NDAs are signed and they become the source of mandate for data collection.
6. **Cost and periodicity:** The amount of effort and cost required for internal benchmarking practice are lower than in case of external benchmarking. Besides, the periodicity of internal benchmarking is as and when required and in external benchmarking, the periodicity is at periodic interval.
7. **Suitability:** External benchmarking practice is best suitable when the organization is new or is venturing into a new area of operation. This practice is also appropriate when the organization wants to benchmark its own performance against its competitors. Internal benchmarking is practiced when the top management in the organization wants to measure relative performance of divisions or units. This practice can also be used to measure average performance of the organization.
8. **Best practices:** In case of external benchmarking, the chances of getting high productivity data were far greater than getting such data from inside the company. Therefore, external data could be closer to best practices. In case of internal benchmarking, this is unlikely to be possible.

SUMMARY

In this chapter, through case studies, assessments of benchmarking practices have been critically appraised to find their suitability for software development projects. In the next chapter, models for productivity and defect density have been developed using data from different projects.

A summary of assessment of benchmarking practices has been shown in Table 9.11.

Table 9.11: A comparative assessment of internal and external benchmarking practices

Characteristics	Internal benchmarking	External benchmarking
Time required	Low	High
Confidentiality	High	Low
Data reliability	High	Low
Acceptability to employees	High	Low
Representing best practice	Low	High
Data gap	Low	High
Possible standardization	Low	High
Challenge factor	Low	High
Non-disclosure agreement	Implicit	Explicit

Adjustment requirement for complexities	Less	High
Depth of insight	High	Low
Level of employee participation (discussion, etc.)	High	Low
Acceptability of qualitative data	More acceptable	Less acceptable
Source of mandate for data	Company directive	Membership of forum, conference, workshop, etc.
Cost	Low	High
Best suitability	For existing business	For new business
Periodicity	As and when needed	At periodic intervals

DISCUSSION POINTS

1. What are the steps involved in internal benchmarking?
2. What are the benefits obtained from internal benchmarking?
3. When should external benchmarking be used?
4. What is the difference between internal and external benchmarking?
5. When should external benchmarking be used?
6. Discuss a business case when both internal and external benchmarking can be used.

10

CMMI and Software Project Management

LEARNING OBJECTIVES

In this chapter, the students would learn:

- What is CMMI?
- Why CMMI is required?
- Different levels of CMMI
- Software project management concepts and CMMI

Introduction

With time the world has come a long way in doing business. Business processes are getting complicated day by day. Every second we witness the birth and demise of many products and services. Every business aims at delivering the product or service of better quality faster than the competitors at a cheaper price. This process of development of increasing complex product/service has resulted in even more complicated processes adopted by the organizations. Not all components of a product/service are developed within the boundary walls of an organization. The development now involves the contribution of many organizations. Some part is developed in-house while some are outsourced. So at this juncture, the integrations of the complicated processes have become a major challenge for the managers. Three major aspects of a process (see Figure 10.1) are as follows:

1. Procedures or methods
2. People
3. Tools and equipments

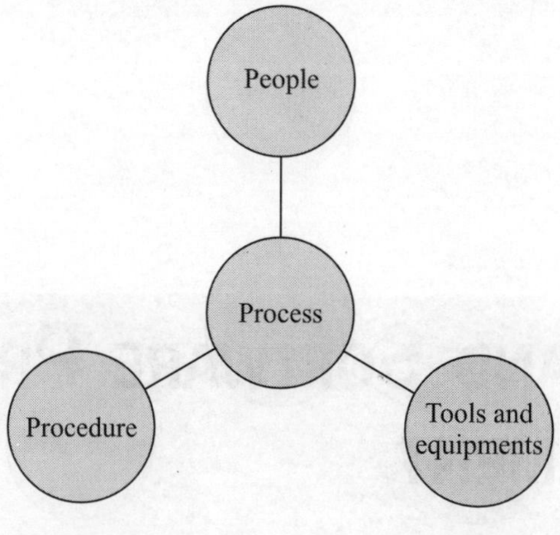

Figure 10.1: Three major aspects of a process

Processes enable the employees to work smarter and help the organization in achieving the business objectives. Excellence in processes materializes into competitive advantage and profitability. There are best practices, methodologies, standards, maturity models, and guidelines that can steer the organizations to achieve excellence in processes. The Software Engineering Institute (SEI) (http://www.sei.cmu.edu) has found several dimensions that an organization can focus on to improve its business, which consists of best practices that address the development and maintenance activities applied to the products and services. Capability maturity model integration (CMMI) focuses on the complete lifecycle of a product or service and proposes ways and measurement to pioneer in the processes (http://www.sei.cmu.edu/cmmi/index.cfm). The philosophy behind the CMMI model is "the quality of a system or product is highly influenced by the quality of the process used to develop and maintain it."

History

The evolution of CMMI (http://en.wikipedia.org/wiki/Capability_Maturity_Model_Integration) into its current state is explained in chronological order in Figure 10.2.

CMMI Framework

The CMMI framework can be divided into three major parts: model, training, and appraisal. There are multiple models under the CMMI framework, and there are some generic components that are common to all CMMI models. These components together are called CMMI Model Foundation (CMF) and are required to be part of each CMMI model. These components along with other applicable material form the CMMI model of a specific interest area such as product or service.

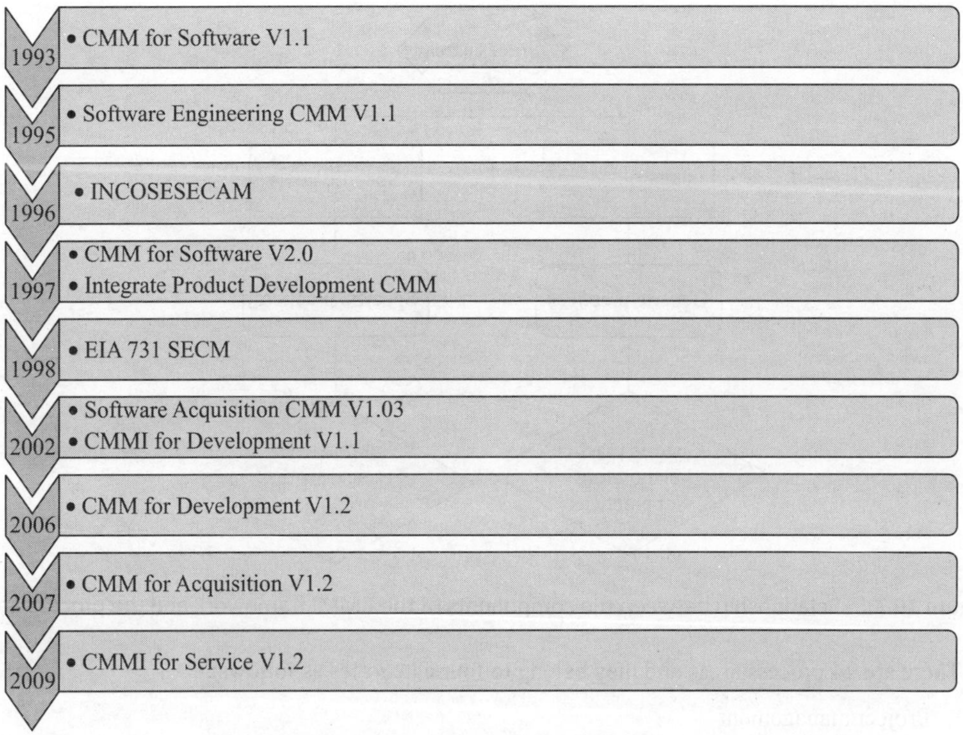

Figure 10.2: Evolution of CMMI

The components of any CMMI can be of three types:

(a) **Required components:** These are the components the organization needs to achieve in order to satisfy the process area. In CMMI, generic goals and specific goals are the required components.

(b) **Expected components:** An organization may implement expected components in order to achieve the required components. These components guide the improvement in processes. Generic and specific practices are the expected components.

(c) **Informative components:** Informative components help the organization in understanding the required and the expected components. Some examples of informative components are subpractices, typical work products, goal and practice titles, goal and practice notes, examples, and references.

Process Area

As per SEI, "A process area is a cluster of related practices in an area that, when implemented collectively, satisfies a set of goals considered important for making improvement in that area." The relationship between the components of the CMMI framework and the process area is shown in Figure 10.3.

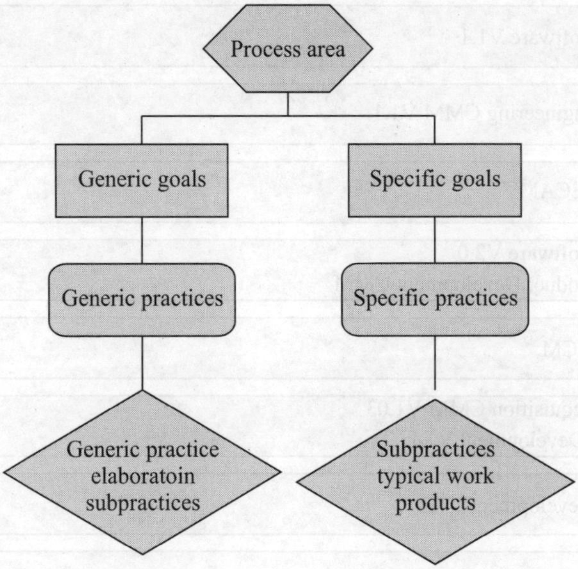

Figure 10.3: Relationship between the components of the CMMI framework and the process area

There are 24 process areas and they belong to four categories as follows:

1. Project management
2. Process management
3. Engineering
4. Support

The process areas are as follows:

- Capacity and availability management (CAM)
- Causal analysis and resolution (CAR)
- Configuration management (CM)
- Decision analysis and resolution (DAR)
- Integrated project management (IPM)
- Incident resolution and prevention (IRP)
- Measurement and analysis (MA)
- Organizational innovation and deployment (OID)
- Organizational process definition (OPD)
- Organizational process focus (OPF)
- Organizational process performance (OPP)
- Organizational training (OT)
- Project monitoring and control (PMC)
- Project planning (PP)
- Process and product quality assurance (PPQA)
- Quantitative project management (QPM)

- Requirements management (REQM)
- Risk management (RSKM)
- Supplier agreement management (SAM)
- Service continuity (SCON)
- Service delivery (SD)
- Service system development (SSD)
- Service system transition (SST)
- Strategic service management (STSM)

Following are the different sections associated with the process area:

- **Purpose statement:** It describes the objective of a process area and also its informative component.
- **Introductory notes:** It describes the major concept and informative component of the process area.
- **Related process area:** This section describes the related process areas and the association with them at a higher level. This is an informative component.
- **Specific goal:** This is one required component of process area and describes the unique characteristics that a process must achieve to satisfy the process area. This is used for appraisal of the process.
- **Generic goals:** Like specific goals, the process needs to achieve few characteristics called generic goals to satisfy the process area; but the difference is the generic goals may be present in other process areas. It is also used for appraisal of any process.
- **Specific practices:** These are the actions considered important for achieving a specific goal. Specific practices are expected to be performed for achievement of success of specific goals of process area.
- **Typical work product:** It lists sample output of a specific practice, and it is an informative component.
- **Subpractice:** It describes the guideline and interpretation of the specific and generic goal and is an informative component of the model.
- **Generic practice:** The objectives of generic practice are same as those of specific practices; the only difference being that these practices can be common for multiple process areas.
- **Generic practice elaboration:** It describes how the generic practice should be uniquely applied to any process area.

CMMI Levels

As per CMMI, for excellence in the processes for the development of product or service, an organization needs to go through some set of evolutionary path. Levels can be referred as the milestones on these paths and can be used as an appraisal parameter for measuring the process maturity. The levels represent the improvement of the organization from an ill-defined state to robust information-driven state, which can be instrumented into realization of the objectives of the organization. The levels can be defined for the whole organization, a small group, or a department in the organization. There are two representations for achieving the levels. One is continuous representation in which a particular process area(s) is improved incrementally. Another one is the staged representation in which a set of related process areas is improved incrementally, addressing the successive process areas.

The levels can be grouped into two categories as follows:

(a) Capability level
(b) Maturity level

Continuous representation uses capability levels, whereas staged representation uses maturity levels.

Capability Level

Capability levels are the means for improving all the processes related to a particular process area. There are six capability levels. Each process area consists of goals and practices as shown in Figure 10.4.

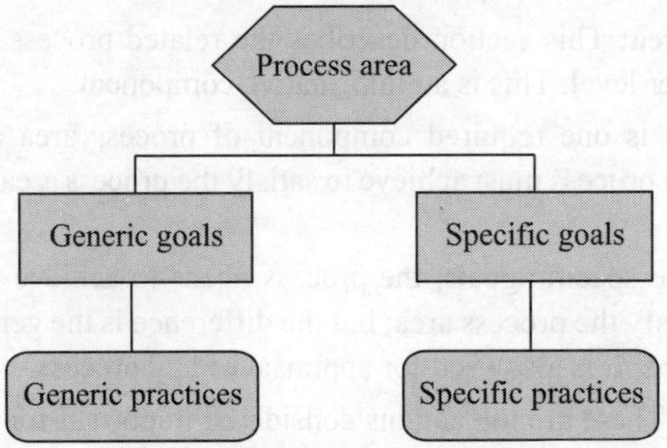

Figure 10.4: Process area

Each capability level contains generic goals and generic practices that an organization needs to adopt to improve a process associated with that process area. With each capability level organization achieves excellence in process. There are six capability levels (see Table 10.1) in CMMI.

Table 10.1: Capability levels

Level	Name
0	Incomplete
1	Performed
2	Managed
3	Defined
4	Quantitatively managed
5	Optimizing

Capability Level 0: Incomplete

A process is said to be incomplete if one or more specific goals are not satisfied for the process area and the process is not finished or partially finished. There is no generic goal for this level, as it is not required to institutionalize an incomplete process.

Capability Level 1: Performed

A process is said to be performed if the specific goals of the process area are performed and it enables the work needed to produce work product/service.

Capability Level 2: Managed

The improvements that have occurred in level 1 are lost if not properly institutionalized. Managed process is basically a performed process, which requires infrastructure in place. Some properties of managed process are as follows:

- Planned and executed in accordance with the policy
- Employs skilled people who have adequate resources to produce controlled outputs
- Involves relevant stakeholders
- Monitored, controlled, and reviewed
- Evaluated for adherence to its process description

Capability Level 3: Defined

Level 3 capability is characterized by a defined process, which is basically a managed process that has been tailored as per the organization standards. It contributes work products, measures, and other process improvement information to the organizational process assets. The basic distinction between level 2 and level 3 is that though level 2 may have standards and procedures, they are generalized for the organization and different projects might follow different standards. Level 3 processes are more consistent and also have some variation with respect to different projects whenever required. Level 3 processes are properly defined and specifies the purpose, inputs, entry criteria, activities, roles, measures, verification steps, outputs, and exit criteria.

Capability Level 4: Quantitatively Managed

Capability level 4 is characterized by a defined process that is managed using statistical and other quantitative methods. Quantitative objectives for quality and process performance are established and used as criteria in managing the process.

Capability Level 5: Optimizing

A process is optimized when a quantitatively managed process is changed as per the inherent requirement of the process. At this level a process is continuously modified using incremental and innovative improvements.

Maturity Level

"A maturity level consists of related specific and generic practices for a predefined set of process areas that improve the organization's overall performance." The maturity level focuses on a set of specific process areas at a time and integrated improvement of all these process area results in overall improvement of the organization. The maturity level indicates the performance of an organization in a particular business environment. With the increase in the maturity levels, an organization achieves performance excellence in a certain subset of organizational process. A major distinction between capability level and maturity level is that maturity level focuses on the improvement of the organization relative to a set of process area whereas capability level represents improvement in a particular process area.

There are five maturity levels (see Figure 10.5) in CMMI.

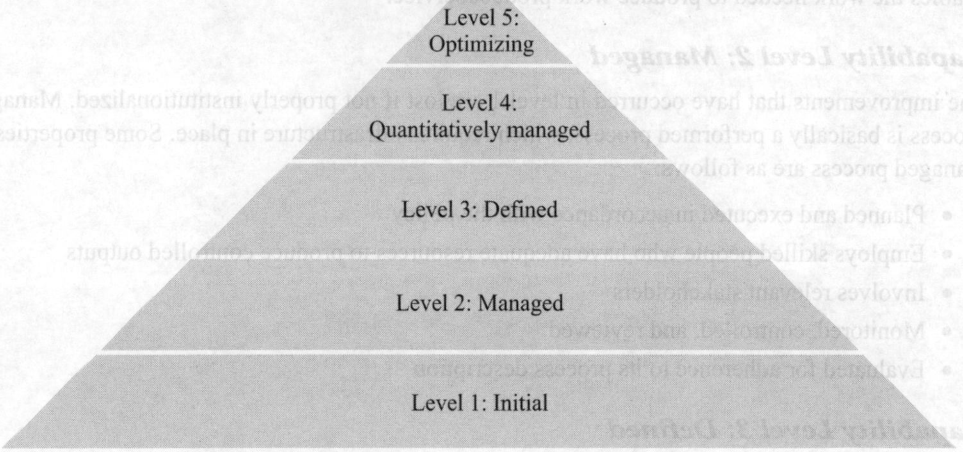

Figure 10.5: Maturity levels

Each maturity level focuses on a few process areas. Table 10.2 lists the process areas related to the maturity levels.

Table 10.2: Process areas in different maturity levels

Initial process	No process area associated with the maturity level 1
Managed process	• Requirements management • Project planning • Project monitoring and control • Supplier agreement management • Measurements and analysis • Process and product quality assurance • Configuration management
Defined process	• Requirements development • Technical solution • Verification • Validation • Product integration • Organizational process focus • Organizational process definition • Organizational training • Integrated project management for IPPD • Integrated supplier management • Risk management • Decision analysis and resolution • Integrated teaming • Organizational environment for integration
Quantitatively managed process	• Quantitative project management • Organizational process performance
Optimizing process	• Causal analysis and resolution • Organizational innovation and deployment

Maturity Level 1: Initial

At this level the processes are chaotic and ad hoc. Processes are not documented and there is no stable environment in the organization. The products and services are designed and delivered by a few exceptionally skilled employees and innovation is very much visible in the outputs. Few characteristics of level 1 maturity are as follows:

- Little scope in repeating the process of a successful project
- Over commitment
- Change of process as per the need

Maturity Level 2: Managed

When an organization achieves maturity level 2, it ensures that the processes are planned and executed as per the policies. The workers are skilled and have access to resources for production. The processes are monitored, controlled, reviewed, and evaluated at a regular interval to check the adherence to policies. The processes are documented and continued even at the time of stress. Milestones are also defined in the processes at this maturity level.

Maturity Level 3: Defined

At maturity level 3, the processes have standards, procedures, tools, and methods and are properly understood and documented. At this level a set of standard processes are defined for the organization and the processes for the projects are designed with these processes as base and performing required tailoring. The policy for tailoring is also documented for the organization.

At level 2, although the processes are standardized, they are different for different projects, whereas at maturity level 3, all the projects are based on some set of standard processes of the organization with required customization. At maturity level 3, a process clearly states the following:

- Purpose
- Inputs
- Entry criteria
- Activities
- Roles
- Measures
- Verification steps
- Outputs
- Exit criteria

Maturity Level 4: Quantitatively Managed

At this level the organization develops the quantitative objectives for quality and performance and the processes are managed as per these values. These quantitative objectives are also used to support fact-based decision making. The objectives are decided based on the needs of the customer, end users, organization, and process implementers. Process variation causes are identified and corrected in the future activities. At maturity level 3, the processes are monitored based on the qualitative parameters, whereas in level 4 more substantial quantitative values are used to monitor the performance.

Maturity Level 5: Optimizing

Maturity level 5 focuses on continually improving the process performance through incremental and innovative process and technological improvements. Quantitative process improvement objectives for the organization are established, continually revised to reflect the changing business objectives, and used as criteria in managing the process improvement. The effects of deployed process improvements are measured and evaluated against the quantitative process improvement objectives. Both the defined processes and the organization's set of standard processes are targets of measurable improvement activities.

The basic difference between maturity level 4 and level 5 is the way the variation in the process is addressed. At maturity level 4, when a variation is detected, the output is predicted based on the quantified quality figures. But at level 5, the organization tries to find the common causes of the variation and changes the processes to remove the variation.

Organizations achieve maturity levels in steps. First, the processes are improved at the project level and then steadily moves toward the most advanced organizational-level process improvement and maturity. When the organization streamlines its business process as per the CMMI model, it is easy to predict the result of the next project looking at the current project. For example, when an organization moves into maturity level 2, it is expected that the processes used in a project would be properly documented and the standard policy would be followed. By climbing the maturity ladder, the organization achieves the generic and specific goals related to some process areas and gets the benefit of process improvement. At the same time, it is also required that an organization proceeds through the maturity levels one by one without skipping any level. Also, it is worth noting that some amount of variation in the model can be made as per the business needs of the organization. For example, in the growth process when an organization moves from level 1 to level 2, it is advised to have process group, whereas Organization Process Focus process area resides at maturity level 3. But it should always be kept in mind that the variation can sometime be risky as the prerequisite for any process area might not have been satisfied.

Process Area, Capability, and Maturity Levels

Process area is comprehended differently in capability and maturity models. In the capability model, each process area passes through different capability level. This model enables an organization to choose a process area and improve it as per the requirement of the business objective. So, two major activities here are as follows: choosing the right process area and deciding how much capability level it should achieve. Some process areas are mandated to achieve certain process capability levels and so an organization cannot randomly pick any process area. So, the organization normally makes a profile of target process areas and the aspired capability level, and defines the generic and specific goals accordingly. Figure 10.6 indicates the process area and the capability maturity in a typical project.

However, in maturity model, every stage has some process areas that need to be satisfied by achieving the related generic and specific goals.

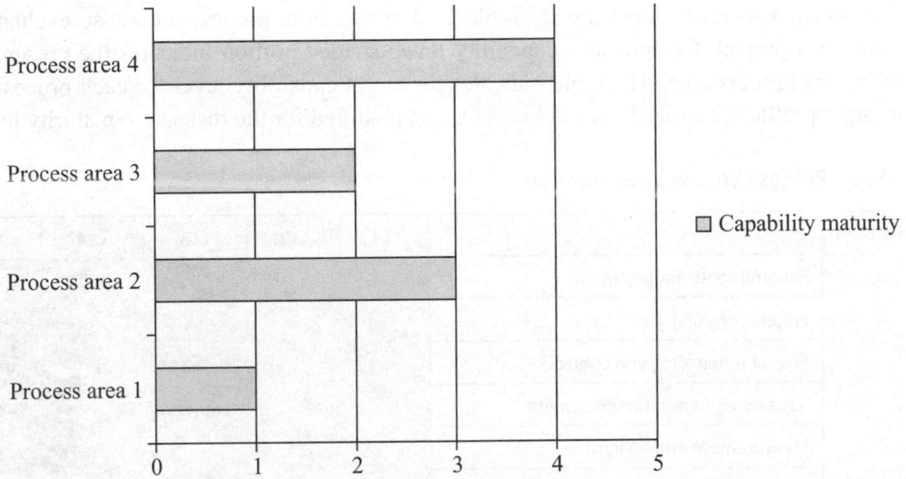

Figure 10.6: Process area and capability maturity

Standard CMMI Appraisal Method for Process Improvement

SCAMPI is a standard method used for appraisal CCMI model. Both the capability level and the maturity level are appraised using this method and rating (level) is one of the major outputs of the method. Appraisal is done in order to find process excellence of the organization.

There are three kinds of appraisal methods: class A, class B, and class C. Class A is a rigorous method and gives the rating as the output. In Class B and C appraisals, less number of data points are used for appraisal. The team which does the assessment also consists of less number of assessors. As a result, unlike class A appraisal no rating is provided for any process area. Usually class B and C are used as preparatory for class A appraisal.

There are certain principles followed strictly for CMMI appraisal:

- Senior management sponsorship
- A focus on the organization's business objectives
- Confidentiality for interviewees
- Use of a documented appraisal method
- Use of a process reference model (e.g., a CMMI model) as a base
- A collaborative team approach
- A focus on actions for process improvement

For appraising capability level, a capability level profile is used. The profile lists the process areas and the capability level achieved by it in the organization and also the target level. It shows the firm's actual progress in process capability. Although the capability level approach gives a good way to rate the process area improvements, the maturity levels have been an effective way of measuring the overall organization improvement. So, there is a need to connect the improvement of the capability level and the maturity level of an organization. Equivalent staging technique is used to enable an organization using the continuous representation for an appraisal to convert a capability level profile into the associated maturity level rating. Table 10.3 shows how process area-wise evaluation is carried out for a project. CL indicates capability level; shaded portion indicates the present level achieved by the process area. The table indicates the target capability level for each process area, and this target profile is required to be achieved to get qualified for the respective maturity level.

Table 10.3: Process area wise evaluation

Maturity level		CL1	CL2	CL3	CL4	CL5
	Requirements management					
	Project planning					
	Project monitoring and control					
2	Supplier agreement management			Target Profile		
	Measurement and analysis					
	Process and product quality assurance					
	Configuration management					
	Requirements development					
	Technical solution					
	Product integration					
	Verification					
	Validation					
3	Organizational process focus		Target Profile			
	Organizational process definition + IPPD					
	Organizational training					
	Integrated project management + IPPD					
	Risk management					
	Decision analysis and resolution					
4	Organizational process performance		Target Profile			
	Quantitative project management					
5	Organizational innovation and deployment	Target Profile				
	Causal analysis and resolution					

CMMI Adoption

Adopting CMMI is a long-term plan and requires dedicated effort to implement. So, strong organization support is utmost necessary and a top-down approach needs to be followed with constant senior management involvement and inspiration. Few tasks of the senior management would be as follows:

- Influence the organization to adopt CMMI
- Implement team selection

- Personal monitoring of process improvement
- Communicating the benefit and being the spokesperson
- Allocating resources

CMMI vs. CMM

This section discusses the differences between CMMI and CMM. The section is helpful to those project managers who have experience in CMM and want to use CMMI for better software project management. This section discusses the scenarios where CMMI has more focus than CMM.

1. CMMI is suitable for system integration, which includes software development as well as hardware integration. CMM only addresses software engineering. For example, in aircraft development, which has multiple systems like flight control, hydraulic, fuel, engine, environment control, undercarriage, avionics system, structures, etc. In each of the sub-system, there is a software component as well as hardware that uses the software. Fuel control system has fuel monitoring and controlling software. It also interfaces with engine control system (based on engine load, the volume of fuel flow is controlled). For these types of system integration, maturity in CMMI can bring in the desired results.
2. In CMM, training is required at the project level, that is, training needs for each project member is to be addressed. In CMMI, training needs at organization level are identified and imparted. This helps in defining the role and responsibility matrix at the organization level.
3. CMMI helps in tracking bidirectional traceability, whereas CMM helps in unidirectional traceability. Bidirectional traceability helps in establishing the link between requirements to set of products' features and across other interfaces.
4. CMMI introduces decision analysis and resolution (DAR) concept, by which the project team has to document its decision related to technology solutions, effective architecture design, decision to develop or buy, onsite–offshore mix, and prioritizing requests during requirement or fixes. This documentation helps in contributing to knowledge management, and the project teams do not have to reinvent the wheel.
5. CMMI has also brought in the concept of quantification of risk management. This quantification helps in determining the cost of risks. Using this cost a threshold value can be determined, where threshold would decide whether the mitigation plan needs to be reviewed by the senior management or it is acceptable to live with the risk. This helps in deciding whether the project team can stay with the risk or implement the mitigation plan.

CMMI and Software Project Management

There are specific process areas in CMMI that need to be followed for project management in CMMI. They are as follows:

- Project planning
- Project monitoring and control
- Supplier agreement management
- Integrated project management (IPPD)
- Integrated supplier management (SS)

- Integrated teaming (IPPD)
- Risk management quantitative project management

These process areas guide a project manager to follow the best practices that have been prescribed in CMMI. Introduction of these practice areas in IT industry has helped the cause of software project management. CMMI comes with a repository of best practices, and by following these best practices, the project teams not only accomplish capability and maturity levels but also benefit in terms of increased productivity, reduced rework, and cost of quality. It has been estimated that 30–40% of project cost are saved. As the project team follows the peer review process, the defects are captured early in project lifecycle, which helps in fixing them at lower cost. It also increases predictability and brings in stability to the project management. With increased capability and maturity levels, accuracy in the estimation of project budgets increases and so also the timeline and schedule of delivery. Periodic reviews (as required by CMMI process areas) increase awareness of project health among the senior management; this helps in effective decision process for managing risks associated with the project execution.

As published in the web site http://www.thedacs.com/databases/roi/, different organizations have gained by following CMMI software project management processes. Boeing has reported 33% decrease in the average cost by following CMMI-prescribed project management process. Boeing has also benefited in the reduction of turnaround time for releases of fixes and reduction in rework cost by 50% and 60%, respectively. Similarly, Lockheed Martin has been competitive by reducing 20% cost of its products as the development cost has come down and productivity increased by 25–30% on an average per project over a period of 3 years. This reduction in development cost has been due to the improved project management process by meeting the requirements of CMMI process areas. During this period, Lockheed Martin has reported 50% reduction in software defects and increase in customer satisfaction.

SUMMARY

CMMI is a powerful tool for process improvement. It can help organizations having few 100 employees to organizations with employees in lakhs. It can significantly improve the product/service delivery of the organization and result in major tool for cost reduction. CMMI model adoptions result in reduction of the number of defects, faster time to market, improvements in estimation capabilities, and better project control. But at the same time it requires thorough planning to achieve process improvement using CMMI model.

DISCUSSION POINTS

1. What are the different stages in CMMI?
2. What is the difference between capability level and maturity level?
3. What is meant by process area?
4. What are the benefits of following CMMI-prescribed project management processes?

11

Project Management in Maintenance Projects

LEARNING OBJECTIVES

In this chapter, the students would learn:

- Process for software maintenance projects
- Managing software maintenance projects
- Project monitoring activities of maintenance projects
- Milestone analysis

Introduction

In this chapter, we will discuss the project management process for software maintenance projects. We will discuss the lifecycle of a maintenance project consisting of project planning, scheduling, tracking, risk analysis, and release management process for the same. The chapter also discusses how to set goals that are in line with the objectives of the customer. It explains the need for process capability baseline and process database and how to use historical data for estimating size, effort, and schedule. These aspects of planning are documented in the project management plan, and this plan is used as a baseline document for monitoring the project. The chapter deals with different processes and activities that are carried out for control and monitoring using the project management plan and statistical tools.

Software Maintenance Project Lifecycle

Software maintenance is the last phase in the software lifecycle process. *Software maintenance* in software engineering is defined as the modification of a software product after delivery to correct faults, to improve performance or other attributes, or to adapt the product to a modified environment (ISO14764). The IEEE/EIA 12207 standard for software lifecycle processes describes the software maintenance as the process of a software product undergoing modification of code and associated documentation due to a problem or the need for improvement. The objective is to modify the existing software product while preserving its integrity.

Software maintenance or sustenance maintains or sustains the software product throughout its operational cycle. Modification requests (MRs) are logged and tracked throughout the cycle. The impact of the proposed MRs is determined; accordingly, code and other artifacts are modified, testing is performed, and finally a new point version (sometimes also called as patch) of the software product is released.

A common perception of maintenance release is that it is merely about fixing bugs. However, studies and surveys have shown that the majority of the maintenance effort is used for noncorrective actions (Pigosky, 1997), which are merely about explaining how a particular functionality or a feature works in the software. Further, to add to this perception, most of the times users submit a bug or a problem, which is in reality a functionality enhancement to the system.

The software maintenance release has both managerial and technical challenges. The key management challenges are as follows: addressing customer priorities, aligning resources, and estimating the time and cost. The key technical challenges are as follows: limited understanding of the software, impact analysis, testing, performance, and maintainability after the changes. An important activity for software maintenance project is project planning, and the program manager must address the issues related to the project planning such as:

- Business planning—at organizational level
- Development planning—at organization level
- Release/version planning—at software level
- Individual software change request planning—at request level

Software product maintenance consists of the following:

(a) Fixing defects (bugs) in the code as reported by the customers
(b) Fixing defects or caveats listed in the previous release notes
(c) Modifying the existing feature as per the customer request
(d) Updating or adding new features as per the customer requirement
(e) Adaptation of the existing software to newer or the latest operating system environment

All changes to the software can be characterized by the above five types of maintenance. Maintenance of the software product becomes more expensive as the software products age.

Software Maintenance Process

Software maintenance is the last stage of the software lifecycle. Once the software product is released and deployed at the customer's site, the customer starts using the product on a regular day-to-day basis. While the product is being used, the customer may find malfunctions in the software, due to the defects in the software, or may like to see certain changes in the existing product or certain enhancements to the existing functionality. On the basis of the priorities, the above-mentioned customer's inputs are addressed in the later releases called "upgrade release" while internally it may be termed as "maintenance release." The maintenance release phase keeps the software up to date with the environment changes and the changing user requirements. The process of handling such requests is called software maintenance release process.

Software product development has overall six different phases. These phases include the following:

- Requirements analysis phase
- Product architecting phase
- Designing, coding, and implementation phase
- Testing and verification phase
- Software release and deployment phase
- Product support and maintenance phase

In order to achieve higher efficiency in the maintenance release phase, the earlier phases should be done with minimum errors so that the product is easily maintainable. Unstructured code, poor documentation, and insufficient knowledge of the system by the software programmers who are working on the maintenance release are some of the major problems that can slowdown the maintenance of the software projects.

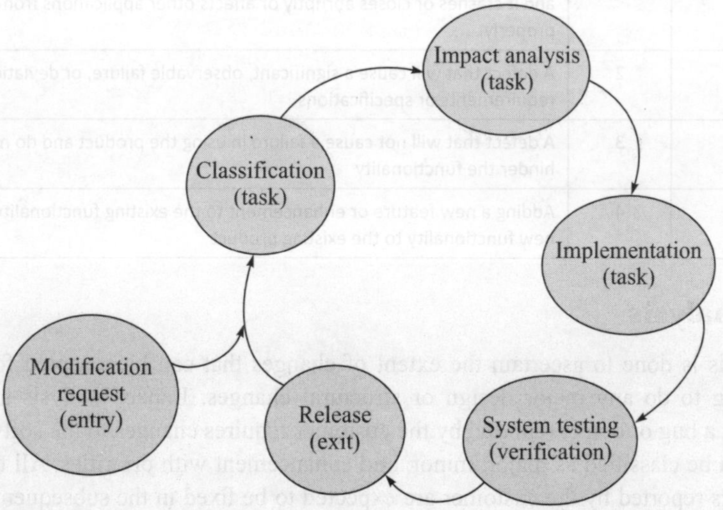

Figure 11.1: Software maintenance process

IEEE/EIA 12207 identifies the primary activities of software maintenance as follows: problem and modification analysis, process implementation, modification implementation, maintenance review/acceptance, migration, and retirement. Practically, the software maintenance project process consists of the following phases (see Figure 11.1):

(a) Modification request (entry)
(b) Classification of requests (tasks)

(c) Impact analysis (tasks)
(d) Implementation (tasks)
(e) Regression testing (and verification)
(f) Release (exit)

Classification of Requests

First and foremost, it is important to classify the MRs received by the customer as well as by the internal teams for further analysis and processing of the requests. Sometimes customer severity and priority may vary from the organizational priority. The customer always wants every request to be addressed at high priority, which is not always possible and his/her high priority request may just be a lack of understanding of the functionality or a totally new enhancement or an additional new feature. Hence, an internal senior management team, which normally consists of representatives from marketing, development, testing, documentation, and related product engineering departments, analyzes the priority of the customer requests before deciding to implement them. A sample classification of MRs is shown in Table 11.1.

Table 11.1: Classification of requests

Category	Severity	Description
Catastrophic/critical	1	A defect that will cause the system or the software unable to function as designed and it crashes or closes abruptly or affects other applications from functioning properly
Major	2	A defect that will cause a significant, observable failure, or deviation from the requirements or specifications
Minor	3	A defect that will not cause a failure in using the product and do not prevent or hinder the functionality
Enhancement	4	Adding a new feature or enhancement to the existing functionality or designing a new functionality to the existing product

Impact Analysis

Impact analysis is done to ascertain the extent of changes that can be accepted for the software without having to do any major design or structural changes. Impact analysis also determines whether or not a bug or defect reported by the customer requires changes to the software.

Defects can be classified as major, minor, and enhancement with priorities. All the priority one and major bugs reported by the customer are expected to be fixed in the subsequent release called maintenance release. Bugs generally do not involve any functionality change. Many a times either writing a few lines of code or modifying minor changes to the existing code would suffice to fix the bug. However, if the major high-priority bug reported by the customer requires significant changes to the functionality of the software, then a detail impact analysis would be required in order to decide whether the changes should be accepted in the next maintenance release or not.

Minor enhancement requests have minor impact on the system functionality. These requests result in the modification of the existing program or addition of few lines to the existing code or simple database changes. These customer requests can be easily accommodated in the maintenance release.

Whether to fix the enhancements (reported as bugs by the customer) or not is decided after conducting an impact analysis. If any enhancement requests have an impact on a large section of the system and involve addition of new modules, interfaces, database tables, or modification to the existing system component, then these changes can go under the next version of software release rather than as maintenance release.

Impact analysis is necessary for the following reasons:

1. To estimate the cost of an MR
    - Understand the cost of the proposed change that is required to fix the bug. Any MR or bug fix to the software involves coding and retesting of the software application, and this involves both hardware and software and human resources allocation. If the MR (defect) has the possibility of affecting large sections of the software and is costlier in terms of resource and time, then the MR need to be re-examined and, if possible, the request needs to be realigned in order to design another safer change.
2. To understand the performance of the software
    - To understand the performance of the software product after the modification has been carried out and the impact on the overall performance of the software after incorporating the changes to the existing software. If the performance is too severe, then the MR can be delayed or the same can be addressed in the forthcoming major release rather than the maintenance release. Also, changes to the software should ensure that it is not exposed to any system threats and thus compromise the confidentiality, integrity, and availability of data. The effect of a modification on the security of the software should be tested during the test and verification process.
3. Impact on testing
    - To determine the parts of the software that needs testing (regression) after the MR has been carried out. The test is also to ensure that the changes have not modified or weakened the existing functionality of the software.

The program manager should decide whether the change request is urgent or a routine request. If the MR is critical and is impacting customer business, then it needs urgent attention and has to be implemented and released to the customer as soon as possible. If it is a routine change, then it can be released in accordance with the release schedule in the project management plan. The program manager, in accordance with the impact analysis committee, decides the priority of the bug and normally gives the same priority rating as the customer although he or she has the right to set a different priority.

The program manager should come out with an overall program plan, which contains the schedule of all the phases such as implementing the changes in code, code review, unit testing, integration testing, system testing and verification, release notes preparation, and software release to the customer. This program plan should be approved by all the stakeholders such as development manager, test manager, configuration manager, and marketing manager of the organization.

The program manager should also address in his/her program plan to clear the backlogs of the defects that are of low priorities and the velocity of the maintenance releases. As the maintenance releases are time bound, all the bugs/defects may not be addressed in one maintenance release. However, there should be a plan and schedule to address the same in the subsequent releases. A recommended maintenance release cycle is once in every 3 months.

The program/project plan should also address a separate plan for an outsourced part, if any feature or part of the software has been outsourced to a different vendor or if there is any hardware or software dependencies. For example, if your software bug fixing/enhancement depends on the operating system, then your schedule should be in accordance with the patch release or maintenance release of the operating system. A sample impact analysis is shown in Table 11.2.

Table 11.2: Sample impact assessment

Category	Severity	Description	Impact	Schedule
Catastrophic/critical	1	A defect that will cause the system or the software unable to function as designed and it crashes or closes abruptly or affects other applications from functioning properly	Direct impact on business and revenues	Schedule fix or patch as soon as possible (within 24 hours)
Major	2	A defect that will cause a significant, observable failure or deviation from the requirements or specifications	No direct impact on the business. Business can still be continued at reduced speed.	Need to be scheduled for next maintenance release
Minor	3	A defect that will not cause a failure in using the product and do not prevent or hinder the functionality	Nil	Can be scheduled for next major software version upgrade
Enhancement	4	Adding a new feature or enhancement to the existing functionality or designing a new functionality to the existing product	Depends on customer priority	Will be decided in consent with the customers

Implementation

Once the defects and the MRs have been approved, the maintenance team implements the change. The goal of this phase is to fix the defects identified and modify the software product. This phase consists of modifying or fixing any feature, algorithms, interface, performing code reviews and performing unit, integration, and system tests. Comprehensive regression testing ensures that the various software components function together properly and that the project implementation meets the system specification.

The main tasks are classified as follows:

- Construction phase
  - o Modify the code and the related interfaces
  - o Code review of the modified code and documents
- Testing phase
  - o Unit and integration test
  - o System and verification test

Construction Phase

Software programmers work on modifying the code to fix the defects identified by the team. Generally, a dedicated team is responsible for this activity. The team is responsible for fixing the defects, based on the priorities, as identified. The main goal is to fix and clear all the backlog bugs in the subsequent maintenance releases. This team may be working on multiple maintenance projects simultaneously. Code review and other related processes are followed as per the organization-defined process.

Testing Phase

Testing phase consists of unit, integration, and system testing. Unit and integration tests are performed by the development team. System testing is done by the system test team. System test ensures a thorough testing, including regression testing of the software product, to ensure that no other previous functionalities have been broken during the defect fixing process.

There are no formal documents that are generated by the development team except unit and integration test reports, which contain all the bugs that are fixed. Release notes are prepared by the system test team. If there are any known issues that were not resolved within a particular maintenance release, then these will be reported in the release notes. A workaround solution will also be given for the known issues, wherever it is possible.

Release and Acceptance

After the system testing phase is complete, the product is released formally to the customer along with the release notes. The release notes consist of installation and configuration details, known issues, workaround and caveats, and bugs that are fixed.

Sometimes a formal acceptance testing, which comprises a series of end-to-end test, is performed by the customer to confirm that the product or system fulfills the acceptance requirements determined by the functional specification in order to safely switchover to the maintenance release. After the acceptance test is complete, the product or the system is considered formally delivered and accepted.

As we discussed, all maintenance activities are similar to those of any software development process. Major activities in maintenance projects consist of analysis, design, coding, testing, and documentation. Maintenance projects must also track requirements (MRs and enhancement requests) as a part of their activities just as is done in development, and update documentation as baselines change. ISO/IEC14764 standard recommends that maintenance projects must adapt to meet the specific organization process. However, for software maintenance projects, some activities or processes are unique as in the following example:

- Problem report system or help desk: an end-user support function that triggers the assessment and prioritization of the MRs.
- MR classification and impact analysis: MR work over a certain size/effort/complexity may be rejected by the maintenance/support teams and rerouted to a development process for the next major release.

- Transition phase: a controlled and coordinated sequence of activities during which software is transferred progressively from the developer to the maintainer; this process becomes more complicated if the projects are outsourced/off-shored.
- Service level agreements (SLAs): specialized, mission-critical, and domain-specific maintenance project contracts

Project Estimation

The methods are the same as any other projects. However, the knowledge of the existing or modifying software product and system is to be considered for the project time estimation. If the team has poor knowledge of the system, then the schedule should accommodate to train the team on the software product.

Software Configuration Management

It is not just sufficient to simply track the MRs. Any changes to the software product must be controlled. The IEEE Standard for Software Maintenance, IEEE1219, describes software configuration management (SCM) as a critical element of the maintenance process. This control is established by implementing and enforcing an approved SCM process. Maintenance team must participate in configuration control review boards meeting to determine the content of the next release/version.

Metrics in Maintenance Projects

There are software measures that are common to all projects: size, effort, schedule, and quality. These measures, which the Software Engineering Institute (SEI) has identified, constitute a good starting point for the maintenance projects. Organization process must determine and decide which measures are appropriate for the organization. IEEE1219-98 suggests measures that are more specific to software maintenance measurement programs, which include the following:

(a) Analyzability: measures of the effort or resources expended in trying to diagnose deficiencies or causes of failure, or in identifying the parts to be modified

(b) Changeability: measures of the maintainer's effort associated with implementing a specified modification

(c) Stability: measures of the unexpected behavior of software, including that encountered during testing

(d) Testability: measures of the maintainer's and user's effort in trying to test the modified software

Certain measures of maintainability of software can be obtained using available commercial tools.

Table 11.3 summarizes the metrics measured for a software maintenance release project in order to calculate the overall efficiency of the project.

Table 11.3: Summary of metrics

Metric	Definition	Formula
Age of open bugs (unresolved)	Average elapsed time from the date the bug was reported	Total of elapsed time (today's date–bug report date)/number of open bugs
Average resolution time	Average elapsed time for the bugs fixed	Sum of elapsed time of each bug/total number of bugs fixed
Mean bug-fix time	Average time taken to fix bugs	Sum of bug fix time of each bug/total number of bugs fixed
Backlog management index	Ratio of number of bugs fixed and delivered during the month to the number of requests received during the month expressed as percentage	(Number of bugs fixed and delivered/number of bugs opened during the month) × 100
Schedule deviation (enhancement requests)	Difference between actual end date and planned end date expressed as the percentage of planned duration (for the enhancement requests)	(Actual end date – planned end date/planned duration) × 100
Not-on-time index	Ratio of number of MRs (bugs) not delivered on time (as per maintenance release schedule) to the total number of MRs delivered (bugs) expressed as percentage	[Number of MRs delivered on time/total number of MRs (bugs) delivered] × 100

Goal Setting, Monitoring, and Control in Maintenance

Just like any other software programs/projects, the program manager is responsible for ensuring that the maintenance projects align with the broader strategy of the organization. This involves setting the goals and objectives, reviewing the individual project plans of the project managers (development and testing), coordinating the planning activity, directing and controlling of company's resources to achieve a specific objective.

The program manager can make use of the management tools, which allows creating and updating the project plans and setting the objectives throughout the lifecycle of the maintenance project. Each individual project manager will create a project plan that will outline and predict the usage of the resources at the beginning of the maintenance project. The program managers track the progress of the projects against the predicted progress of individual plans and use that information for better allocation of the resources. These plans are reviewed and updated for any changes in scheduling or release dates, during the regular program meetings, and in program steering committee that define the program's connection to the overall business strategy.

Defect Prevention Activities in Maintenance Projects

Defect prevention (DP) is a strategy applied to identify the root causes of defects and prevents them from recurring. DP activities are a mechanism for propagating the knowledge of lessons learned in-between projects. Organizations will have an established software process to carry out the software projects; however, this process is enhanced when DP methodologies are implemented, which will help organization process to improve quality, productivity, and reduce costs.

Some of the DP activities include the following:

- Extensive reviews
- Proper regression testing
- Monitoring and tracking defects
- Configuration controls

Key Issues in Software Maintenance

Software maintenance projects provide unique technical and management challenges. One of the challenges is to identify the resources that can work on software containing 500K lines of code that the software engineer did not develop. Planning for a future release, while coding the next maintenance release and also sending out emergency patches for the current release to the customers, makes the entire process challenging. The main challenges in the software maintenance projects are described below.

Limited Knowledge

How quickly a software engineer can understand the software application and make a change or a correction in the software which he or she did not develop? Research indicates that nearly 40–60% of the effort is spent on understanding the software to be modified.

Testing

How much to test? The cost of complete testing on a major piece of software can be expensive in terms of time and money. Regression testing and selective retesting of a software component to verify that the modifications have not caused unintended effects is very important in maintenance projects. Many times it is challenging to coordinate tests on test beds when different members of the maintenance team are working on different problems at the same time. Hence, automation testing plays an important role for maintenance release projects, as it can reduce the time of the entire lifecycle by running tests on 24/7 basis.

Organization Structure

The maintenance team (once software is operational in the field) and the team that developed the software are not necessarily the same. The decision of whether or not to have separate software maintenance function teams depends on priorities and process within the software engineering organizations. What is important is the delegation or assignment of the maintenance responsibility to a single group or person, regardless of the organization's structure. One of the challenges in maintenance projects is to attract and keep software engineers. Maintenance is often not viewed as a glamorous work. As a result, software maintenance personnel are frequently viewed as second-class citizens and therefore the morale suffers. Hence, the frequent movement of these engineers to different projects within the organization keeps the attrition low.

Off-shoring

Outsourcing is a major industry. Many large enterprises are outsourcing entire portfolio of software systems, including software maintenance. To reduce the risk, often the outsourcing option is selected for less mission-critical software product. The challenges for large enterprises are to define the scope of maintenance services required. The scope will help in defining service level agreement (SLA) with the vendors who have agreed to provide maintenance services.

SUMMARY

This chapter dealt with the project management concepts in a maintenance project. A maintenance project starts after development and implementation of code at the customer place. After the warranty period is over, the customer has to enter into an agreement for maintenance of the programs or code. This process of maintenance involves fixing of bugs or defects as being reported during daily operations. Maintenance projects also involve minor as well as major enhancement of the features of existing applications so as to meet the business requirements. However, it requires a systematic and process-oriented approach, which project management concepts, as explained in this chapter, address them. The chapter also dealt with maintenance project management for off-shored maintenance activities.

DISCUSSION POINTS

1. Please explain the lifecycle stages in release management. How is it different from a development project?
2. How do you set quality goals for maintenance projects?
3. Describe estimation process for maintenance projects.
4. How do you carry out DP activities in maintenance projects?
5. What are the different metrics in maintenance projects and what decisions do you take based on these metrics?

CASE STUDY

ISL is a leading Indian multinational in providing customized solution to the customers. It has over 50,000 employees worldwide and uses onsite–offshore model to service its customers in more than 35 countries. The organization bagged its first project, which was worth 100 million dollars, in banking industry, and was to be executed over a period of 2 years. This is the first time that the organization was awarded such a big project, and the management wanted to set appropriate goals for productivity. The goals for productivity were set by using current performance capability in other projects. ISL is a multinational software development organization that has headquarters in Chennai, with a total of 13 development centers in India. Out of these, six are in Chennai, three in Mumbai, two in Hyderabad, one in Gurgaon, and one in Bangalore. It has offices in 13 other countries and more than 7500 employees in India alone. It provides solutions to banking and financial institutions and uses state of the architecture called service-oriented architecture (SOA) to develop software. During the last two decades of its existence, it has grown to become a leader in providing solutions to a number of Fortune 500 companies. Relationship management with its customers is one of the best in the industry, as this relationship is based on providing a cost advantage to the customers with quality and reliability with the flexibility of meeting delivery schedule while being able to incorporate any change requests.

The software developed by ISL helped in boundary-less banking with robust security features. The solution of using SOA architecture helped the customers to bank anytime, anywhere, and on any platform. This has reduced the cost of ownership for this software for its customers, as the customers did not have to invest in upgrading their platform. In the fifth year of operation, the organization bagged its first maintenance project in Australia. As this was an existing customer account, the organization wanted to decide the productivity rate at which the maintenance team for the new customer account was to perform. The organization had published process capability baseline using database from completed projects. The capability baseline had average values of productivity, schedule variation, time to turnaround for defects, etc. However, the customer had its own capability baseline where metrics such as productivity, turnaround time, etc., had values higher than that published by ISL. Niyati was the project manager for this account. She was asked to set the project goals for this maintenance project.

The goal-setting process for a maintenance project followed the steps as described here. Niyati had to follow these steps before setting the goals. The steps are scalable and can be used in other maintenance projects engaged in offshore support mode. The case study described here is from real life and has been successfully adopted in many projects engaged in similar maintenance projects. Niyati, a project manager with 12 years of experience, had her job well cut out. On one hand, she had to come to the terms with the capability of the project team members. On the other hand, she had to meet the requirements of a demanding customer. The customer had been with ISL for more than 5 years and revenue earned from different projects from the same customer had been high. In one particular quarter, the revenue earned from the customer had amounted to one-fifth of the total revenue, and hence Niyati had no choice but to meet the customer needs for productivity and turnaround time.

Niyati, at first, took time to study the performance values demanded by the customer. Compared to latest ISL's process capability baseline, customer's demand for productivity was higher by 7% and average turnaround time for critical defects was less by 9%. The team given to Niyati was a mixture of experienced and inexperienced persons. Technology was not new and some of the experienced persons had worked in the same domain applications in the development phase of the project.

Niyati arranged for training sessions for inexperienced team members by using her experienced team members, who had worked in the development phase of the project. The sessions conducted by the experienced persons covered technology, domain, and application-related knowledge. The trainers then conducted quizzes to evaluate knowledge assimilation in different areas. Also, feedbacks from participants were taken to measure the effectiveness of trainers. This was done to increase the competency level of the team members to meet the challenges posed by the customer. The learning curve, which is usually a flat one for new projects (meaning it takes quite some time to assimilate knowledge), was a steep one (which indicates that knowledge assimilation was quicker and effective). This increased the confidence and the moral level of the team. At this moment, Niyati called for a project team meeting with an agenda to set goals for the team and requested all stakeholders such as infrastructure, travel, visa, and human resources departments to attend the meeting. Also, senior management, who would be part of project review process, was invited to attend. This ensured that at the end of the meeting all the stakeholders would accept the goals that have been set for the project team and would work in unison to fulfill these goals.

After setting the goals, which were in line with the customer expectations, a roadmap was drawn that would indicate the gradual increase of performance level from current capability level to the desired level. The roadmap was shared with the customer later on that indicated the time and resources required to reach the desired level of competency. The roadmap not only helped to ease the stress on the team members to achieve desired stress but also made the process transparent to the customers, which improved customer relations. At the end of 6 months, when customers reviewed the status, the entire team got accolades from the customer and the learning from this goal-setting process was shared as best practices in other projects as well.

12

PROJECT MANAGEMENT IN SOFTWARE PRODUCT DEVELOPMENT

LEARNING OBJECTIVES

In this chapter, the students would learn:

- Process for software product development
- Project management for software product developments
- Project monitoring activities of product development
- Milestone analysis

INTRODUCTION

Software product management deals with the processes dealing with the inception stage of a product until customer delivery, and then upgrade the existing products to provide features that will provide maximum possible value to the customers as well as to the manufacturers. Thus, a software product, apart from providing value to the manufacturers and customers, provides a memorable experience to the end users. A product can be a combination of applications, solutions, materials, and services bundled together. Product management leads to the concepts of portfolio management, product road map, product implementation, and marketing strategy. Because of these possible combinations, the roles of project manager, product manager, and portfolio managers are blurred. In software product development, a project is executed to develop a product. During this execution, a project manager has to deliver "a release" or "a product" while meeting project goals of schedule, effort, cost, and quality.

In a product development scenario, there are three distinct roles: product manager, project manager, and portfolio manager. A product manager manages one or more products from the idea generation stage to sun setting of the product (sun setting implies that the life of the product is over). His/her goal is to maximize business value for all concerned. Thus, he/she coordinates with marketing, development and engineering teams, and quality and support teams to make the product a success. The product manager has a higher role compared to the project manager in that he/she (product manager) has to have a wider business responsibility compared with the project manager. The product manager decides features to be developed in a product, provides a road map for product development, and determines pricing strategy of a product.

The project manager has always a contract with the product manager to execute a project. The contract specifies the terms of reference for specifying goals such as schedule, effort, and quality for completing the development process. He/she is responsible for quality and compliance to defined development process within an organization. His/her team also is answerable for defects reported from customer site and provides support for fixing bugs reported after implementation. He/she prepares project plan and executes it in consultation with the product manager.

The portfolio manager, basically, decides on marketing strategies for selling a product or a suite of products. He/she finds potential market and determines the target customers in consultation with the product manager. He is also an expert in understanding market trends and meets the existing customers on regular basis to improve product features. These information are provided to the product manager who then decides the product road maps, which are developed by the project manager.

For executing projects, the project manager can use software development models as described in Chapter 1. These models represent software development models that have been in practice for long time. However, for software product development, where the development team is located at offshore locations, these models do not help in addressing the issues faced by the offshore team. An offshore–onsite model is used when the company wants to leverage on highly skilled workers available in offshore locations at low cost. The customers are based at onsite and the requirements are gathered at onsite. The requirements are then passed on to the offshore team to develop, test, and deliver them to the customer. In the course of developing these requirements, the customer may change the requirements and these changed requirements need to be developed and delivered as per the negotiated schedule. The existing software development models are not in a position to take care of such dynamic situation and often lead to delay in time schedule and spending more time while developing the products than agreed upon earlier with the customer.

For an organization that develops software products in offshore–onsite business model, it has been observed that the following points become critical:

1. Excellent communication protocol between offshore–onsite teams;
2. Availability of domain knowledge at offshore with the project team;
3. Availability of expertise for carrying out requirement analysis and design with offshore project team;
4. Continuous interaction with customers from offshore team (both oral and written communication);
5. Availability of iterative testing skills in the project team and at low cost;
6. Ability to deal with small, medium, and large customers using the same development model;
7. Ability to accommodate change requests during development life cycle without affecting timeline as negotiated with customers.

To address these teething problems while developing products for software applications, project management in product development process assumes importance. The product development process has to take care of the issues faced by existing models while being able to produce high quality of deliverables.

Project Management in Product Development

Product management process against other software development models lays emphasis on iterative testing. This means that packets are tested even during the requirement phase. A packet consists of already developed functionalities that have been tested and ready to be used. These packets are designed and developed in such a manner that they are independent of each other. Similar requirements received from different customers are grouped together and formed into these packets. This helps in reducing the time required to develop these requirements again.

As the product development progresses in its lifecycle phase, the testing of packets continues till the products are delivered to the customer. Using this methodology, products are developed in "packets." After building these packets, not only each packet is tested thoroughly but also these are integrated and testing is carried out for each new product. The entire product is developed and delivered through an "integrated team" approach. The methodology has four phases. In phase 1, contract is signed with the customer, and based on the contract an integrated team is developed. The contract is quite significant in product management process as the entire scope is determined at this stage. Even though change requests are accommodated later on, this helps the organization in tracking the extra effort required to develop these change requests. This also helps in billing accurately to the customer. After the contract is signed and purchase order is received, requirement gathering and analysis of requirements are carried out. In phase 2, detailed design specifications and test scripts are written based on the requirement analysis. Phase 3 primarily takes care of development of packets and testing. And finally, installation, user training, user acceptance testing, and transition to support happen in phase 4. Each of these phases is described here and a schematic diagram is given in Figure 12.1.

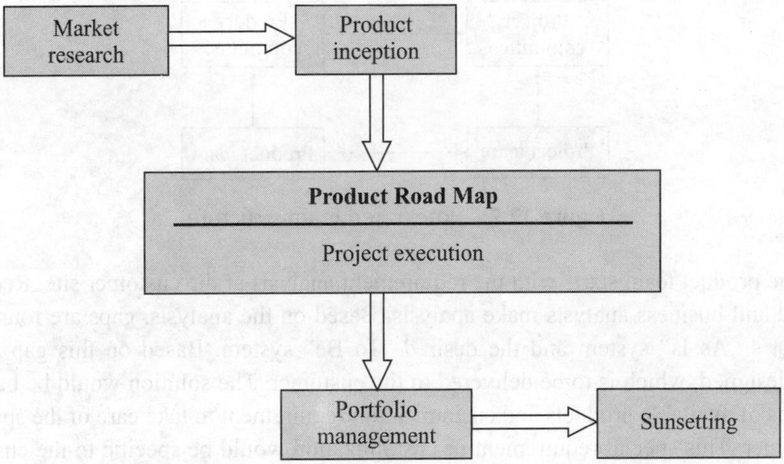

Figure 12.1: Phases in product development process

The Integrated Team Approach

The product management process also addresses how an organization puts together a project team to deliver a product. This concept is called as the integrated project team approach. The integrated team consists of project committee, product committee, product team (all these are based near the customer site), and project team based at offshore. Project committee works with the marketing team in pre-sales activities; it helps the marketing team to clarify any doubts that a prospect will raise during the initial discussion period. Once a prospect is turned into customer, it is the responsibility of the product committee to provide a detailed estimation, negotiate with the customer, and then enter into a detailed contract. The contract, apart from other things, will highlight the scope, the timeline of delivery, and the total effort that would be spent for execution of the project. The offshore project team reports to this committee. The project committee reports to the solution director who has the overall responsibility for providing the products to the customer.

The product committee largely consists of domain experts, who based on market research, and interaction with customers and industry experts, would design different "packets." The packets, as explained earlier, will be independent to each other and would be integrated by offshore product team. These integrated packets would be delivered to the customer. The product committee would also define what is known as roadmap for each product. The roadmap for the products consists of timeline for developing different features. These features would be the part of the packets and would be developed by the product team. The product team directly reports to this product committee. Both product committee and product teams are based near the customer site.

Product offshore team has a primary responsibility of integrating packets, iterative testing, and delivering the final integrated products to the customers. The team has expertise in testing and integration of packets. A schematic organization structure is shown in Figure 12.2.

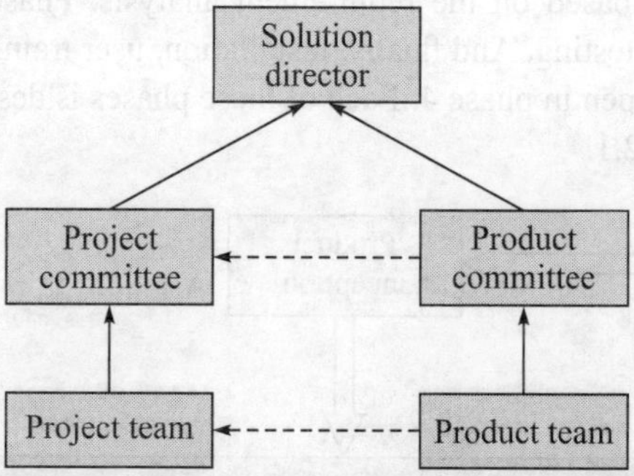

Figure 12.2: Integrated team structure

Phase 1: The product team starts with the requirement analysis at the customer site. Requirements are gathered and business analysts make analysis. Based on the analysis, gaps are found between the customer's "As Is" system and the desired "To Be" system. Based on this gap analysis, a solution is designed, which is to be delivered to the customer. The solution would be based on the combinations of available products and customization requirement to take care of the special needs of the customer. This special requirement or customization would be specific to the customer and hence is not required to be part of the product roadmap. Timeline for delivery of these products are matched with respect to the roadmap so that the final project delivery schedule can be adhered to.

Phase 2: Once the gap analysis is done, the complete solution is divided into "packets"; some of these packets would be in the form of available products while the customization packet has to be developed specific to the customer needs. Each packet is designed in such a manner that they become standalone components that can be integrated with each other. Detailed specifications are prepared in line with the requirements analysis done in phase 1. Test cases are prepared in the current phase with test scenarios so that all the functionalities required can be tested.

Each lifecycle stage has deliverables, and output from one stage is fed into the next stage. At the completion of all LC stages, software is delivered to the customer. So if one stage has a faulty output, it will only have a cascading effect on the next stage and the faults will get compounded. These faults are issues, as they are called in software development projects, and are injected into the software during the course of project execution. The causes for injecting these issues could be lack of complete understanding of the customer's requirements and communication gap between the development team and the end users. These deficiencies would lead to spending effort for reworking the application later on. Also, the customer may not like the look and feel of the software that will be developed resulting in rework of the software. All these are termed as issues in software parlance, and they need to be reworked by the development team as per the customer's specifications and requirements. This rework not only lead to the extra amount of time needed for completing the project assignment, which delays schedule of delivery of the application, but also results in development team spending extra efforts than initially estimated and it means extra cost of software development. As a result it is necessary that the team take initiatives to prevent these issues well in advance. During phase 2, a lot of emphasis is given on upfront activities such as design and test case preparation. Domain experts need to reduce rework effort by preventing defect injection at earlier stage, and review design specifications and test cases.

Phase 3: A product development should start with purchase order being awarded to the vendor organization. A customer would typically provide a statement of authorization where he/she (customer) would authorize the vendor organization to develop software as per his/her (customer's) requirement. The vendor would also be asked to provide estimation for the project. To arrive at the final estimation, vendor would gather requirements from the customer and get details on the functionalities that need to be developed. For estimating total effort and schedule required to complete the project, standard estimation techniques are available. Some of the techniques available are function point, Delphi, COCOMO, and simple medium and complex (SMC) classification technique. However, an organization, which has well-defined processes and has achieved maturity in implementing the processes, will have approved and documented predefined estimation technique. Using approved predefined estimation technique, a project should calculate effort and time period required for completing the project.

Before entering into a contract with any customer, a detailed estimation is carried out. This estimation is then sent to the customer for approval. Table 12.1 shows a sample estimation method used at 3IS software where the requirements are considered at micro level and then classified as low/medium/high/very high.

Table 12.1: Estimation method

Req #	Description	L/M/H/VH	Hours	Comment
001.008	Same day effective dating—add group node	L	5	Add another screen to same day effective dating

003.010	Virtual cutoff notification	H	30	Change to cust prof—new event type (4) Profile XML (3) Cutoff administrator (4) Cutoff scheduler (3) Cutoff executor (3) Manual profile export (1) Cutoff monitor (3) EOC report (2) Trigger XSD (1) Profile XSD (1)
015.013	Send notification to edge on days Final batch	H	30	The interval to retry must be configurable Profile option (3) Script to set option (2) Profile export (3) Cutoff scheduler (4) End of day (3) Toronto EOD (3) Box complete stager (20)
018.058	Fixed message to mail out instructions page	L	5	Change to mail out
018.059	Delphi software upgrade	VH	60	
018.067	Batch maintenance module header	L	5	Batch maintenance utility (5) Menu file (1)
019.071	Eliminate blank field for envelope	M	15	DDE/EDE (7) Key verify (3) Batch edit (7) TFC batch export (2)
018.020	Government flip checkbox	L	5	Template script update
019.054	Forced match report	M	15	Force match app (7) Force match report (5) Menu file (1)
99.001	TMS database update documentation	L	5	
99.002	Import/Export updates	L	5	
99.003	Eliminate system use of user fields	H	30	Approx 17 apps @ 2 days each
	Mitek 3.1 Car upgrade	M	15	
Scale	L = 1–10 hours	6 × 5	30	
	M = 11–20 hours	3 × 15	45	
	H = 21–40 hours	3 × 30	90	
	VH = 41–80 hours	1 × 60	60	
	Total 3IS		**225**	

Each lifecycle stage in product management process has defined deliverables. These deliverables ensure that proper and effective documentation is carried out without making these activities as overhead. Quality system documentation (QSD), an internal system that details all the procedures and processes, is used as a reference while developing software using the product development process. QSD is internal to the organization and is used as induction training material to new entrants at all levels. This ensures that employees at all levels are familiar with the deliverables expected out of them. Table 12.2 lists key deliverables in RITE model.

Table 12.2: List of key deliverables in product management process

Life stages in product management	Required deliverables
At contract/project initiation	Statement of work/contract
Project start-up, ongoing revisions to the project plan	Project plan and iteration plan
Client sign off on RD	Requirements definition
Following RD delivery	Detail design document
Logical day test plan at project initiation, test scripts at design	Test plan and scripts
Upon completion of each iteration	Test results
Ongoing throughout the testing process	Issues list
Upon client delivery	Training materials
Upon client delivery	Customer/user documentation
Upon transition to support	Project transition documentation Lessons learnt documentation

It is important that within the initial phase of the project, the project team reviews, assesses, and incorporates the deliverables and activities that are appropriate for that project into the project plan.

Phase 4: In this phase, deployment of the products is carried out at the customer site. Once all the packets are designed and developed, they are integrated with each other. These packets include standalone components from different products and the customized component to meet the special requirement of the customer. Each packet, after its completion, is tested with packets developed earlier. As a result, testing happens at each stage of packet development, which is one of the unique features of this methodology. Thus, each packet goes through repetitive testing process, which is quite different than other software development models (as discussed in the "Introduction" section). After testing is completed, user acceptance test is carried out at the customer site. On successful completion of testing, the solution is then implemented at the customer location.

SUMMARY

During the last 50 years, software development as a business has seen phenomenal growth. Different models have been developed to streamline and codify the developmental process. There are different models such as applicable to different situations. The processes can be different for products, services, and solutions. In this chapter, project management processes for developing software products have been explained. This method lays emphasis on iterative testing environment to achieve high quality and time-bounded software delivery by using a repeatable packet of software components. The model is also dynamic in terms of accommodating change request without affecting the timeline for delivery. The concept can be tried out in other organization that have off-shore onsite business model. It will also be interesting to see how this model is applicable for solutions and services.

The product management process is different from known software models practiced in other development organizations. The product management described here can be used for any size of the application development. The effort spent is optimized as there is no need to spend time on developing a prototype; while taking advantage of features of iterative model, it accommodates change requests. The difference is in saving time as change request can be accommodated at later stages in this model while meeting all functional and performance requirements of the customer. Thus, while effort overrun is minimized, solutions are delivered as per the schedule. As a result the customer is able to use the delivered solution for his business processes while keeping the total cost of ownership (cost of buying solution, hardware cost, and cost for maintenance of code) at the lowest level, which results in customer satisfaction. Customer satisfaction ensures further business growth potential for the vendor organization and also becomes a reference for prospects.

DISCUSSION POINTS

1. What are the different software development models available?
2. How software product development management is different from software project management?
3. Describe product management process.
4. What is meant by packet development?
5. What is iterative testing?
6. What are the benefits of product management process?

CASE STUDY

3IS Software is a leader in providing software products for use in remittance and payment processing industry and has been in existence for last 25 years. It had revolutionized the image-based payment processing industry by providing simple-to-install and easy-to-maintain core applications that are capable of meeting specific customer needs. The customer profile of the company includes regional and money-center banks, insurance companies and mutual funds, credit card and student loan processors, telecom, utilities, government, and nonprofit organizations. 3IS has been a dominant player in software products business (the other two software businesses are known as software solutions and services). The company has been in development of such products particularly for very large organizations. In fact, as of March 2007, 88 Fortune 500 companies have been in its list of clients.

From the beginning, 3IS has not been quite satisfied with the various models of software development practiced by other competing companies and also with the models as available in the published materials. A brief review at the company from time to time has shown the relative strengths and weakness of various models based on which the company has concluded that direct applications of such models will not adequately fulfill its software quality and efficiency goals.

Using product management process, 3IS Software has achieved customer satisfaction as issues were addressed and all functional requirements were met. The end deliverables were robust as the packets were tested in every iteration of development. Even though at the outset it might seem that it would take more time to deliver the product compared to other software development models, still at the end, rework is reduced as the team was able to capture issues earlier through testing. This not only helps to foster a good relationship with the customer but also ensures that we receive good reference from our customers. The product management process thus ensures that all the issues are detected and fixed before each build so that the final delivery have less issues and are more robust and also ensures that all the functional requirements including change requests of the customer are incorporated into the system, tested comprehensively, and finally released as a robust system.

Being compliant with the product management process has also ensured that quality processes are compliant with SEI CMMI processes. Compliant to SEI CMMI model is an indicator that organization processes are matured and are performed consistently. When the organization decided to go for assessment for SEI CMMI, internal processes were assessed at level 3, indicating that the processes are stable. An indicator called process compliance index (explanation beyond the scope of this chapter), which is used to indicate the level of compliance to CMMI processes, significantly improved (by 50%) over a period of 3 months after adopting RITE model while meeting business goals. Other benefit obtained from RITE model was reduction in issues related to software configuration management. The number of issues related to configuration reduced by 30%.

Table 12.3 indicates process compliance benefits that were achieved over a period of time. The benefits indicate that apart from meeting business goal, the organization was also compliant to CMMI processes. In May 2006, 3IS Software was assessed at SEI CMMI level 3 at their Chennai location where RITE methodology is adopted for development. These results are available in the company internal documents and also available for verification.

Table 12.3: Benefits obtained through product management process

	Jan–Mar 2006	Apr–Jun 2006
Process compliance index	2.3	3.38
Configuration issues/person hour	3.32	2.2

Annexure

A

SAMPLE PROJECT ESTIMATION

ID	Name	Duration	Start	Finish	Predecessors	Outline level
1	Wyndham.com website development	97.833d	1/28/2002 8:00	6/12/2002 15:40		1
2	Project initiation	15.d	1/28/2002 8:00	2/15/2002 17:00		2
3	System setup and familiarization	10.d	1/28/2002 8:00	2/8/2002 17:00		3
4	Software environment setup	10.d	1/28/2002 8:00	2/8/2002 17:00		4
5	Weblogic upgrade 5.1–6.1	10.d	1/28/2002 8:00	2/8/2002 17:00		5
6	Interwoven Upgrade 4.5-5.0	5.d	1/28/2002 8:00	2/1/2002 17:00		5
7	Test preview functionality	1.d	2/4/2002 8:00	2/4/2002 17:00		5
8	Demo preview functionality	1.d	2/5/2002 8:00	2/5/2002 17:00	7	5
9	Prepare baseline	1.d	1/31/2002 8:00	1/31/2002 17:00		4
10	Baseline latest code	1.d	1/31/2002 8:00	1/31/2002 17:00		5

11	Baseline latest documentation	1.d	1/31/2002 8:00	1/31/2002 17:00		5
12	System appreciation and gap analysis	10.d	1/28/2002 8:00	2/8/2002 17:00		4
13	Architecture familiarization	10.d	1/28/2002 8:00	2/8/2002 17:00		5
14	Offshore environment setUp	15.d	1/28/2002 8:00	2/15/2002 17:00		3
15	VPN connectivity	15.d	1/28/2002 8:00	2/15/2002 17:00		4
16	Development environment—Weblogic	1.d	1/28/2002 8:00	1/28/2002 17:00		4
17	Development Environ—Personalization	1.d	1/28/2002 8:00	1/28/2002 17:00		4
18	Source control —define strategy	1.d	1/28/2002 8:00	1/28/2002 17:00		4
19	Review source control strategy	1.d	1/29/2002 8:00	1/29/2002 17:00	18	4
20	Setup source control environment	1.d	1/30/2002 8:00	1/30/2002 17:00	19	4
21	Identification of iteration-1 features	1.d	1/28/2002 8:00	1/28/2002 17:00		3
22	Team site configuration	2.d	2/27/2002 8:00	2/28/2002 17:00		2
23	Create userIDs on Solaris	1.d	2/27/2002 8:00	2/27/2002 17:00		3
24	Setup roles in TeamSite	1.d	2/28/2002 8:00	2/28/2002 17:00	23	3
25	Define deployment strategy	6.d	3/11/2002 8:00	3/18/2002 17:00		2
26	Study existing documentation	2.d	3/11/2002 8:00	3/12/2002 17:00		3
27	Prepare deployment plan Document	3.d	3/13/2002 8:00	3/15/2002 17:00	26	3
28	Review deployment plan	1.d	3/18/2002 8:00	3/18/2002 17:00	27	3
29	Signoff on deployment plan	.d	3/18/2002 17:00	3/18/2002 17:00	28	3
30	Workflow definition	23.333d	2/14/2002 8:00	3/19/2002 10:40		2
31	Define workflow process	.d	2/14/2002 8:00	2/14/2002 8:00		3
32	Workflow 1	23.333d	2/14/2002 8:00	3/19/2002 10:40	31	3
33	Code workflow	1.d	2/14/2002 8:00	2/14/2002 17:00		4
34	Test workflow	1.d	2/15/2002 8:00	2/15/2002 17:00	33	4
35	Document workflow	5.d	2/18/2002 8:00	2/22/2002 17:00	34	4
36	Modify workflow and documentation	2.d	2/26/2002 8:00	2/27/2002 17:00	35	4
37	Workflow documentation ready for review	.d	2/27/2002 17:00	2/27/2002 17:00	36	4
38	Review and signoff workflow document	.154d	2/28/2002 8:00	2/28/2002 9:14	37	4
39	Signoff workflow document	.d	2/28/2002 9:14	2/28/2002 9:14	38	4

40	Update workflow	1.d	3/15/2002 8:00	3/15/2002 17:00		4
41	QA of workflow process	1.333d	3/18/2002 8:00	3/19/2002 10:40	40	4
42	Workflow process signoff	.d	3/19/2002 10:40	3/19/2002 10:40	41	4
43	Environment ready	.d	2/15/2002 8:00	2/15/2002 8:00		2
44	Iteration-1 development	46.d	2/15/2002 8:00	4/19/2002 17:00	3,43	2
45	ASP development	17.d	3/8/2002 8:00	4/1/2002 17:00		3
46	ASP review for special offers	1.d	3/8/2002 8:00	3/8/2002 17:00		4
47	ASP review for functionality—special offers	1.d	3/15/2002 8:00	3/15/2002 17:00		4
48	ASP modifications for special offers	1.d	3/14/2002 8:00	3/14/2002 17:00		4
49	ASP signoff for special offers	.d	3/14/2002 17:00	3/14/2002 17:00	48	4
50	ASP review for help, site search, e-mail list subscriptions, property locator	2.d	3/12/2002 8:00	3/13/2002 17:00		4
51	ASP modifications for help, site search, e-mail list subscriptions, property locator	2.d	3/14/2002 8:00	3/15/2002 17:00	50	4
52	ASP signoff for help, site search, e-mail list subscriptions, property locator	.d	3/15/2002 17:00	3/15/2002 17:00	51	4
53	Submit ASPs for review	.d	3/14/2002 8:00	3/14/2002 8:00		4
54	ASP review for informative content	1.d	3/15/2002 8:00	3/15/2002 17:00	53	4
55	ASP modifications for informative content	1.d	3/18/2002 8:00	3/18/2002 17:00	54	4
56	ASP signoff for informative content	.d	3/18/2002 17:00	3/18/2002 17:00	55	4
57	ASP Review for product line homepages	1.d	3/25/2002 8:00	3/25/2002 17:00		4
58	ASP modifications for product line homepages	1.d	3/26/2002 8:00	3/26/2002 17:00	57	4
59	ASP signoff for product line homepages	.d	3/26/2002 17:00	3/26/2002 17:00	58	4
60	ASP review for Wyndham New York website	1.d	3/25/2002 8:00	3/25/2002 17:00		4
61	ASP modifications for Wyndham New York website	1.d	3/26/2002 8:00	3/26/2002 17:00	60	4
62	ASP signoff for Wyndham New York website	.d	3/26/2002 17:00	3/26/2002 17:00	61	4
63	ASP review for travel agent services	1.d	3/25/2002 8:00	3/25/2002 17:00		4

64	ASP modifications for travel agent services	1.d	3/26/2002 8:00	3/26/2002 17:00	63	4
65	ASP signoff for travel agent services	.d	3/26/2002 17:00	3/26/2002 17:00	64	4
66	ASP review for meetings and weddings	1.d	3/27/2002 8:00	3/27/2002 17:00		4
67	ASP modifications for meetings and weddings	1.d	3/28/2002 8:00	3/28/2002 17:00	66	4
68	ASP signoff for meetings and weddings	.d	3/28/2002 17:00	3/28/2002 17:00	67	4
69	ASP review for destinations and interests	1.d	3/27/2002 8:00	3/27/2002 17:00		4
70	ASP modifications for destinations and interests	1.d	3/28/2002 8:00	3/28/2002 17:00	69	4
71	ASP signoff for destinations and interests	.d	3/28/2002 17:00	3/28/2002 17:00	70	4
72	ASP review for corporate ad pages	1.d	3/27/2002 8:00	3/27/2002 17:00		4
73	ASP modifications for corporate ad pages	1.d	3/28/2002 8:00	3/28/2002 17:00	72	4
74	ASP signoff for corporate ad pages	.d	3/28/2002 17:00	3/28/2002 17:00	73	4
75	ASP review for WOTW—travel tips	1.d	3/29/2002 8:00	3/29/2002 17:00		4
76	ASP modifications for WOTW—travel tips	1.d	4/1/2002 8:00	4/1/2002 17:00	75	4
77	ASP signoff for WOTW—travel tips	.d	4/1/2002 17:00	4/1/2002 17:00	76	4
78	ASP review for WOTW—Cary's Book Club	1.d	3/29/2002 8:00	3/29/2002 17:00		4
79	ASP modifications for WOTW—Cary's Book Club	1.d	4/1/2002 8:00	4/1/2002 17:00	78	4
80	ASP signoff for WOTW—Cary's Book Club	.d	4/1/2002 17:00	4/1/2002 17:00	79	4
81	ASP review for WOTW—content	1.d	3/29/2002 8:00	3/29/2002 17:00		4
82	ASP modifications for WOTW—content	1.d	4/1/2002 8:00	4/1/2002 17:00	81	4
83	ASP signoff for WOTW—content	.d	4/1/2002 17:00	4/1/2002 17:00	82	4
84	ASP review for corporate information	1.d	3/29/2002 8:00	3/29/2002 17:00		4
85	ASP modifications for corporate information	1.d	4/1/2002 8:00	4/1/2002 17:00	84	4
86	ASP signoff for corporate information	.d	4/1/2002 17:00	4/1/2002 17:00	85	4
87	ASP reviews completed	.d	4/1/2002 17:00	4/1/2002 17:00	45	3

88	WBR main page and WBR content	24.d	2/15/2002 8:00	3/20/2002 17:00		3
89	Feature analysis	1.d	2/18/2002 8:00	2/18/2002 17:00		4
90	Development	14.d	2/19/2002 8:00	3/8/2002 17:00	89	4
91	Create DCTs	3.d	2/19/2002 8:00	2/21/2002 17:00		5
92	JSPs corresponding to PT ready	.d	2/22/2002 8:00	2/22/2002 8:00	93SS	5
93	Create presentation templates	2.d	2/22/2002 8:00	2/25/2002 17:00	91	5
94	DCTs and templates ready	.d	2/25/2002 17:00	2/25/2002 17:00	93	5
95	Prepare test plan for feature	1.d	2/27/2002 8:00	2/27/2002 17:00		5
96	Review test plan	.25d	3/7/2002 8:00	3/7/2002 10:00		5
97	Signoff test Plan	.d	3/7/2002 10:00	3/7/2002 10:00	96	5
98	Create JSPs	8.d	2/19/2002 8:00	2/28/2002 17:00		5
99	Develop Java classes	13.d	2/19/2002 8:00	3/7/2002 17:00		5
100	Fix defects	1.d	3/8/2002 8:00	3/8/2002 17:00	99	5
101	Feature development complete	.d	3/8/2002 17:00	3/8/2002 17:00	90	4
102	Create and enter content, preview	23.d	2/15/2002 8:00	3/19/2002 17:00		4
103	Create content	7.d	2/15/2002 8:00	2/25/2002 17:00		5
104	Finalize boiler plates	.d	2/26/2002 17:00	2/26/2002 17:00	103	5
105	Update ASPs	1.d	2/27/2002 8:00	2/27/2002 17:00	104	5
106	Review ASPs	1.d	2/28/2002 8:00	2/28/2002 17:00	105	5
107	Review ASPs	1.d	3/4/2002 8:00	3/4/2002 17:00		5
108	Signoff ASPs	.d	3/5/2002 8:00	3/5/2002 8:00	107	5
109	Review and signoff of DCTs	1.d	2/28/2002 8:00	2/28/2002 17:00		5
110	Signoff of DCTs	.d	2/28/2002 17:00	2/28/2002 17:00	109	5
111	Enter all content	3.d	3/13/2002 8:00	3/15/2002 17:00	110,108	5
112	Internal review of content	3.d	3/13/2002 8:00	3/15/2002 17:00	111SS	5
113	Content entry complete	.d	3/15/2002 17:00	3/15/2002 17:00	112	5
114	Review presentation templates	1.d	3/18/2002 8:00	3/18/2002 17:00	113	5
115	Content and template QA	1.d	3/19/2002 8:00	3/19/2002 17:00	114	5
116	Signoff presentation templates	.d	3/18/2002 17:00	3/18/2002 17:00	114	5
117	Deploy content to development environment	1.d	3/20/2002 8:00	3/20/2002 17:00	102	4
118	Test and integrate feature into website	3.d	3/11/2002 8:00	3/13/2002 17:00	90	4
119	WBR main page and WBR content—feature ready for QA	.d	3/18/2002 8:00	3/18/2002 8:00		4

120	WBR main page and WBR content—QA of feature	1.d	3/18/2002 8:00	3/18/2002 17:00	119	4
121	WBR main page and WBR content—feature complete	.d	3/20/2002 17:00	3/20/2002 17:00	88	3
122	Wyndham by request membership	18.d	2/26/2002 8:00	3/21/2002 17:00		3
123	Feature analysis	1.d	2/26/2002 8:00	2/26/2002 17:00	93	4
124	Development	12.9d	2/26/2002 17:00	3/15/2002 16:12	123	4
125	Create DCTs	1.d	2/27/2002 8:00	2/27/2002 17:00	123	5
126	JSPs corresponding to PT ready	.d	2/26/2002 17:00	2/26/2002 17:00		5
127	Create presentation templates	2.d	3/1/2002 8:00	3/4/2002 17:00	140	5
128	DCTs and templates ready	.d	3/4/2002 17:00	3/4/2002 17:00	127	5
129	Prepare test plan for feature	1.d	2/28/2002 8:00	2/28/2002 17:00	125	5
130	Review test plan	.9d	3/15/2002 8:00	3/15/2002 16:12		5
131	Signoff test Plan	.d	3/15/2002 16:12	3/15/2002 16:12	130	5
132	Create JSPs	8.d	2/27/2002 8:00	3/8/2002 17:00		5
133	Develop Java classes	5.d	2/27/2002 8:00	3/5/2002 17:00		5
134	Feature development complete	.d	3/15/2002 16:12	3/15/2002 16:12	124	4
135	Create content, preview	15.d	2/27/2002 8:00	3/19/2002 17:00		4
136	Create content	10.d	3/1/2002 8:00	3/15/2002 8:00	143SF	5
137	Finalize boilerplates	.d	2/27/2002 8:00	2/27/2002 8:00		5
138	Update ASPs	1.d	2/27/2002 8:00	2/27/2002 17:00	137	5
139	Review ASPs	1.d	2/28/2002 8:00	2/28/2002 17:00	138	5
140	Signoff ASPs	.d	2/28/2002 17:00	2/28/2002 17:00	139	5
141	Review and signoff DCTs	1.d	2/28/2002 8:00	2/28/2002 17:00	125	5
142	Signoff of DCTs	.d	2/28/2002 17:00	2/28/2002 17:00	141	5
143	Enter content	1.d	3/15/2002 8:00	3/15/2002 17:00		5
144	Content entry complete	.d	3/15/2002 17:00	3/15/2002 17:00	143	5
145	Review TPLs	.5d	3/18/2002 8:00	3/18/2002 12:00	144	5
146	Template QA	1.d	3/18/2002 13:00	3/19/2002 12:00	145	5
147	Rework TPLs	1.d	3/18/2002 13:00	3/19/2002 12:00	145	5
148	Signoff of TPLs	.d	3/19/2002 12:00	3/19/2002 12:00	147	5
149	Internal review of content	1.d	3/18/2002 8:00	3/18/2002 17:00	143	5
150	Content entry complete	.d	3/18/2002 17:00	3/18/2002 17:00	149	5
151	Content QA	1.d	3/19/2002 8:00	3/19/2002 17:00	149SS+1 day	5

152	Deploy content to development environment	1.d	3/20/2002 8:00	3/20/2002 17:00	135	4
153	Test and integrate feature into website	3.d	3/18/2002 8:00	3/20/2002 17:00	124,143	4
154	Feature ready for QA	.d	3/20/2002 17:00	3/20/2002 17:00	153	4
155	QA of feature	1.d	3/21/2002 8:00	3/21/2002 17:00	154	4
156	Wyndham By request membership—feature complete	.d	3/21/2002 17:00	3/21/2002 17:00	122	3
157	Additional functionality for WBR	9.d	3/18/2002 8:00	3/28/2002 17:00		3
158	Finalize requirements for forgot password	.d	3/18/2002 8:00	3/18/2002 8:00		4
159	Forgot password	2.d	3/18/2002 8:00	3/19/2002 17:00	158	4
160	Special offers browser	3.d	3/25/2002 8:00	3/27/2002 17:00		4
161	Test additional functionality	1.d	3/28/2002 8:00	3/28/2002 17:00	160	4
162	Signoff additional functionality	.d	3/28/2002 17:00	3/28/2002 17:00	161	4
163	Wyndham.com homepage	46.d	2/15/2002 8:00	4/19/2002 17:00		3
164	Redesign homepage	10.d	2/15/2002 8:00	2/28/2002 17:00		4
165	Wyndham.com Homepage redesign complete	.d	2/28/2002 17:00	2/28/2002 17:00	164	4
166	Update ASPs	2.d	3/18/2002 8:00	3/19/2002 17:00		4
167	Review ASPs	1.d	3/20/2002 8:00	3/20/2002 17:00	166	4
168	Rework ASPs	1.d	3/21/2002 8:00	3/21/2002 17:00	167	4
169	Signoff ASPs	.d	3/21/2002 17:00	3/21/2002 17:00	168	4
170	Feature analysis	4.d	3/26/2002 8:00	3/29/2002 17:00	169,226	4
171	Development	6.d	3/29/2002 17:00	4/8/2002 17:00	170,169	4
172	Create DCTs	2.d	4/1/2002 8:00	4/2/2002 17:00	170	5
173	DCTs ready	.d	3/29/2002 17:00	3/29/2002 17:00		5
174	JSPs corresponding to PT ready	.d	4/3/2002 8:00	4/3/2002 8:00	175SS	5
175	Create presentation templates	4.d	4/3/2002 8:00	4/8/2002 17:00	172	5
176	DCTs and templates ready	.d	4/8/2002 17:00	4/8/2002 17:00	175	5
177	Prepare test plan for feature	1.d	4/3/2002 8:00	4/3/2002 17:00	172	5
178	Review test plan	.8d	4/4/2002 8:00	4/4/2002 15:24	177	5
179	Create JSPs	2.d	4/1/2002 8:00	4/2/2002 17:00		5
180	Develop Java classes	2.d	4/1/2002 8:00	4/2/2002 17:00		5
181	Third party integration	1.d	4/3/2002 8:00	4/3/2002 17:00	180	5
182	Feature development complete	.d	4/8/2002 17:00	4/8/2002 17:00	171	4
183	Create content, preview	26.d	3/14/2002 8:00	4/18/2002 17:00		4

184	Create content	20.d	3/14/2002 8:00	4/11/2002 8:00	188SF	5
185	Review DCTs	1.d	4/9/2002 8:00	4/9/2002 17:00	176	5
186	Rework DCTs	1.d	4/10/2002 8:00	4/10/2002 17:00	185	5
187	Signoff of DCTs	.d	4/10/2002 17:00	4/10/2002 17:00	186	5
188	Enter content for testing	1.d	4/11/2002 8:00	4/11/2002 17:00	187	5
189	Test content entry complete	.d	4/11/2002 17:00	4/11/2002 17:00	188	5
190	Review of TPLs	1.d	4/12/2002 8:00	4/12/2002 17:00	189	5
191	Template QA	1.d	4/15/2002 8:00	4/15/2002 17:00	190	5
192	Template rework	1.d	4/15/2002 8:00	4/15/2002 17:00	190	5
193	Signoff of TPLs	.d	4/15/2002 17:00	4/15/2002 17:00	192	5
194	Enter all content	2.d	4/16/2002 8:00	4/17/2002 17:00	193	5
195	Internal review of content	2.d	4/16/2002 8:00	4/17/2002 17:00	194SS	5
196	Content entry complete	.d	4/17/2002 17:00	4/17/2002 17:00	195	5
197	Content QA	2.d	4/17/2002 8:00	4/18/2002 17:00	195SS+1 day	5
198	Deploy content to development environment	1.d	4/19/2002 8:00	4/19/2002 17:00	183	4
199	Test and integrate feature into website	3.d	4/12/2002 8:00	4/16/2002 17:00	171,188	4
200	Feature ready for QA	.d	4/16/2002 17:00	4/16/2002 17:00	199	4
201	QA of feature	2.d	4/17/2002 8:00	4/18/2002 17:00	200	4
202	Wyndham.com homepage, corporate ad pages—feature complete	.d	4/19/2002 17:00	4/19/2002 17:00	163	3
203	Special offers	29.d	2/26/2002 8:00	4/5/2002 17:00		3
204	Feature analysis	3.d	3/5/2002 8:00	3/7/2002 17:00	128	4
205	Development	11.d	3/8/2002 8:00	3/22/2002 17:00		4
206	Create DCTs	2.d	3/13/2002 8:00	3/14/2002 17:00		5
207	DCTs ready	.d	3/14/2002 17:00	3/14/2002 17:00	206	5
208	JSPs corresponding to PT ready	.d	3/19/2002 8:00	3/19/2002 8:00		5
209	Create presentation templates	3.d	3/19/2002 8:00	3/21/2002 17:00	208	5
210	DCTs and templates ready	.d	3/21/2002 17:00	3/21/2002 17:00	209	5
211	Prepare test plan for feature	1.d	3/15/2002 8:00	3/15/2002 17:00	206	5
212	Review test plan	.889d	3/18/2002 8:00	3/18/2002 16:07	211	5
213	Create JSPs	8.d	3/8/2002 8:00	3/19/2002 17:00	204	5
214	Develop Java classes	3.d	3/20/2002 8:00	3/22/2002 17:00	213	5
215	Feature development complete	.d	3/22/2002 17:00	3/22/2002 17:00	205	4

216	Create content, preview	24.d	2/26/2002 8:00	3/29/2002 17:00		4
217	Create content	15.d	2/26/2002 8:00	3/19/2002 8:00	221SF	5
218	DCT review	1.d	3/15/2002 8:00	3/15/2002 17:00	207	5
219	Rework DCTs based on review	1.d	3/18/2002 8:00	3/18/2002 17:00	218	5
220	Signoff of DCTs	.d	3/18/2002 17:00	3/18/2002 17:00	219	5
221	Enter content for testing	2.d	3/19/2002 8:00	3/20/2002 17:00	220	5
222	Test content entry complete	.d	3/20/2002 17:00	3/20/2002 17:00	221	5
223	Review and signoff of TPLs	1.d	3/21/2002 8:00	3/21/2002 17:00	222	5
224	Template QA	1.d	3/22/2002 8:00	3/22/2002 17:00	223	5
225	Rework TPLs	1.d	3/25/2002 8:00	3/25/2002 17:00	224	5
226	Signoff of TPLs	.d	3/25/2002 17:00	3/25/2002 17:00	225	5
227	Enter all content	3.d	3/26/2002 8:00	3/28/2002 17:00	226	5
228	Internal review of content	3.d	3/26/2002 8:00	3/28/2002 17:00	227SS	5
229	Content entry complete	.d	3/28/2002 17:00	3/28/2002 17:00	228	5
230	Content QA	3.d	3/27/2002 8:00	3/29/2002 17:00	228SS+1 day	5
231	Deploy content to development environment	5.d	4/1/2002 8:00	4/5/2002 17:00	216	4
232	Test and integrate feature into website	3.d	3/25/2002 8:00	3/27/2002 17:00	205,221	4
233	Feature ready for QA	.d	3/27/2002 17:00	3/27/2002 17:00	232	4
234	QA of feature	2.d	3/28/2002 8:00	3/29/2002 17:00	233	4
235	Special offers—feature complete	.d	4/5/2002 17:00	4/5/2002 17:00	203	3
236	Help	24.d	3/1/2002 8:00	4/3/2002 17:00		3
237	Feature analysis	2.d	3/14/2002 8:00	3/15/2002 17:00		4
238	Development	7.d	3/14/2002 8:00	3/22/2002 17:00	237	4
239	Create DCTs	2.d	3/18/2002 8:00	3/19/2002 17:00		5
240	DCTs ready	.d	3/19/2002 17:00	3/19/2002 17:00	239	5
241	Create JSPs	3.d	3/14/2002 8:00	3/18/2002 17:00	237	5
242	JSPs corresponding to PT ready	.d	3/18/2002 17:00	3/18/2002 17:00	241	5
243	Create presentation templates	2.d	3/20/2002 8:00	3/21/2002 17:00	240	5
244	Document usage instructions	1.d	3/22/2002 8:00	3/22/2002 17:00	243	5
245	DCTs and templates ready	.d	3/22/2002 17:00	3/22/2002 17:00	244	5
246	Prepare test plan for feature	1.d	3/18/2002 8:00	3/18/2002 17:00	237	5
247	Review test plan	.9d	3/19/2002 8:00	3/19/2002 16:12	246	5
248	Create Java classes	2.d	3/18/2002 8:00	3/19/2002 17:00		5

249	Feature development complete	.d	3/22/2002 17:00	3/22/2002 17:00	238	4
250	Create content, preview	23.d	3/1/2002 8:00	4/2/2002 17:00		4
251	Create content	15.d	3/1/2002 8:00	3/22/2002 8:00	255SF	5
252	DCT review	1.d	3/20/2002 8:00	3/20/2002 17:00	240	5
253	Update DCT based on review	1.d	3/21/2002 8:00	3/21/2002 17:00	252	5
254	Signoff of DCTs	.d	3/21/2002 17:00	3/21/2002 17:00	253	5
255	Enter content for testing	1.d	3/22/2002 8:00	3/22/2002 17:00	254	5
256	Test content entry complete	.d	3/22/2002 17:00	3/22/2002 17:00	255	5
257	Review and signoff of TPLs	1.d	3/25/2002 8:00	3/25/2002 17:00	256	5
258	Template QA	1.d	3/26/2002 8:00	3/26/2002 17:00	257	5
259	Rework TPLs	1.d	3/27/2002 8:00	3/27/2002 17:00	258	5
260	Signoff of TPLs	.d	3/27/2002 17:00	3/27/2002 17:00	259	5
261	Enter all content	4.d	3/28/2002 8:00	4/2/2002 17:00	260	5
262	Internal review of content	4.d	3/28/2002 8:00	4/2/2002 17:00	261SS	5
263	Content entry complete	.d	4/2/2002 17:00	4/2/2002 17:00	262	5
264	Content QA	4.d	3/27/2002 8:00	4/1/2002 17:00	228SS+1 day	5
265	Deploy content to development environment	1.d	4/3/2002 8:00	4/3/2002 17:00	250	4
266	Test and integrate feature into website	3.d	3/25/2002 8:00	3/27/2002 17:00	238,255	4
267	Feature ready for QA	.d	3/27/2002 17:00	3/27/2002 17:00	266	4
268	QA of feature	2.d	3/28/2002 8:00	3/29/2002 17:00	267	4
269	Help—feature complete	.d	4/3/2002 17:00	4/3/2002 17:00	236	3
270	Lanyon feed	12.833d	3/15/2002 8:00	4/2/2002 15:40		3
271	Develop update script	3.d	3/15/2002 8:00	3/19/2002 17:00		4
272	Test update script	2.d	3/20/2002 8:00	3/21/2002 17:00	271	4
273	Setup and test batch process	2.d	3/22/2002 8:00	3/25/2002 17:00	272	4
274	Prepare process documentation	3.d	3/26/2002 8:00	3/28/2002 17:00	273	4
275	Prepare test plan for feature	1.d	3/29/2002 8:00	3/29/2002 17:00	274	4
276	Review test plan and documentation	.833d	4/1/2002 8:00	4/1/2002 15:40	275	4
277	Set up environment for Lanyon process	.5d	3/15/2002 8:00	3/15/2002 12:00		4
278	Set up FTP server in DMZ	.5d	3/15/2002 8:00	3/15/2002 12:00		5
279	Lanyon process ready for QA	.d	4/1/2002 15:40	4/1/2002 15:40	277,276	4
280	QA Lanyon process	1.d	4/1/2002 15:40	4/2/2002 15:40	279	4

281	Signoff of Lanyon process	.d	4/2/2002 15:40	4/2/2002 15:40	280	4
282	Lanyon feed—feature complete	.d	4/2/2002 15:40	4/2/2002 15:40	270	3
283	Hotel homepages	42.d	2/15/2002 8:00	4/15/2002 17:00		3
284	Feature analysis	1.d	2/22/2002 8:00	2/22/2002 17:00		4
285	Development	18.d	2/25/2002 8:00	3/20/2002 17:00	284	4
286	Create DCTs and TPLs	10.d	2/25/2002 8:00	3/8/2002 17:00	284	5
287	Property	1.d	2/25/2002 8:00	2/25/2002 17:00		6
288	DCT	1.d	2/25/2002 8:00	2/25/2002 17:00		7
289	Lanyon DCTs	1.d	2/25/2002 8:00	2/25/2002 17:00		6
290	DCT	1.d	2/25/2002 8:00	2/25/2002 17:00		7
291	Additional info	1.d	2/25/2002 8:00	2/25/2002 17:00		6
292	DCT	1.d	2/25/2002 8:00	2/25/2002 17:00		7
293	Property DCTs and TPLs ready	.d	2/25/2002 17:00	2/25/2002 17:00	287,289,291	6
294	Detail	1.d	2/25/2002 8:00	2/25/2002 17:00		6
295	DCT	1.d	2/25/2002 8:00	2/25/2002 17:00		7
296	FAQ	.5d	2/26/2002 8:00	2/26/2002 12:00		6
297	DCT	.5d	2/26/2002 8:00	2/26/2002 12:00	295	7
298	Guest room	1.d	2/26/2002 13:00	2/27/2002 12:00		6
299	DCT	1.d	2/26/2002 13:00	2/27/2002 12:00	297	7
300	Suggested itineraries	1.d	2/25/2002 8:00	2/25/2002 17:00		6
301	DCT	1.d	2/25/2002 8:00	2/25/2002 17:00		7
302	Local events	1.d	2/26/2002 8:00	2/26/2002 17:00		6
303	DCT	1.d	2/26/2002 8:00	2/26/2002 17:00	301	7
304	All hotel page DCTs ready	.d	2/27/2002 12:00	2/27/2002 12:00	294,296,298,300	6
305	Develop PTs for Lanyon and additional Info DCTs	1.d	3/8/2002 8:00	3/8/2002 17:00		6
306	Develop PTs for detail area, FAQ, and guest rooms	1.d	3/8/2002 8:00	3/8/2002 17:00		6
307	Prepare test plan for feature	1.d	3/18/2002 8:00	3/18/2002 17:00		5
308	Review test plan	.667d	3/19/2002 8:00	3/19/2002 14:20	307	5
309	Create JSPs	5.d	2/25/2002 8:00	3/1/2002 17:00		5
310	Develop Java classes	10.d	2/25/2002 8:00	3/8/2002 17:00		5
311	Third party integration	8.d	3/11/2002 8:00	3/20/2002 17:00		5
312	Integration to intellicast for weather functionality	2.d	3/11/2002 8:00	3/12/2002 17:00	310	6
313	Towne interface	2.d	3/13/2002 8:00	3/14/2002 17:00	312	6

314	Vicinity interface	2.d	3/15/2002 8:00	3/18/2002 17:00	313	6
315	Viator interface	1.d	3/19/2002 8:00	3/19/2002 17:00	314	6
316	Mpoint interface	1.d	3/20/2002 8:00	3/20/2002 17:00	315	6
317	Feature development complete	.d	3/20/2002 17:00	3/20/2002 17:00	285	4
318	Create content, preview	40.d	2/15/2002 8:00	4/11/2002 17:00		4
319	Create content	10.d	2/15/2002 8:00	2/28/2002 17:00	329SF	5
320	Create spreadsheet for boilerplates	.d	2/27/2002 8:00	2/27/2002 8:00		5
321	Update boilerplate text	1.d	3/6/2002 8:00	3/6/2002 17:00	320	5
322	Finalize boilerplates	.d	3/6/2002 8:00	3/6/2002 8:00	321	5
323	Update ASPs	2.d	3/6/2002 8:00	3/7/2002 17:00	322	5
324	Review ASPs	1.d	3/8/2002 8:00	3/8/2002 17:00	323	5
325	Signoff ASPs	.d	3/8/2002 17:00	3/8/2002 17:00	324	5
326	Review and signoff DCTs	2.5d	2/26/2002 8:00	2/28/2002 12:00		5
327	Property DCTs	1.d	2/26/2002 8:00	2/26/2002 17:00	293	6
328	Remaining DCTs	1.d	2/27/2002 13:00	2/28/2002 12:00	304	6
329	Enter content for testing	2.d	2/27/2002 8:00	2/28/2002 17:00	327	5
330	Test content entry complete	.d	2/28/2002 17:00	2/28/2002 17:00	329	5
331	Review and signoff of TPLs	1.d	3/1/2002 8:00	3/1/2002 17:00	330	5
332	Template QA	1.d	3/4/2002 8:00	3/4/2002 17:00	331	5
333	Rework TPLs	1.d	3/5/2002 8:00	3/5/2002 17:00	332	5
334	Signoff of TPLs	.d	3/5/2002 17:00	3/5/2002 17:00	333	5
335	Enter all content	31.5d	2/27/2002 8:00	4/11/2002 12:00		5
336	Enter content for hotel main pages and additional information	30.d	2/27/2002 8:00	4/9/2002 17:00	327	6
337	Enter content for all other pages	30.d	2/28/2002 13:00	4/11/2002 12:00	328	6
338	Internal review of content	25.d	2/27/2002 8:00	4/2/2002 17:00	335SS	5
339	Content entry complete	.d	4/2/2002 17:00	4/2/2002 17:00	338	5
340	Content QA	30.d	3/1/2002 8:00	4/11/2002 17:00	338SS+2 days	5
341	Deploy content to development environment	2.d	4/12/2002 8:00	4/15/2002 17:00	318	4
342	Test and integrate feature into website	3.d	3/21/2002 8:00	3/25/2002 17:00	285,329	4
343	Feature ready for QA	.d	3/25/2002 17:00	3/25/2002 17:00	342	4
344	QA of feature	2.d	3/26/2002 8:00	3/27/2002 17:00	343	4
345	Hotel homepages—feature complete	.d	4/15/2002 17:00	4/15/2002 17:00	283	3

346	Hotel navigation bar	10.5d	3/14/2002 8:00	3/28/2002 12:00		3
347	Create DCT	2.d	3/14/2002 8:00	3/15/2002 17:00		4
348	Create XML	1.d	3/18/2002 8:00	3/18/2002 17:00	347	4
349	Review DCT	1.d	3/19/2002 8:00	3/19/2002 17:00	348	4
350	Rework DCT and XML	1.d	3/20/2002 8:00	3/20/2002 17:00	349	4
351	Signoff DCT	.d	3/20/2002 17:00	3/20/2002 17:00	350	4
352	Generate default DCRs for all hotels	.5d	3/21/2002 8:00	3/21/2002 12:00	351	4
353	Update DCRs for specific hotels	5.d	3/21/2002 13:00	3/28/2002 12:00	352	4
354	Test integration with property pages	1.d	3/21/2002 13:00	3/22/2002 12:00	352	4
355	Informative content	21.5d	3/4/2002 8:00	4/2/2002 12:00		3
356	Feature analysis	1.d	3/18/2002 8:00	3/18/2002 17:00	304	4
357	Development	2.8d	3/19/2002 8:00	3/21/2002 15:24	356	4
358	Create DCTs	1.d	3/19/2002 8:00	3/19/2002 17:00	356	5
359	JSPs corresponding to PT ready	.d	3/19/2002 17:00	3/19/2002 17:00	358	5
360	Create presentation templates	1.d	3/20/2002 8:00	3/20/2002 17:00	359	5
361	DCTs and templates ready	.d	3/20/2002 17:00	3/20/2002 17:00	360	5
362	Prepare test plan for feature	1.d	3/20/2002 8:00	3/20/2002 17:00	358	5
363	Review test plan	.8d	3/21/2002 8:00	3/21/2002 15:24	362	5
364	Feature development complete	.d	3/21/2002 15:24	3/21/2002 15:24	357	4
365	Create content, preview	20.5d	3/4/2002 8:00	4/1/2002 12:00		4
366	Create content	15.d	3/4/2002 8:00	3/25/2002 8:00	370SF	5
367	Review DCTs	1.d	3/21/2002 8:00	3/21/2002 17:00	361	5
368	Rework DCTs	1.d	3/22/2002 8:00	3/22/2002 17:00	367	5
369	Signoff of DCTs	.d	3/22/2002 17:00	3/22/2002 17:00	368	5
370	Enter content for testing	1.d	3/25/2002 8:00	3/25/2002 17:00	369	5
371	Test content entry complete	.d	3/25/2002 17:00	3/25/2002 17:00	370	5
372	Review and signoff of TPLs	1.d	3/26/2002 8:00	3/26/2002 17:00	371	5
373	Template QA	.5d	3/27/2002 8:00	3/27/2002 12:00	372	5
374	Rework TPLs	1.d	3/27/2002 13:00	3/28/2002 12:00	373	5
375	Signoff of TPLs	.d	3/28/2002 12:00	3/28/2002 12:00	374	5
376	Enter all content	1.d	3/28/2002 13:00	3/29/2002 12:00	375	5
377	Internal review of content	1.d	3/28/2002 13:00	3/29/2002 12:00	376SS	5
378	Content entry complete	.d	3/29/2002 12:00	3/29/2002 12:00	377	5

379	Content QA	1.d	3/29/2002 13:00	4/1/2002 12:00	377SS+1 day	5
380	Deploy content to development environment	1.d	4/1/2002 13:00	4/2/2002 12:00	365	4
381	Test and integrate feature into website	1.d	3/26/2002 8:00	3/26/2002 17:00	357,370	4
382	Feature ready for QA	.d	3/26/2002 17:00	3/26/2002 17:00	381	4
383	QA of feature	1.d	3/27/2002 8:00	3/27/2002 17:00	382	4
384	Informative content—feature complete	.d	4/2/2002 12:00	4/2/2002 12:00	355	3
385	Site search	31.5d	2/18/2002 8:00	4/2/2002 12:00		3
386	Feature analysis	2.d	2/18/2002 8:00	2/19/2002 17:00		4
387	Development	21.d	2/20/2002 8:00	3/20/2002 17:00		4
388	Redesign look and feel	1.d	3/15/2002 8:00	3/15/2002 17:00		5
389	Create DCTs	1.d	3/18/2002 8:00	3/18/2002 17:00	291,388	5
390	Create presentation templates	2.d	3/19/2002 8:00	3/20/2002 17:00	389	5
391	DCTs and templates ready	.d	3/20/2002 17:00	3/20/2002 17:00	390	5
392	Prepare test plan for feature	1.d	3/19/2002 8:00	3/19/2002 17:00	389	5
393	Review test plan	.8d	3/20/2002 8:00	3/20/2002 15:24	392	5
394	Create JSPs	4.d	2/20/2002 8:00	2/25/2002 17:00		5
395	Develop Java classes	2.d	2/20/2002 8:00	2/21/2002 17:00		5
396	Third party integration	5.d	2/22/2002 8:00	2/28/2002 17:00		5
397	Inktomi search engine	5.d	2/22/2002 8:00	2/28/2002 17:00	395	6
398	Feature development complete	.d	3/20/2002 17:00	3/20/2002 17:00	387	4
399	Create content, preview	26.d	2/25/2002 8:00	4/1/2002 17:00		4
400	Create content	20.d	2/25/2002 8:00	3/25/2002 8:00	404SF	5
401	Review DCTs	1.d	3/21/2002 8:00	3/21/2002 17:00	391	5
402	Rework DCTs	1.d	3/22/2002 8:00	3/22/2002 17:00	401	5
403	Signoff of DCTs	.d	3/22/2002 17:00	3/22/2002 17:00	402	5
404	Enter content for testing	1.d	3/25/2002 8:00	3/25/2002 17:00	403	5
405	Test content entry complete	.d	3/25/2002 17:00	3/25/2002 17:00	404	5
406	Review and signoff of TPLs	1.d	3/26/2002 8:00	3/26/2002 17:00	405	5
407	Template QA	1.d	3/27/2002 8:00	3/27/2002 17:00	406	5
408	Rework TPLs	1.d	3/28/2002 8:00	3/28/2002 17:00	407	5
409	Signoff of TPLs	.d	3/28/2002 17:00	3/28/2002 17:00	408	5
410	Enter all content	1.d	3/29/2002 8:00	3/29/2002 17:00	409	5
411	Internal review of content	1.d	3/29/2002 8:00	3/29/2002 17:00	410SS	5

412	Content entry complete	.d	3/29/2002 17:00	3/29/2002 17:00	411	5
413	Content QA	1.d	4/1/2002 8:00	4/1/2002 17:00	411SS+1 day	5
414	Deploy content to development environment	.5d	4/2/2002 8:00	4/2/2002 12:00	399	4
415	Test and integrate feature into website	3.d	3/26/2002 8:00	3/28/2002 17:00	387,404	4
416	Feature ready for QA	.d	3/28/2002 17:00	3/28/2002 17:00	415	4
417	QA of feature	2.d	3/29/2002 8:00	4/1/2002 17:00	416	4
418	Site Search—feature complete	.d	2/15/2002 8:00	2/15/2002 8:00		3
419	Email list subscriptions	28.d	2/25/2002 13:00	4/4/2002 12:00		3
420	Feature analysis	.5d	3/21/2002 8:00	3/21/2002 12:00	361	4
421	Development	6.d	3/21/2002 13:00	3/29/2002 12:00		4
422	Create DCTs	1.d	3/21/2002 13:00	3/22/2002 12:00	420	5
423	JSPs corresponding to PT ready	.d	3/22/2002 12:00	3/22/2002 12:00	422	5
424	Create database update script	1.d	3/22/2002 13:00	3/25/2002 12:00	423	5
425	DCTs and Templates ready	.d	3/25/2002 12:00	3/25/2002 12:00	424	5
426	Prepare test plan for feature	1.d	3/22/2002 13:00	3/25/2002 12:00	422	5
427	Review test plan	.5d	3/25/2002 13:00	3/25/2002 17:00	426	5
428	Create JSPs	2.d	3/21/2002 13:00	3/25/2002 12:00	420	5
429	Develop Java classes	4.d	3/25/2002 13:00	3/29/2002 12:00	428	5
430	Third party integration	4.d	3/22/2002 8:00	3/27/2002 17:00		5
431	CheetahMail technical interface agreement ready	.d	3/22/2002 8:00	3/22/2002 8:00		6
432	Develop CheetahMail interface	2.d	3/22/2002 8:00	3/25/2002 17:00	431	6
433	CheetahMail development complete	.d	3/25/2002 17:00	3/25/2002 17:00	432	6
434	Integrate and test CheetahMail interface	2.d	3/26/2002 8:00	3/27/2002 17:00	433,432	6
435	Feature development complete	.d	3/29/2002 12:00	3/29/2002 12:00	421	4
436	Create content, preview	23.d	2/25/2002 13:00	3/28/2002 12:00		4
437	Create content	22.d	2/25/2002 13:00	3/27/2002 13:00	441SF	5
438	Review DCTs	1.d	3/25/2002 13:00	3/26/2002 12:00	425	5
439	Rework DCTs	1.d	3/26/2002 13:00	3/27/2002 12:00	438	5
440	Signoff of DCTs	.d	3/27/2002 12:00	3/27/2002 12:00	439	5
441	Enter content	1.d	3/27/2002 13:00	3/28/2002 12:00	440	5
442	Content entered	.d	3/28/2002 12:00	3/28/2002 12:00	441	5

443	Deploy content to development environment	.5d	3/28/2002 13:00	3/28/2002 17:00	436	4
444	Test and integrate feature into website	3.d	3/29/2002 13:00	4/3/2002 12:00	421,441	4
445	Feature ready for QA	.d	4/3/2002 12:00	4/3/2002 12:00	444	4
446	QA of feature	1.d	4/3/2002 13:00	4/4/2002 12:00	445	4
447	Email list subscriptions—feature complete	.d	4/4/2002 12:00	4/4/2002 12:00	419	3
448	Customer interface	36.5d	2/15/2002 8:00	4/8/2002 12:00		3
449	Feature analysis	1.d	3/25/2002 13:00	3/26/2002 12:00	424	4
450	Development	12.5d	3/15/2002 8:00	4/2/2002 12:00		4
451	Create DCTs	1.d	3/26/2002 13:00	3/27/2002 12:00	449	5
452	JSPs corresponding to PT ready	.d	3/27/2002 12:00	3/27/2002 12:00	451	5
453	Create presentation templates	1.d	3/27/2002 13:00	3/28/2002 12:00	452	5
454	DCTs and templates ready	.d	3/28/2002 12:00	3/28/2002 12:00	453	5
455	Prepare test plan for feature	1.d	3/27/2002 13:00	3/28/2002 12:00	451	5
456	Review test plan	.5d	3/28/2002 13:00	3/28/2002 17:00	455	5
457	Create JSPs	2.d	3/26/2002 13:00	3/28/2002 12:00	449	5
458	Develop Java classes	3.d	3/28/2002 13:00	4/2/2002 12:00	457	5
459	Third party integration	.d	3/15/2002 8:00	3/15/2002 8:00		5
460	CheetahMail database migration	.d	3/15/2002 8:00	3/15/2002 8:00		6
461	Feature development complete	.d	4/2/2002 12:00	4/2/2002 12:00	450	4
462	Create content, preview	33.5d	2/15/2002 8:00	4/3/2002 12:00		4
463	Create content	20.d	3/4/2002 13:00	4/1/2002 13:00	467SF	5
464	Review DCTs	1.d	3/28/2002 13:00	3/29/2002 12:00	454	5
465	Rework DCTs	1.d	3/29/2002 13:00	4/1/2002 12:00	464	5
466	Signoff of DCTs	.d	4/1/2002 12:00	4/1/2002 12:00	465	5
467	Enter content	1.d	4/1/2002 13:00	4/2/2002 12:00	466	5
468	Test content entry complete	.d	2/15/2002 8:00	2/15/2002 8:00		5
469	Review and signoff of TPLs	1.d	2/15/2002 8:00	2/15/2002 17:00		5
470	Template QA	1.d	2/18/2002 8:00	2/18/2002 17:00	469	5
471	Rework TPLs	1.d	2/19/2002 8:00	2/19/2002 17:00	470	5
472	Signoff of TPLs	.d	2/19/2002 17:00	2/19/2002 17:00	471	5
473	Internal review of content	1.d	4/1/2002 13:00	4/2/2002 12:00	467SS	5
474	Content entry complete	.d	4/2/2002 12:00	4/2/2002 12:00	473	5
475	Content QA	1.d	4/2/2002 13:00	4/3/2002 12:00	474	5

476	Deploy content to development environment	1.d	4/3/2002 13:00	4/4/2002 12:00	462	4
477	Test and integrate feature into website	3.d	4/2/2002 13:00	4/5/2002 12:00	450,467	4
478	Feature ready for QA	.d	4/5/2002 12:00	4/5/2002 12:00	477	4
479	QA of feature	1.d	4/5/2002 13:00	4/8/2002 12:00	478	4
480	Customer interface—feature complete	.d	4/8/2002 12:00	4/8/2002 12:00	448	3
481	Start WBE integration	.d	3/19/2002 8:00	3/19/2002 8:00		3
482	Web booking engine integration	29.5d	2/20/2002 8:00	4/2/2002 12:00		3
483	WBE 3.0 installed in test	.d	2/20/2002 8:00	2/20/2002 8:00		4
484	Feature analysis	1.d	3/19/2002 8:00	3/19/2002 17:00	483,481	4
485	Finalize interface definitions	2.d	3/20/2002 8:00	3/21/2002 17:00	484	4
486	Prepare test plan for feature	1.d	3/22/2002 8:00	3/22/2002 17:00	485	4
487	Review test plan	1.5d	3/25/2002 8:00	3/26/2002 12:00	486	4
488	Test feature in development	3.d	3/26/2002 13:00	3/29/2002 12:00	487	4
489	Feature ready for QA	.d	3/29/2002 12:00	3/29/2002 12:00	488	4
490	QA of feature	2.d	3/29/2002 13:00	4/2/2002 12:00	489	4
491	Web booking engine integration—feature complete	.d	4/2/2002 12:00	4/2/2002 12:00	482	3
492	Ramky returns offshore	.d	3/4/2002 8:00	3/4/2002 8:00		3
493	Property locator	21.125d	3/4/2002 8:00	4/2/2002 9:00		3
494	Feature Analysis	1.d	3/4/2002 8:00	3/4/2002 17:00	492	4
495	Development	15.125d	3/5/2002 8:00	3/26/2002 9:00		4
496	Create JSPs	5.d	3/5/2002 8:00	3/11/2002 17:00	494	5
497	Develop Java classes	8.d	3/12/2002 8:00	3/21/2002 17:00	496	5
498	Prepare test plan for feature	1.d	3/22/2002 8:00	3/22/2002 17:00	497	5
499	Review test plan	.125d	3/25/2002 8:00	3/25/2002 9:00	498	5
500	Third party integration	1.d	3/25/2002 9:00	3/26/2002 9:00	499	5
501	Feature development complete	.d	3/26/2002 9:00	3/26/2002 9:00	495	4
502	Test and integrate feature into website	3.d	3/26/2002 9:00	3/29/2002 9:00	501	4
503	Feature ready for QA	.d	3/29/2002 9:00	3/29/2002 9:00	502	4
504	QA of feature	2.d	3/29/2002 9:00	4/2/2002 9:00	503	4
505	Property locator—feature complete	.d	4/2/2002 9:00	4/2/2002 9:00	493	3
506	Administrative functions	26.d	3/4/2002 8:00	4/8/2002 17:00		3

507	Feature analysis	3.d	3/4/2002 8:00	3/6/2002 17:00		4
508	Prototype	2.d	3/7/2002 8:00	3/8/2002 17:00	507	4
509	Onsite review of prototype	1.d	3/11/2002 8:00	3/11/2002 17:00	508	4
510	Prepare design document	2.d	3/12/2002 8:00	3/13/2002 17:00	509	4
511	Review design	1.d	3/14/2002 8:00	3/14/2002 17:00	510	4
512	Design signoff	.d	3/14/2002 17:00	3/14/2002 17:00	511	4
513	Development	16.d	3/7/2002 8:00	3/28/2002 17:00		4
514	Prepare test plan for feature	1.d	3/7/2002 8:00	3/7/2002 17:00	507	5
515	Review test plan	.5d	3/8/2002 8:00	3/8/2002 12:00	514	5
516	Create JSPs	5.d	3/15/2002 8:00	3/21/2002 17:00	512	5
517	Develop Java classes	5.d	3/22/2002 8:00	3/28/2002 17:00	516	5
518	Feature development complete	.d	3/28/2002 17:00	3/28/2002 17:00	513	4
519	Test and integrate feature into website	3.d	3/29/2002 8:00	4/2/2002 17:00	518	4
520	Onsite integration	2.d	4/3/2002 8:00	4/4/2002 17:00	519	4
521	Feature ready for QA	.d	4/4/2002 17:00	4/4/2002 17:00	520	4
522	QA of feature	2.d	4/5/2002 8:00	4/8/2002 17:00	521	4
523	Administrative functions—feature complete	.d	4/8/2002 17:00	4/8/2002 17:00	506	3
524	Iteration 1 release	80.833d	1/28/2002 8:00	5/20/2002 15:40		2
525	CMS—configuration management plan	4.6d	3/14/2002 8:00	3/20/2002 13:48		3
526	Document CMS environment setup	2.d	3/14/2002 8:00	3/15/2002 17:00		4
527	Review plan	1.d	3/18/2002 8:00	3/18/2002 17:00	526	4
528	Customer review of CMS config plan	.6d	3/19/2002 8:00	3/19/2002 13:48	527	4
529	Revise document	1.d	3/19/2002 13:48	3/20/2002 13:48	528	4
530	Signoff CMS configuration plan	.d	3/20/2002 13:48	3/20/2002 13:48	529	4
531	Prepare integration test plan	15.d	2/25/2002 8:00	3/15/2002 17:00		3
532	Integration test plan complete	.d	3/15/2002 17:00	3/15/2002 17:00	531	3
533	Review integration test plan	1.6d	3/18/2002 8:00	3/19/2002 13:48	532	3
534	Signoff integration test plan	.d	3/19/2002 13:48	3/19/2002 13:48	533	3
535	Iteration 1 development complete	.d	4/2/2002 15:40	4/2/2002 15:40	101,134,215,249, 364,398,435,461, 501,518,282,491	3
536	Integration testing	10.d	4/2/2002 15:40	4/16/2002 15:40	535	3

537	Iteration 1 integration testing complete	.d	4/16/2002 15:40	4/16/2002 15:40	536	3
538	Documentation updates	10.d	4/16/2002 15:40	4/30/2002 15:40	535,537	3
539	Load tester joins onsite team	.d	4/8/2002 8:00	4/8/2002 8:00		3
540	Training on load testing	1.636d	4/8/2002 8:00	4/9/2002 14:06	539	3
541	Iteration 1 ready for QA testing	.d	4/16/2002 15:40	4/16/2002 15:40	121,156,235,269, 282,384,418,447, 480,491,505,523, 537	3
542	QA testing in development environment	5.d	4/16/2002 15:40	4/23/2002 15:40	541	3
543	Prepare for move to QA	57.833d	1/28/2002 8:00	4/17/2002 15:40		3
544	Document installation instructions	1.d	4/16/2002 15:40	4/17/2002 15:40	537	4
545	Develop installation script	1.d	1/28/2002 8:00	1/28/2002 17:00		4
546	Test install process	1.d	1/28/2002 8:00	1/28/2002 17:00		4
547	Review installation instructions	.5d	1/28/2002 8:00	1/28/2002 12:00		4
548	Signoff installation instructions	.d	1/28/2002 8:00	1/28/2002 8:00		4
549	QA dependencies	5.d	4/8/2002 8:00	4/15/2002 8:00		3
550	FTCRS 11.2b—QA complete	.d	4/8/2002 8:00	4/8/2002 8:00		4
551	WBE 3.0—QA complete	.d	4/15/2002 8:00	4/15/2002 8:00		4
552	Prepare QA environment	54.d	1/28/2002 8:00	4/11/2002 17:00		3
553	Test environment setup in development	42.d	1/28/2002 8:00	3/26/2002 17:00		4
554	Setup and test multicast clustering	3.d	3/18/2002 8:00	3/20/2002 17:00		5
555	Configure node manager	2.d	3/21/2002 8:00	3/22/2002 17:00	554	5
556	Identify testing requirements for clustering	2.d	3/15/2002 8:00	3/18/2002 17:00		5
557	Develop test scripts for testing clustering	2.d	1/28/2002 8:00	1/29/2002 17:00		5
558	Test BigIP configuration	5.d	3/19/2002 8:00	3/25/2002 17:00		5
559	Setup and test system and domain logs	2.d	3/25/2002 8:00	3/26/2002 17:00	555	5
560	Document procedures	43.d	1/28/2002 8:00	3/27/2002 17:00		4
561	Prepare OS upgrade documentation	1.d	3/15/2002 8:00	3/15/2002 17:00		5
562	Prepare Weblogic install documentation	1.d	3/18/2002 8:00	3/18/2002 17:00	561	5
563	Prepare multicase clustering setup documentation	1.d	3/21/2002 8:00	3/21/2002 17:00	554	5

564	Prepare BigIP configuration documentation	1.d	3/26/2002 8:00	3/26/2002 17:00	558	5
565	Prepare node manager configuration documentation	1.d	1/28/2002 8:00	1/28/2002 17:00		5
566	Prepare system/domain log setup documentation	1.d	3/27/2002 8:00	3/27/2002 17:00	559	5
567	Install OS, Weblogic, and Apache on QA boxes	4.d	3/28/2002 8:00	4/2/2002 17:00	560	4
568	Configure Weblogic servers	2.d	4/3/2002 8:00	4/4/2002 17:00	567	4
569	QA environment—hardware setup	.d	4/4/2002 17:00	4/4/2002 17:00	568	4
570	Deploy application in QA	2.d	4/5/2002 8:00	4/8/2002 17:00	569	4
571	Promote content to QA environment	3.d	4/9/2002 8:00	4/11/2002 17:00	570	4
572	QA testing in QA environment	5.d	4/23/2002 15:40	4/30/2002 15:40	552,542,549	3
573	Load testing	10.d	4/23/2002 15:40	5/7/2002 15:40	572SS	3
574	User acceptance testing	5.d	4/30/2002 15:40	5/7/2002 15:40	572	3
575	Acceptance of WBR	.d	5/7/2002 15:40	5/7/2002 15:40	574	3
576	Prepare production environment	9.d	5/7/2002 15:40	5/20/2002 15:40	575	3
577	Install OS, Weblogic, and Apache on production boxes	4.d	5/7/2002 15:40	5/13/2002 15:40		4
578	Configure Weblogic servers	2.d	5/13/2002 15:40	5/15/2002 15:40	577	4
579	Production environment—hardware setup	.d	5/15/2002 15:40	5/15/2002 15:40	578	4
580	Create	1.d	5/15/2002 15:40	5/16/2002 15:40	579	4
581	Deploy application in production	2.d	5/16/2002 15:40	5/20/2002 15:40	580	4
582	WBR Ready for production	.d	5/20/2002 15:40	5/20/2002 15:40	576	3
583	Iteration-2 development	69.d	2/8/2002 17:00	5/16/2002 17:00	3	2
584	Product line homepages	41.d	3/4/2002 13:00	4/30/2002 12:00		3
585	Feature analysis	1.d	3/28/2002 13:00	3/29/2002 12:00	453	4
586	Development	5.d	3/29/2002 13:00	4/5/2002 12:00	585	4
587	Create DCTs	2.d	3/29/2002 13:00	4/2/2002 12:00	585	5
588	JSPs corresponding to PT ready	.d	4/2/2002 12:00	4/2/2002 12:00	587	5
589	Create presentation templates	2.d	4/2/2002 13:00	4/4/2002 12:00	588	5
590	DCTs and templates ready	.d	4/4/2002 12:00	4/4/2002 12:00	589	5
591	Prepare test plan for feature	1.d	4/2/2002 13:00	4/3/2002 12:00	587	5
592	Review test plan	.75d	4/3/2002 13:00	4/4/2002 10:00	591	5
593	Create JSPs	5.d	3/29/2002 13:00	4/5/2002 12:00		5

594	Develop Java classes	2.d	3/29/2002 13:00	4/2/2002 12:00		5
595	Third party integration	1.d	4/2/2002 13:00	4/3/2002 12:00	594	5
596	Feature development complete	.d	4/5/2002 12:00	4/5/2002 12:00	586	4
597	Create content, preview	35.d	3/4/2002 13:00	4/22/2002 12:00		4
598	Create content	25.d	3/4/2002 13:00	4/8/2002 13:00	602SF	5
599	Review DCTs	1.d	4/4/2002 13:00	4/5/2002 12:00	590	5
600	Rework DCTs	1.d	4/5/2002 13:00	4/8/2002 12:00	599	5
601	Signoff of DCTs	.d	4/8/2002 12:00	4/8/2002 12:00	600	5
602	Enter content for testing	1.d	4/8/2002 13:00	4/9/2002 12:00	601	5
603	Test content entry complete	.d	4/9/2002 12:00	4/9/2002 12:00	602	5
604	Review and signoff of TPLs	1.d	4/9/2002 13:00	4/10/2002 12:00	603	5
605	Template QA	1.d	4/10/2002 13:00	4/11/2002 12:00	604	5
606	Rework TPLs	1.d	4/11/2002 13:00	4/12/2002 12:00	605	5
607	Signoff of TPLs	.d	4/12/2002 12:00	4/12/2002 12:00	606	5
608	Enter all content	5.d	4/12/2002 13:00	4/19/2002 12:00	607	5
609	Internal review of content	5.d	4/12/2002 13:00	4/19/2002 12:00	608SS	5
610	Content entry complete	.d	4/19/2002 12:00	4/19/2002 12:00	609	5
611	Content QA	5.d	4/15/2002 13:00	4/22/2002 12:00	609SS+1 day	5
612	Deploy content to development environment	1.d	4/22/2002 13:00	4/23/2002 12:00	597	4
613	Test and integrate feature into website	3.d	4/23/2002 13:00	4/26/2002 12:00	586,612	4
614	Feature ready for QA	.d	4/26/2002 12:00	4/26/2002 12:00	613	4
615	QA of feature	2.d	4/26/2002 13:00	4/30/2002 12:00	614	4
616	Product line homepages—feature complete	.d	4/30/2002 12:00	4/30/2002 12:00	584	3
617	Wyndham New York webste	41.d	3/6/2002 13:00	5/2/2002 12:00		3
618	Feature analysis	1.d	4/4/2002 13:00	4/5/2002 12:00	589	4
619	Development	6.d	4/5/2002 13:00	4/15/2002 12:00	618	4
620	Create DCTs	2.d	4/5/2002 13:00	4/9/2002 12:00	618	5
621	JSPs corresponding to PT ready	.d	4/9/2002 12:00	4/9/2002 12:00	620	5
622	Create presentation templates	4.d	4/9/2002 13:00	4/15/2002 12:00	621	5
623	DCTs and templates ready	.d	4/15/2002 12:00	4/15/2002 12:00	622	5
624	Prepare test plan for feature	1.d	4/9/2002 13:00	4/10/2002 12:00	620	5
625	Review test plan	.8d	4/10/2002 13:00	4/11/2002 10:24	624	5
626	Create JSPs	5.d	4/5/2002 13:00	4/12/2002 12:00		5

627	Develop Java classes	2.d	4/5/2002 13:00	4/9/2002 12:00		5
628	Third party integration	1.d	4/9/2002 13:00	4/10/2002 12:00	627	5
629	Feature development complete	.d	4/15/2002 12:00	4/15/2002 12:00	619	4
630	Create content, preview	40.d	3/6/2002 13:00	5/1/2002 12:00		4
631	Create content	30.d	3/6/2002 13:00	4/17/2002 13:00	635SF	5
632	Review DCTs	1.d	4/15/2002 13:00	4/16/2002 12:00	623	5
633	Rework DCTs	1.d	4/16/2002 13:00	4/17/2002 12:00	632	5
634	Signoff of DCTs	.d	4/17/2002 12:00	4/17/2002 12:00	633	5
635	Enter content for testing	1.d	4/17/2002 13:00	4/18/2002 12:00	634	5
636	Test content entry complete	.d	4/18/2002 12:00	4/18/2002 12:00	635	5
637	Review and signoff of TPLs	1.d	4/18/2002 13:00	4/19/2002 12:00	636	5
638	Template QA	1.d	4/19/2002 13:00	4/22/2002 12:00	637	5
639	Rework TPLs	1.d	4/22/2002 13:00	4/23/2002 12:00	638	5
640	Signoff of TPLs	.d	4/23/2002 12:00	4/23/2002 12:00	639	5
641	Enter all content	5.d	4/23/2002 13:00	4/30/2002 12:00	640	5
642	Internal review of content	5.d	4/23/2002 13:00	4/30/2002 12:00	641SS	5
643	Content entry complete	.d	4/30/2002 12:00	4/30/2002 12:00	642	5
644	Content QA	5.d	4/24/2002 13:00	5/1/2002 12:00	642SS+1 day	5
645	Deploy content to development environment	1.d	5/1/2002 13:00	5/2/2002 12:00	630	4
646	Test and integrate feature into website	3.d	4/18/2002 13:00	4/23/2002 12:00	619,635	4
647	Feature ready for QA	.d	4/23/2002 12:00	4/23/2002 12:00	646	4
648	QA of feature	2.d	4/23/2002 13:00	4/25/2002 12:00	647	4
649	Wyndham New York website—feature complete	.d	5/2/2002 12:00	5/2/2002 12:00	617	3
650	Travel agent services	47.d	2/27/2002 13:00	5/3/2002 12:00		3
651	Feature analysis	1.d	4/15/2002 13:00	4/16/2002 12:00	622	4
652	Development	5.d	4/16/2002 13:00	4/23/2002 12:00	651	4
653	Create DCTs	2.d	4/16/2002 13:00	4/18/2002 12:00	651	5
654	JSPs corresponding to PT ready	.d	4/18/2002 12:00	4/18/2002 12:00	653	5
655	Create presentation templates	2.d	4/18/2002 13:00	4/22/2002 12:00	654	5
656	DCTs and templates ready	.d	4/22/2002 12:00	4/22/2002 12:00	655	5
657	Prepare test plan for feature	1.d	4/18/2002 13:00	4/19/2002 12:00	653	5
658	Review test plan	.75d	4/19/2002 13:00	4/22/2002 10:00	657	5
659	Create JSPs	5.d	4/16/2002 13:00	4/23/2002 12:00		5

660	Develop Java classes	2.d	4/16/2002 13:00	4/18/2002 12:00		5
661	Third party integration	1.d	4/18/2002 13:00	4/19/2002 12:00	660	5
662	Feature development complete	.d	4/23/2002 12:00	4/23/2002 12:00	652	4
663	Create content, preview	46.d	2/27/2002 13:00	5/2/2002 12:00		4
664	Create content	40.d	2/27/2002 13:00	4/24/2002 13:00	668SF	5
665	Review DCTs	1.d	4/22/2002 13:00	4/23/2002 12:00	656	5
666	Rework DCTs	1.d	4/23/2002 13:00	4/24/2002 12:00	665	5
667	Signoff of DCTs	.d	4/24/2002 12:00	4/24/2002 12:00	666	5
668	Enter content for testing	1.d	4/24/2002 13:00	4/25/2002 12:00	667	5
669	Test content entry complete	.d	4/25/2002 12:00	4/25/2002 12:00	668	5
670	Review and signoff of TPLs	1.d	4/25/2002 13:00	4/26/2002 12:00	669	5
671	Template QA	1.d	4/26/2002 13:00	4/29/2002 12:00	670	5
672	Rework TPLs	1.d	4/29/2002 13:00	4/30/2002 12:00	671	5
673	Signoff of TPLs	.d	4/30/2002 12:00	4/30/2002 12:00	672	5
674	Enter all content	1.d	4/30/2002 13:00	5/1/2002 12:00	673	5
675	Internal review of content	1.d	4/30/2002 13:00	5/1/2002 12:00	674SS	5
676	Content entry complete	.d	5/1/2002 12:00	5/1/2002 12:00	675	5
677	Content QA	1.d	5/1/2002 13:00	5/2/2002 12:00	676	5
678	Deploy content to development environment	1.d	5/2/2002 13:00	5/3/2002 12:00	663	4
679	Test and integrate feature into website	3.d	4/25/2002 13:00	4/30/2002 12:00	652,668	4
680	Feature ready for QA	.d	4/30/2002 12:00	4/30/2002 12:00	679	4
681	QA of feature	2.d	4/30/2002 13:00	5/2/2002 12:00	680	4
682	Travel agent services—feature complete	.d	5/3/2002 12:00	5/3/2002 12:00	650	3
683	Corporate ad pages	34.d	4/1/2002 8:00	5/16/2002 17:00		3
684	Feature analysis	4.d	4/1/2002 8:00	4/4/2002 17:00		4
685	Development	6.d	4/4/2002 17:00	4/12/2002 17:00	684	4
686	Create DCTs	2.d	4/5/2002 8:00	4/8/2002 17:00	684	5
687	DCTs ready	.d	4/4/2002 17:00	4/4/2002 17:00		5
688	JSPs corresponding to PT ready	.d	4/12/2002 17:00	4/12/2002 17:00	689	5
689	Create presentation templates	4.d	4/9/2002 8:00	4/12/2002 17:00	686	5
690	DCTs and templates ready	.d	4/12/2002 17:00	4/12/2002 17:00	689	5
691	Prepare test plan for feature	1.d	4/9/2002 8:00	4/9/2002 17:00	686	5
692	Review test plan	.8d	4/10/2002 8:00	4/10/2002 15:24	691	5

693	Create JSPs	2.d	4/5/2002 8:00	4/8/2002 17:00		5
694	Develop Java classes	2.d	4/5/2002 8:00	4/8/2002 17:00		5
695	Third party integration	1.d	4/9/2002 8:00	4/9/2002 17:00	694	5
696	Feature development complete	.d	4/12/2002 17:00	4/12/2002 17:00	685	4
697	Create content, preview	23.d	4/15/2002 8:00	5/15/2002 17:00		4
698	Create content	20.d	4/18/2002 8:00	5/15/2002 17:00	702	5
699	Review DCTs	1.d	4/15/2002 8:00	4/15/2002 17:00	690	5
700	Rework DCTs	1.d	4/16/2002 8:00	4/16/2002 17:00	699	5
701	Signoff of DCTs	.d	4/16/2002 17:00	4/16/2002 17:00	700	5
702	Enter content for testing	1.d	4/17/2002 8:00	4/17/2002 17:00	701	5
703	Test content entry complete	.d	4/17/2002 17:00	4/17/2002 17:00	702	5
704	Review of TPLs	1.d	4/18/2002 8:00	4/18/2002 17:00	703	5
705	Template QA	1.d	4/19/2002 8:00	4/19/2002 17:00	704	5
706	Template rework	1.d	4/19/2002 8:00	4/19/2002 17:00	704	5
707	Signoff of TPLs	.d	4/19/2002 17:00	4/19/2002 17:00	706	5
708	Enter all content	2.d	4/22/2002 8:00	4/23/2002 17:00	707	5
709	Internal review of content	2.d	4/22/2002 8:00	4/23/2002 17:00	708SS	5
710	Content entry complete	.d	4/23/2002 17:00	4/23/2002 17:00	709	5
711	Content QA	2.d	4/23/2002 8:00	4/24/2002 17:00	709SS+1 day	5
712	Deploy content to development environment	1.d	5/16/2002 8:00	5/16/2002 17:00	697	4
713	Test and integrate feature into website	3.d	4/18/2002 8:00	4/22/2002 17:00	685,702	4
714	Feature ready for QA	.d	4/22/2002 17:00	4/22/2002 17:00	713	4
715	QA of feature	2.d	4/23/2002 8:00	4/24/2002 17:00	714	4
716	Corporate ad pages—feature complete	.d	5/16/2002 17:00	5/16/2002 17:00	683	3
717	Destinations and interests	47.d	3/5/2002 13:00	5/9/2002 12:00		3
718	Feature analysis	1.d	4/22/2002 13:00	4/23/2002 12:00	655	4
719	Development	3.75d	4/23/2002 13:00	4/29/2002 10:00	718	4
720	Create DCTs	2.d	4/23/2002 13:00	4/25/2002 12:00		5
721	JSPs corresponding to PT ready	.d	4/25/2002 12:00	4/25/2002 12:00	720	5
722	Create presentation templates	1.d	4/25/2002 13:00	4/26/2002 12:00	721	5
723	DCTs and templates ready	.d	4/26/2002 12:00	4/26/2002 12:00	722	5
724	Prepare test plan for feature	1.d	4/25/2002 13:00	4/26/2002 12:00	720	5
725	Review test plan	.75d	4/26/2002 13:00	4/29/2002 10:00	724	5

726	Create JSPs	2.d	4/23/2002 13:00	4/25/2002 12:00		5
727	Integration with 10Best	1.d	4/25/2002 13:00	4/26/2002 12:00	726	5
728	Feature development complete	.d	4/29/2002 10:00	4/29/2002 10:00	719	4
729	Create content, preview	46.d	3/5/2002 13:00	5/8/2002 12:00		4
730	Create content	40.d	3/5/2002 13:00	4/30/2002 13:00	734SF	5
731	Review DCTs	1.d	4/26/2002 13:00	4/29/2002 12:00	723	5
732	Rework DCTs	1.d	4/29/2002 13:00	4/30/2002 12:00	731	5
733	Signoff of DCTs	.d	4/30/2002 12:00	4/30/2002 12:00	732	5
734	Enter content for testing	1.d	4/30/2002 13:00	5/1/2002 12:00	733	5
735	Test content entry complete	.d	5/1/2002 12:00	5/1/2002 12:00	734	5
736	Review and signoff of TPLs	1.d	5/1/2002 13:00	5/2/2002 12:00	735	5
737	Template QA	1.d	5/2/2002 13:00	5/3/2002 12:00	736	5
738	Rework TPLs	1.d	5/3/2002 13:00	5/6/2002 12:00	737	5
739	Signoff of TPLs	.d	5/6/2002 12:00	5/6/2002 12:00	738	5
740	Enter all content	1.d	5/6/2002 13:00	5/7/2002 12:00	739	5
741	Internal review of content	1.d	5/6/2002 13:00	5/7/2002 12:00	740SS	5
742	Content entry complete	.d	5/7/2002 12:00	5/7/2002 12:00	741	5
743	Content QA	1.d	5/7/2002 13:00	5/8/2002 12:00	742	5
744	Deploy content to development environment	1.d	5/8/2002 13:00	5/9/2002 12:00	729	4
745	Test and integrate feature into website	3.d	5/1/2002 13:00	5/6/2002 12:00	719,734	4
746	Feature ready for QA	.d	5/6/2002 12:00	5/6/2002 12:00	745	4
747	QA of feature	1.d	5/6/2002 13:00	5/7/2002 12:00	746	4
748	Destinations and interests—feature complete	.d	5/9/2002 12:00	5/9/2002 12:00	717	3
749	Corporate information	48.5d	3/11/2002 13:00	5/16/2002 17:00		3
750	Feature analysis	1.d	4/26/2002 13:00	4/29/2002 12:00	722	4
751	Development	7.d	4/29/2002 13:00	5/8/2002 12:00	750	4
752	Create DCTs	2.d	4/29/2002 13:00	5/1/2002 12:00		5
753	JSPs corresponding to PT ready	.d	5/1/2002 12:00	5/1/2002 12:00	752	5
754	Create presentation templates	1.d	5/1/2002 13:00	5/2/2002 12:00	753	5
755	DCTs and templates ready	.d	5/2/2002 12:00	5/2/2002 12:00	754	5
756	Prepare test plan for feature	1.d	5/1/2002 13:00	5/2/2002 12:00	752	5
757	Review test plan	1.d	5/2/2002 13:00	5/3/2002 12:00	756	5
758	Create JSPs	7.d	4/29/2002 13:00	5/8/2002 12:00		5

759	Develop Java classes	2.d	4/29/2002 13:00	5/1/2002 12:00		5
760	Third party integration	2.d	5/1/2002 13:00	5/3/2002 12:00	759	5
761	Feature development complete	.d	5/8/2002 12:00	5/8/2002 12:00	751	4
762	Create content, preview	48.d	3/11/2002 13:00	5/16/2002 12:00		4
763	Create content	40.d	3/11/2002 13:00	5/6/2002 13:00	767SF	5
764	Review DCTs	1.d	5/2/2002 13:00	5/3/2002 12:00	755	5
765	Rework DCTs	1.d	5/3/2002 13:00	5/6/2002 12:00	764	5
766	Signoff of DCTs	.d	5/6/2002 12:00	5/6/2002 12:00	765	5
767	Enter content for testing	1.d	5/6/2002 13:00	5/7/2002 12:00	766	5
768	Test content entry complete	.d	5/7/2002 12:00	5/7/2002 12:00	767	5
769	Review and signoff of TPLs	1.d	5/7/2002 13:00	5/8/2002 12:00	768	5
770	Template QA	1.d	5/8/2002 13:00	5/9/2002 12:00	769	5
771	Signoff of TPLs	.d	5/9/2002 12:00	5/9/2002 12:00	770	5
772	Enter all content	4.d	5/9/2002 13:00	5/15/2002 12:00	771	5
773	Internal review of content	4.d	5/9/2002 13:00	5/15/2002 12:00	772SS	5
774	Content entry complete	.d	5/15/2002 12:00	5/15/2002 12:00	773	5
775	Content QA	4.d	5/10/2002 13:00	5/16/2002 12:00	773SS+1 day	5
776	Deploy content to development environment	.5d	5/16/2002 13:00	5/16/2002 17:00	762	4
777	Test and integrate feature into website	3.d	5/8/2002 13:00	5/13/2002 12:00	751,767	4
778	Feature ready for QA	.d	5/13/2002 12:00	5/13/2002 12:00	777	4
779	QA of feature	2.d	5/13/2002 13:00	5/15/2002 12:00	778	4
780	Corporate information—feature complete	.d	5/16/2002 17:00	5/16/2002 17:00	749	3
781	Meetings and weddings	32.d	3/20/2002 8:00	5/2/2002 17:00		3
782	Feature analysis	1.d	4/15/2002 8:00	4/15/2002 17:00	690	4
783	Development	8.d	4/16/2002 8:00	4/25/2002 17:00	782	4
784	Create DCTs	2.d	4/16/2002 8:00	4/17/2002 17:00	782	5
785	Create presentation templates	2.d	4/18/2002 8:00	4/19/2002 17:00	784	5
786	DCTs and templates ready	.d	4/19/2002 17:00	4/19/2002 17:00	785	5
787	Prepare test plan for feature	1.d	4/18/2002 8:00	4/18/2002 17:00	784	5
788	Review test plan	.75d	4/19/2002 8:00	4/19/2002 15:00	787	5
789	Create JSPs	5.d	4/16/2002 8:00	4/22/2002 17:00		5
790	Develop Java classes	2.d	4/23/2002 8:00	4/24/2002 17:00	789	5
791	Third party integration	1.d	4/25/2002 8:00	4/25/2002 17:00	790	5

792	Feature development complete	.d	4/25/2002 17:00	4/25/2002 17:00	783	4
793	Create content, preview	31.d	3/20/2002 8:00	5/1/2002 17:00		4
794	Create content	25.d	3/20/2002 8:00	4/24/2002 8:00	798SF	5
795	Review DCTs	1.d	4/22/2002 8:00	4/22/2002 17:00	786	5
796	Rework DCTs	1.d	4/23/2002 8:00	4/23/2002 17:00	795	5
797	Signoff of DCTs	.d	4/23/2002 17:00	4/23/2002 17:00	796	5
798	Enter content for testing	1.d	4/24/2002 8:00	4/24/2002 17:00	797	5
799	Test content entry complete	.d	4/24/2002 17:00	4/24/2002 17:00	798	5
800	Review and signoff of TPLs	1.d	4/25/2002 8:00	4/25/2002 17:00	799	5
801	Template QA	1.d	4/26/2002 8:00	4/26/2002 17:00	800	5
802	Rework TPLs	1.d	4/29/2002 8:00	4/29/2002 17:00	801	5
803	Signoff of TPLs	.d	4/29/2002 17:00	4/29/2002 17:00	802	5
804	Enter all content	1.d	4/30/2002 8:00	4/30/2002 17:00	803	5
805	Internal review of content	1.d	4/30/2002 8:00	4/30/2002 17:00	804SS	5
806	Content entry complete	.d	4/30/2002 17:00	4/30/2002 17:00	805	5
807	Content QA	1.d	5/1/2002 8:00	5/1/2002 17:00	806	5
808	Deploy content to development environment	1.d	5/2/2002 8:00	5/2/2002 17:00	793	4
809	Test and integrate feature into website	3.d	4/26/2002 8:00	4/30/2002 17:00	783,798	4
810	Feature ready for QA	.d	4/30/2002 17:00	4/30/2002 17:00	809	4
811	QA of feature	2.d	5/1/2002 8:00	5/2/2002 17:00	810	4
812	Meetings and weddings—feature complete	.d	5/2/2002 17:00	5/2/2002 17:00	781	3
813	WOTW—travel tips	28.d	3/5/2002 8:00	4/11/2002 17:00		3
814	Start WOTW	.d	3/25/2002 17:00	3/25/2002 17:00	226	4
815	Feature analysis	1.d	3/26/2002 8:00	3/26/2002 17:00	814	4
816	Development	5.d	3/27/2002 8:00	4/2/2002 17:00	815	4
817	Create DCTs	1.d	3/27/2002 8:00	3/27/2002 17:00	815	5
818	JSPs corresponding to PT ready	.d	3/27/2002 17:00	3/27/2002 17:00	817	5
819	Create presentation templates	1.d	3/28/2002 8:00	3/28/2002 17:00	818	5
820	DCTs and Templates ready	.d	3/28/2002 17:00	3/28/2002 17:00	819	5
821	Prepare test plan for feature	1.d	3/28/2002 8:00	3/28/2002 17:00	817	5
822	Review test plan	.75d	3/29/2002 8:00	3/29/2002 15:00	821	5
823	Create JSPs	5.d	3/27/2002 8:00	4/2/2002 17:00		5
824	Develop Java classes	2.d	3/27/2002 8:00	3/28/2002 17:00		5

825	Third party integration	1.d	3/29/2002 8:00	3/29/2002 17:00	824		5
826	Feature development complete	.d	4/2/2002 17:00	4/2/2002 17:00	816		4
827	Create content, preview	27.d	3/5/2002 8:00	4/10/2002 17:00			4
828	Create content	20.d	3/5/2002 8:00	4/2/2002 8:00	832SF		5
829	Review DCTs	1.d	3/29/2002 8:00	3/29/2002 17:00	820		5
830	Rework DCTs	1.d	4/1/2002 8:00	4/1/2002 17:00	829		5
831	Signoff of DCTs	.d	4/1/2002 17:00	4/1/2002 17:00	830		5
832	Enter content for testing	1.d	4/2/2002 8:00	4/2/2002 17:00	831		5
833	Test content entry complete	.d	4/2/2002 17:00	4/2/2002 17:00	832		5
834	Review and signoff of TPLs	1.d	4/3/2002 8:00	4/3/2002 17:00	833		5
835	Template QA	1.d	4/4/2002 8:00	4/4/2002 17:00	834		5
836	Rework TPLs	1.d	4/5/2002 8:00	4/5/2002 17:00	835		5
837	Signoff of TPLs	.d	4/5/2002 17:00	4/5/2002 17:00	836		5
838	Enter all content	2.d	4/8/2002 8:00	4/9/2002 17:00	837		5
839	Internal review of content	2.d	4/8/2002 8:00	4/9/2002 17:00	838SS		5
840	Content entry complete	.d	4/9/2002 17:00	4/9/2002 17:00	839		5
841	Content QA	2.d	4/9/2002 8:00	4/10/2002 17:00	839SS+1 day		5
842	Deploy content to development environment	1.d	4/11/2002 8:00	4/11/2002 17:00	827		4
843	Test and integrate feature into website	3.d	4/3/2002 8:00	4/5/2002 17:00	816,832		4
844	Feature ready for QA	.d	4/5/2002 17:00	4/5/2002 17:00	843		4
845	QA of feature	2.d	4/8/2002 8:00	4/9/2002 17:00	844		4
846	WOTW—travel tips—feature complete	.d	4/11/2002 17:00	4/11/2002 17:00	813		3
847	WOTW—Cary's Book Club	32.d	3/4/2002 8:00	4/16/2002 17:00			3
848	Feature analysis	1.d	3/29/2002 8:00	3/29/2002 17:00	819		4
849	Development	5.d	4/1/2002 8:00	4/5/2002 17:00	848		4
850	Create DCTs	1.d	4/1/2002 8:00	4/1/2002 17:00	848		5
851	JSPs corresponding to PT ready	.d	4/1/2002 17:00	4/1/2002 17:00	850		5
852	Create presentation templates	2.d	4/2/2002 8:00	4/3/2002 17:00	851		5
853	DCTs and templates ready	.d	4/3/2002 17:00	4/3/2002 17:00	852		5
854	Prepare test plan for feature	1.d	4/2/2002 8:00	4/2/2002 17:00	850		5
855	Review test plan	.75d	4/3/2002 8:00	4/3/2002 15:00	854		5
856	Create JSPs	5.d	4/1/2002 8:00	4/5/2002 17:00			5
857	Develop Java classes	2.d	4/1/2002 8:00	4/2/2002 17:00			5

858	Third party integration	1.d	4/3/2002 8:00	4/3/2002 17:00	857	5
859	Feature development complete	.d	4/5/2002 17:00	4/5/2002 17:00	849	4
860	Create content, preview	31.d	3/4/2002 8:00	4/15/2002 17:00		4
861	Create content	25.d	3/4/2002 8:00	4/8/2002 8:00	865SF	5
862	Review DCTs	1.d	4/4/2002 8:00	4/4/2002 17:00	853	5
863	Rework DCTs	1.d	4/5/2002 8:00	4/5/2002 17:00	862	5
864	Signoff of DCTs	.d	4/5/2002 17:00	4/5/2002 17:00	863	5
865	Enter content for testing	1.d	4/8/2002 8:00	4/8/2002 17:00	864	5
866	Test content entry complete	.d	4/8/2002 17:00	4/8/2002 17:00	865	5
867	Review and signoff of TPLs	1.d	4/9/2002 8:00	4/9/2002 17:00	866	5
868	Template QA	1.d	4/10/2002 8:00	4/10/2002 17:00	867	5
869	Rework TPLs	1.d	4/11/2002 8:00	4/11/2002 17:00	868	5
870	Signoff of TPLs	.d	4/11/2002 17:00	4/11/2002 17:00	869	5
871	Enter all content	1.d	4/12/2002 8:00	4/12/2002 17:00	870	5
872	Internal review of content	1.d	4/12/2002 8:00	4/12/2002 17:00	871SS	5
873	Content entry complete	.d	4/12/2002 17:00	4/12/2002 17:00	872	5
874	Content QA	1.d	4/15/2002 8:00	4/15/2002 17:00	873	5
875	Deploy content to development environment	1.d	4/16/2002 8:00	4/16/2002 17:00	860	4
876	Test and integrate feature into website	3.d	4/9/2002 8:00	4/11/2002 17:00	849,865	4
877	Feature ready for QA	.d	4/11/2002 17:00	4/11/2002 17:00	876	4
878	QA of feature	2.d	4/12/2002 8:00	4/15/2002 17:00	877	4
879	WOTW—Cary's Book Club—feature complete	.d	4/16/2002 17:00	4/16/2002 17:00	847	3
880	WOTW—content	50.d	2/22/2002 8:00	5/2/2002 17:00		3
881	Feature analysis	1.d	4/4/2002 8:00	4/4/2002 17:00	852	4
882	Development	8.d	4/5/2002 8:00	4/16/2002 17:00	881	4
883	Create DCTs	4.d	4/5/2002 8:00	4/10/2002 17:00	881	5
884	JSPs corresponding to PT ready	.d	4/10/2002 17:00	4/10/2002 17:00	883	5
885	Create presentation templates	4.d	4/11/2002 8:00	4/16/2002 17:00	884	5
886	DCTs and templates ready	.d	4/16/2002 17:00	4/16/2002 17:00	885	5
887	Prepare test plan for feature	1.d	4/11/2002 8:00	4/11/2002 17:00	883	5
888	Review test plan	.75d	4/12/2002 8:00	4/12/2002 15:00	887	5
889	Create JSPs	1.d	4/5/2002 8:00	4/5/2002 17:00		5
890	Develop Java classes	1.d	4/5/2002 8:00	4/5/2002 17:00		5

891	Third party integration	1.d	4/8/2002 8:00	4/8/2002 17:00	890	5
892	Feature development complete	.d	4/16/2002 17:00	4/16/2002 17:00	882	4
893	Create content, preview	49.d	2/22/2002 8:00	5/1/2002 17:00		4
894	Create content	40.d	2/22/2002 8:00	4/19/2002 8:00	898SF	5
895	Review DCTs	1.d	4/17/2002 8:00	4/17/2002 17:00	886	5
896	Rework DCTs	1.d	4/18/2002 8:00	4/18/2002 17:00	895	5
897	Signoff of DCTs	.d	4/18/2002 17:00	4/18/2002 17:00	896	5
898	Enter content for testing	1.d	4/19/2002 8:00	4/19/2002 17:00	897	5
899	Test content entry complete	.d	4/19/2002 17:00	4/19/2002 17:00	898	5
900	Review and signoff of TPLs	1.d	4/22/2002 8:00	4/22/2002 17:00	899	5
901	Template QA	1.d	4/23/2002 8:00	4/23/2002 17:00	900	5
902	Rework TPLs	1.d	4/24/2002 8:00	4/24/2002 17:00	901	5
903	Signoff of TPLs	.d	4/24/2002 17:00	4/24/2002 17:00	902	5
904	Enter all content	4.d	4/25/2002 8:00	4/30/2002 17:00	903	5
905	Internal review of content	4.d	4/25/2002 8:00	4/30/2002 17:00	904SS	5
906	Content entry complete	.d	4/30/2002 17:00	4/30/2002 17:00	905	5
907	Content QA	4.d	4/26/2002 8:00	5/1/2002 17:00	905SS+1 day	5
908	Deploy content to development environment	1.d	5/2/2002 8:00	5/2/2002 17:00	893	4
909	Test and integrate feature into website	3.d	4/22/2002 8:00	4/24/2002 17:00	882,898	4
910	Feature ready for QA	.d	4/24/2002 17:00	4/24/2002 17:00	909	4
911	QA of feature	2.d	4/25/2002 8:00	4/26/2002 17:00	910	4
912	WOTW—content—feature complete	.d	5/2/2002 17:00	5/2/2002 17:00	880	3
913	Polls	21.d	4/17/2002 8:00	5/15/2002 17:00		3
914	Feature analysis	1.d	4/17/2002 8:00	4/17/2002 17:00	886	4
915	Development	8.d	4/18/2002 8:00	4/29/2002 17:00	914	4
916	Create DCTs	4.d	4/18/2002 8:00	4/23/2002 17:00	914	5
917	JSPs corresponding to PT ready	.d	4/23/2002 17:00	4/23/2002 17:00	916	5
918	Create presentation templates	4.d	4/24/2002 8:00	4/29/2002 17:00	917	5
919	DCTs and templates ready	.d	4/29/2002 17:00	4/29/2002 17:00	918	5
920	Prepare test plan for feature	1.d	4/24/2002 8:00	4/24/2002 17:00	916	5
921	Review test plan	.75d	4/25/2002 8:00	4/25/2002 15:00	920	5
922	Create JSPs	1.d	4/18/2002 8:00	4/18/2002 17:00		5
923	Develop Java classes	1.d	4/18/2002 8:00	4/18/2002 17:00		5

924	Third party integration	1.d	4/19/2002 8:00	4/19/2002 17:00	923	5
925	Feature development complete	.d	4/29/2002 17:00	4/29/2002 17:00	915	4
926	Create content, preview	11.d	4/30/2002 8:00	5/14/2002 17:00		4
927	Create content	1.d	5/3/2002 8:00	5/3/2002 17:00	931	5
928	Review DCTs	1.d	4/30/2002 8:00	4/30/2002 17:00	919	5
929	Rework DCTs	1.d	5/1/2002 8:00	5/1/2002 17:00	928	5
930	Signoff of DCTs	.d	5/1/2002 17:00	5/1/2002 17:00	929	5
931	Enter content for testing	1.d	5/2/2002 8:00	5/2/2002 17:00	930	5
932	Test content entry complete	.d	5/2/2002 17:00	5/2/2002 17:00	931	5
933	Review and signoff of TPLs	1.d	5/3/2002 8:00	5/3/2002 17:00	932	5
934	Template QA	1.d	5/6/2002 8:00	5/6/2002 17:00	933	5
935	Rework TPLs	1.d	5/7/2002 8:00	5/7/2002 17:00	934	5
936	Signoff of TPLs	.d	5/7/2002 17:00	5/7/2002 17:00	935	5
937	Enter all content	4.d	5/8/2002 8:00	5/13/2002 17:00	936	5
938	Internal review of content	4.d	5/8/2002 8:00	5/13/2002 17:00	937SS	5
939	Content entry complete	.d	5/13/2002 17:00	5/13/2002 17:00	938	5
940	Content QA	4.d	5/9/2002 8:00	5/14/2002 17:00	938SS+1 day	5
941	Deploy content to development environment	1.d	5/15/2002 8:00	5/15/2002 17:00	926	4
942	Test and integrate feature into website	3.d	5/3/2002 8:00	5/7/2002 17:00	915,931	4
943	Feature ready for QA	.d	5/7/2002 17:00	5/7/2002 17:00	942	4
944	QA of feature	2.d	5/8/2002 8:00	5/9/2002 17:00	943	4
945	Polls—feature complete	.d	5/15/2002 17:00	5/15/2002 17:00	913	3
946	Download documents	9.8d	4/15/2002 8:00	4/26/2002 15:24		3
947	Feature analysis	1.d	4/15/2002 8:00	4/15/2002 17:00		4
948	Development	3.8d	4/16/2002 8:00	4/19/2002 15:24	947	4
949	Develop Java classes	2.d	4/16/2002 8:00	4/17/2002 17:00		5
950	Prepare test plan for feature	1.d	4/18/2002 8:00	4/18/2002 17:00	949	5
951	Review test plan	.8d	4/19/2002 8:00	4/19/2002 15:24	950	5
952	Feature development complete	.d	4/19/2002 15:24	4/19/2002 15:24	948	4
953	Test and integrate feature into website	3.d	4/19/2002 15:24	4/24/2002 15:24	952	4
954	Feature ready for QA	.d	4/24/2002 15:24	4/24/2002 15:24	953	4
955	QA of feature	2.d	4/24/2002 15:24	4/26/2002 15:24	954	4
956	Download documents—feature complete	.d	4/26/2002 15:24	4/26/2002 15:24	946	3

957	Reports	7.d	2/11/2002 8:00	2/19/2002 17:00		3
958	Install WebTrends	3.d	2/11/2002 8:00	2/13/2002 17:00		4
959	Testing	2.d	2/14/2002 8:00	2/15/2002 17:00	958	4
960	Feature ready for QA	.d	2/15/2002 17:00	2/15/2002 17:00	959	4
961	QA of feature	2.d	2/18/2002 8:00	2/19/2002 17:00	960	4
962	Reports—feature complete	.d	2/8/2002 17:00	2/8/2002 17:00		3
963	WebMiles	1.d	4/26/2002 15:24	4/29/2002 15:24		3
964	Feature analysis	1.d	4/26/2002 15:24	4/29/2002 15:24	956	4
965	WebMiles—feature complete	.d	4/29/2002 15:24	4/29/2002 15:24	963	3
966	Contests/sweepstakes	.5d	3/18/2002 8:00	3/18/2002 12:00		3
967	Feature analysis	.5d	3/18/2002 8:00	3/18/2002 12:00		4
968	Contests/sweepstakes—feature complete	.d	3/18/2002 12:00	3/18/2002 12:00	966	3
969	Iteration 2 release	41.d	4/16/2002 15:40	6/12/2002 15:40		2
970	Update integration test plan for Phase 2	5.d	4/16/2002 15:40	4/23/2002 15:40	537	3
971	Review integration test plan	1.d	4/23/2002 15:40	4/24/2002 15:40	970	3
972	Ready to start Integration Testing	.d	5/8/2002 12:00	5/8/2002 12:00	971,182,317,596, 629,662,728,761, 792,826,859,892, 956,962,965,968	3
973	Integration testing	10.d	5/8/2002 13:00	5/22/2002 12:00	972	3
974	QA dependencies	.d	5/7/2002 15:40	5/7/2002 15:40		3
975	WBR (Iteration 1)—QA Complete	.d	5/7/2002 15:40	5/7/2002 15:40	575	4
976	Prepare QA environment	2.d	5/20/2002 15:40	5/22/2002 15:40	974	3
977	Deploy application in QA	2.d	5/20/2002 15:40	5/22/2002 15:40	582	4
978	Deploy dependencies in QA	.d	5/22/2002 15:40	5/22/2002 15:40	977	4
979	QA environment ready	.d	5/22/2002 15:40	5/22/2002 15:40	976	3
980	Load testing	10.d	5/22/2002 15:40	6/5/2002 15:40	979	3
981	QA testing	10.d	5/22/2002 15:40	6/5/2002 15:40	973,979	3
982	User acceptance testing	5.d	6/5/2002 15:40	6/12/2002 15:40	981	3
983	Documentation updates	10.d	5/22/2002 13:00	6/5/2002 12:00	973	3
984	Acceptance of Wyndham.com	.d	6/5/2002 15:40	6/5/2002 15:40	981	3
985	Wyndham.com ready for production	.d	6/5/2002 15:40	6/5/2002 15:40	984	3
986	Project end	.d	6/12/2002 15:40	6/12/2002 15:40	1	1

Annexure

B

Template For Data Collection

General details								
Report no.								
Project code								
Project type								
Type of project contract								
Business domain								
Platform details								
Report date								
Prepared by								
Reviewed by								
Authorized by								
Recipients of report								

Project manager/ programmer analyst								
Business manager/ delivery manager								
Peak team size								
Project duration								
Project estimated Start date								
Project estimated end date								
Project re-estimated end date								
Project actual start date								
Project actual end date								
			Effort Distribution					
Stage	Effort spent for the activity	Review effort	Rework effort	Total effort for stage	% of total effort	Estimated effort for the stage (from project plan)	% deviation (between estimated and actuals)	Reasons for deviation, if any
LC stages								
Requirements								
High level design								
Detailed design								
Build								
Coding								

Unit test planning								
Unit testing								
Total—build								
Integration test								
Integration test planning								
Integration testing								
Total—integration testing								
System test								
System test planning								
System testing								
Total—system testing								
Acceptance test								
Acceptance test planning								
Acceptance testing								
Total—acceptance testing								
Total—LC stages								
Mgmt stages								
Project management								
Training								
CM								
Misc								
Total—mgmt stages								

Total effort (person hours)							
Total effort (person months)							
Stage detected	Stage injected (origin)	No. of critical defects detected by the QC activity	No. of major defects detected by the QC activity	No. of minor defects detected by the QC activity	No. of cosmetic defects detected by the QC activity	No. of defects detected by the QC activity	Review effectiveness
Requirements review							
HLD review							
Detailed design review							
Code review							
Unit testing							
Integration testing							
System testing							
Acceptance testing							
Defect distribution (stage detected)							
Stage detected (reviews and testing)							
Required review							
Design review							
Code review							

UT								
IT								
ST								
AT								
Total								
Defect distribution (severity)								
Severity								
Critical								
Major								
Minor								
Cosmetic								
Total								

Template for effort data collection per employee

Employee no.	Employee name	Activity code	Activity description	Date	Effort planned	Effort spent		

Annexure C

PROJECT SUMMARY

PROJECT OVERVIEW

Provide a brief description of the project such as project type, platform, domain, project start date, project finish date, name of project managers, etc., and commitments made to the customer—schedule with milestones to be delivered, effort, scope, etc.

Assumptions made while planning, estimating, scheduling which were included in the proposal

Lifecycle stage	Deliverables	Responsible (Onsite/Offshore/Customer)	Applicable areas for structured decision techniques

Tailoring Notes

Deviations from standard process	Added/modified/deleted	Reasons for deviations

Change Request Process

Describe the mechanism for change request process.

Estimated Size and Effort

Basis for estimation

Specify the estimation method used—please describe the estimation model
Specify the average build effort required for each of the program function/type

Estimated efforts	
Program/function	**Effort**

Size

Mention the size of application in terms of S/M/C, SLOC, or FP

Size	
Number of simple units	
Number of medium units	
Number of complex units	
Number of function points	

Effort for Each Lifecycle Stage of the Project

Specify the effort distribution across the different LC stages for the whole project

Activity	Estimated/Effort	
	Person days	**% of total effort**
Requirements analysis		
High level design		

Detailed design		
Build—coding		
Build—independent unit test		
Integration test (including integration planning)		
System test (including system test planning)		
Acceptance test (including installation and warranty)		
Project management		
Configuration management		
Project specific training		
Others		
Total estimated effort for the project		100%

Computer Resources

Hardware/software				
PCs/MAC/workstations	**Required #**	**Date**	**Actual #**	**Date**

Team members—people by role				
Description	**Required #**	**Date**	**Actual #**	**Date**

Training Plan

Training area	Duration	Role
Technical		
Business domain		

Process related		

Interface with other groups

Mention any specific commitments/participation from and dependencies with other groups (SQA, Communication Design Group, E & R, CCD, other projects, DP teams of similar projects)

Project Goals

To set the project goal, project shall

1. Identify needs and priorities of customer, end users, and other relevant stakeholders
2. Identify sources to define project goals
3. Define project goals
4. Resolve conflicts among the goals

Goals	Source	Basis for setting goals	Value	Constraints, if any
Product quality				
Quality (acceptance defect density)				
Process quality				
Requirements review				
Design review				
Code review				
Service quality				
Schedule				
Service level agreements, if any				

Estimates of defects injected

Work product	Estimated number of defects	Basis for estimation
Requirements and design		
Code		
Total		

Schedule

Schedule details	
	•
	•

Project Tracking

Task Tracking

Mention how the tasks are scheduled, who assigns the tasks to team members and how, and how their status is tracked.

Activity	Procedure
Task scheduling	•
Task assignment	•
Task status tracking	•
Program level tracking estimated vs actual	•
Project meeting Mention the frequency	•
Causal analysis meeting Mention the frequency	•

Review by Senior Management (BM/DM)

S. no.	Item for review	Frequency of review
1	Schedule	
2	Project plan	
3	Milestone report	

Status Reporting

Status reports	
Report to	**Frequency**
Business manager/delivery manager	
Customer	

Insert here templates of status reports.

The status report should contain the following minimum set of fields:

Communication Protocol

The PM will escalate issues in the following order, if they remain unresolved at the previous level for the threshold period.

Escalation at customer's end		
Threshold period	**Name of person** **To whom the issue should be escalated**	**Designation of the person**

The customer will escalate issues in the following order, if they remain unresolved at the previous level for the threshold period.

Escalation at vendor's end		
Threshold period	**Name of person** **To whom the issue should be escalated**	**Designation of the person**

Roles and responsibilities of stakeholders

Role	Responsibilities
Customer	•
BM	•
DM	•
PM	•
PA	•
DPT	•
SE	•
CC	•
SQA	•

Annexure

D

Sample Status Report

Weekly Status Update: <Project Code>

Table of Contents

List of resolved tickets for the week
List of open tickets
List of frozen tickets

The status of tickets may be:

- **Unassigned**—We have received the request and are in the process of identifying the best method to resolve.
- **Active**—Technical support is working to resolve this ticket.
- **Awaiting client input**—We have communicated to you that before we can pursue the issue any further, we need additional information.
- **Active II**—A different skill set or coding is needed to address the problem. The problem is being handled by appropriate resources.
- **Awaiting upload**—A program has been fixed as part of the resolution for the problem. The fixed program has to be uploaded to your production environment. The date scheduled for upload will be indicated here or separately.

Frozen—An issue which need not be looked at everyday. This can be an enhancement or a recurring issue that needs review on a regular basis.

The status of enhancements are one of the following:

TBE—The time it will take to complete the enhancement is in the process of being estimated by the engineering team.

Roadmap—The engineering team has determined that this enhancement will be incorporated into the product in a future patch release.

TBQ—The management is calculating the quote based on the resources needed and the time it will take to complete this enhancement.

Quoted—The quote for this enhancement has been sent to the customer and is awaiting your approval within 30 days.

Approved—The enhancement has been approved by the customer and is in the process of being scheduled for completion.

Scheduled—The enhancement has been scheduled for completing on the designated date and is awaiting completion.

If you have any questions please do not hesitate to contact us.
Best regards,
Name:

Support Issues and Bugs

Resolved support issues

Ticket #	7215
Bug ID	6976
Priority	Critical
Request type	Data integrity error(s)
Created on	3/7/00 9:19:55 AM
Ticket summary	(e-mail received 06 Mar 00:)

Transaction: wh857

Desc: When a work order is created and create move flag is set to "Y" on the screen, wh857 releases the work order. If release is not complete (i.e., if the entire work order cannot be released), cOMPL_TASKED flag is set to "N" so that wh857 can release the work order again automatically. Sometimes, this flag is 'N' even after the entire work order is released. Because of this, wh857 picks up this work order again and again.

I have one work order (work order #0006734) that is processed by wh857 for more than 17500 times. Since I have setup print code to print work order on in work order type table, each time wh857 picks up this work order, it also submits whbu503. Hence, for this work order, whbu503 was submitted 17500 times.

Fix required:

1. Please do not log job request unless the entire work order is released.

2. Update the "COMPL_TASKED" flag to "Y" once the entire work order is released.

We need this fix immediately. This is affecting the performance of the system drastically.

Thanks

Name:

Resolved on 3/22/00 4:32:47 pm

Resolution Bug fixed and uploaded

Sample Status Report for Senior Management

Besides periodic status reporting by projects to the senior management (typically BM), some special analyses have to be done at defined milestones (selected milestones are defined in the project management plan). This template defines the minimum that must be reported at the milestones as defined in the project plan. The milestone could be specific time intervals for maintenance projects. This time interval must be mentioned in the project plan.

Project name	
End date of project	
Milestone name	
Milestone date	
Milestone description	

1. Overall Quality and Productvity

Type of requests	Quality for the period of current report	Goals set	Quality as per the previous report	Productivity for the period of current report	Productivity as per the previous report	Reason for deviation, if any
Enhancements						
Bug fixes						

2. Schedule

S. no.	Description	Planned date for delivery	Actual date of delivery	If deviation is more than limit set for project (or standard limit as defined in process capability baseline)	
				Reasons for slippage	Actions taken to bring project schedule back in control

Bug fixes

(a) Turnaround time

Priority	No. of requests received	Average turnaround time of closed requests (elapsed days)	Goals set	*If deviation is more than the limit set for the project	
				Reasons for deviation	Actions taken to bring project schedule back in control
Priority 1					
Priority 2					
Priority 3					

*As mentioned in the project plan

(b) Age of open requests

Priority	No. of requests received	Average age of open requests (elapsed days)	Goals set	Number of requests beyond limits	
				Reasons for deviations	Actions taken to bring the "Age" back in control
Priority 1					
Priority 2					
Priority 3					

3. Effort

S. no.	Description	Estimated total effort	Actual total effort	*If deviation of actual vs. estimated is more than the limit set for the project (or standard limit in process capability baseline), provide	
				Reason for overrun	action taken

* As mentioned in the project plan.

4. Defects

For quality control activities since last report:

QC activity	Est. effort from MSP	Actual effort	Est. no. of defects	Actual defects	*If deviation of actual vs. estimated is more than the limit set for the project (or standard limit in process capability baseline), provide		
					Reason for deviation	Action proposed/taken	Impact on quality goal of the project

5. Defect Prevention Activities

5.1 Status of the action items

S. no.	Action items planned	Status	Remarks

5.2 Benefits of solutions implemented

S. no.	Solutions implemented	Expected benefits in		Actual benefits	
		Quality	Productivity	Quality	Productivity

6. Requirements Change Tracking

Total no. of major requirement changes to date	Total no. of minor requirement changes to date	Total (estimated) effort impact in person hrs on the overall project		Total (estimated) schedule impact in elapsed days on the overall project		Cumulative effort overrun to date in person hrs	Percentage of Requirement change effort billed	Reasons for not billing the remaining Requirement change effort
		For major changes	For minor changes	For major changes	For minor changes			

7. Service Level Agreements (SLA)

If any service level agreements are missed,

- Reasons for missing SLA
- Action taken

8. Risks

Status in previous report			Risk item	Status of mitigation actions	Current status		
Probability	Impact	Exposure			Probability	Impact	Exposure

9. Customer Complaints

No. of customer complaints raised:
No. of customer complaints closed:
No. of customer complaints open:

10. Training Activities

Planned:
Actual:

11. Issues with the Team

Review participants (of this doc):
Prepared by:
Date:

Annexure

E

SAMPLE CONFIGURATION MANAGEMENT PLAN

1. CM PLANNING

This document describes the configuration management of (PROJECT NAME) CM. The objective of this document is to ensure that all documents are generated by (PROJECT NAME):

1.1 Directory Overview

The directory structure given below shall be followed in each module. The consolidated baseline area of the offshore module is the (PROJECT NAME) quality group baseline area, which combines the baseline documents of all the modules, that is, each MODULE shall have a baseline area in which documents related to the projects and work specific to that module shall be stored. Replica of the documents, which are identified to be stored in the consolidated baseline area as per the table given in Section 1.2, from each module shall be stored in the consolidated baseline area for the CM, which is in offshore module.

In case of modules other than the offshore module, copies of all documents that are baselined are stored in /RELEASE area temporarily at time of baseline in the MODULE. On 15th and the last day of each month the documents shall be sent to offshore for baselining. The /RECEIVE area is where the docs received from other modules are stored temporarily till they are moved to appropriate directory. Each module will have the /RELEASE and /RECEIVE area for this exchange of documents.

1.2 Configuration Items and Storage Areas

1.2.1 Naming Conventions

Extension (ext) could be xls/doc/ppt/mpp/rtf/mps.

1.2.2 Major Storage Areas

WORKAREA / REVIEWAREA: <MODULE Server>\(PROJECT NAME)\WORK
BASELINEAREA<MODULE Server>\(PROJECT NAME)\BASELINE
CONSOLIDATED BASELINEAREA (As mentioned in Section 1.1, the consolidated baseline area is in Offshore):<MODULE Server>\(PROJECT NAME)\(PROJECT NAME)_BASELINE
RELEASE AREA(where copies of all baselined items are stored before sending to the consolidated baseline area in Offshore): <MODULE Server>\(PROJECT NAME)\RELEASE
TEMPORARY STORAGE AREA FOR DOCS RECEIVED FROM OTHER MODULE's: <MODULE Server>\(PROJECT NAME)\RECEIVE

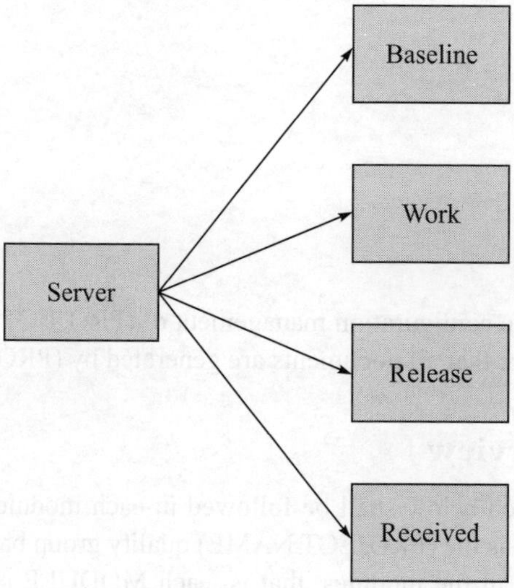

1.2.3 (PROJECT NAME) MODULE Servers

Configuration items	Naming conventions	Work/Review	MODULE Baseline	(PROJECT NAME) Baseline
		WORKAREA\	BASELINEAREA\	CONSOLIDATED BASELINEAREA\
Process improvement plan of the CM	(PROJECT NAME)_PIP_<yyyy>.ext	(PROJECT NAME)_Mgmt\ CM_Plan	(PROJECT NAME)_Mgmt\Plan\ CM_Plan	(PROJECT NAME)_Mgmt\Plan\CM_Plan
CM plan for CM	(PROJECT NAME)_CMPlan.doc	(PROJECT NAME)_Mgmt\ CM_Plan	(PROJECT NAME)_Mgmt\Plan\ CM_Plan	(PROJECT NAME)_Mgmt\Plan\CM_Plan
CM audit reports of CM	(PROJECT NAME)_ CMAuditReport_<mmm><yyyy>.ext	(PROJECT NAME)_Mgmt\ CMAuditReports	(PROJECT NAME)_Mgmt\ CMAuditReports\	(PROJECT NAME)_Mgmt\ CMAuditReports\<MODULE Name>\
Customer feedback	CustomerFeedback_<mmm><yyyy>. ext	NA	(PROJECT NAME)_Mgmt\ CustomerFeedback	(PROJECT NAME)_Mgmt\ CustomerFeedback
Mini assessment reports of the CM	<project code>_MiniAssessmentRep ort_<mmm><yyyy>.ext	(PROJECT NAME)_Mgmt\ MiniAssessmentReports	(PROJECT NAME)_Mgmt\ MiniAssessmentReports	(PROJECT NAME)_Mgmt\ MiniAssessmentReports\<MODULE Name>\
Metric analysis reports of CM	<project code>_MetricAnalysisRepor t_<mmm><yyyy>.ext	Processdeployment\<Quality name>\<project code>	MetricAnalysisReports\Abandoned MetricAnalysisReports\Dev MetricAnalysisReports\Reengg MetricAnalysisReports\Mnt	MetricAnalysisReports\Abandoned MetricAnalysisReports\Dev MetricAnalysisReports\Reengg MetricAnalysisReports\Mnt
GR head report to CM head	GR HEADReport_<CM name>_<mmm><yyyy>.ext	(PROJECT NAME)_Mgmt\GR HEADReports	(PROJECT NAME)_Mgmt\GR HEADReports	(PROJECT NAME)_Mgmt\GR HEADReports
QUALITY report to BM/ DM/GR head	QUALITYMailId_ QUALITYReport_<mmm><yyyy>.ext	\(PROJECT NAME)_Mgmt\ QUALITYReports\<QUALITY MailId>\	(PROJECT NAME)_Mgmt\ QUALITYReports	NA
Minutes of meeting with CMHead/BM/ DM	MOM_<CMHead/ BMName>_<mmm><yyyy>.ext	(PROJECT NAME)_Mgmt\MOM	(PROJECT NAME)_Mgmt\MOM	NA

Configuration items	Naming conventions	Work/Review	MODULE Baseline	(PROJECT NAME) Baseline
		WORKAREA\	BASELINEAREA\	CONSOLIDATED BASELINEAREA\
Domain Plans of each QUALITY within CM	<QUALITYMailId>_DomainPlan.ext	(PROJECT NAME)_Mgmt \<QUALITY MailId>	(PROJECT NAME)_Mgmt\Plan\ Oth_Plan	NA
QUALITY Schedule for the month	<QUALITYMailid>_ Schedule_<mmm><yyyy>.mpp	(PROJECT NAME)_Mgmt\ Schedule	NA	NA
Templates	Descriptive name of the template	(PROJECT NAME)_Mgmt\ Templates	(PROJECT NAME)_Mgmt\Templates	(PROJECT NAME)_Mgmt\Templates
Presentations	Descriptive name of the presentation	(PROJECT NAME)_Mgmt\ Presentations	(PROJECT NAME)_Mgmt\ Presentations	(PROJECT NAME)_Mgmt\Presentations
Trend charts	Descriptive name of the chart	(PROJECT NAME)_Mgmt\ charts	(PROJECT NAME)_Mgmt\charts	(PROJECT NAME)_Mgmt\charts
Trackers like project map, performance-experience map, etc	(PROJECT NAME)_<MODULE Name>_<Descriptive name of tracker>	\(PROJECT NAME)_Mgmt\ Trackers	NA	NA
WIP reports	(PROJECT NAME)_<MODULE Name>_<descriptive name of report>	\(PROJECT NAME)_Mgmt\ Reports	NA	NA
PQUALITY activity related records	Descriptive name of the doc	(PROJECT NAME)_Mgmt\ PQUALITY	(PROJECT NAME)_Mgmt\PQUALITY	NA
SEPG work	Descriptive name of the doc	SEPG\<Initiative title>	SEPG\<Initiative title>	NA
QUALITY plan of the projects	<Project code>_QUALITYPlan.ext	Processdeployment\<QUALITY MailId>\<project code>	NA	NA

Configuration items	Naming conventions	Work/Review	MODULE Baseline	(PROJECT NAME) Baseline
		WORKAREA\	BASELINEAREA\	CONSOLIDATED BASELINEAREA\
Compliance check reports of the projects	<projectcode>_ compcheck_<mmm><yyyy>.ext	Processdeployment\<QUALITY MailId>\<project code>	Processdeployment\<QUALITY MailId>\<project code>	NA
Mail	Project related mails:<project code>. pst QUALITY mailing list mails and other mails: <Quality mailid>.pst	Processdeployment \<QUALITYMailId>\ Mail\	NA	NA
Documents collected from projects such as plans, causal analysis reports, checklists, etc.	Name of the doc as given by the project	Processdeployment\<QUALITY MailId>\<project code>\Docs	NA	NA
Same docs as above for closed projects	Same as above	Processdeployment\ Archive\<project code>\Docs	NA	NA
Archives	Project archive to be named as <Project code>_<QUALITYMailId>_ ARCHIVE QD Archive to be named as < QUALITYMailId >_ FROM<mmm><yyyy>_ TO<mmm><yyyy>	NA	Under CCD control	Under CCD control

1.3 Version/Revision Numbering

Following documents should have revision history:

- Process Improvement Plan
- CM Plan
- CM Audit Reports
- Domain Plans
- Mini Assessment Reports
- Metric Analysis Report
- GR HEADReport
- QUALITYReport to BM/GR HEAD
- Compliance Check reports

All documents should start with version 0.00a. After each change, the document is changed to 0.00b (c, etc.). After the document is reviewed, the version is changed to 1.00 for the first time. Later depending on the volume of changes, version is changed to 1.01 if the changes are minor, or 2.00, if it goes through a major change or after a number of minor changes accumulate, and the document is reviewed again.

1.4 Movement of Configuration Items Through Their Storage Areas

1.4.1 Process Improvement Plan

Prepare/Update by GR HEAD→Review by CMHead, QD Head, (BMs)→Baseline

1.4.2 CM Plan

Prepare by QUALITY/GR HEAD→Review by GR HEAD→Baseline

1.4.3 CM Audit Reports

Prepare CM Audit Reports→Discuss the CM audit issues with team→Track issues to closure→Baseline

1.4.4 Domain Plan

Prepared by QUALITY/GR HEAD→Review by GR HEAD/QD Head→Baseline

1.4.5 Mini Assessment Reports

Prepared by the Assessor→Reviewed by the project→Baseline

1.4.6 Metric Analysis Report

Prepared by PL→Review by QUALITY→Review by SIGMA→Update PDB by QUALITY→Authorize the Report and PDB entry by SIGMA

1.4.7 GR HEAD Report

Prepared by GR HEAD→Baseline

1.4.8 QUALITY Report

Prepared by QUALITY→Sent to BM/GR HEAD→Baseline

1.4.9 MOM

Prepare by QUALITY/GR HEAD→Baseline

1.4.10 QUALITY Plan

Prepare by QUALITY for each project→Baseline

1.4.11 QUALITY Schedule

Prepare by QUALITY for each project→Review by PL/GR HEAD→Baseline

1.4.12 Compliance check report

Prepare by QUALITY→Issues are tracked to closure by PL→Baseline

1.5 Access Rights

Mentioned as part of Section 1.2.

Documents will be shared across QD based on the need and will be sent based on requestor location/size by either mail or FTP or any other suitable methods.

Baseline copy of (PROJECT NAME) CM Plan will be made available through QUALITY Portal.

1.6 Reconciliation

The reconciliation of documents that are baselined is done in the following manner:

1. The document that is to be baselined is moved into baseline area of that MODULE and a copy of it is stored in the /RELEASE area. On the 15th and the last day of each month all the documents in the release area are zipped and sent across to Offshore for baselining at the CM level. This zip file is retained until the next CM audit and then deleted.

1.7 Release

Release is made only after the work product completion check is done. (PROJECT NAME)_CM Plan will be released through QUALITY portal.

1.7.1 Verification of Work Product Completion

- Ensure review comments are updated in the document
- Revision history of the doc is updated with the evidence of been updated after review
- Ensure work product is spell checked and free from grammatical errors
- Ensure work product is presentable in both soft and hard copy form
- Follows the documentation standard of Infosys
- Placed in the appropriate folder identified as per this CM Plans
- Ensure archival is done as per this plan

1.8 Status Accounting

Status of the configuration item will be known by the folder in which the files exist (WORKAREA/REVIEWAREA/BASELINEAREA) and content of the revision history of the document.

1.9 Backup

Storage area to be backed up	Backup media	Numbering scheme	Backup		Checking backup files	
			Frequency	Responsibility	Frequency	Responsibility
WORKAREA AND BASELINE AREA	Tape	As per CCD Standards	Daily	CCD	2 months	CC

- If LAPTOP is used, the WORKAREA has to be updated at least once in a week (My Briefcase feature of windows to be used to do this).

1.10 Archival

Archival of the project artifacts and QD artifacts to follow the archival procedure in QUALITY MANUAL. Specific differences to the procedure are given below.

1.10.1 Archival of Project Artifacts

QUALITY to archive the following artifacts for each of the project that is supported:

- QUALITY Plan
- QUALITY Schedule
- Compliance check reports
- Defect/effort analysis done for the project
- All the mails on the project with PL, BM, CM Head, and GR HEAD

Archival to be done on closure of the project and at 15 months interval for long duration projects for all the artifacts of last 12 months.

1.10.2 Archival of QD Artifacts

Following QD artifacts are to be archived:

- Domain Plans
- Mini Assessment Reports
- Metric Analysis Reports
- GR HEAD Report
- QUALITY Report to BM/GR HEAD
- Minutes of meeting with CMHead/BM
- All mails to and from BMs/CM Head/other GR HEADs

Archival to be done at 15 months interval for all the artifacts of previous 12 months leaving last 3 months data for use.

1.11 CM Tools Used

No tools identified and used.

2. Configuration Audit

CC or Back up CC will do CM audit once a month. This audit will include baseline, work product completion, and functional audit.

3. Roles and Responsibilities

3.1 Roles

Name	Mail-id	Role
Nitin GK	Nitingk	GR HEAD
Kedar Tirth	Kedarnath	QUALITY, CC (CMne)
Savita P	Savitap	QUALITY
Venkatesh	Nkvenkatesh	QUALITY, CC (Blore)
Srinivas Poosarla	SrinivasP	QUALITY, CC (BBSR)
Subramanian KRV	SubramanianKRV	QUALITY, CC (Mlore)
Ananthan G	AnanthanG	QUALITY, CC (Chennai)

3.2 Responsibilities of Configuration Controller (CC)

- CM orientation to group
- Configuration item status tracking
- Ensuring backups and archival

- Conducting CM audits as planned
- Generating CM audit reports
- Tracking CM audit discrepancies to closure

3.3 CM Audit Checklist

During the CM audit following can be looked into:

- Are file naming and storage areas maintained as per this plan?
- Are the CIs followed the workflow?
- Are version number as per plan?
- Are access rights sufficient to provide change control and as per plan?
- Are CM audits conducted as per plan and all issues are tracked closure?
- Are there any recurrence of CM audit issues?

4. Compliance Audit Reports

Compliance audit reports shall contain the following:

- Date of audit and duration
- Name of the auditor and auditee
- Artifacts seen during the audit
- Focus area of the audit
- Description of issues and their priority (High/Medium/Low)
- Facility to update the following by PL
- Assign issues to someone in the project
- Corrective action planned
- Target date to close the issue
- Correction action verified date and by whom
- Status of issue (Open/Closed/Abandoned)

5. Mail Organization

GR HEAD and QUALITY to maintain correspondences to CM head, QD head, BMs, and SIGMA group. Suggested format is that within <QUALITYmailid>.pst create subfolders for

- Each BMs (mail-id) that the QUALITY/GR HEAD interacts with
- Communication with QD Head and/or CM Head
- For SIGMA

If a QUALITY supports multiple CMs, there must be one .pst file for each of the CM/Initiative that he/she supports with naming like <QUALITYMailId>_<CM Name>/<Initiative name>.pst. The abbreviation for the initiative is to be obtained from the initiative anchors.

6. Terms and Abbreviations

Abbreviations	Expansion
BM	Business manager
CC	Configuration controller
CCD	Computers and Communication Department
CI	Configuration item
CM	Configuration management
DM	Delivery manager
GR HEAD	Group leader
MOM	Minutes of meeting
PDB	Process database
MODULE	Development center
CM	Practice units
QD	Quality Department
QUALITY MANUAL	Quality system documentation
SIGMA	Special interest group for metric analysis
(PROJECT NAME)	Canada and East Coast of North America
QUALITY	Software quality advisor

7. References

Annexure
F

CHANGE REQUEST TEMPLATE

Request number		Customer reference number	
Change category			
Change specification			
Impact on the project a. Schedule b. Effort c. Cost			
Impacted work products			
Status of the change			
Date requested			
Date approved/rejected			
Date to be delivered by			
Date completed			
Comments			

Approved by

Annexure G

DETAILS

RESOURCE TABLE

ID	Name	Initials	Type	Material label	Group	Email address	Windows user account	Max units	Standard rate	Cost per use	Notes
1	Guneet	G	Work		CMS			100%	$0.00/hr	$0.00	
2	Wyndham	W	Work					100%	$0.00/hr	$0.00	
3	Offshore	O	Work		Java/JSP			100%	$0.00/hr	$0.00	
4	Kaushal	K	Work		CMS			100%	$0.00/hr	$0.00	
5	Venkat	V	Work		Java/JSP			100%	$0.00/hr	$0.00	
6	Load Tester	L	Work		Testing			100%	$0.00/hr	$0.00	
7	Ramky	R	Work		Java/JSP			100%	$0.00/hr	$0.00	
8	Nick	N	Work		Content			100%	$0.00/hr	$0.00	

9	Kathi	K	Work		Content			100%	$0.00/hr	$0.00	
10	John	J	Work		Content			100%	$0.00/hr	$0.00	
11	Julie	J	Work		QA			100%	$0.00/hr	$0.00	
12	Mike	M	Work		Content			100%	$0.00/hr	$0.00	
13	Chris	C	Work		Java/JSP			100%	$0.00/hr	$0.00	
14	Mahesh	M	Work		Management			100%	$0.00/hr	$0.00	
15	Kapil	K	Work		Java/JSP			100%	$0.00/hr	$0.00	
16	Rajnish	R	Work		Java/JSP			100%	$0.00/hr	$0.00	
17	Jason	J	Work		QA			100%	$0.00/hr	$0.00	
18	Virginia	V	Work		Content			100%	$0.00/hr	$0.00	
19	Stella	S	Work		Management			100%	$0.00/hr	$0.00	
20	Charlie	C	Work		Management			100%	$0.00/hr	$0.00	
21	Cherry	C	Work		Management			100%	$0.00/hr	$0.00	
22	Ramki	r	Work					100%	$0.00/hr	$0.00	
23	Doug	D	Work					100%	$0.00/hr	$0.00	
24	Anthony	A	Work					100%	$0.00/hr	$0.00	
25	Carlie	c	Work					100%	$0.00/hr	$0.00	
26	Joe Yurko	J	Work					100%	$0.00/hr	$0.00	
27	Joe	j	Work					100%	$0.00/hr	$0.00	
28	Aletta	A	Work					100%	$0.00/hr	$0.00	
29	Erik	E	Work					100%	$0.00/hr	$0.00	
30	Justin	J	Work					100%	$0.00/hr	$0.00	
31	Eric steen	e	Work					100%	$0.00/hr	$0.00	
32	Eric	E	Work					100%	$0.00/hr	$0.00	
33	Naveen	N	Work					100%	$0.00/hr	$0.00	
34	Kiran	K	Work					100%	$0.00/hr	$0.00	
35	Swati	S	Work					100%	$0.00/hr	$0.00	
36	Arun	A	Work					100%	$0.00/hr	$0.00	
37	Jayadev	J	Work					100%	$0.00/hr	$0.00	
38	Raky	R	Work					100%	$0.00/hr	$0.00	
39	Iran	i	Work					100%	$0.00/hr	$0.00	

Assignment Table

Task name	Resource Nname	% work complete	Work	Units
Source control—define strategy	Rajnish	100%	8 hrs	100%
Review source control strategy	Kapil	100%	8 hrs	100%
Setup source control environment	Kiran	100%	8 hrs	100%
Create userIDs on Solaris	Anthony	100%	2 hrs	25%
Setup roles in TeamSite	Kaushal	100%	2 hrs	25%
Study existing documentation	Mahesh	0%	16 hrs	100%
Prepare deployment plan document	Mahesh	0%	24 hrs	100%
Review deployment plan	carlie	0%	8 hrs	100%
Review deployment plan	Cherry	0%	8 hrs	100%
Review deployment plan	Mahesh	0%	8 hrs	100%
Code workflow	Kaushal	100%	8 hrs	100%
Test workflow	Kaushal	100%	8 hrs	100%
Modify workflow and documentation	Kaushal	100%	16 hrs	100%
Review and signoff workflow document	Julie	100%	0.3 hrs	25%
Review and signoff workflow document	John	100%	1.23 hrs	100%
Review and signoff workflow document	Kathi	100%	1.23 hrs	100%
Review and signoff workflow document	Cherry	100%	1.23 hrs	100%
Update workflow	Kaushal	0%	2 hrs	25%
QA of workflow process	Jason	0%	2.67 hrs	25%
QA of workflow process	Julie	0%	1.33 hrs	100%
ASP review for special offers	Virginia	100%	8 hrs	100%
ASP review for special offers	John	100%	8 hrs	100%
ASP review for special offers	Mahesh	100%	8 hrs	100%
ASP Review for functionality—special offers	John	0%	2 hrs	25%
ASP modifications for special offers	Swati	100%	8 hrs	100%
ASP review for help, site search, e-mail list subscriptions, property locator	Virginia	100%	16 hrs	100%
ASP review for help, site search, e-mail list subscriptions, property locator	John	100%	16 hrs	100%
ASP review for help, site search, e-mail list subscriptions, property locator	Mahesh	100%	16 hrs	100%
ASP modifications for help, site search, e-mail list subscriptions, property locator	Swati	0%	16 hrs	100%
ASP review for informative content	Virginia	0%	8 hrs	100%

ASP review for informative content	John	0%	8 hrs	100%
ASP review for informative content	Mahesh	0%	8 hrs	100%
ASP modifications for informative content	Swati	0%	8 hrs	100%
ASP review for product line homepages	Virginia	0%	8 hrs	100%
ASP review for product line homepages	John	0%	8 hrs	100%
ASP review for product line homepages	Mahesh	0%	8 hrs	100%
ASP modifications for product line homepages	Swati	0%	8 hrs	100%
ASP review for Wyndham New York website	Virginia	0%	8 hrs	100%
ASP review for Wyndham New York website	John	0%	8 hrs	100%
ASP review for Wyndham New York website	Mahesh	0%	8 hrs	100%
ASP modifications for Wyndham New York website	Swati	0%	8 hrs	100%
ASP review for travel agent services	Virginia	0%	8 hrs	100%
ASP review for travel agent services	John	0%	8 hrs	100%
ASP review for travel agent services	Mahesh	0%	8 hrs	100%
ASP modifications for travel agent services	Swati	0%	8 hrs	100%
ASP review for meetings and weddings	Virginia	0%	8 hrs	100%
ASP review for meetings and weddings	John	0%	8 hrs	100%
ASP review for meetings and weddings	Mahesh	0%	8 hrs	100%
ASP modifications for meetings and weddings	Swati	0%	8 hrs	100%
ASP review for destinations and interests	Virginia	0%	8 hrs	100%
ASP review for destinations and interests	John	0%	8 hrs	100%
ASP review for destinations and interests	Mahesh	0%	8 hrs	100%
ASP modifications for destinations and interests	Swati	0%	8 hrs	100%
ASP review for corporate ad pages	Virginia	0%	8 hrs	100%
ASP review for corporate ad pages	John	0%	8 hrs	100%
ASP review for corporate ad pages	Mahesh	0%	8 hrs	100%
ASP modifications for corporate ad pages	Swati	0%	8 hrs	100%
ASP review for WOTW—travel tips	Virginia	0%	8 hrs	100%
ASP review for WOTW—travel tips	John	0%	8 hrs	100%
ASP review for WOTW—travel tips	Mahesh	0%	8 hrs	100%
ASP modifications for WOTW—travel tips	Swati	0%	8 hrs	100%
ASP review for WOTW—Cary's Book Club	Virginia	0%	8 hrs	100%
ASP review for WOTW—Cary's Book Club	John	0%	8 hrs	100%
ASP review for WOTW—Cary's Book Club	Mahesh	0%	8 hrs	100%
ASP modifications for WOTW—Cary's Book Club	Swati	0%	8 hrs	100%

ASP review for WOTW—content	Virginia	0%	8 hrs	100%
ASP review for WOTW—content	John	0%	8 hrs	100%
ASP review for WOTW—content	Mahesh	0%	8 hrs	100%
ASP modifications for WOTW—content	Swati	0%	8 hrs	100%
ASP review for corporate information	Virginia	0%	8 hrs	100%
ASP review for corporate information	John	0%	8 hrs	100%
ASP review for corporate information	Mahesh	0%	8 hrs	100%
ASP modifications for corporate information	Swati	0%	8 hrs	100%
Feature analysis	Guneet	100%	8 hrs	100%
Create DCTs	Guneet	100%	24 hrs	100%
Create presentation templates	Guneet	100%	16 hrs	100%
Prepare test plan for feature	Arun	100%	8 hrs	100%
Review test plan	Mahesh	0%	2 hrs	100%
Review test plan	Julie	0%	2 hrs	100%
Create JSPs	Arun	100%	64 hrs	100%
Develop Java classes	Arun	100%	104 hrs	100%
Fix defects	Arun	100%	8 hrs	100%
Create content	Virginia	100%	56 hrs	100%
Update ASPs	Swati	100%	8 hrs	100%
Review ASPs	John	100%	8 hrs	100%
Review ASPs	Virginia	100%	8 hrs	100%
Review ASPs	Kathi	100%	8 hrs	100%
Review and signoff of DCTs	John	100%	8 hrs	100%
Review and signoff of DCTs	Virginia	100%	8 hrs	100%
Review and signoff of DCTs	Chris	100%	8 hrs	100%
Enter all content	Nick	0%	24 hrs	100%
Internal review of content	Nick	0%	24 hrs	100%
Review presentation templates	Nick	0%	8 hrs	100%
Content and template QA	Julie	0%	2 hrs	25%
Deploy content to development environment	Guneet	0%	8 hrs	100%
Test and integrate feature into website	Venkat	100%	24 hrs	100%
WBR main page and WBR content—QA of feature	Julie	0%	4 hrs	50%
Feature analysis	Guneet	100%	8 hrs	100%
Create DCTs	Guneet	100%	8 hrs	100%
Create presentation templates	Guneet	100%	16 hrs	100%

Prepare test plan for feature		Arun	100%	8 hrs	100%
Review test plan		Mahesh	0%	3.6 hrs	50%
Review test plan		Julie	0%	0.4 hrs	100%
Create JSPs		Arun	100%	64 hrs	100%
Develop Java classes		Arun	100%	40 hrs	100%
Create content		Virginia	100%	80 hrs	100%
Update ASPs		Swati	100%	8 hrs	100%
Review ASPs		John	100%	8 hrs	100%
Review ASPs		Virginia	100%	8 hrs	100%
Review and signoff DCTs		John	100%	8 hrs	100%
Review and signoff DCTs		Virginia	100%	8 hrs	100%
Review and signoff DCTs		Chris	100%	8 hrs	100%
Enter content		Nick	0%	8 hrs	100%
Review TPLs		Nick	0%	4 hrs	100%
Template QA		Julie	0%	2 hrs	25%
Rework TPLs		Kiran	0%	8 hrs	100%
Internal review of content		Nick	0%	8 hrs	100%
Content QA		Julie	0%	2 hrs	25%
Deploy content to development environment		Guneet	0%	8 hrs	100%
Test and integrate feature into website		Guneet	0%	24 hrs	100%
Test and integrate feature into website		Venkat	0%	24 hrs	100%
QA of feature		Julie	0%	2 hrs	25%
Test additional functionality		Julie	0%	2 hrs	25%
Redesign homepage		Mike	100%	80 hrs	100%
Redesign homepage		John	100%	80 hrs	100%
Update ASPs		Swati	0%	16 hrs	100%
Review ASPs		John	0%	8 hrs	100%
Review ASPs		Virginia	0%	8 hrs	100%
Rework ASPs		Swati	0%	8 hrs	100%
Feature analysis		Guneet	0%	32 hrs	100%
Create DCTs		Guneet	0%	16 hrs	100%
Create presentation templates		Guneet	0%	32 hrs	100%
Prepare test plan for feature		Swati	0%	8 hrs	100%
Review test plan		Mahesh	0%	3.2 hrs	50%
Review test plan		Julie	0%	0.8 hrs	100%

Create JSPs	Swati	0%	16 hrs	100%
Develop Java classes	Swati	0%	16 hrs	100%
Third party integration	Swati	0%	8 hrs	100%
Create content	Virginia	0%	160 hrs	100%
Review DCTs	John	0%	8 hrs	100%
Review DCTs	Virginia	0%	8 hrs	100%
Review DCTs	Chris	0%	8 hrs	100%
Rework DCTs	Guneet	0%	8 hrs	100%
Enter content for testing	Nick	0%	8 hrs	100%
Review of TPLs	John	0%	8 hrs	100%
Template QA	Julie	0%	4 hrs	50%
Template rework	Guneet	0%	8 hrs	100%
Template rework	Kiran	0%	8 hrs	100%
Enter all content	Nick	0%	16 hrs	100%
Internal review of content	John	0%	16 hrs	100%
Content QA	Julie	0%	4 hrs	25%
Deploy content to development environment	Guneet	0%	8 hrs	100%
Test and integrate feature into website	Guneet	0%	24 hrs	100%
Test and integrate feature into website	Venkat	0%	24 hrs	100%
QA of feature	Julie	0%	4 hrs	25%
Feature analysis	Guneet	0%	24 hrs	100%
Create DCTs	Guneet	0%	16 hrs	100%
Create presentation templates	Guneet	0%	24 hrs	100%
Prepare test plan for feature	Jayadev	0%	8 hrs	100%
Review test plan	Julie	0%	0.45 hrs	100%
Review test plan	Mahesh	0%	3.55 hrs	50%
Create JSPs	Jayadev	0%	64 hrs	100%
Develop Java classes	Jayadev	0%	24 hrs	100%
Create content	John	0%	120 hrs	100%
DCT Review	John	0%	8 hrs	100%
DCT Review	Virginia	0%	8 hrs	100%
DCT Review	Chris	0%	8 hrs	100%
Rework DCTs based on review	Guneet	0%	4 hrs	50%
Rework DCTs based on review	Kiran	0%	4 hrs	50%
Enter content for testing	Nick	0%	16 hrs	100%

Review and signoff of TPLs	John	0%		8 hrs	100%
Template QA	Julie	0%		4 hrs	50%
Rework TPLs	Kiran	0%		8 hrs	100%
Rework TPLs	Guneet	0%		8 hrs	100%
Enter all content	Nick	0%		24 hrs	100%
Internal review of content	John	0%		24 hrs	100%
Content QA	Julie	0%		8 hrs	33%
Deploy content to development environment	Guneet	0%		40 hrs	100%
Test and integrate feature into website	Guneet	0%		24 hrs	100%
Test and integrate feature into website	Venkat	0%		24 hrs	100%
QA of feature	Julie	0%		4 hrs	25%
Feature analysis	Aletta	0%		16 hrs	100%
Create DCTs	Aletta	0%		16 hrs	100%
Create JSPs	Ramky	100%		24 hrs	100%
Create presentation templates	Aletta	0%		16 hrs	100%
Document usage instructions	Aletta	0%		2 hrs	25%
Prepare test plan for feature	Ramky	100%		8 hrs	100%
Review test plan	Mahesh	0%		3.6 hrs	50%
Review test plan	Julie	0%		3.6 hrs	100%
Create Java classes	Ramky	100%		16 hrs	100%
Create content	Virginia	0%		120 hrs	100%
DCT review	John	0%		8 hrs	100%
DCT review	Virginia	0%		8 hrs	100%
DCT review	Chris	0%		8 hrs	100%
Update DCT based on review	Aletta	0%		2 hrs	25%
Enter content for testing	Nick	0%		8 hrs	100%
Review and signoff of TPLs	John	0%		8 hrs	100%
Template QA	Julie	0%		2 hrs	25%
Rework TPLs	Aletta	0%		8 hrs	100%
Enter all content	Nick	0%		32 hrs	100%
Internal review of content	John	0%		32 hrs	100%
Content QA	Julie	0%		4 hrs	13%
Deploy content to development environment	Guneet	0%		8 hrs	100%
Test and integrate feature into website	Guneet	0%		24 hrs	100%
Test and integrate feature into website	Venkat	0%		24 hrs	100%

QA of feature	Julie	0%	2 hrs	13%
Develop update script	Kiran	0%	24 hrs	100%
Test update script	Kaushal	0%	16 hrs	100%
Setup and test batch process	Kaushal	0%	16 hrs	100%
Prepare process documentation	Kiran	100%	24 hrs	100%
Prepare test plan for feature	Kiran	0%	8 hrs	100%
Review test plan and documentation	Mahesh	0%	5 hrs	75%
Review test plan and documentation	Julie	0%	1 hr	100%
Set up FTP server in DMZ	Eric	0%	4 hrs	100%
QA Lanyon process	Julie	0%	4 hrs	50%
Feature analysis	Kaushal	0%	8 hrs	100%
DCT	Kaushal	100%	8 hrs	100%
DCT	Kaushal	100%	8 hrs	100%
DCT	Kaushal	100%	8 hrs	100%
DCT	Kaushal	100%	8 hrs	100%
DCT	Kaushal	100%	4 hrs	100%
DCT	Kaushal	100%	8 hrs	100%
DCT	Kiran	100%	8 hrs	100%
DCT	Kiran	100%	8 hrs	100%
Develop PTs for Lanyon and additional info DCTs	Kiran	100%	8 hrs	100%
Develop PTs for detail area, FAQ, and guest rooms	Kaushal	100%	8 hrs	100%
Prepare test plan for feature	Arun	100%	8 hrs	100%
Review test plan	Julie	0%	1.33 hrs	100%
Review test plan	Mahesh	0%	2.67 hrs	50%
Create JSPs	Arun	100%	40 hrs	100%
Develop Java classes	Arun	100%	80 hrs	100%
Integration to intellicast for weather functionality	Swati	0%	16 hrs	100%
Towne interface	Kiran	0%	16 hrs	100%
Vicinity interface	Ramky	0%	16 hrs	100%
Viator interface	Kiran	0%	8 hrs	100%
mpoint interface	Kiran	0%	8 hrs	100%
Create content	Virginia	0%	80 hrs	100%
Create spreadsheet for boilerplates	Offshore	0%	0 hrs	100%
Update boilerplate text	Virginia	100%	8 hrs	100%
Update ASPs	Swati	0%	16 hrs	100%

Review ASPs	John	0%	8 hrs	100%
Review ASPs	Virginia	0%	8 hrs	100%
Property DCTs	John	100%	8 hrs	100%
Property DCTs	Virginia	100%	8 hrs	100%
Property DCTs	Chris	100%	8 hrs	100%
Remaining DCTs	John	100%	8 hrs	100%
Remaining DCTs	Virginia	100%	8 hrs	100%
Remaining DCTs	Chris	100%	8 hrs	100%
Enter content for testing	Nick	0%	16 hrs	100%
Review and signoff of TPLs	John	0%	8 hrs	100%
Template QA	Julie	0%	4 hrs	50%
Rework TPLs	Kiran	0%	8 hrs	100%
Enter content for hotel main pages and additional information	Nick	0%	240 hrs	100%
Enter content for all other pages	Nick	0%	240 hrs	100%
Internal review of content	John	0%	200 hrs	100%
Content QA	Julie	0%	40 hrs	17%
Deploy content to development environment	Kaushal	0%	16 hrs	100%
Test and integrate feature into website	Kaushal	0%	24 hrs	100%
QA of feature	Julie	0%	16 hrs	100%
Create DCT	Kaushal	0%	16 hrs	100%
Create XML	Kaushal	0%	8 hrs	100%
Review DCT	John	0%	8 hrs	100%
Review DCT	Nick	0%	8 hrs	100%
Rework DCT and XML	Kaushal	0%	8 hrs	100%
Generate default DCRs for all hotels	Kaushal	0%	4 hrs	100%
Update DCRs for specific hotels	Nick	0%	40 hrs	100%
Test integration with property pages	Kaushal	0%	8 hrs	100%
Feature analysis	Kaushal	0%	8 hrs	100%
Create DCTs	Kaushal	0%	8 hrs	100%
Create presentation templates	Kaushal	0%	8 hrs	100%
Prepare test plan for feature	Swati	0%	8 hrs	100%
Review test plan	Mahesh	0%	3.2 hrs	50%
Review test plan	Julie	0%	0.8 hrs	100%
Create content	Virginia	0%	120 hrs	100%
Review DCTs	John	0%	8 hrs	100%

Review DCTs	Virginia	0%	8 hrs	100%
Review DCTs	Chris	0%	8 hrs	100%
Rework DCTs	Kaushal	0%	8 hrs	100%
Enter content for testing	Nick	0%	8 hrs	100%
Review and signoff of TPLs	John	0%	8 hrs	100%
Template QA	Julie	0%	1 hr	25%
Rework TPLs	Kaushal	0%	8 hrs	100%
Enter all content	Nick	0%	8 hrs	100%
Internal review of content	John	0%	8 hrs	100%
Content QA	Julie	0%	2 hrs	25%
Deploy content to development environment	Kaushal	0%	8 hrs	100%
Test and integrate feature into website	Venkat	0%	8 hrs	100%
QA of feature	Julie	0%	2 hrs	25%
Feature analysis	Ramky	100%	16 hrs	100%
Feature analysis	Offshore	100%	16 hrs	100%
Redesign look and feel	John	0%	8 hrs	100%
Create DCTs	Kiran	100%	8 hrs	100%
Create presentation templates	Kiran	100%	16 hrs	100%
Prepare test plan for feature	Ramky	100%	8 hrs	100%
Review test plan	Julie	0%	0.8 hrs	100%
Review test plan	Mahesh	0%	3.2 hrs	50%
Create JSPs	Ramky	100%	32 hrs	100%
Develop Java classes	Ramky	100%	16 hrs	100%
Inktomi search engine	Ramky	100%	40 hrs	100%
Create content	Virginia	0%	160 hrs	100%
Review DCTs	John	0%	8 hrs	100%
Review DCTs	Virginia	0%	8 hrs	100%
Review DCTs	Chris	0%	8 hrs	100%
Rework DCTs	Kaushal	0%	8 hrs	100%
Enter content for testing	Nick	0%	8 hrs	100%
Review and signoff of TPLs	John	0%	8 hrs	100%
Template QA	Julie	0%	2 hrs	25%
Rework TPLs	Kiran	0%	8 hrs	100%
Enter all content	Nick	0%	8 hrs	100%
Internal review of content	John	0%	8 hrs	100%

Content QA	Julie	0%	2 hrs	25%
Deploy content to development environment	Kaushal	0%	4 hrs	100%
Test and integrate feature into website	Venkat	0%	24 hrs	100%
Test and integrate feature into website	Kaushal	0%	24 hrs	100%
QA of feature	Julie	0%	4 hrs	25%
Feature analysis	Ramky	0%	4 hrs	100%
Feature analysis	Offshore	0%	4 hrs	100%
Create DCTs	Kaushal	0%	8 hrs	100%
Create database update script	Ramky	0%	8 hrs	100%
Prepare test plan for feature	Ramky	0%	8 hrs	100%
Review test plan	Mahesh	0%	2 hrs	50%
Review test plan	Julie	0%	2 hrs	100%
Create JSPs	Ramky	0%	16 hrs	100%
Develop Java classes	Ramky	0%	32 hrs	100%
Third party integration	Offshore	0%	32 hrs	100%
Develop CheetahMail interface	Ramky	0%	16 hrs	100%
Create content	Virginia	0%	176 hrs	100%
Review DCTs	John	0%	8 hrs	100%
Review DCTs	Virginia	0%	8 hrs	100%
Review DCTs	Chris	0%	8 hrs	100%
Rework DCTs	Kaushal	0%	8 hrs	100%
Enter content	Nick	0%	8 hrs	100%
Deploy content to development environment	Kaushal	0%	4 hrs	100%
Test and integrate feature into website	Venkat	0%	24 hrs	100%
Test and integrate feature into website	Kaushal	0%	24 hrs	100%
QA of feature	Julie	0%	2 hrs	25%
Feature analysis	Kaushal	0%	8 hrs	100%
Create DCTs	Kaushal	0%	8 hrs	100%
Create presentation templates	Kaushal	0%	8 hrs	100%
Prepare test plan for feature	Ramky	0%	8 hrs	100%
Review test plan	Julie	0%	1 hr	100%
Review test plan	Mahesh	0%	1 hr	25%
Create JSPs	Ramky	0%	16 hrs	100%
Develop Java classes	Ramky	0%	24 hrs	100%
Third party integration	Ramky	0%	0 hrs	100%

Create content	Virginia	0%	160 hrs	100%
Review DCTs	John	0%	8 hrs	100%
Review DCTs	Virginia	0%	8 hrs	100%
Review DCTs	Chris	0%	8 hrs	100%
Rework DCTs	Kaushal	0%	8 hrs	100%
Enter content	Nick	0%	8 hrs	100%
Review and signoff of TPLs	John	0%	8 hrs	100%
Template QA	Julie	0%	2 hrs	25%
Rework TPLs	Kaushal	0%	8 hrs	100%
Internal review of content	John	0%	8 hrs	100%
Content QA	Julie	0%	2 hrs	25%
Deploy content to development environment	Kaushal	0%	8 hrs	100%
Test and integrate feature into website	Kaushal	0%	24 hrs	100%
Test and integrate feature into website	Venkat	0%	24 hrs	100%
QA of feature	Julie	0%	2 hrs	25%
Feature analysis	Venkat	0%	8 hrs	100%
Finalize interface definitions	Venkat	0%	16 hrs	100%
Prepare test plan for feature	Jayadev	0%	8 hrs	100%
Review test plan	Julie	0%	1 hr	100%
Review test plan	Mahesh	0%	3 hrs	25%
Test Feature in development	Venkat	0%	24 hrs	100%
QA of feature	Julie	0%	4 hrs	25%
Feature analysis	Ramky	0%	8 hrs	100%
Create JSPs	Ramky	100%	40 hrs	100%
Develop Java classes	Ramky	100%	64 hrs	100%
Prepare test plan for feature	Ramky	0%	8 hrs	100%
Review test plan	Mahesh	0%	1 hr	100%
Review test plan	Julie	0%	1 hr	100%
Third party integration	Ramky	0%	8 hrs	100%
Test and integrate feature into website	Venkat	0%	24 hrs	100%
QA of feature	Julie	0%	4 hrs	25%
Feature analysis	Kiran	0%	24 hrs	100%
Feature analysis	Chris	0%	24 hrs	100%
Prototype	Kiran	100%	16 hrs	100%
Onsite review of prototype	Mahesh	0%	8 hrs	100%

Onsite review of prototype	Kathi	0%	8 hrs	100%
Onsite review of prototype	Doug	0%	8 hrs	100%
Onsite review of prototype	Chris	0%	8 hrs	100%
Prepare design document	Kiran	100%	16 hrs	100%
Review design	Mahesh	0%	8 hrs	100%
Review design	Kapil	0%	8 hrs	100%
Review design	Doug	0%	8 hrs	100%
Review design	Chris	0%	8 hrs	100%
Prepare test plan for feature	Chris	0%	8 hrs	100%
Review test plan	Mahesh	0%	2 hrs	50%
Review test plan	Julie	0%	2 hrs	100%
Create JSPs	Chris	0%	40 hrs	100%
Develop Java classes	Chris	0%	40 hrs	100%
Test and integrate feature into website	Chris	0%	24 hrs	100%
Onsite integration	Venkat	0%	16 hrs	100%
Onsite integration	Chris	0%	16 hrs	100%
QA of feature	Julie	0%	4 hrs	25%
Document CMS environment setup	Guneet	0%	8 hrs	50%
Review plan	Mahesh	0%	2 hrs	25%
Customer review of CMS config plan	Cherry	0%	1.8 hrs	38%
Customer review of CMS config plan	joe	0%	0.6 hrs	100%
Customer review of CMS config plan	Kapil	0%	0.6 hrs	100%
Revise document	Guneet	0%	4 hrs	50%
Prepare Integration test plan	Kiran	0%	120 hrs	100%
Review Integration test plan	Mahesh	0%	6.4 hrs	50%
Review Integration test plan	Julie	0%	1.6 hrs	100%
Training on load testing	Load Tester	0%	6.55 hrs	50%
Training on load testing	Jason	0%	0.73 hrs	100%
Training on load testing	Julie	0%	0.73 hrs	100%
QA testing in development environment	Julie	0%	40 hrs	100%
QA testing in development environment	Jason	0%	40 hrs	100%
Document Installation instructions	Venkat	0%	8 hrs	100%
Develop installation script	Venkat	0%	8 hrs	100%
Test install process	Venkat	0%	8 hrs	100%

Review installation instructions	Venkat	0%	2 hrs	50%
Review installation instructions	Anthony	0%	2 hrs	100%
FTCRS 11.2b—QA complete	Stella	0%	0 hrs	100%
WBE 3.0—QA complete	Stella	0%	0 hrs	100%
Setup and test multicast clustering	Erik	0%	24 hrs	100%
Configure node manager	Erik	0%	16 hrs	100%
Identify testing requirements for clustering	Kapil	0%	16 hrs	100%
Develop test scripts for testing clustering	Chris	0%	16 hrs	100%
Test BigIP configuration	Justin	0%	40 hrs	100%
Setup and test system and domain logs	Erik	0%	16 hrs	100%
Prepare OS upgrade documentation	Erik	0%	2 hrs	25%
Prepare Weblogic install documentation	Erik	0%	2 hrs	25%
Prepare multicase clustering setup documentation	Erik	0%	4 hrs	50%
Prepare BigIP configuration documentation	Justin	0%	4 hrs	50%
Prepare node manager configuration documentation	Erik	0%	2 hrs	25%
Prepare system/domain log setup documentation	Erik	0%	2 hrs	25%
Install OS, Weblogic, and Apache on QA boxes	Anthony	0%	32 hrs	100%
Configure Weblogic servers	Anthony	0%	16 hrs	100%
Deploy application in QA	Venkat	0%	16 hrs	100%
Deploy application in QA	Anthony	0%	16 hrs	100%
Promote content to QA environment	Guneet	0%	24 hrs	100%
Promote content to QA environment	Kaushal	0%	24 hrs	100%
QA testing in QA environment	Julie	0%	40 hrs	100%
QA testing in QA environment	Jason	0%	40 hrs	100%
Load Testing	Load Tester	0%	80 hrs	100%
User acceptance testing	John	0%	40 hrs	100%
User acceptance testing	Mike	0%	40 hrs	100%
Install OS, weblogic, and Apache on production boxes	Anthony	0%	32 hrs	100%
Configure Weblogic servers	Anthony	0%	16 hrs	100%
Deploy application in production	Anthony	0%	16 hrs	100%
Feature analysis	Kaushal	0%	8 hrs	100%
Create DCTs	Kaushal	0%	16 hrs	100%
Create presentation templates	Kaushal	0%	16 hrs	100%
Prepare test plan for feature	Offshore	0%	8 hrs	100%
Review test plan	Mahesh	0%	3 hrs	50%

Review test plan	Julie	0%	1 hr	100%
Create JSPs	Offshore	0%	40 hrs	100%
Develop Java classes	Offshore	0%	16 hrs	100%
Third party integration	Offshore	0%	8 hrs	100%
Third party integration	Kaushal	0%	8 hrs	100%
Create content	Virginia	0%	200 hrs	100%
Review DCTs	John	0%	8 hrs	100%
Review DCTs	Virginia	0%	8 hrs	100%
Review DCTs	Chris	0%	8 hrs	100%
Rework DCTs	Kaushal	0%	8 hrs	100%
Enter content for testing	Nick	0%	8 hrs	100%
Review and signoff of TPLs	John	0%	8 hrs	100%
Template QA	Julie	0%	2 hrs	25%
Rework TPLs	Kaushal	0%	8 hrs	100%
Enter all content	Nick	0%	40 hrs	100%
Internal review of content	John	0%	40 hrs	100%
Content QA	Julie	0%	6 hrs	15%
Deploy content to development environment	Kaushal	0%	8 hrs	100%
Test and integrate feature into website	Kaushal	0%	24 hrs	100%
QA of feature	Julie	0%	4 hrs	25%
Feature analysis	Kaushal	0%	8 hrs	100%
Create DCTs	Kaushal	0%	16 hrs	100%
Create presentation templates	Kaushal	0%	32 hrs	100%
Prepare test plan for feature	Offshore	0%	8 hrs	100%
Review test plan	Mahesh	0%	3.2 hrs	50%
Review test plan	Julie	0%	0.8 hrs	100%
Create JSPs	Offshore	0%	40 hrs	100%
Develop Java classes	Offshore	0%	16 hrs	100%
Third party integration	Offshore	0%	8 hrs	100%
Third party integration	Kaushal	0%	8 hrs	100%
Create content	Virginia	0%	240 hrs	100%
Review DCTs	John	0%	8 hrs	100%
Review DCTs	Virginia	0%	8 hrs	100%
Review DCTs	Chris	0%	8 hrs	100%
Rework DCTs	Kaushal	0%	8 hrs	100%

Enter content for testing	Nick	0%	8 hrs	100%
Review & signoff of TPLs	John	0%	8 hrs	100%
Template QA	Julie	0%	2 hrs	25%
Rework TPLs	Kaushal	0%	8 hrs	100%
Enter all content	Nick	0%	40 hrs	100%
Internal review of content	John	0%	40 hrs	100%
Content QA	Julie	0%	4 hrs	10%
Deploy content to development environment	Kaushal	0%	8 hrs	100%
Test and integrate feature into website	Kaushal	0%	24 hrs	100%
QA of feature	Julie	0%	2 hrs	13%
Feature analysis	Kaushal	0%	8 hrs	100%
Create DCTs	Kaushal	0%	16 hrs	100%
Create presentation templates	Kaushal	0%	16 hrs	100%
Prepare test plan for feature	Offshore	0%	8 hrs	100%
Review test plan	Mahesh	0%	3 hrs	50%
Review test plan	Julie	0%	1 hr	100%
Create JSPs	Offshore	0%	40 hrs	100%
Develop Java classes	Offshore	0%	16 hrs	100%
Third party integration	Offshore	0%	8 hrs	100%
Third party integration	Kaushal	0%	8 hrs	100%
Create content	Virginia	0%	320 hrs	100%
Review DCTs	John	0%	8 hrs	100%
Review DCTs	Virginia	0%	8 hrs	100%
Review DCTs	Chris	0%	8 hrs	100%
Rework DCTs	Kaushal	0%	8 hrs	100%
Enter content for testing	Nick	0%	8 hrs	100%
Review and signoff of TPLs	John	0%	8 hrs	100%
Template QA	Julie	0%	2 hrs	25%
Rework TPLs	Kaushal	0%	8 hrs	100%
Enter all content	Nick	0%	8 hrs	100%
Internal review of content	John	0%	8 hrs	100%
Content QA	Julie	0%	2 hrs	25%
Deploy content to development environment	Guneet	0%	8 hrs	100%

Test and integrate feature into website	Kaushal	0%	24 hrs	100%
QA of feature	Julie	0%	4 hrs	25%
Feature analysis	Offshore	0%	32 hrs	100%
Create DCTs	Offshore	0%	16 hrs	100%
Create presentation templates	Offshore	0%	32 hrs	100%
Prepare test plan for feature	Offshore	0%	8 hrs	100%
Review test plan	Mahesh	0%	3.2 hrs	50%
Review test plan	Julie	0%	0.8 hrs	100%
Create JSPs	Offshore	0%	16 hrs	100%
Develop Java classes	Offshore	0%	16 hrs	100%
Third party integration	Offshore	0%	8 hrs	100%
Create content	Virginia	0%	160 hrs	100%
Review DCTs	John	0%	8 hrs	100%
Review DCTs	Virginia	0%	8 hrs	100%
Review DCTs	Chris	0%	8 hrs	100%
Rework DCTs	Guneet	0%	8 hrs	100%
Enter content for testing	Nick	0%	8 hrs	100%
Review of TPLs	John	0%	8 hrs	100%
Template QA	Julie	0%	4 hrs	50%
Template rework	Guneet	0%	8 hrs	100%
Enter all content	Nick	0%	16 hrs	100%
Internal review of content	John	0%	16 hrs	100%
Content QA	Julie	0%	4 hrs	25%
Deploy content to development environment	Guneet	0%	8 hrs	100%
Test and integrate feature into website	Guneet	0%	24 hrs	100%
Test and integrate feature into website	Venkat	0%	24 hrs	100%
QA of feature	Julie	0%	4 hrs	25%
Feature analysis	Kaushal	0%	8 hrs	100%
Create DCTs	Kaushal	0%	16 hrs	100%
Create presentation templates	Kaushal	0%	8 hrs	100%
Prepare test plan for feature	Offshore	0%	8 hrs	100%
Review test plan	Mahesh	0%	3 hrs	50%
Review test plan	Julie	0%	1 hr	100%
Create JSPs	Offshore	0%	16 hrs	100%
Integration with 10Best	Offshore	0%	8 hrs	100%

Create content	Virginia	0%	320 hrs	100%
Review DCTs	John	0%	8 hrs	100%
Review DCTs	Virginia	0%	8 hrs	100%
Review DCTs	Chris	0%	8 hrs	100%
Rework DCTs	Kaushal	0%	8 hrs	100%
Enter content for testing	Nick	0%	8 hrs	100%
Review and signoff of TPLs	John	0%	8 hrs	100%
Template QA	Julie	0%	2 hrs	25%
Rework TPLs	Kaushal	0%	8 hrs	100%
Enter all content	Nick	0%	8 hrs	100%
Internal review of content	John	0%	8 hrs	100%
Content QA	Julie	0%	2 hrs	25%
Deploy content to development environment	Kaushal	0%	8 hrs	100%
Test and integrate feature into website	Kaushal	0%	24 hrs	100%
QA of feature	Julie	0%	2 hrs	25%
Feature analysis	Kaushal	0%	8 hrs	100%
Create DCTs	Kaushal	0%	16 hrs	100%
Create presentation templates	Kaushal	0%	8 hrs	100%
Prepare test plan for feature	Offshore	0%	8 hrs	100%
Review test plan	Mahesh	0%	0.25 hrs	3%
Review test plan	Julie	0%	3.75 hrs	100%
Create JSPs	Offshore	0%	56 hrs	100%
Develop Java classes	Offshore	0%	16 hrs	100%
Third party integration	Offshore	0%	16 hrs	100%
Create content	Virginia	0%	320 hrs	100%
Review DCTs	John	0%	8 hrs	100%
Review DCTs	Virginia	0%	8 hrs	100%
Review DCTs	Chris	0%	8 hrs	100%
Rework DCTs	Kaushal	0%	8 hrs	100%
Enter content for testing	Nick	0%	8 hrs	100%
Review and signoff of TPLs	John	0%	8 hrs	100%
Template QA	Julie	0%	2 hrs	25%
Enter all content	Nick	0%	32 hrs	100%
Internal review of content	John	0%	32 hrs	100%
Content QA	Julie	0%	4 hrs	13%

Deploy content to development environment	Guneet	0%	4 hrs	100%
Test and integrate feature into website	Venkat	0%	24 hrs	100%
Test and integrate feature into website	Kaushal	0%	24 hrs	100%
QA of feature	Julie	0%	2 hrs	13%
Feature analysis	Offshore	0%	8 hrs	100%
Create DCTs	Offshore	0%	16 hrs	100%
Create presentation templates	Offshore	0%	16 hrs	100%
Prepare test plan for feature	Offshore	0%	8 hrs	100%
Review test plan	Mahesh	0%	3 hrs	50%
Review test plan	Julie	0%	1 hr	100%
Create JSPs	Offshore	0%	40 hrs	100%
Develop Java classes	Offshore	0%	16 hrs	100%
Third party integration	Offshore	0%	8 hrs	100%
Third party integration	Kaushal	0%	8 hrs	100%
Create content	Virginia	0%	200 hrs	100%
Review DCTs	John	0%	8 hrs	100%
Review DCTs	Virginia	0%	8 hrs	100%
Review DCTs	Chris	0%	8 hrs	100%
Rework DCTs	Kaushal	0%	8 hrs	100%
Enter content for testing	Nick	0%	8 hrs	100%
Review and signoff of TPLs	John	0%	8 hrs	100%
Template QA	Julie	0%	2 hrs	25%
Rework TPLs	Kaushal	0%	8 hrs	100%
Enter all content	Nick	0%	3 hrs	100%
Internal review of content	John	0%	8 hrs	100%
Content QA	Julie	0%	2 hrs	25%
Deploy content to development environment	Kaushal	0%	8 hrs	100%
Test and integrate feature into website	Kaushal	0%	24 hrs	100%
QA of feature	Julie	0%	4 hrs	25%
Feature analysis	Guneet	0%	8 hrs	100%
Create DCTs	Guneet	0%	8 hrs	100%
Create presentation templates	Guneet	0%	8 hrs	100%
Prepare test plan for feature	Offshore	0%	8 hrs	100%
Review test plan	Mahesh	0%	3 hrs	50%
Review test plan	Julie	0%	1 hr	100%

Create JSPs	Offshore	0%	40 hrs	100%
Develop Java classes	Offshore	0%	16 hrs	100%
Third party integration	Offshore	0%	8 hrs	100%
Create content	Virginia	0%	160 hrs	100%
Review DCTs	John	0%	8 hrs	100%
Review DCTs	Virginia	0%	8 hrs	100%
Review DCTs	Chris	0%	8 hrs	100%
Rework DCTs	Guneet	0%	8 hrs	100%
Enter content for testing	Nick	0%	8 hrs	100%
Review and signoff of TPLs	John	0%	8 hrs	100%
Template QA	Julie	0%	2 hrs	25%
Rework TPLs	Guneet	0%	8 hrs	100%
Enter all content	Nick	0%	16 hrs	100%
Internal review of content	John	0%	16 hrs	100%
Content QA	Julie	0%	2 hrs	13%
Deploy content to development environment	Guneet	0%	8 hrs	100%
Test and integrate feature into website	Guneet	0%	24 hrs	100%
Test and integrate feature into website	Venkat	0%	24 hrs	100%
QA of feature	Julie	0%	2 hrs	13%
Feature analysis	Guneet	0%	8 hrs	100%
Create DCTs	Guneet	0%	8 hrs	100%
Create presentation templates	Guneet	0%	16 hrs	100%
Prepare test plan for feature	Offshore	0%	8 hrs	100%
Review test plan	Mahesh	0%	3 hrs	50%
Review test plan	Julie	0%	1 hr	100%
Create JSPs	Offshore	0%	40 hrs	100%
Develop Java classes	Offshore	0%	16 hrs	100%
Third party integration	Offshore	0%	8 hrs	100%
Create content	Virginia	0%	200 hrs	100%
Review DCTs	John	0%	8 hrs	100%
Review DCTs	Virginia	0%	8 hrs	100%
Review DCTs	Chris	0%	8 hrs	100%
Rework DCTs	Guneet	0%	8 hrs	100%
Enter content for testing	Nick	0%	8 hrs	100%
Review and signoff of TPLs	John	0%	8 hrs	100%

Template QA	Julie	0%	2 hrs	25%
Rework TPLs	Guneet	0%	8 hrs	100%
Enter all content	Nick	0%	8 hrs	100%
Internal review of content	John	0%	8 hrs	100%
Content QA	Julie	0%	2 hrs	25%
Deploy content to development environment	Guneet	0%	8 hrs	100%
Test and integrate feature into website	Guneet	0%	24 hrs	100%
Test and integrate feature into website	Venkat	0%	24 hrs	100%
QA of feature	Julie	0%	2 hrs	13%
Feature Analysis	Guneet	0%	8 hrs	100%
Create DCTs	Guneet	0%	32 hrs	100%
Create presentation templates	Guneet	0%	32 hrs	100%
Prepare test plan for feature	Offshore	0%	8 hrs	100%
Review test plan	Mahesh	0%	3 hrs	50%
Review test plan	Julie	0%	1 hr	100%
Create JSPs	Offshore	0%	8 hrs	100%
Develop Java classes	Offshore	0%	8 hrs	100%
Third party integration	Offshore	0%	8 hrs	100%
Create content	Virginia	0%	320 hrs	100%
Review DCTs	John	0%	8 hrs	100%
Review DCTs	Virginia	0%	8 hrs	100%
Review DCTs	Chris	0%	8 hrs	100%
Rework DCTs	Guneet	0%	8 hrs	100%
Enter content for testing	Nick	0%	8 hrs	100%
Review and signoff of TPLs	John	0%	8 hrs	100%
Template QA	Julie	0%	2 hrs	25%
Rework TPLs	Guneet	0%	8 hrs	100%
Enter all content	Nick	0%	32 hrs	100%
Internal review of content	John	0%	32 hrs	100%
Content QA	Julie	0%	4 hrs	13%
Deploy content to development environment	Guneet	0%	8 hrs	100%
Test and integrate feature into website	Guneet	0%	24 hrs	100%
Test and integrate feature into website	Venkat	0%	24 hrs	100%
QA of feature	Julie	0%	2 hrs	13%
Feature Analysis	Guneet	0%	8 hrs	100%

Create DCTs	Guneet	0%	32 hrs	100%
Create presentation templates	Guneet	0%	32 hrs	100%
Prepare test plan for feature	Offshore	0%	8 hrs	100%
Review test plan	Mahesh	0%	3 hrs	50%
Review test plan	Julie	0%	1 hr	100%
Create JSPs	Offshore	0%	8 hrs	100%
Develop Java classes	Offshore	0%	8 hrs	100%
Third party integration	Offshore	0%	8 hrs	100%
Create content	Virginia	0%	8 hrs	100%
Review DCTs	John	0%	8 hrs	100%
Review DCTs	Virginia	0%	8 hrs	100%
Review DCTs	Chris	0%	8 hrs	100%
Rework DCTs	Guneet	0%	8 hrs	100%
Enter content for testing	Nick	0%	8 hrs	100%
Review and signoff of TPLs	John	0%	8 hrs	100%
Template QA	Julie	0%	2 hrs	25%
Rework TPLs	Guneet	0%	8 hrs	100%
Enter all content	Nick	0%	32 hrs	100%
Internal review of content	John	0%	32 hrs	100%
Content QA	Julie	0%	4 hrs	13%
Deploy content to development environment	Guneet	0%	8 hrs	100%
Test and integrate feature into website	Guneet	0%	24 hrs	100%
Test and integrate feature into website	Venkat	0%	24 hrs	100%
QA of feature	Julie	0%	2 hrs	13%
Feature Analysis	Offshore	0%	8 hrs	100%
Develop Java classes	Offshore	0%	16 hrs	100%
Prepare test plan for feature	Offshore	0%	8 hrs	100%
Review test plan	Mahesh	0%	3.2 hrs	50%
Review test plan	Julie	0%	0.8 hrs	100%
Test and integrate feature into website	Venkat	0%	24 hrs	100%
QA of feature	Julie	0%	2 hrs	13%
Install WebTrends	Chris	0%	24 hrs	100%
Testing	Chris	0%	16 hrs	100%
QA of feature	Julie	0%	2 hrs	13%
Feature analysis	Offshore	0%	8 hrs	100%

Feature analysis	Offshore	0%	4 hrs	100%
Update integration test plan for phase 2	Offshore	0%	40 hrs	100%
Review integration test plan	Julie	0%	4 hrs	50%
Review integration test plan	Mahesh	0%	4 hrs	50%
Deploy application in QA	Kaushal	0%	16 hrs	100%
Deploy application in QA	Guneet	0%	16 hrs	100%
Deploy application in QA	Venkat	0%	16 hrs	100%
Deploy application in QA	Kapil	0%	16 hrs	100%
Load testing	Load Tester	0%	80 hrs	100%
QA testing	Julie	0%	80 hrs	100%
QA testing	Jason	0%	80 hrs	100%
User acceptance testing	John	0%	40 hrs	100%

Info Table

Microsoft project	**Template ID:**	**9876543210**
Microsoft project is a project management program designed to help you plan and manage your projects and communicate project information.		
Whether you have a simple list of tasks or want to coordinate activities across multiple projects, Microsoft project makes it easy to get started and learn as you go.		
With this template you can export data to Excel to perform more advanced numerical analysis. Then you can import project data back into Microsoft project to perform standard project tasks, such as: * Seeing your tasks linked in a Gantt chart * Seeing how much work each person on the team has assigned to them		
You can easily import this information back into Microsoft project and keep working without reentering data.		

GLOSSARY

Acceptance criteria

The criteria that a system or component must satisfy in order to be accepted by a user, customer, or other authorized entity.

Acceptance testing

1. Formal testing conducted to determine whether or not a system satisfies its acceptance criteria and to enable the customer to determine whether or not to accept the system.
2. Formal testing conducted to enable a user, customer, or other authorized entity to determine whether to accept a system or component.

Application software

Software designed to fulfill specific needs of a user, for example, software for navigation, payroll, or process control.

Audit planning

It is a process of preparing an audit plan with the following details: lead auditor, auditee (the person to be audited), approver of the planning process, and the timeline for auditing.

Audit strategy

An audit strategy is developed by considering the internal control system required for the business model followed by the organization in question. Audit strategy will decide the frequency of audits and functional areas to be covered by audit, and will take into account statutory and regulatory requirements as well as customers' requirements.

Benchmarking principle

A process of finding, adapting, and implementing outstanding practices.

Benchmarking

Benchmarking is the process of comparing processes and performance results of an organization with another that is widely considered to be a best in class industry standard benchmark or best practice.

Bottom-up estimation

It figures out how long each generic task or building block would take, based on some kind of historical evidence (again, the importance of tracking).

Business process

A collection of logically associated activities that use the resources of the organization to provide defined results in support of the organization's objectives.

Capability level

This level indicates the organization's capability relative to a process area in CMMI.

Causal analysis

A technique to identify and understand the reasons why things are as they are and hence enabling focus of change activity. The basic rule of this is to find causes that you can treat rather than treat the symptoms.

Change management

A defined process for creating changes to a project plan.

CMMI

Capability maturity model integration (CMMI) has been developed by Carnegie Mellon Software Engineering Institute (SEI). This is useful in software engineering and organizational development process and for effective process improvement.

Code review

The code review flag signifies whether or not a code review was conducted as a result of a defect. The value is either "Y," signifying that a code review had occurred, or "N," signifying that a code review had not occurred.

Compliance

This refers to adherence to standard or statutory regulations.

Configuration control board

A board established to endorse all projected changes to an approved baseline.

Configuration controller

A system of procedures that monitors emerging project scope against the scope baseline. It requires documentation and management approval on any change to the baseline.

Configuration item

Component of a configuration that has a well distinct function and elected for configuration management.

Configuration management

A procedure for applying technical and administrative direction and supervision to identify and document in detail the functional and physical characteristics of a configuration item or system, control changes to those characteristics, record and report change processing and implementation status, and verify obedience with precise requirements.

Contract

An agreement is termed as a contract, which means the clauses in a contract are bound by legal agreement that is enforceable in a court of law.

Corrective maintenance

Maintenance performed to correct faults in hardware or software.

Design

Creates a blueprint for the design with the necessary specifications for the hardware, software, people, and data resources.

Effectiveness

It is a measure of whether or not and to what extent the set goals have been achieved. In project management, effectiveness is a strategic criterion.

Enhancement

A request is classified as enhancement when there is a need for adding a new feature or enhancement to the existing functionality or designing a new functionality to the existing product.

Estimation

A general definition: "Estimation is the process of establishing a reliable analytical model of a project." A specific definition: "Estimation is the process of establishing values for critical parameters in an analytical model of a project."

External audit

Periodic or specific purpose checks conducted by external party (external to organization). These are conducted by certified or qualified auditors.

External benchmarking

External benchmarking compares processes and performance of an organization with similar organizations either in the same industry or outside the industry.

Function point

A standard metric for the relative size and complexity of a software system. It is used to estimate the relative size and complexity of software in the early stages of development—analysis and design. The size is determined by identifying the components of the system as seen by the end user: the inputs, outputs, inquiries, interfaces to other systems, and logical internal files.

Impact analysis

Impact analysis is done to ascertain the extent of changes that can be accepted for the software without having to do any major design or structural changes.

Internal audit

These audits are conducted by certified or trained auditors from the organization; these audits are conducted as per the requirement of the defined processes at organization level or before an external audit is to be conducted to ensure that the projects are compliant to the defined processes.

Internal benchmarking

Internal benchmarking compares processes and performance of different projects and business units and finds best practices within the organization.

Knowledge transfer

The process of capturing and recording all relevant details about an application with an objective of providing remote maintenance on the application.

Maintenance (projects)

Projects that involve only maintenance support for software already developed.

Maintenance phase

The period of time in the software lifecycle during which a software product is employed in its operational environment, monitored for satisfactory performance, and modified as necessary to correct performance, and modified as necessary to correct problems or to respond to changing requirements.

Maintenance plan

A document produced by the maintenance projects, wherein the procedures for the maintenance and monitoring of the project are laid down.

Maintenance

1. The process of modifying a software system or component after delivery to correct faults, improve performance or other attributes, or adapt to a changed environment.
2. The process of retaining a hardware system or component in, or restoring it to, a state in which it can perform its required functions.

Major defect

A defect that will cause a significant, observable failure or deviation from the requirements or specifications is classified as major defect.

Maturity level

This level indicates the level of maturity that an organization exhibits with respect to process areas in CMMI.

MBT

Model-based testing is the automatic generation of efficient test procedures/vectors using models of system. An example of MBT is a finite state machine (FSM) model of a simple phone system. This model is of a phone that can call out. Nodes are states of the phone. Edges indicate actions that the user can take (these are inputs to the system). Test cases specify a sequence of inputs, the states the system is expected to be in after each action, and the value of all outputs of the system.

Metrics

Parameters or measures of quantitative appraisal used for measurement, comparison, or tracking performance or production.

Milestone analysis

A technique that helps to recognize a few key milestones in the project (e.g., commissioning of a certain phase, handover, etc.) and to monitor the finish dates of these milestones during the project.

Minor defect

A defect that will not cause a failure in using the product and do not prevent or hinder the functionality is classified as minor defect.

Non-conformance report

This is a report that details the deviations from compliance specifications and is prepared at the end of an audit.

Pareto analysis

A formal technique for finding the changes that will give the biggest benefits. A simple technique that helps to identify the most important problem to solve and gives you a score showing how severe the problem is. It uses the idea that by doing 20% of work you can generate 80% of the advantage of doing the entire job.

Process area

In CMMI for software development, there are 24 process areas indicating the aspects of product and service development that should be covered by institutional processes.

Process capability baseline

A documented characterization of the range of expected results that would normally be achieved by following a specific process under typical circumstances. A process capability baseline is typically established at an organizational level.

Process database

It is a process of collecting and recording data in a systematic manner.

Productivity

The amount of output per unit of input (labor, equipment, and capital). For example, productivity might be measured in a factory based on the number of hours it takes to produce a good, while in the service sector productivity might be measured based on the revenue generated by an employee divided by his/her salary.

Project control

A project management function that involves comparing real performance with planned performance and taking corrective measures to produce the desired outcome when significant differences exist.

Project management plan

A management summary document that gives the essentials of a project in terms of its objectives, justification, and how the objectives are to be achieved. It should describe how all the major activities under each project management function are to be accomplished, including that of overall project control.

Project management

The art of expressing and organizing human and material resources throughout the life of a project by using modern management techniques to achieve the predetermined objectives of scope, quality, time, cost, and participant satisfaction.

Project monitor

Judging of recent project status with what was intended to be done to recognize and report any variation.

Quality assurance

This is a planned and systematic approach for providing confidence to the management that features of a product and quality of service are suitable for its defined purpose.

Quality control

Quality control is the discipline that deals with testing the suitability of functions developed with respect to the customer requirements.

Quality

Quality is defined by the customers and refers to the features and requirements that have been defined by the customer in either an explicit or implicit manner.

Requirement analysis

It is the process of comprehending the customer needs and expectations from a proposed system or application.

Review effectiveness

Review effectiveness is quite difficult to define. When you hold a review, say for the software requirement specification, then you would have a total number of defects discovered and you also know the number of pages in the document. So, to first order, you could divide the total number of defects by the number of pages and derive a defect density measure for the document. But that number by itself doesn't tell you a whole lot. You need to have a good understanding of the expected number of defects per page coming out of a review. That number would come from your historical data. But this number still doesn't yield an effectiveness measure. So you have to look for defects that were missed by the review in downstream activities such as testing and other reviews.

RFI (request for information)

A request for information (RFI) is a process to collect and document information about the capabilities of various suppliers against specific requirements.

RFP (request for proposal)

A request for proposal (referred to as RFP) is an invitation for intended suppliers to submit a proposal on specific requirements. The invitation could be sent to specific suppliers (approved vendors) or public bidding process.

RFQ (request for quotation)

The purpose of RFQ is to invite suppliers into a bidding process to bid against specific requirements.

Risk management

Risk management is a process of identification, assessment, and quantification of risks so that resources can be used optimally.

Risk mitigation

Risk mitigation includes finding out ways to prevent risks from occurring or to find alternate ways to avoid the problems from happening.

Risk plan

A risk management plan is a document prepared at the initial stages of project planning to foresee risks, estimate the impact, and create response plans to mitigate them.

Schedule

Defined as planned dates for performing the schedule activities and for meeting the schedule milestone.

Software maintenance projects

Software maintenance in software engineering is defined as the modification of a software product after delivery. The reason for these changes requires could be for technical reasons (such as correcting a fault) or functional (enhancing present capabilities of the software).

Software project management

It is a class of computer applications specifically designed to assist with planning and controlling resources, costs, and schedule of a project in order to fulfill the business requirements.

SOW (statement of work)

A statement of work (SOW) is a document that documents roles and responsibilities, deliverables, and timeline that a supplier will have to execute for a customer.

SPIN benchmarking practices

SPIN (software process improvement network) is a forum consisting of group of software professionals from different organizations. There are different SPIN forums at international and national levels such as SPIN Hyderabad, SPIN Bangalore, etc.

Stakeholders

Stakeholders are an integral part of a project. They are the end users or clients, the people from whom requirements will be drawn, the people who will influence the design and, ultimately, the people who will reap the benefits of your completed project. There are different types of stakeholders: executive, end user, expert. Executive stakeholders are the persons who pay the bills. Typically, they are managers or directors who are involved with the commercial objectives for the project. End users are the persons who are going to use the product. Sometimes you need input from experts in other fields. They can be people like graphic designers, support reps, sales, or sometime lawyers and accountants.

Status reporting

A written report given to both the project team and to a responsible person on a regular basis stating the position of an activity, work package, or whole project.

System integration

System integration implies that both hardware and software required for a product are in compatible mode so that final functionalities can be met.

Tailoring

Documented rules that provide guidance for adapting the organization's standard software process with the specific project requirements.

Testing strategy

The organization's current best practice for performing software system test. The software testing strategy is a vital process that contains part of the software development lifecycle. The test plan forms the part of the project documentation. The test documentation is designed to create test cases to meet the requirements of the application for functional fit, system stability, platform stability, usability, and performance.

Testing

Evaluates the system's actual functionality in relation to the expected or intended functionality.

Top-down estimation

It starts with the methodology, considering the phases, and builds the model (including a generic work-breakdown structure) according to which it assigns specific roles—which have different cost levels to these generic tasks.

Turnaround time

The process of or time needed for performing a task, especially receiving, completing, and returning an assignment. Period for completing a process cycle (such as repair or replacement of a component or equipment) is commonly expressed as an average of previous such periods.

Validation

This is the process of providing evidence that a product or a process conforms to the defined user needs, requirements, and/or specifications under defined operating conditions.

Verification

It is the process that proves the system (or subsystem or component), meets its requirements, and matches the design. It may be determined by test, analysis, inspection, or demonstration. It starts with the integration activities at the component level. It progresses through the subsystem development to the verification of the entire system. Final verification for system acceptance is done with the installed system.

BIBLIOGRAPHY

Abrahamsson, H., Ahlgren, B., Alonso, J., Anderson, Anders., and Kreuger, P., (2002). A Multi-path Routing Algorithm for IP Networks Based on Flow Optimization. In: Proceedings QofIS'02/ICQT'02, Proceedings of the 3rd International Conference on Quality of Future Internet Services and Internet Charging and QoS Technologies, 2nd International Conference on from QoS Provisioning to QoS Charging.

Abrahamsson, P., Salo, O., Ronkainen, J., Warsta, J. (2002). Agile Software Development Methods: Review and Analysis. VTT Publications, 478.

Abrahamsson, P., Warsta, J., Siponen, M.T., Ronkainen, J. (2003). New Directions on Agile Methods: A Comparative Analysis. Proceedings of ICSE'03, pp. 244–254.

Abran, A., Idri, A. (2001). Fuzzy Logic Based Set of Measures for Software Project Similarity: Validation and Possible Improvements. In: Seventh International Software Metrics Symposium (METRICS'01).

A Guide to Project Management Body of Knowledge (PMBOK), www.pmi.org

Albrecht, A.J. (1979). Software Function, Source Lines of Code, and Development Effort Prediction: A Software Science Validation. IEEE Transactions on Software Engineering. Vol. SE-9, no. 6, pp. 639–648.

Armstrong, J.S. (2006). Findings from Evidence-Based Forecasting: Methods for Reducing Forecast Error. International Journal of Forecasting, Vol. 22, no. 3, 2006, pp. 583–659.

Aydin, C. (2005). Evaluating the Organizational Impact of Healthcare Information Systems. Health Informatics, Part I, pp. 5–29.

Belz, F.C. (1986). Applying the Spiral Model: Observations on Developing System Software, In: Proceedings of the 4th Annual Conference on Ada.

Berczuk, S.P. (2003). Software Configuration Management Patterns: Effective Teamwork, Practical Integration. Boston, MA: Addison-Wesley.

Bersoff, E.H. (1997). Elements of Software Configuration Management. Los Alamitos, CA: IEEE Computer Society Press.

Blanc, Accurate Parametrization of Conics by NURBS November 1996 (Vol. 16, No. 6).

Boehm, B. (1970). Build it Twice. Proceedings of ICSE9.

Boehm, B. (1981). Software Engineering Economics. Prentice-Hall. ISBN 0-13-822122-7, pp. 41–42, 254.

Boehm, B. (1985). A Spiral Model of Software Development and Enhancement. 2nd International Software Process Workshop. Coto de Caza, Trabuco Canyon, USA.

Boehm, B. (1986). A Spiral Model of Software Development and Enhancement. ACM SIGSOFT Software Engineering Notes (SEN).

Boehm, B.W. (1988). A Spiral Model of Software Development and Enhancement. Computer. Vol. 21, no 5. pp. 61–72.

Boehm, B., Belz, F.C. (1988). Applying Process Programming to the Spiral Model. Proceedings of Fourth Software Process Workshop, IEEE.

Boehm, B. (1996a). Escaping the Software Tar Pit: Model Clashes and How to Avoid Them, ACM SIGSOFT Software Engineering Notes, Vol. 24, no. 1.

Boehm, B. (1996b). Anchoring the Software Process. IEEE Software, July 1996, pp.73–82.

Boehm, B., Turner, R. (2004). Balancing Agility and Discipline: A Guide for the Perplexed. Boston, MA: Addison-Wesley. ISBN 0-321-18612-5, Appendix A, pp. 165–194.

Borodzicz, E. (2005). Risk, Crisis and Security Management. New York: Wiley.

Chrissis, M.B., Konard, M., Shrum, S. (2003). CMMI Guidelines for Process Integration and Product Improvement, Pearson.

Cleland, D.I., Gareis, R. (2006). Global Project Management Handbook. McGraw-Hill Professional.

Cohen, D., Lindvall, M., Costa, P. (2004). An Introduction to Agile Methods. In: Advances in Computers (pp. 1–66). New York: Elsevier Science.

Dinsmore, P.C., et al. (2005). The Right Projects Done Right!. John Wiley and Sons.

Dorfman, M.S. (2007). Introduction to Risk Management and Insurance (9th ed.). Englewood Cliffs, NJ: Prentice Hall.

Futrell, R.T., Shafer, D.F., and Shafer, L.I. (2002). Quality Software Project Management. New Jersey: Prentice Hall PTR.

Grady, R. (1992). Practical Software Metrics for Project Management and Process Improvement. Prentice Hall PTR.

Haag., S., Baltzan, P., Phillips, A. (2006). Business driven technology, New York: McGraw-Hill/ Irwin.

http://www.mcbreen.ab.ca/talks/CAMUG.pdf. 2003.

http://www.ifpug.org.

http://www.nesma.nl/section/home/

Hubbard, D. (2009). The Failure of Risk Management: Why It's Broken and How to Fix It. John Wiley & Sons, p. 46.

Humphrey, W. (1989). Managing the Software Process. Addison-Wesley.

International Standards Organization. (1987). ISO 9001, Quality Systems-Model for Quality Assurance in Design/Development, Production, Installation, and Services.

Ireland, L.R. (2006). Project Management. McGraw-Hill Professional.

Jacobson, M.J. (1994). Issues in Hypertext and Hypermedia Research: Toward a Framework for Linking Theory-to-Design. Journal of Educational Multimedia and Hypermedia, vol. 3, no. 2, pp. 141–154.

Jalote, P. (2000). Use of Metrics in High Maturity Organizations, SEPG2K, Seattle.

James, M. (1980). Rapid Application Development, Macmillan Coll Div, ISBN 0-02-376775-8.

Jones, C. (1996). Applied Software Measurement—Assuring Productivity and Quality (2nd ed.). McGraw Hill.

Jones, G.R. (1986). Socialization Tactics, Self-Efficacy, and Newcomers' Adjustments to Organizations. Academy of Management Journal, Vol. 29, no.2, pp. 262–279.

Larman, C., Basili, V.R. (2003). Iterative and Incremental Developments: A Brief History, Computer, Vol. 36, no. 6, pp. 47–56.

Lempel, A. (2003). Compression of Individual Sequences Via Variable-Rate Coding. IEEE Transactions on Information Theory, Vol. 24, Issue No. 5.

Livary, J. (1987). A Hierarchical Spiral Model for the Software Process. ACM Software Engineering Notes, pp. 35–37.

Lock, D. (2007). Project Management (9th ed.). Gower Publishing Ltd.

McConnell, J. (1996). Active Learning and Its Use in Computer Science. In: ITiCSE '96 Proceedings of the 1st Conference on Integrating Technology into Computer Science Education.

Michael, A., Ziglio, E., ed. (1996). Gazing Into the Oracle: The Delphi Method and Its Application to Social Policy and Public Health. London: Jessica Kingsley Publishers.

Mills, H.D. (1973). On the structure of a computing profession. In: SIGCSE '73 Proceedings of the Third SIGCSE Technical Symposium on Computer Science Education.

Neighbors, J.M. (1980). Software Construction Using Components, Department of Information and Computer Science, Doctoral Dissertation, University of California, Irvine.

Raccoon, L.B.S. (1995a). The Complexity Gap. CM SIGSOFT Software Engineering Notes. Vol. 20, no. 3.

Raccoon, L.B.S. (1995b). The Chaos Model and the Chaos Life Cycle, ACM Software Engineering Notes, ACM Press, Vol. 20, no. 1, pp. 55–66.

Royce, W. (1970). Managing the Development of Large Software Systems. In: Proceedings of IEEE WESCON, pp. 1–9.

Scrum (1986). An SOA-Based Software Development Management System. In: Proceedings WI '06 Proceedings of the 2006 IEEE/WIC/ACM International Conference on Web Intelligence.

Symons, F.J.W. (1988). Modelling and Analysis of Communication Protocols Using Numerical Petri Nets. Dissertation Abstracts International Part B: Science and Engineering [diss. Abst. Int. Pt. B—Sci. & Eng.], Vol. 49, No. 1, 489 pp.

Whitmire, S.A. (1992). 3-D Function Points: Scientific and Real Time Extensions to Function Points. In: Proceedings of 1992 Pacific Northwest Software Quality Conference.

INDEX

K

L

M

N

O

P

Q